HISTORICAL DICTIONARIES
OF PEOPLE AND CULTURES
Jon Woronoff, Series Editor

Historical Dictionary of the Kurds

Michael M. Gunter

*Historical Dictionaries of People and
Cultures, No. 1*

The Scarecrow Press, Inc.
Lanham, Maryland, and Oxford
2004

SCARECROW PRESS, INC.

Published in the United States of America
by Scarecrow Press, Inc.
A wholly owned subsidiary of
The Rowman & Littlefield Publishing Group, Inc.
4501 Forbes Boulevard, Suite 200, Lanham, Maryland 20706
www.scarecrowpress.com

PO Box 317
Oxford
OX2 9RU, UK

British Library Cataloguing in Publication Information Available

Library of Congress Cataloging-in-Publication Data

Gunter, Michael M.
  Historical dictionary of the Kurds / Michael M. Gunter.
    p. cm. — (Historical dictionaries of people and cultures; no. 1)
  Includes bibliographical references.
  ISBN 0-8108-4870-8
  1. Kurds—History—Dictionaries. I. Title. II. Series.
DS59.K86 G86 2003
956.6'7'003—dc21

2003011652

*To my wife Judy,
my daughter Heidi, my son Michael, his wife Linda,
and their new daughter Ansleigh Morgan Gunter.*

Contents

Editor's Foreword

In today's world of sovereign states, there is not much tolerance for a "people" without a state, even when the people is larger than the populations of many states. This applies most decidedly to the Kurds, some 25 million strong, depending on the count, who are divided among three large multipeople states in the Middle East and a growing diaspora in Europe and North America. This is their first misfortune. The second is that the Kurds developed a sense of nationhood too late, after the region had been carved up, which only frightened the countries they lived in traditionally. The reaction was more often repression, if not outright warfare, rather than accommodation and provision of reasonable autonomy. But the third, and worst, misfortune is that the Kurds, while recognizing one another as branches of the same family, are still deeply divided in their allegiances and sometimes fight one another more bitterly than they fight those who dominate them. Thus, while the situation can improve for the Kurdish people and the fall of Sadam Hussein is exceptionally promising, there is always a cause to fear a reversal and new setbacks.

Writing about a "people" is not as easy as writing about a state. It is necessary, first, to show where the people resided at various times in the past, what holds them together and what divides them, and how they manage to survive as a coherent group in a world of states. Only then can one concentrate on the persons, places, and events that mark their history or consider how they survive economically, maintain privileged social relations with one another and relate to outsiders, and preserve their culture, language, and religion. Thus while writing about a people is hard to do, it can be done, indeed, has been done very successfully in the *Historical Dictionary of the Kurds,* with its introduction providing an overall view plus a look at more specific circumstances, a substantial dictionary going into the essential details, and the chronology, which traces a longer and more impressive history than many would expect. Naturally, there is much more to be said about the Kurds, so the bibliography offers many helpful leads.

Aside from the sheer difficulty in gathering the basic information, when writing about a people—especially the Kurds—it is necessary to maintain a proper balance between different groups and factions and between the people and its neighbors. This is often harder for an insider than for an outsider, but the outsider must compensate by having a keen understanding of and strong affinity for the subject. That is certainly the case for the author of this book, Michael M. Gunter, who has been studying and teaching about the region for more than three decades. He is presently professor of political science at the Tennessee Technological University and a leading authority not only on the Kurds but also on the Armenians and Turks. Dr. Gunter has written numerous articles and chapters as well as general books on the Kurdish question, the Kurds in Iraq, and the Kurds in Turkey. This historical dictionary sums up the situation in another form, one that is particularly handy and will doubtless prove very useful for all those who want to know more about the Kurds, including many Kurds, I am sure. It is thus the ideal first volume for our new series on peoples.

Jon Woronoff
series editor

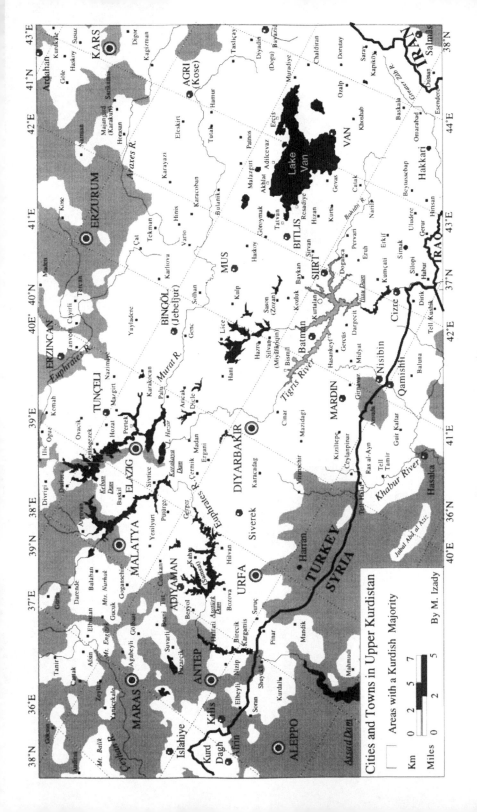

Cities and Towns in Upper Kurdistan

Areas with a Kurdish Majority

By M. Izady

Km 0 2 5 7

Miles 0 2 5

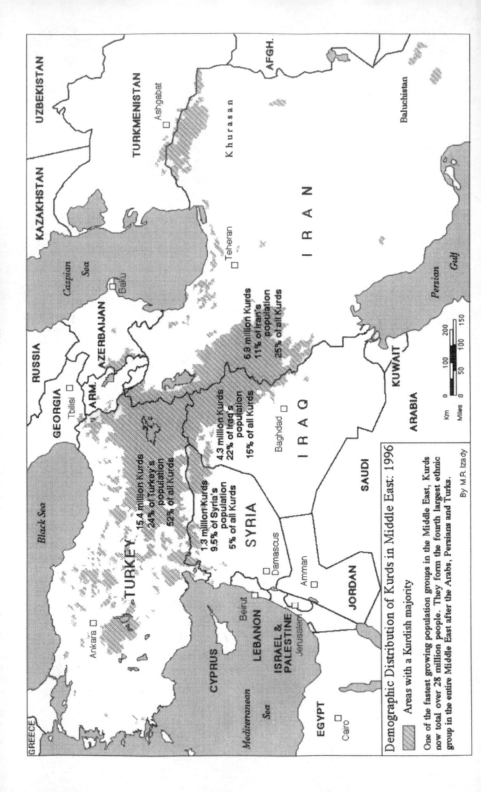

Demographic Distribution of Kurds in Middle East: 1996

Areas with a Kurdish majority

One of the fastest growing population groups in the Middle East, Kurds now total over 28 million people. They form the fourth largest ethnic group in the entire Middle East after the Arabs, Persians and Turks.

By M.R. Izady

Map labels:

GREECE

UZBEKISTAN

KAZAKHSTAN

TURKMENISTAN
Ashgabat

RUSSIA

GEORGIA
Tbilisi

ARM.

AZERBAIJAN
Baku

Caspian Sea

Khurasan

AFGH.

Baluchistan

I R A N
Teheran

Black Sea

15.4 million Kurds
24% of Turkey's population
52% of all Kurds

TURKEY
Ankara

6.8 million Kurds
11% of Iran's population
25% of all Kurds

4.3 million Kurds
22% of Iraq's population
15% of all Kurds

I R A Q
Baghdad

KUWAIT

Persian Gulf

1.3 million Kurds
9.5% of Syria's population
5% of all Kurds

SYRIA
Damascus

SAUDI ARABIA

Mediterranean Sea

CYPRUS

LEBANON
Beirut

ISRAEL & PALESTINE
Jerusalem

Amman

JORDAN

EGYPT
Cairo

Km   0   50   100   150   200
Miles 0 50 100 150

Cities and Towns in Lower Kurdistan.

Areas with a Kurdish Majority

Km 0   25   50   75

Miles 0   25   50

By M. Izady

Preface

This historical dictionary of the Kurds contains mainly historical and political entries, with an emphasis on topics closer to the present day. Nevertheless, I have sought to include the most important earlier names and events, too. In addition, I have included a number of entries on important cultural, economic, and social topics, among others. As an aid to readers, many of the entries have extensive cross-references in boldface type. There inevitably is a certain amount of subjectivity when choosing topics for entries. Furthermore, I am sure that I have simply neglected to provide entries on topics that deserved to be included. Therefore, I welcome suggestions from readers for additional entries in any future edition.

In writing a dictionary on the Kurds in the English language, I have attempted to simplify the transliteration of names and terms as much as possible. Given the rich variety of spellings among Western scholars and the linguistic differences among the Kurds themselves, it was not possible to be completely consistent in my transliterations. Rather, I have used spellings that are most comfortable to me, an English-speaking reader and writer. Although the purist might object, the result should be that readers will be easily able to identify quickly what they are reading about.

In some cases, Kurds and those who write about them most commonly use the Kurdish term, while in others they use the English. To compound the inconsistency, Kurdish acronyms are sometimes commonly employed with full English terms. The Kurdistan Workers Party, commonly known by its Kurdish acronym, PKK, is a good example. By contrast, the Kurdistan Democratic Party (KDP) and the Patriotic Union of Kurdistan (PUK) are usually known by both their English full names and their English acronyms. Therefore, by seeking to use the terms that seem to me most common, I have not been consistent in regard to language. Nevertheless, the result is that I have used terms that readers should most easily recognize. In most entries, I have sought to use both full Kurdish and English names upon first mention.

Another problem of consistency involves the birth and death years in many of the entries on persons. Because of the unsettled conditions usually prevailing in Kurdistan, even today, many Kurds simply do not know when they were born. Therefore, I have not been able to list dates for all my person entries. This problem becomes even greater for historical figures. Nevertheless, I have been able to establish the dates for a number of persons and have entered them when I could. The result is an obvious inconsistency in my entries, although they have the merit of giving as much information as they can. Again, I would welcome comments from my readers, some of whom may undoubtedly help fill in a few of the numerous gaps here.

In writing this historical dictionary, I have always sought to be as objective as possible without being egregiously politically correct. Therefore, I have offered many criticisms both overt and implied of the states in which the Kurds live, as well as of the Kurds themselves. To do otherwise would have overly sanitized and missed much of the essence of the subject with which I am dealing. In addition, of course, I am writing about a subject about which writings are inherently very emotional and subjective. As a Westerner and an American, my relative objectivity is possibly an advantage I possess that will make up for some of the lapses in understanding I inevitably suffer from in not being a Kurd.

I have learned a great deal from my friendships and acquaintances with other scholars who have written about the Kurds, as well as many Kurdish leaders. The scholarly writings of Martin van Bruinessen, Mehrdad Izady, and David McDowall, among many others, have been especially helpful. I have also learned much from such activists as Barham Salih and Najmaldin Karim. Special thanks are due to Mehrdad Izady for the detailed maps he provided for this historical dictionary and the understanding he gave me on many points. Lokman I. Meho also helped me with several dates and suggested some historical entries. I, of course, am entirely to blame for any misunderstandings, misinterpretations, or sheer errors that inevitably have crept into my book. Again, I welcome comments from my readers so that I can make necessary corrections in any future edition. My e-mail address is mgunter@tntech.edu.

Acronyms and Abbreviations

AKIN	American Kurdish Information Network
AI	Amnesty International
AKP	Adalet ve Kalkinma Partisi (Justice and Development Party [Turkey])
ARGK	Artes-I Rizgariye Geli Kurdistan (Kurdistan Peoples Liberation Army)
CIA	Central Intelligence Agency (United States)
DDKD	Devrimci Demokratik Kultur Dernekleri (Revolutionary Democratic Cultural Associations)
DDKO	Devrimci Dogu Kultur Ocaklari (Revolutionary Eastern Cultural Hearths)
DEP	Demokrasi Partisi (Democracy Party)
DEHAP	Demokratik Halkin Partisi (Democratic Peoples Party)
DISK	Devrimci Isci Sendikalari Konfederasyonu (Revolutionary Workers Unions Confederation [Turkey])
DKP	Demokratik Kitle Partisi (Democratic Mass Party)
ECHR	European Court of Human Rights
ERNK	Eniye Rizgariye Navata Kurdistan (Kurdistan National Liberation Front)
EU	European Union
GAP	Guneydogu Anadolu Projesi (Southeast Anatolia Project)
HADEP	Halkin Demokrasi Partisi (Peoples Democracy Party)
HEP	Halkin Emek Partisi (Peoples Labor Party)
HRK	Hazen Rizgariya Kurdistan (Kurdistan Freedom Brigades)
ICP	Iraqi Communist Party
IKF	Iraqi Kurdistan Front
IMK	Islamic Movement of Kurdistan
INC	Iraqi National Congress
JITEM	Gendarmerie Intelligence and Counter Terrorist Service (Turkey)

KADEK	Kurdistan Azadi Demokrasi Kongire (Kurdistan Freedom and Democracy Congress)
KDP	Kurdistan Democratic Party (Iraq)
KDPI	Kurdistan Democratic Party of Iran
KDPT	Kurdistan Democratic Party of Turkey
KHRP	Kurdish Human Rights Project (Great Britain)
KNC	Kurdish National Congress of North America
KNK	Kongra Netewiya Kurdistan (Kurdistan National Congress)
KPDP	Kurdistan Popular Democratic Party
KRG	Kurdistan Regional Government
KUK	Kurdistan Ulusal Kurtulusculari (Kurdistan National Liberationists)
MGK	Milli Guvenlik Kurulu (National Security Council [Turkey])
MIT	Milli Istihbarat Teshilati (National Intelligence Organization [Turkey])
NATO	North Atlantic Treaty Organization
OHAL	Emergency Rule (Turkey)
ONW	Operation Northern Watch
OPC	Operation Provide Comfort
OSCE	Organization for Security and Cooperation in Europe
PASOK	Kurdish Socialist Party (Iraq)
PKDW	Parlamana Kurdistane Li Derveyi Welat (Kurdistan Parliament in Exile)
PKK	Partiya Karkaren Kurdistan (Kurdistan Workers Party)
PPKK	Kurdistan Pesheng Karkaren Partiya (Kurdistan Vanguard Workers Party)
PSK	Kurdistan Socialist Party (Turkey)
PUK	Patriotic Union of Kurdistan
TIKKO	Turkiye Isci Koylu Kurtulus Ordusu (Turkish Workers–Peasants Liberation Army)
TOBB	Chamber of Commerce and Commodity Exchange (Turkey)
UN	United Nations
WKI	Washington Kurdish Institute

Chronology

401 B.C.E. Kardouchoi harass retreating Greeks, as recorded by Xenophon in *Anabasis*.

Mid-7th century C.E. Kurds are Islamicized. Saladin (most famous Kurd) battles Crusaders and establishes Ayyubid dynasty in Egypt and Syria.

1514 Battle of Chaldiran establishes Ottoman–Persian Empire frontier in Kurdistan.

1543–1603 Sharaf Khan Bitlisi is the author of the Kurdish history, *Sharafnama*.

1639 Treaty of Zuhab between the Ottoman and Persian Empires formally establishes their borders.

Late 17th century Ahmad-i Khani (1650–1706) writes *Mem u Zin*, the Kurdish national epic.

1811 Maulana Khalid begins to establish Naqshbandi Sufi order in what is now Iraqi Kurdistan.

1840s Barzanis establish themselves in Barzan.

1847 Badr Khan Beg, ruler of last semi-independent Kurdish emirate, surrenders to Ottomans.

1880 Sheikh Ubeydullah of Nehri's unsuccessful revolt.

1891 Ottoman Sultan Abdul Hamid II creates *Hamidiye*, Kurdish cavalry.

1914–18 Kurds support Ottomans in World War I.

1916 Sykes–Picot Agreement divides Middle East and thus Kurdistan.

1918 U.S. president Woodrow Wilson proclaims Fourteen Points. British create Iraq; Sheikh Mahmud Barzinji begins decade of unsuccessful revolts in Iraq.

1919–22 Ismail Agha Simko leads large revolts in Persia. Kurds support Turkish War of Independence.

1920s Red Kurdistan (Lachin) established in the Soviet Union.

1920 Stillborn Treaty of Sevres provides for possible Kurdish independence.

1923 Definitive Treaty of Lausanne fails to mention Kurds.

1925 Turkey crushes Sheikh Said's rebellion. "Mountain Turks" (Kurds) repressed.

1927 **October:** Khoybun is established as a pan-Kurdish party.

1930 Turkey crushes Kurdish rebellion in Ararat area. Mulla Mustafa Barzani (1903–79) begins to emerge in Iraq as preeminent Kurdish leader of the 20th century. **July:** Iranian Kurdish leader Ismail Agha Simko is assassinated by Iran.

1936–38 Turkey crushes Kurdish rebellion in Dersim (Tunceli).

1936 Saadabad Pact seeks to control Kurds.

1946 Mahabad Republic of Kurdistan exists in Iran. **16 August:** (Iraqi) Kurdistan Democratic Party (KDP) is formed.

1947 **31 March:** Qazi Muhammad is hanged by Iran.

1947–58 Mulla Mustafa Barzani is exiled in the Soviet Union.

1955 Baghdad Pact is created, in part to control the Kurds.

1958 **October:** Mulla Mustafa Barzani returns to Iraq.

1961 **September:** Fighting begins between Barzani-led Iraqi Kurds and Iraqi government.

Mid-1960s Fighting occurs between Barzani and KDP Politburo.

1970 March Manifesto in Iraq theoretically promises Kurdish autonomy.

1974 Renewed fighting occurs between Iraqi Kurds and Iraqi government.

1975 **March:** Algiers Agreement between Iraq and Iran ends Iranian support for Iraqi Kurds. Final defeat of Mulla Mustafa Barzani occurs. His son, Massoud Barzani (1946–), eventually emerges as his successor.

1975 **1 June:** Jalal Talabani (1933–) creates (Iraqi) Patriotic Union of Kurdistan (PUK).

1978 **27 November:** Abdullah (Apo) Ocalan creates Kurdistan Workers Party (PKK) in Turkey.

1979 **January:** The shah leaves Iran; Ayatollah Ruhollah Khomeini assumes power. **16 July:** Saddam Hussein becomes president of Iraq.

1980 **12 September:** Turkish military coup occurs, followed by crackdown on Kurds.

1980–88 Iran–Iraq War involves the Kurds in both states.

1982 **November:** Current Turkish constitution contains many provisions repressing the Kurds.

1984 **15 August:** PKK insurgency in Turkey begins.

1985 **March:** PKK establishes Kurdistan National Liberation Front (ERNK). **April:** Village guards created in Turkey.

1986 **October:** PKK establishes Kurdistan Peoples Liberation Army (ARGK).

1987 **Summer:** Emergency rule established in southeastern Turkey.

1987–88 Saddam Hussein's genocidal *Anfal* campaigns against Iraqi Kurds.

1988 **16 March:** Iraq launches chemical attack against Halabja. **May:** Iraqi Kurdistan Front is created.

1989 **13 July:** Iranian Kurdish leader Abdul Rahman Ghassemlou is assassinated.

1990 **June:** Peoples Labor Party (HEP) is created in Turkey as legal Kurdish party.

1991 Gulf War, Iraqi Kurdish uprising, and mass Kurdish refugee flight. United States creates Operation Provide Comfort, safe haven, and no-fly zone, resulting in de facto Kurdish state in northern Iraq. U.N. Security Council Resolution 688 condemns Iraqi repression of Iraqi Kurds. Antiterrorism law (Turkey) makes peaceful advocacy of Kurdish rights a crime. **November:** Suleyman Demirel becomes Turkish prime minister and recognizes the "Kurdish reality."

1992 **19 May:** Elections are held in Iraqi Kurdistan. **June–July:** Kurdistan Regional Government (KRG) is created in Iraqi Kurdistan. **October 4:** Turkey, KDP, and PUK begin fight against PKK in Iraqi Kurdistan. KRG parliament declares Iraqi Kurdistan a constituent state in a federal Iraq. **October 27:** The opposition Iraqi National Congress (INC) is formed.

1993 **March–May:** PKK implements unilateral cease-fire in Turkey. **17 April:** Turkish President Turgut Ozal suddenly dies in office. **May:** Suleyman Demirel becomes president of Turkey. **June:** Peoples Labor Party (HEP) is banned in Turkey. Democracy Party (DEP) succeeds it. **December:** Fighting occurs between PUK and Islamists in Iraqi Kurdistan.

1994 **March:** DEP is banned and Leyla Zana is imprisoned. Peoples Democracy Party (HADEP) takes its place in Turkey.

1994–98 KDP–PUK civil war occurs in Iraqi Kurdistan.

1995 **March:** INC fails in coup attempt in Iraq after U.S. Central Intelligence Agency withdraws its support. **12 April:** Kurdistan Parliament in Exile is created in Europe. **14 April:** United Nations Security Council Resolution 986 establishes oil-for-food program that allows Iraq to sell limited amount of oil. Iraqi Kurds eventually begin to receive 13 percent of the funds. **May:** MED-TV begins to broadcast to the Middle East. **August:** The report of the Chamber of Commerce and Commodity Exchange (TOBB Report) on PKK and Kurds is released in Turkey. PKK attacks KDP in Iraqi Kurdistan.

1996 **31 August:** Saddam's troops enter Iraqi Kurdistan to help KDP fight against PUK.

1997 **1 January:** Operation Northern Watch succeeds Operation Provide Comfort in enforcing no-fly zone over Iraqi Kurdistan.

1998 **20 February:** United Nations Security Council Resolution 1153 dramatically increases amount of oil Iraq is allowed to sell. **17 Sep-**

tember: Washington Accord ends KDP–PUK civil war. **October:** Syria expels Ocalan.

1998–99 Ocalan seeks asylum in Europe.

1999 **16 February:** Turkey captures Ocalan in Kenya and returns him to Turkey. Ocalan calls for democracy in Turkey and an end to armed struggle. **May:** Kurdistan National Congress succeeds Kurdistan Parliament in Exile. **29 June:** Turkey sentences Ocalan to death for treason. **July:** MEDYA-TV begins to broadcast as successor to MED-TV. **September:** Ocalan renews call for end to PKK's armed struggle and also calls for PKK to evacuate its fighters from Turkey. **December:** European Union (EU) accepts Turkey as candidate member; Ocalan's death sentence is put on hold.

2000 **May:** Reform-minded Ahmet Necdet Sezer is elected president in Turkey. **September and December:** PUK fights against PKK in Iraqi Kurdistan.

2001 **18 February:** Francis Hariri, a leading Christian member of KDP, is assassinated in Iraqi Kurdistan by Islamic extremists. **September:** Heavy fighting occurs between PUK and Jund al-Islam.

2002 **February:** PKK renames itself Kurdistan Freedom and Democracy Congress (KADEK). **August:** Turkish parliament passes reform legislation abolishing the death penalty and providing for Kurdish education and broadcasting to meet EU standards for admission. However, the implementation of these reforms remains uncertain. **October:** Ocalan's death sentence is commuted to life imprisonment. Reunified KRG parliament meets and reaffirms a federal status for Iraqi Kurdistan in a post-Saddam Iraq. **3 November:** Moderate Islamist AK Partisi (AKP) wins tremendous electoral victory in Turkey and establishes a majority government. **December:** Turkey ends Emergency Rule in last two provinces still having it. **14–17 December:** Major Iraqi opposition conference held in London amid U.S. threats to invade Iraq and declares post-Saddam Iraq will be a democratic, parliamentary, and federal state.

2003 **February:** Iraqi Kurds fear Turkey will occupy Iraqi Kurdistan in agreement with United States as part of U.S. war against Iraq. **March:** Turkey's Constitutional Court bans pro-Kurdish HADEP. **19 March:** United States launches war against Iraq.

Introduction

Although a large majority within the mountainous Middle East where Turkey, Iran, Iraq, and Syria meet, the Kurds have been gerrymandered into being mere minorities within the existing states they inhabit. The desire of many Kurds for statehood, or at least cultural autonomy within the states they now inhabit, has led to an almost continuous series of Kurdish revolts since the creation of the modern Middle East following World War I and constitutes the Kurdish problem or question.

The 25–28 million Kurds form the largest nation in the world without its own independent state. Since the end of the Gulf War in 1991 and the creation of a de facto state of Kurdistan in northern Iraq, the Kurdish problem has become increasingly important in Middle Eastern and even international politics. Turkey's application for admission to the European Union (EU) has also served to make the Kurdish issue more significant. If the Arab–Israeli dispute slowly winds down, the Kurdish issue will bid to replace it as the leading factor of instability in the geostrategically important Middle East. Furthermore, since the Kurds sit on a great deal of the Middle East's oil and possibly even-more-important water resources, the Kurdish issue will become even more important in the new century.

LAND AND PEOPLE

Geography

Kurdistan, or the land of the Kurds, constitutes the geographical area in the Middle East where the states of Turkey, Iran, Iraq, and Syria converge and in which the majority of the people are ethnic Kurds. There are also significant enclaves of Kurds living in the Iranian province of

Khurasan east of the Caspian Sea and in central Anatolia. Large numbers of Kurds also live in Turkey's three biggest cities: Istanbul, Ankara, and Izmir. In addition, Kurds live in Armenia, Azerbaijan, and Turkmenistan, across the border from the Iranian province of Khurasan. Given various political, economic, and social vicissitudes, the geographic extent of Kurdistan has varied considerably over the centuries. Although semi-independent Kurdish emirates such as Ardalan existed into the middle of the 19th century, there has never been an independent Kurdistan in the modern sense of an independent state. Before World War I, Kurdistan was divided between the Ottoman Empire (mostly) and the Persian Empire. Following World War I, Kurdistan was divided among five different states. Although only approximations can be cited, Turkey has the largest portion of Kurdistan (43 percent), followed by Iran (31 percent), Iraq (18 percent), Syria (6 percent), and the former Soviet Union (now mainly Armenia and Azerbaijan—2 percent).

Mountains are the most prominent geographic characteristic of landlocked Kurdistan. Indeed, a famous Kurdish proverb explains that "the Kurds have no friends but the mountains." This means that, although their rugged mountainous terrain contributes heavily to the lack of Kurdish unity, these mountains also have defined Kurdish history and culture and have protected the Kurds from being fully conquered or assimilated by the Turks to the north, Iranians to the east, and Arabs to the south and west. The Zagros range constitutes the most important portion of these mountains, running northwest to southeast like a spinal column through much of the land. Portions of the Taurus, Pontus, and Amanus Mountains also rise within Kurdistan.

Climate

The climate of these mountains has been described as bracing throughout the year. While northern Kurdistan has the highest average elevation, central Kurdistan enjoys a lower elevation and thus a warmer, even relatively balmy, climate. The mean annual temperatures in Kurdistan exhibit great variations according to the elevation. Although summers remain pleasantly cool in the mountains, in the lower elevations they can be oppressively hot and humid. Winters in most areas are bitterly cold and snowy.

These climatic contrasts have been sharpened by the loss of the forests that once covered the land, but succumbed to overgrazing, logging for fuel or construction, and the effects of war. In strong contrast to most other parts of the Middle East, much of Kurdistan enjoys adequate and regular rainfall.

Population

The Kurds are a largely Sunni Muslim, Indo-European–speaking people. Thus they are quite distinct ethnically from the Turks and Arabs, but related to the Iranians, with whom they share the *Newroz* (new year) holiday at the beginning of spring. No precise figure for the Kurdish population exists because most Kurds tend to exaggerate their numbers, while the states in which they live undercount them for political reasons. In addition, a significant number of Kurds have partially or fully assimilated into the larger Arab, Turkish, or Iranian populations surrounding them. Furthermore, debate continues whether such groups as the Lurs, Bakhtiyaris, and others are Kurds or not. Thus there is not even complete agreement on who is a Kurd.

Nevertheless, a reasonable estimate is that there are 12 to 15 million Kurds in Turkey (18 to 23 percent of the population), 6.5 million in Iran (11 percent), 3.5 to 4 million in Iraq (17 to 20 percent), and 1 million in Syria (9 percent). (Mehrdad Izady has listed slightly higher figures on one of his maps he has so kindly allowed me to use in this volume.) At least 200,000 Kurds also live in parts of the former Soviet Union (some claim as many as 1 million largely assimilated Kurds live there) and recently a Kurdish diaspora of more than 1 million has risen in western Europe. More than half of this diaspora is concentrated in Germany. Some 20,000 Kurds live in the United States. (However, it must again be noted that these figures are simply estimates, given the lack of accurate demographic statistics.) Finally, it should be noted that numerous minorities also live in Kurdistan. These minorities include Christian groups such as the Armenians, Assyrians, Turkomans, Turks, Arabs, and Iranians, among others.

The Kurds themselves are notoriously divided geographically, politically, linguistically, tribally, and ideologically. As noted above, their mountains and valleys divide the Kurds as much as they ethnically stamp them. Whatever their exact origin, it is clear that racially the Kurds today constitute a mixture of various groupings, the result of earlier invasions and migrations.

Also, the Kurdish language (which is related to Iranian) has two main variants: Kurmanji (or Bahdinani), spoken mainly in the northwest of Kurdistan (Turkey and the Bahdinan or Barzani area of northwest Iraqi Kurdistan), and Sorani, spoken mainly in the southeast of Kurdistan. In addition, Dimili (Zaza) is spoken in parts of Turkish Kurdistan, while Gurani is spoken in sections of Iraqi and Iranian Kurdistan. Finally, there are numerous subdialects of each of these four main dialects. These Kurdish-language variants are only partially mutually understandable, a situation that adds to the many divisions in Kurdish society.

Tribalism, too, has prevented Kurdish unity. Indeed, the tribe has probably received more loyalty than any sense of Kurdish nationalism. In all of the Kurdish revolts of the 20th century, for example, significant numbers of Kurds have supported the government because of their tribal antipathies for those rebelling. In Iraq, these progovernment Kurds have been derisively referred to as *josh* (little donkeys), while in recent years the Turkish government created a progovernment militia of Kurds called village guards. Similarly, the aghas (feudal landlords or tribal chieftains) and sheikhs (religious leaders) continue to command allegiances inconsistent with the full development of a modern sense of nationalism.

Economy

Although many Kurds were historically nomadic, very few continue to practice such a lifestyle today. Many Kurds now farm and raise livestock. Corn, barley, rice, cotton, and sugar beets are valuable crops. In addition, the best tobacco in Turkey and Iraq is grown in Kurdistan. Animal husbandry (goats, sheep, cows, and buffaloes) has been and still is a mainstay. Because of recent wars, many Kurds also now live in urban areas.

Blessed with large reserves of water (in the Turkish and Iraqi parts) and oil (in the Iraqi section), Kurdistan has great economic and geostrategic importance. Despite being economically underdeveloped compared to the non-Kurdish areas of Turkey, Iran, Iraq, and Syria, Kurdistan witnessed a tremendous amount of economic, political, and social modernization during the 20th century. Indeed, Iraqi Kurdistan's economy surpassed that of the rest of Iraq in the late 1990s due to the oil-for-food program funds it received from the sale of Iraqi oil through the United Nations. Similar hopes have yet to materialize for Turkish Kurdistan, however, despite the Guneydogu Anadolu Projesi (GAP), or Southeast Anatolia Project, for harnessing the Euphrates and Tigris Rivers through the construction of gigantic dams. The Turkish, Iranian, and Syrian portions of Kurdistan still lag greatly behind economically.

HISTORICAL BACKGROUND

The origin of the Kurds is uncertain, although some scholars believe them to be the descendants of various Indo-European tribes that settled in the area as many as 4,000 years ago. The Kurds themselves claim to be the descendants of the Medes, who helped overthrow the Assyrian Empire in 612 B.C.E., and also recite interesting myths about their origins involving King Solomon, *jinn,* and other magical agents. Many believe that the Kardouchoi, mentioned in his *Anabasis* by Xenophon as having given his 10,000 a mauling as they retreated from Persia in 401 B.C.E., were the ancestors of the Kurds.

In the seventh century C.E., the conquering Arabs applied the name "Kurds" to the mountainous people they Islamicized in the region, and history also records that the famous Saladin (Salah al-Din), who fought so chivalrously and successfully against the Christian Crusaders and Richard the Lionhearted, was a Kurd.

Early in the 16th century, most of the Kurds loosely fell under Ottoman Turkish rule, while the remainder were placed under the Persians. In 1596, Sharaf Khan Bitlisi completed the *Sharafnama,* a very erudite history of the ruling families of the Kurdish emirates. Ahmad-i Khani wrote *Mem u Zin,* the Kurdish national epic, during the following century and is seen by some as an early advocate of Kurdish nationalism. Badr Khan Beg, the ruler of the last semi-independent Kurdish emirate of Botan, surrendered to the Ottomans in 1847. Some scholars argue that Sheikh Ubeydullah's unsuccessful revolt in 1880 represented the first indication of modern Kurdish nationalism, while others consider it little more than a tribal–religious disturbance.

Turkey

In 1891, Ottoman sultan Abdul Hamid II created the *Hamidiye,* a modern progovernment Kurdish cavalry that proved to be an important stage in the emergence of modern Kurdish nationalism. Nevertheless, the Kurds supported the Ottomans in World War I and Mustafa Kemal (Ataturk) during the Turkish War of Independence following that conflict.

During World War I, one of U.S. president Woodrow Wilson's Fourteen Points (Number 12) declared that the non-Turkish minorities of the Ottoman Empire should be granted the right of "autonomous development." The stillborn Treaty of Sevres signed in August 1920 provided for "local autonomy for the predominantly Kurdish areas" (Article 62) and in Article 64 even looked forward to the possibility that "the Kurdish peoples" might be granted "independence from Turkey." Turkey's quick revival under Ataturk—ironically enough with considerable Kurdish help as the Turks played well on the theme of Islamic unity—altered the entire situation. The subsequent and definitive Treaty of Lausanne in July 1923 recognized the modern Republic of Turkey with no special provisions for the Turkish Kurds.

Ataturk's creation of a secular and purely Turkish state led to the first of three great Kurdish revolts, beginning with the rising in 1925 of Sheikh Said, the hereditary chief of the powerful Naqshbandi Sufi Islamic order. Sheikh Said's rebellion was both nationalistic and religious, as it also favored the reinstatement of the caliphate. After some initial successes, Sheikh Said was crushed and hanged. In 1927, Khoybun (Independence), a transnational Kurdish party that had been founded that year in Lebanon, helped to launch another major uprising under General Ihsan Nuri Pasha in the Ararat area that also was completely crushed, this time with Iranian cooperation. Finally, the Dersim (now called Tunceli) rebellion from 1936 to the end of 1938, led by Sheikh Sayyid Riza until his death in 1937, also ended in a total Kurdish defeat.

Although many Kurdish tribes either supported the Turkish government or were at least neutral in these rebellions, the Turkish authorities decided to eliminate anything that might suggest a separate Kurdish nation. A broad battery of social and constitutional devices was employed to achieve this goal. In some cases what can only be termed pseudotheoretical justifications were offered to defend what was being done. Thus the so-called Sun theory taught that all languages derived from one original primeval Turkic language in central Asia. Isolated in the mountain fastnesses of eastern Anatolia, the Kurds had simply forgotten their mother tongue. The much-abused and -criticized appellation "Mountain Turks," used when referring to the Turkish Kurds, served as a code term for these actions. Everything that recalled a separate Kurdish identity was to be abolished, including language, clothing, and names.

The present constitution (from 1982) contains a number of specific provisions that seek to limit even speaking or writing in Kurdish. Its preamble, for example, declares: "The determination that no protection shall be afforded to thoughts or opinions contrary to Turkish national interests, the principle of the existence of Turkey as an indivisible entity." Two articles ban the spoken and written usage of the Kurdish language without specifically naming it.

Although restrictions on the usage of the Kurdish language were eased following the Gulf War in 1991, Article 8 of a new Anti-Terrorism law that entered into force in April 1991 made it possible to consider academics, intellectuals, and journalists speaking up peacefully for Kurdish rights to be engaging in terrorist acts. Similarly, under Article 312 of the Turkish Penal Code, mere verbal or written support for Kurdish rights could lead one to be charged with "provoking hatred or animosity between groups of different race, religion, region, or social class." Yasar Kemal, one of Turkey's most famous novelists and an ethnic Kurd, was indicted in 1995 for violating these provisions of what some have termed "thought crime."

Since the 1970s, an increasing portion of Turkey's population of ethnic Kurds has actively demanded cultural, linguistic, and political rights as Kurds. The government has ruthlessly suppressed these demands for fear they would lead to the breakup of the state itself. This official refusal to brook any moderate Kurdish opposition helped encourage extremism and the creation of the Partiya Karkaren Kurdistan (PKK), or Kurdistan Workers Party, headed by Abdullah (Apo) Ocalan, on 27 November 1978. In August 1984, the PKK officially launched its insurgency that by the beginning of 2000 had resulted in more than 37,000 deaths, the partial or complete destruction of as many as 3,000 villages, and the internal displacement of some 3 million people.

For a short period in the early 1990s, Ocalan actually seemed close to achieving a certain degree of military success. In the end, however, he overextended himself, while the Turkish military spared no excesses in containing him. Slowly but steadily, the Turks marginalized the PKK's military threat. Ocalan's ill-advised decision in August 1995 to also attack Massoud Barzani's Kurdistan Democratic Party (KDP) in northern Iraq because of its support for Turkey further sapped his strength. The final blow came when Turkey threatened to go to war against Syria in October 1998 unless Damascus expelled Ocalan from his longtime sanctuary in that country.

Ocalan fled to Italy, but U.S. pressure on behalf of its NATO ally Turkey led Italy and others to reject Ocalan as a terrorist undeserving of political asylum or negotiation. Indeed for years the United States had given Turkey intelligence training and weapons to battle against what it saw as the "bad" Kurds of Turkey, while ironically supporting the "good" Kurds of Iraq against Saddam Hussein. Ocalan was finally captured in Kenya on 16 February 1999, flown back to Turkey for a sensational trial, and sentenced to death for treason.

Instead of making a hard-line appeal for renewed struggle during his trial, Ocalan issued a remarkable statement that called for the implementation of true democracy to solve the Kurdish problem within the existing borders of a unitary Turkey. To demonstrate his sincerity, he also ordered his guerrillas to evacuate Turkey. Thus, far from ending Turkey's Kurdish problem, Ocalan's capture began a process of implicit bargaining between the state and many of its citizens of Kurdish ethnic heritage as represented by the PKK and the Peoples Democracy Party (HADEP). HADEP had been founded in 1994 as a legal Kurdish party and had elected numerous mayors in the Kurdish areas during the local elections held shortly after Ocalan's capture.

At the same time, Harold Hongju Koh, the U.S. assistant secretary of state for democracy, human rights, and labor, visited Turkey and met with a wide variety of people. Although recognizing Turkey's right to defend itself against the PKK, he also argued that one could oppose terrorism and still support human rights. He further maintained that far from hurting Turkey's territorial integrity, now that the PKK's military threat had been defeated, an inclusive policy that acknowledged human rights would strengthen the Turkish state by giving its Kurdish ethnic community a genuine stake in their country's future.

At this point, Turkish candidacy for membership in the European Union (EU) entered the picture, when in December 1999 the EU finally accepted Turkey as a candidate member. If implemented, EU membership would fulfill Ataturk's ultimate hope for a strong, united, and democratic Turkey joined to the West. However, until Turkey successfully implemented the so-called Copenhagen Criteria of minority rights for its Kurdish ethnic population and suspended Ocalan's death sentence to conform with EU standards, which banned capital punishment, it was clear that Turkey's long-treasured candidacy would be only a pipe dream.

Although the election of Ahmet Necdet Sezer, a reform-minded judge, as Turkey's new president in May 2000 demonstrated a willingness to seek new, bolder approaches, there are unfortunately still powerful forces in Turkey that do not want further democratization because they fear it would threaten their privileged positions as well as Turkey's territorial integrity. Thus Turkey's passage of reform legislation in August 2002 allowing significant Kurdish cultural rights in theory and the commutation of Ocalan's death sentence to life imprisonment in October 2002 have not solved the continuing Kurdish problem in Turkey. It also remains to be seen what the tremendous electoral victory of the moderate Islamist Adalet ve Kalkinma Partisi (AK Party, or AKP) on 3 November 2002 will bring.

As of March 2003, however, little further progress on the Kurdish issue seems to have occurred. Indeed, there were even signs that the PKK (which had changed its name to the Kurdistan Freedom and Democracy Congress, KADEK, as of February 2002) might resume the military struggle.

Iraq

The Kurds in Iraq have been in an almost constant state of revolt ever since Great Britain artificially created Iraq—according to the Sykes–Picot Agreement of World War I—out of the former Ottoman *vilayets* (provinces) of Mosul, Baghdad, and Basra. There are three major reasons for this rebellious situation.

First, in Iraq the Kurds long constituted a greater proportion of the population than they did in any other state they inhabited. Despite their smaller absolute numbers compared to Kurds in Turkey and Iran, they represented a larger critical mass in Iraq, a situation that enabled them to play a more important role there than they did in Turkey and Iran.

Second, as an artificial, new state, Iraq had less legitimacy as a political entity than did Turkey and Iran, two states that had existed in one form or another for many centuries, despite their large Kurdish minorities. Thus discontent and rebellion came easier for the Iraqi Kurds. Third, Iraq was further divided by a Sunni–Shiite Muslim division not present in Turkey or Iran. This predicament further called into question Iraq's future.

For its part, the Iraqi government has always feared the possibility of Kurdish separatism. Kurdish secession would not only deplete the Iraqi population, but it would also set a precedent that the Shiites, some 55 percent of the population, might follow and would thus threaten the very future of the Iraqi state. In addition, since for many years approximately two-thirds of the oil production and reserves as well as much of the fertile land were located in the Kurdish area, the government believed that Kurdish secession would strike at the economic heart of the state. Thus were sown the seeds of a seemingly irreconcilable struggle between Iraq and its Kurdish minority.

To further their goals, the British, who held Iraq as a mandate from the League of Nations, invited a local Kurdish leader, Sheikh Mahmud Barzinji of Sulaymaniya, to act as their governor in the Kurdish *vilayet* of Mosul. Despite his inability to overcome the division among the Kurds, Sheikh Mahmud almost immediately proclaimed himself "King of Kurdistan," revolted against British rule, and began secret dealings with the Turks. In a precursor to subsequent defeats at the hands of the Iraqi government in Baghdad, the British Royal Air Force successfully bombed the sheikh's forces, putting down several of his uprisings during the 1920s.

Although the Treaty of Sevres (1920) held out the possibility of Kurdish independence, as mentioned above, the definitive Treaty of Lausanne (1923) made no mention of the Kurds. What is more, the British already had decided to attach the largely Kurdish *vilayet* of Mosul to Iraq because of its vast oil resources. The British believed that this was the only way Iraq could be made viable.

With the final defeat of Sheikh Mahmud in 1931, Mulla Mustafa Barzani began to emerge as the leader almost synonymous with the Kurdish movement in Iraq. Although the Barzanis' power was originally founded on their religious authority as Naqshbandi sheikhs, they also became noted for their fighting abilities and still wear a distinctive turban with red stripes. For more than half a century, Mulla Mustafa Barzani fought the Iraqi government in one way or another. Despite his inherent conservatism and tribal mentality, he was the guiding spirit of the Kurdistan Democratic Party (KDP), founded on 16 August 1946, spent a decade of exile in the Soviet Union (1947–58), and at the height of his power in the early 1970s negotiated the March Manifesto of 1970, which theoretically provided for Kurdish autonomy under his rule. Intra-Kurdish infighting against such other leaders as Ibrahim Ahmad and his son-in-law Jalal Talabani and continuing government opposition, however, finally helped lead to Barzani's defeat in 1975. Barzani's defeat also occurred because the United States and Iran withdrew their support in return for Iraqi concessions, an action U.S. national security advisor Henry Kissinger cynically explained as necessary covert action not to be confused with missionary work.

Following Barzani's collapse in March 1975, his son Massoud Barzani eventually emerged as the new leader of the KDP, while Talabani established his Patriotic Union of Kurdistan (PUK) on 1 June 1975. Divided by philosophy, geography, dialect, and ambition, Barzani's KDP and Talabani's PUK have alternated between cooperation and bloody conflict ever since. They also have suffered grievously from such horrific repression as Saddam Hussein's genocidal Anfal campaigns of 1987–88 and the chemical attack against the city of Halabja on 16 March 1988.

After the Gulf War and the failure of the ensuing Kurdish uprising in March 1991, the mass flight of Kurdish refugees to the mountains reluctantly forced the United States to create a safe haven and no-fly zone in which a de facto Kurdish state began to develop in northern Iraq. In addition, the unprecedented United Nations Security Council Resolution 688 of 5 April 1991 condemned "the repression of the Iraqi civilian population . . . in Kurdish populated areas" and demanded "that Iraq . . . immediately end this repression." As symbolic as the resolution may have been, never before had the Kurds received such official international mention and protection.

Despite the de facto Kurdish state that emerged in northern Iraq following Saddam Hussein's defeat in the Gulf War, the KDP and PUK actually fought a civil war against each other from 1994 to 1998. As a result of this internal Kurdish fighting, there were two separate rump governments in Iraqi Kurdistan after 1994: the KDP's in Irbil and the

PUK's in Sulaymaniya. Inevitably, the resulting instability and power vacuum drew in neighboring Turkey and Iran, among others such as the United States, Syria, and of course, Iraq, since for reasons of state none of the powers wanted to see a Kurdish state established in northern Iraq.

The United States finally brokered a cease-fire by bringing Barzani and Talabani together in Washington in September 1998. The Kurds also began to receive 13 percent of the receipts from the oil Iraq was allowed to sell after 1995. Peace, relative prosperity, and democracy began to grow in the de facto state of Kurdistan in northern Iraq. In October 2002, the reunified parliament of the de facto Kurdish state met for the first time since 1994 and declared that Iraqi Kurdistan would be a federal state in a post-Saddam Iraq.

During the fall of 2002, however, U.S. president George W. Bush demanded that Saddam Hussein disarm, threatening a coalition war to disarm Iraq if Saddam did not. Early in 2003, war appeared likely, and there was a great deal of speculation concerning the Kurdish future in a post-Saddam Iraq. Although most Iraqi Kurds seem to support the idea of removing Saddam Hussein, they did not approve of a U.S. plan to allow Turkish troops to enter Iraqi Kurdistan in the event of a war, because such an occurrence might threaten the very existence of the de facto Kurdish state. Turkey, however, feared that the Iraqi Kurds offered an increasingly dangerous model for the Kurds in Turkey that might reignite their military struggle. On 19 March 2003, the United States finally launched a war against Iraq, one that quickly overthrew Saddam Hussein's regime. Until a new supposedly federal government that would allow the Kurds a large amount of self-government was established in Iraq, the Kurdistan Regional Government (KRG) continued to function. Thus, the future of the Iraqi Kurds remained very uncertain as of this writing.

Iran

Although twice as many Kurds live in Iran as in Iraq, the Kurdish national movement in Iran has enjoyed much less success, due in part to the relatively greater long-term strength of the Iranian governments. This, however, did not prevent Ismail Agha Simko from leading major Kurdish revolts in the 1920s that ended only when the Iranian government treacherously assassinated him under false pretenses of negotiation in 1930.

This Iranian technique of solving its Kurdish problem was used again on 13 July 1989, when Iranian agents assassinated the leader of the Kurdistan Democratic Party of Iran (KDPI), Abdul Rahman Ghassemlou, in Vienna while supposedly negotiating with him. On 17 September 1992, Iranian agents also assassinated Ghassemlou's successor, Sadegh Sharafkandi, while he was dining at a restaurant in Berlin. Earlier, the KDPI's revolt against the Ayatollah Ruhollah Khomeini's new government had been completely smashed by the superior Iranian forces by 1981.

Despite these failures, the Iranian Kurds are famous among their Kurdish brethren for having established the only Kurdish state in the 20th century, the short-lived Mahabad Republic of Kurdistan (January–December 1946). After this rump Kurdish state was destroyed, however, its president, Qazi Muhammad, was summarily hanged on 31 March 1947, a blow from which the Iranian Kurds still have not completely recovered.

Syria

Approximately a million Kurds live in Syria, a much smaller number than in Turkey, Iraq, or Iran. Although the largest minority in Syria, the Kurds there live in three noncontiguous areas and have been much less successfully organized and developed than in the other three states. Many Kurds in Syria have even been denied Syrian citizenship. The repressive Baathist Party under Hafez Assad (and since 2000 his son Bashar Assad) have also kept a close watch on the Kurds. A government decree in September 1992, for example, prohibited the registration of children with Kurdish first names. Kurdish cultural centers, bookshops, and similar activities have been banned. Indeed, some have suspected that in return for giving the Kurdistan Workers Party (PKK) sanctuary in Syria for many years, the PKK kept the lid on Syrian Kurdish unrest. For all these reasons, therefore, the Kurds in Syria are not as important a problem as they are in the other three states.

THE FUTURE

Despite the seemingly ceaseless conflicts of the past century, most Kurds in Turkey would probably still be satisfied with meaningful cultural rights and real democracy. In Iran and Syria, the lesser-developed

Kurdish movements would also be more than pleased with such a result. In Iraq, however—due to the incredible incompetence of Saddam Hussein, who brought upon himself the Gulf War of 1991, and thus the resulting institution of a de facto state of Kurdistan in northern Iraq—the Iraqi Kurds will probably be satisfied with nothing less than a federal solution in any post-Saddam Iraq.

As described above, Kurdish aspirations seem better placed, but still highly problematic, in Turkey and Iraq. To the extent that the fledgling democracy in Iran continues to develop, however, one might also hold out hopes for greater Kurdish cultural rights in that state, too. Even Syria has demonstrated a modicum of hope for modest Kurdish rights now that its longtime strongman Hafez Assad has died and his possibly more progressive son Bashar Assad has succeeded him. Only time will tell, however, whether this occurs.

Any Kurdish independence and even more pan-Kurdish unity remain unlikely, however, because each of the neighboring states bitterly opposes it as a threat to its own territorial integrity. The United States, although protecting the de facto state of Kurdistan in northern Iraq with a no-fly zone, also opposes independence for it because of Turkey's attitude and the U.S. fear that Kurdish independence would destabilize the geostrategically important Middle East. Given the current uncertain situation regarding the future of a post-Saddam Iraq, the Kurdish situation there remains highly uncertain for the future. What is certain, however, is the increasing importance of the Kurds for the future of the Middle East and international politics.

The Dictionary

– A –

ABDUL SALAM II (Sheikh of Barzan) (c. 1882–c. 1915). The older brother of the legendary **Mulla Mustafa Barzani** and thus an uncle of the current **Barzani** leader, **Massoud Barzani**. The Barzani tribe Abdul Salam II headed was known for its religious and military leadership. Abdul Salam himself was called "the Sheikh of the Christians" because of his tolerance. He also was known as a representative of nascent Kurdish nationalism during the waning days of the **Ottoman Empire**. He was captured and hanged by the Ottomans during the early years of World War I.

ABDULLAH, HAMZA (c. 1915–2000). Elected the first secretary general of the **Kurdistan Democratic Party (KDP)** of **Iraq** at its first congress on 16 August 1946. Thus he was in effect the second in command under **Mulla Mustafa Barzani**, who was chosen as the president of the KDP. During his relatively short and checkered career, Hamza Abdullah was seen as close to the **Iraqi Communist Party**, which was quite powerful in the 1950s. He also was an intraparty opponent of **Ibrahim Ahmad** and was finally retired permanently by Barzani in 1959. Abdullah was still living at the end of the 20th century, but he played no further political role.

ABDURRAHMAN, MUHAMMAD "SAMI" (1932–). "Sami," as he is popularly known, has been an important Iraqi Kurdish leader since the later days of **Mulla Mustafa Barzani**. He was trained in Britain as an engineer. Shortly after Barzani's defeat and exile in 1975, Sami joined Barzani's two sons, **Idris Barzani** and **Massoud Barzani**, to form the KDP/Provisional Command. Differences with

1

the more traditional Idris led to the more progressive Sami leaving the **Kurdistan Democratic Party (KDP)** (as it was now once again called) to form his own **Kurdistan Popular Democratic Party (KPDP)** in 1981. During the negotiations between the Iraqi government and the **Iraqi Kurdistan Front** in the spring and summer of 1991, Sami was one of the Kurdish representatives.

The KPDP did very poorly in the Iraqi Kurdish elections held in May 1992. After an attempt to reinvigorate his fortunes by combining with two other minor Kurdish parties as the **Kurdistan Unity Party**, Sami rejoined the KDP in 1993. He has played an important role since then and is currently the deputy prime minister in the KDP **Kurdistan Regional Government**. In 2002, Sami Abdurrahman suffered a minor stroke, but he was soon able to return to work.

ABU al-FIDA (1273–1331). An ethnic Kurd who was a Syrian prince born into the **Ayyubid** family. He enjoyed a great reputation as a man of letters. Two of his works stand out: the *Mukhtasar tarikh al-bashar* is a universal history covering the pre-Islamic and Islamic periods up to 1329; the *Takwin al-Buldan* is a descriptive geography containing physical and mathematical information in tabular form. Both are largely compilations that Abu al-Fida rearranged and supplemented.

Following the suppression of the Ayyubid principality of Hamah in 1299, Abu al-Fida remained in the service of its Mamluk governors and a friend of the sultan. Eventually, he was appointed as the governor of Hamah for life and given precedence over all other governors in Syria.

AGHA (AGA). Leaders of Kurdish **tribes**, clans, or lineages who usually live with their tribe. Most aghas have a guest house where travelers can rest and be entertained. Aghas and **sheikhs** (religious leaders) are traditional Kurdish leaders and as such are seen in Turkey especially as reactionary impediments to modernization and democracy. However, many current Kurdish leaders originally come from agha or sheikh backgrounds.

AHL-I HAQQ (People of the Truth or Spirit). Ancient indigenous Kurdish **religion** that still persists in Iraqi and Iranian Kurdistan, where with some exceptions it corresponds with **Gurani**-speaking Kurds. It is also called **Kakai**, Yarsanism, Aliullahi, or Alli-Ilahi (those who deify Ali). It shares many tenets with the practice of **Alevis** and **Yezidis**. Its use of religious dissimulation (*taquiya*, similar to that practiced by the Shiites) to confuse opponents and thus survive probably helps identify it with more mainstream Shiism. The main Ahl-i Haqq shrine at Baba Yadigar is also venerated by Shiite Kurds. *See also GHULAT.*

AHMAD, IBRAHIM (1914–2000). Longtime Iraqi Kurdish rival of **Mulla Mustafa Barzani**, as well as the father-in-law and political mentor of **Jalal Talabani**. He graduated from the faculty of law at the University of Baghdad and published his thesis on Arab-Kurdish relations in 1937. Although he flirted with communism—as did many Kurdish intellectuals in those days—and even spent three years in prison for communist activities in the early 1950s, Ahmad can best be described as a leftist Kurdish nationalist.

With brief interruptions, he served as the secretary general of the **Kurdistan Democratic Party (KDP)** from 1953 to 1964. With Jalal Talabani, Ahmad led the **KDP Politburo** faction, a leftist, intellectual Marxist-oriented wing, during the 1960s against the more conservative and traditional tribal wing of the KDP associated with Barzani. Eventually, Ahmad was defeated, although his beliefs were taken up by the younger Talabani and his **Patriotic Union of Kurdistan (PUK)**, established in 1975. Ahmad lived many years in exile in London, from where he continued to be active in Kurdish causes right up until his death as an old and honored Kurdish nationalist.

AK KOYUNLU (WHITE SHEEP). One of two rival Turkoman federations or dynasties (the other being the Kara Koyunlu, or Black Sheep) that ruled parts of Kurdistan during much of the 15th century after the death of Timur Lang in 1404. Early on, the Sunni Ak Koyunlu had Amed (**Diyarbakir**) as their capital, while the Shia Kara Koyunlu had their center northeast of Lake Van. The Kurds did not play a major role in the armed struggles of the two.

In 1467, the able Ak Koyunlu leader Uzun Hasan destroyed the rival Kara Koyunlu federation and eventually extended his power over most of Kurdistan. According to the *Sharafnama*, Uzun Hasan then "took it upon himself to exterminate the leading families of Kurdistan, especially those who had shown themselves devoted to or subjects of the Kara Koyunlu sultans." He made his new capital in Tabriz in what is now **Iran**. In 1502, after Uzun Hasan's death, the Iranian Safavid leader Ismail destroyed the Ak Koyunlu and proclaimed himself shah.

AK PARTISI (AKP). The AKP (Justice and Development Party) is a moderate **Islamist** party formed in **Turkey** in 2001 after a previous Islamist party (the Fazilet or Virtue Party) had been banned. AK is an acronym for the Turkish words for justice and development, and by itself means in Turkish white, clean, or honest.

In November 2002, the AKP won a landslide victory in the Turkish national elections and formed the first majority government in 20 years. All of the parties in the previous parliament were swept out of office due to their failure to gain at least 10 percent of the vote. The severe economic and resulting social crisis Turkey was suffering from was the main reason for this development. Recep Tayyip Erdogan, the leader of the AKP and former mayor of Istanbul, was not able immediately to become the new prime minister, however, because of an earlier conviction for incitement to hate. In the meantime, his deputy, Abdullah Gul, served as prime minister. In March 2003, Erdogan finally became prime minister, while Gul took over as the foreign minister.

Although only time can tell, the AKP's victory promised to redefine Turkish politics and possibly offer some positive solutions to Turkey's Kurdish problem. On 1 March 2003, however, the Turkish parliament voted against allowing U.S. troops to use Turkey as a base from which to attack Iraq in the **Gulf War II**. This action seemed to foreclose Turkey's opportunity to help occupy northern Iraq as a U.S. ally in the war against Iraq. It also deprived Turkey of badly needed U.S. economic credits. The AKP was in danger of seeming to be foundering in disarray.

AKRAD. The Arabic plural for the word for Kurd.

ALA RIZGARI (Flag of Liberation). One of the numerous small Kurdish parties or groups during the unsettled decade of the 1970s in

Turkey, Ala Rizgari split off from the Marxist **Rizgari** in 1979. This new splinter group was sometimes described as Trotskyist and was mostly nonviolent, more flexible in its political position, and also more censorious of the **Soviet Union** than was Rizgari.

ALEVIS. Practitioners of a heterodox form of Islam in **Turkey** that some would consider beyond the Islamic pale. They are also referred to as Qizilbash, or Red Heads, for the distinctive red turbans they historically wore. Alevi beliefs are a mixture of pre-Islamic, Zoroastrian, Turkoman shaman, and Shia ideas. The Alevis share many common tenets with the **Ahl-i Haqq** religion, such as the veneration of the Prophet Muhammad's son-in-law, Ali. Along with the **Yezidis**, these religions are also sometimes referred to as the **Cult of Angels**.

The *jam (cam)* is the main religious observance of both Alevis and the Ahl-i Haqq and takes the place of the mosque as the religious gathering place. Also, both use the term *pir* for their religious leaders. Orthodox Muslims sometimes accuse Alevis of sexual promiscuity from the erroneous belief that Alevis share their women at their communal religious ceremony of the candle blown out.

Historically, the Qizilbash supported the Safavid **Persian** Shah Ismail and constituted a large part of his army when he advanced against the **Ottomans** in the early 16th century. Thus the Sunni Ottomans saw the Qizilbash as bitter enemies and killed as many as 40,000 after their victory at the Battle of **Chaldiran** in 1514. The Qizilbash, however, survived, and at least 10 percent of the population in Turkey today is Alevi, while claims go as high as 30 percent.

The term Qizilbash is an epithet of abuse in modern Turkey. Alevis are sometimes persecuted by the Sunni majority, and thus they tend to espouse liberal causes. The deadly riots that killed several hundred in Kahramanmaras in southeastern Turkey on Christmas Day in 1978 partially involved the Qizilbash. Many Zaza speakers in Turkey are Alevis and constitute a majority in the province of **Dersim**, now called Tunceli. Alevi Kurds in Turkey are a minority within a minority.

ALGIERS AGREEMENT (ACCORD). In March 1975, **Iraq** and **Iran** signed an agreement in Algiers under which Iran halted its support for the revolt of **Mulla Mustafa Barzani** in return for joint usage of the Shatt al-Arab River. Without Iranian aid, Barzani's long-time on-again, off-again revolt quickly collapsed and the great Kurdish leader was forced into exile, where he died in 1979. The Algiers Agreement is still remembered by Kurds as a great disaster and evidence of foreign betrayal. *See also* KISSINGER, HENRY.

ALTUN, RIZA. One of the original members of the **Kurdistan Workers Party** (PKK), and long a close confidant of the party's leader **Abdullah Ocalan**. Altun served a severe nine years in the **Diyarbakir** prison. After Ocalan's capture in 1999, Altun was named to the PKK's presidential council to act for Ocalan.

AMED. *See* DIYARBAKIR.

AMERICAN KURDISH INFORMATION NETWORK (AKIN). Small, but active Kurdish lobby in Washington, D.C., headed by Kani Xulam, a Turkish Kurdish exile. It often takes positions similar to those of the **Kurdistan National Liberation Front**, the public relations and propaganda organization of the **Kurdistan Workers Party**.

AMIN, NOSHIRWAN MUSTAFA (1943–). For many years, a top assistant of **Jalal Talabani**, the leader of the **Patriotic Union of Kurdistan (PUK)**. The PUK was originally established in June 1975 by combining Amin's Komala, a Marxist group, with the Socialist Movement of Kurdistan, led by **Ali Askari**.

AMNESTY INTERNATIONAL (AI). Private nongovernmental international organization that works to prevent some of the gravest violations by governments of people's fundamental **human rights**. It was founded in 1961. AI's main focus is freeing all prisoners of conscience; ensuring fair and prompt trials for political prisoners; abolishing the death penalty, torture, and other cruel treatment of prisoners; and ending extrajudicial executions. Thus AI has been a major actor supporting human rights for the Kurds. As a result, it has been strongly criticized by governments accused of violating Kurdish human rights. AI has also worked to correct human rights violations committed by various Kurdish organizations, such as occurred during the **Kurdistan Democratic Party–Patriotic Union of Kurdistan** fighting in northern **Iraq** in the mid-1990s. In 1977, AI was awarded the Nobel Peace Prize.

ANFAL. The Anfal operations in 1988 were a series of genocidal assaults on the Iraqi Kurdish population that had supported **Iran** during the **Iran–Iraq War** (1980–88). Led by **Ali Hassan Majid, Saddam Hussein**'s cousin and at that time defense minister, the Anfal operations resulted in some 180,000 deaths by execution and **chemical** attacks such as at the Iraqi Kurdish city of **Halabja** in March 1988. Some 2,000–3,000 villages were destroyed and many more Kurds were exiled to "model villages" and to the south of **Iraq**. Thousands of official Iraqi documents testifying to the extent of the slaughter were captured during the Kurdish uprising in 1991 and they were eventually transferred to the University of Colorado at Boulder in the **United States**, where some have been translated and published by the **Human Rights Watch**/Middle East. The term "Anfal" comes from the Koran, where it is the title of the eighth *sura* (chapter), and means "spoils of battle." By using the term, the Iraqis were attempting to provide a religious justification for what they were doing.

ANNAZIDS. The Annazids were a Kurdish dynasty that flourished from 991 to 1117 in the frontier regions between **Iraq** and **Iran**. They existed along with numerous other principalities of Iranian origin during the period of the **Buwayhids (Buyids)**. Abu al-Fath Muhammad bin Annaz established the dynasty and ruled in Hulwan, situated at the beginning of the pass leading up to the Iranian plateau.

The Arabic names and titles of most of the Annazids indicated their Arab links. The Annazids were seminomadic, living in tents but also possessing fortified settled areas for protection.

ANSAR AL-ISLAM. Meaning "Supporters of Islam," an organization originally created in 2001 out of several smaller Kurdish **Islamist** extremist groups in northern **Iraq**. Its membership includes Kurds, Arabs, and Afghans. At first, it called itself Jund al-Islam (Soldiers of Islam), but it changed its name in 2002. Many believe that Ansar al-Islam has connections to al-Qaida. Others dispute this contention. Apparently, some of Ansar's members did receive training at al-

Qaida's bases in Afghanistan. The **United States** claims that Ansar has received financial support from al-Qaida and has experimented with the deadly chemical agent, ricin.

The group established itself in the mountains near **Halabja** next to the border with **Iran**. It modeled itself after the Taliban in Afghanistan, ruled with a deeply conservative religious bent, and sponsored terror and war against the secular **Patriotic Union of Kurdistan (PUK)**. Savage fighting occurred between the two in the fall of 2001 and again in the fall of 2002. Ansar mutilated the bodies of some of its victims and in April even came close to assassinating **Barham Salih**, the prime minister of the PUK administration in **Sulaymaniya**. In February 2003, Ansar did treacherously assassinate another PUK official, Shawkat Haji Mushir, as he was attempting to negotiate with it.

Ansar al-Islam has prohibited electronic devices such as television and radio, mandates beards for men, and requires women to wear full-length gowns that cover their faces. Mulla Fatih Kraker, its founder and first leader, was arrested in the Netherlands in September 2002. Mulla Mohammad Hasan reputedly became the new leader. The group also has a 15-member *shura,* or leadership council, which operates from the village of Beyara. Early in 2003, Ansar was thought to have approximately 600 fighters. Some, however, believed the total was larger. The group runs training camps offering lessons on infantry weapons, tactics, suicide bombing, and assassination. In addition, it videotapes combat operations and announces its battlefield accomplishments on a web site at www.ansarislam.com.

In February 2003, Colin Powell, the U.S. secretary of state, declared in a speech to the **United Nations** Security Council that Ansar al-Islam was testing **chemical weapons** and had connections with **Saddam Hussein**. Although some of these claims seem rather exaggerated, it was clear that Ansar al-Islam was a serious threat to the PUK and any possible attack by the United States against Iraq that was directed near Ansar's stronghold in northern Iraq. During the **Gulf War II**, U.S. and Kurdish troops routed Ansar, but some of its elements seemed to have escaped to Iran, possibly to fight again another day. See *also* ISLAMIC MOVEMENT OF KURDISTAN.

ANTER, MUSA (1922–92). Famous Kurdish intellectual and writer in **Turkey** who was murdered in September 1992, almost certainly by a member of the **Hizbullah–Contras**, a clandestine, government-sponsored group murdering Kurdish civilians believed to be supporting the **Kurdistan Workers Party**, and Kurdish nationalist causes.

ANTI-TERRORIST LAW (Turkey). Article 8 of the Anti-Terrorist Law, which entered into force in 1991, made it possible to consider academics, intellectuals, and journalists speaking up peacefully for Kurdish rights and other causes in **Turkey** to be engaging in terrorist acts punishable by imprisonment. Although Article 8 has been subsequently modified, **human rights** abuses against those advocating Kurdish rights and democracy continue in Turkey.

APO. *See* OCALAN, ABDULLAH.

APOCULAR. Named for the leader **Abdullah (Apo) Ocalan**, the Apocular, or "followers of Apo," was an early name for the **Kurdistan Workers Party.**

ARARAT REVOLT (1927–30). One of three great Kurdish revolts during the early years of the Turkish Republic, the other two being the **Sheikh Said** revolt in 1925 and the **Dersim** revolt in 1936–38. The revolt around Mt. Ararat in easternmost **Turkey** was planned by the **Khoybun**, a new Kurdish party based in **Syria**. The **Armenian** Dashnak Party and the International Minority Movement in the **Soviet Union** helped with funds.

Ihsan Nuri was chosen to head a trained, nontribal fighting force in an attempt to move away from the failed tribal uprisings. Nevertheless, various tribal chieftains joined the revolt, including the Jelali tribe, who lived in the region. A government was formed and in the first clashes the Kurds defeated the Turks. Eventually, however, the Turks were able to crush the revolt because of their superior resources. In addition, Turkey obtained border modifications with **Iran**, which allowed Turkey to surround the Kurdish rebels and cut off their retreat into nearby Iran.

ARDALAN. An old Kurdish **emirate** that by the 14th century ruled large amounts of territory on either side of the central **Zagros Mountains**. According to the *Sharafnama*, Baba Ardalan was a descendant of the earlier **Marwanid** Kurdish dynasty.

In more recent times, along with the rival **Babans**, Ardalan dominated the territory on either side of what is today the Iraqi–Iranian border. In the 19th century, Ardalan corresponded roughly with the present Iranian province of **Kordestan**. The *walis* (governors) of Ardalan, with their capital at Sinna (now known as Sanandaj), were hereditary rulers known for their loyalty to the **Persian Empire**. They epitomized the decentralized system of rule the later Safavids and their Qajar successors employed. The literary language of Ardalan was Haurami, a **Gurani** dialect. Under the patronage of the Ardalan court, a large body of Kurdish **literature** was produced in Gurani.

ARGK. *See* KURDISTAN PEOPLES LIBERATION ARMY.

ARMED PROPAGANDA. This term was used by various violent leftist groups in **Turkey**, including the **Kurdistan Workers Party**, during the 1960s and 1970s to refer to violent attacks against certain unpopular state targets. Hopefully, such attacks would attract public attention and show that the state was incapable of protecting its own. The people then would gain the courage to side with the revolution.

ARMENIANS. The Armenians are an ancient Indo-European-speaking people who lived in eastern Anatolia until World War I and still inhabit the Caucasus Mountains. In 301 C.E., they became the first people to adopt Christianity as the official state religion. A catholicos (pope) heads the Armenian Gregorian (Apostolic) Church in Armenia, and a rival cilician (sis) catholicos sits in Lebanon. Armenians' historic homeland partially overlaps with the Kurds'. Over the years, much bloodshed has occurred between the historically nomadic Kurds and the sedentary Armenians. During World War I, the Armenians suffered at the hands of the **Ottoman** Turks what many consider to have been genocide. Kurdish brigands played a notorious role in these events.

Since both saw **Turkey** as an enemy after World War I, however, some proposed an alliance between the Armenians and Kurds against Turkey. A small amount of cooperation apparently has occurred. From 1973 to 1984, some 30 Turkish diplomats or members of their immediate families were assassinated by Armenian terrorists. In 1991, upon the breakup of the **Soviet Union**, Armenia became an independent state. More than 3 million Armenians currently live in Armenia, while a diaspora of another 3 million live in various successor Soviet states, the **United States**, **France**, and numerous other places.

ASHIRET. Term from Arabic used throughout Kurdistan to denote an entire tribe or even confederation of tribes. *Ashiret* also conveys the meaning of being tribal as opposed to being nontribal. In recent decades, the number of tribal Kurds has dramatically declined due to the forces of modernization. In Iraqi Kurdistan, for example, maybe 60 percent of the Kurds claimed a tribal affiliation as recently as 1960. By the late 1980s, this proportion had probably fallen to approximately 20 percent. A similar pattern exists elsewhere, especially in **Turkey**. However, the governments sometimes encourage progovernment tribes as a divide-and-rule tactic. The progovernment **Bucaks** in Turkey remain an excellent, but not unique, example.

Kurdish tribes are not easy to define because they vary in time and place, and in size, structure, and internal organization. In the 19th century, for example, the very term "Kurd" meant tribespeople who spoke Kurdish. This imprecision regarding tribe is indicated in the various words used by Kurds to denote a tribal group: *il, ashira, qabila, taifa, tira, oba, hawz,* and so forth. In general, these different terms range from tribal confederations down to clan, septs, or sections. Tribes are usually defined by kinship, real or mythical. Most Kurdish tribal groups claim descent from a hero of the early Islamic period. *See also* BARADUST; BARZANIS; HARKIS; JAF; KALHUR; MUKRI; SHABANKARA; SHIKAK; SHILLET; SINDJABI; SURCHI; ZIBARIS.

ASKARI, ALI (?–1978). Ali Askari was one of **Mulla Mustafa Barzani**'s most capable commanders. After 1975, he became a prominent leader in the **Patriotic Union of Kurdistan (PUK).** During **Kurdistan Democratic Party**–PUK fighting in 1978, Askari was captured and executed by the KDP. This event still embitters intra-Kurdish relations between the two main Iraqi Kurdish parties.

ASSYRIANS. A rather recent term used by a still partially Aramaic-speaking, **Christian** minority who have historically lived among the Kurds, with whom they have often, but not always, had bad, subservient relations. Assyrians claim descent from the ancient Assyrian Empire and call their ancestral land Beth Nahrain. A substantial proportion of the Assyrians probably come from the same racial stock as their Muslim neighbors.

Assyrians belong to the Nestorian Church, which had broken theologically with the Roman Catholic Church in 431 after the Council of Ephesus rejected the teachings of Nestorius, the patriarch of Constantinople. The Nestorians saw Christ as two distinct persons, divine and human, and argue that the Father begot Jesus as God, while Mary bore him as a man. Thus the Nestorians opposed using the title "Mother of God" for Mary.

At one time, the Nestorians extended as far east as China, where they built a famous monument in Xian in 781. The Nestorians possibly gave rise to the medieval legends of Prester John, a Christian king supposedly living somewhere in the east who might be a potential ally for the West in its struggle against Islam.

The Nestorians, however, were reduced by persecutions and never recovered from Timur Lang's attacks in the 14th century. They eventually shrank to a community largely concentrated in the mountains of **Hakkari** in what is now southeastern **Turkey**. Nevertheless, as recently as around 1870 there were some 97,000 Assyrians living in Hakkari, of whom 52,000 were tribally organized and thus not subservient to the Kurds, who numbered some 165,000 in Hakkari. The Assyrians were led by a patriarch called the mar shamun. During the 19th century, the Assyrians suffered numerous massacres at the hands of the Kurds, the depredations of **Badr Khan Beg** in the 1840s being a prime example.

During World War I, many Assyrians died supporting the Allies. After the war, **Great Britain** resettled most of them in the Kurdish areas of northern **Iraq**. The Kurds greatly resented this intrusion and the Assyrian levy, a special military group of some 5,000 Assyrians trained by the British to help uphold their rule in northern Iraq. In

1933, Kurds and Iraqi nationalist army officers massacred many Assyrians and destroyed them as a military force. In recent decades, most Assyrians have emigrated to the **United States** and Europe. There are about 50,000 still living in northern Iraq, where in recent years the Assyrian Democratic Movement (Zowaa) has joined the **Iraqi Kurdistan Front** and cooperated with the **Kurdistan Democratic Party**. Both the parliament of the **Kurdistan Regional Government** in Iraqi Kurdistan and the **Kurdistan National Congress** (backed by the **Kurdistan Workers Party**) have Assyrian representatives. **MED-TV** and its successor, MEDYA-TV, have both broadcast Aramaic-language newscasts. Problems concerning finances, education, and land remain, however.

Most observers would include among the Assyrians other small Christian groups such as the **Chaldeans**, who were converted in modern times by the **French** to Roman Catholicism, and the **Syrian** Orthodox (Suryani) or Jacobites, who are a Monophysite Christian sect like the **Armenian** Apostolic Church and the Coptic Church in Egypt. The Monophysites believe that Christ contained only a single, wholly divine nature. They were declared heretical by the Council of Chalcedon in 451.

ATAC, HALIL (ABU BAKIR). A leading member of the **Kurdistan Workers Party (PKK)** for many years. In the 1990s, he served on the party's leadership council (politburo) and was also chosen to serve on its presidential council to act for **Abdullah Ocalan**, the PKK's leader, after Ocalan's capture in 1999. During the 1990s, Atac also commanded **Kurdistan Peoples Liberation Army** units in the Turkish provinces of Batman and **Bitlis**, called Garzan by the Kurds.

ATATURK, MUSTAFA KEMAL (1881–1938). Figure who remains revered by Turks as the founder of the modern Republic of **Turkey** out of the ashes of the defeat and disintegration of the **Ottoman Empire** following World War I. Kurds, however, see Ataturk as the author of the racist and assimilationist policies pursued against them to this day by Turkey.

During World War I, Mustafa Kemal established a reputation at the Battle of Gallipoli as one of the very few successful Ottoman leaders. After the war, he broke with the sultan and brilliantly led the

Turkish War of Independence against the invading Greeks. He abolished the sultanate in 1923 and the caliphate in 1924. His ultimate goal was to establish a modern and secular Turkish nation–state and achieve the "level of contemporary civilization." Famous reforms included establishing a secular state, adopting the Latin script, abolishing the fez, adopting surnames, and establishing women's rights. In foreign affairs, he pursued a policy of conciliation and neutrality.

To implement and secure his reforms, however, he established a unitary state that a Kurdish presence threatened to divide and destroy. In 1925, Ataturk crushed the **Sheikh Said** rebellion and deported many Kurds to the west in an effort to dilute their presence and begin to assimilate them. A decree banned all Kurdish schools, organizations, and publications, as well as religious fraternities and *madrasahs*, which were the last source of education for most Kurds. During the 1930s, the basic principles of **Kemalism** led to an extreme form of Turkish nationalism that had no place for Kurdish ethnic consciousness. Indeed, the very words "Kurds" and "Kurdistan" were abolished from the official state discourse. Use of the term **"Mountain Turks"** when referring to the Turkish Kurds served as a code for these actions. Thus the heritage of this great man for nationalist Kurds is largely one of degradation and racism.

AUTONOMOUS REGION. This is the term variously used by the Iraqi government to refer to the political structure it established in northern Iraq in 1974 to allow the Kurds a certain amount of autonomy. **Mulla Mustafa Barzani** refused to accept what he saw as a betrayal of the 1970 **March Manifesto** and war resumed, ultimately leading to Barzani's defeat. Despite all that has since occurred, the Iraqi government continues to maintain the theoretical structure for the Autonomous Region in the north.

AVEBURY, ERIC (1928–). For a number of years, Lord Avebury has been a prominent British activist and author using his position in the House of Lords and as chairman of the Parliamentary Human Rights Group to pursue various Kurdish **human rights** causes.

AYYUBIDS. A famous Islamic dynasty established by the illustrious **Saladin (Salah al Din)** in Egypt in 1171, and who at their brief height also held sway in greater **Syria, Iraq,** and Yemen. The Ayyubids replaced the Fatimids and were in turn replaced by the Mamluks of Egypt in 1252.

The Ayyubids are one of the five Kurdish dynasties mentioned by **Sharaf Khan Bitlisi** in the *Sharafnama* as enjoying royalty. Clearly, however, the Ayyubids thought of themselves as Muslims first, rather than as ethnic Kurds. Other Ayyubids ruled in Syria until 1260. Indeed, the Kurdish writer–prince **Abu al-Fida**, who was followed by his son, ruled Hamah in Syria until 1342. The later rulers (**meliks**) of **Hasankeyf** in modern **Turkey** were also in charge of an Ayyubid successor state.

AZADI. Kurdish word that means "freedom" or "liberty." It has been used as the name of various Kurdish groups and journals. For example, it was the name of the organization associated with the uprising by **Sheikh Said** in 1925. This Azadi consisted mainly of experienced military men and was headquartered in Erzurum in eastern **Turkey**.

Azadi was also the name of the journal of the Kurdish Section of the **Iraqi Communist Party** for many years.

– B –

BAATH PARTY (BAATHISTS). A transnational Arab party ("baath" in Arabic means resurrection) founded in Damascus in 1940 by Michel Aflaq, a Syrian Orthodox Christian intellectual, and Salah al-Din Baitar, a Sunni Muslim Syrian intellectual. The party's historic goals were to achieve Arab unity under secularism and socialism. So-called national sections of the party ruled in **Iraq** and Syria until the United States removed Saddam Hussein from power in April 2003, but the two sections were embittered enemies. The Baath Party came to power in Iraq for nine months in 1963, when it helped to overthrow **Abdul Karim Kassem**. It resumed power in July 1968 and held it until April 2003.

Saddam Hussein increasingly began to wield power and became the party's leader by 1979. The party's fortunes effectively became those of him and Iraq. Under Saddam Hussein, the Baathists made Iraq into a militarily powerful state that was finally able to crush the rebellious Kurds in 1975. To do this, however, Saddam Hussein increasingly used tactics of terror and murder, and against the Kurds **genocide**, effectively turning Iraq into a police state. Ultimately, the Baathists under Saddam Hussein overreached themselves militarily in the **Iran–Iraq War** of the 1980s and the **Gulf War** of 1991 against the **United States** and its allies, following Iraq's invasion of Kuwait.

BABAN. This Kurdish **emirate** played an important role in what is now northern **Iraq** from roughly 1550 until its final demise in 1850. According to the *Sharafnama* of Sharaf Khan Bitlisi, the first chief and eponymous founder of the Baban line was Pir Budak Babe, but his line was soon extinguished. A line claiming a legendary descent from Keghan, a Frank woman captured in battle, then succeeded. Baba Sulayman emerged in 1677 and over the years was followed by 17 additional Baban *mirs* or pashas.

Although it pursued an opportunistic strategy, for most of the time, Baban was nominally subject to the **Ottoman Empire**. Its ruling *mir* received the high Turkish title of pasha early in the 17th century, many decades before this title was given to others in his position. Qara Cholan was Baban's capital until it was moved to **Sulaymaniya** in 1785. The emirate of **Ardalan** in what is now **Iran** was its longtime rival. Abdullah Pasha, the last Baban *mir,* was deposed in 1850.

BADJWAN (BADJALAN, BADJURAN). The Badjwan are a small Kurdish community living some 45 kilometers southeast of **Mosul** who profess **Ahl-i Haqq** or **Kakai** beliefs and are thus sometimes referred to as a *ghulat,* or extremist Shiite sect. They speak a **Gurani** dialect. The Badywan are closely identified with the **Shabak**, but are tribally organized, while the latter are not. Intermarriage among the two communities and others of similar beliefs has somewhat blurred distinctions between them in recent years.

BADR FORCE. A military force of some 5,000–10,000 fighters of the Iraqi Shiite Supreme Council for the Islamic Revolution in Iraq, an Iraqi opposition group created in 1982 and based in Iran. Its Badr Force was formed in 1983. Elements of the Badr Force were employed near **Sulaymaniya** in northern Iraq in 1995. This was done through an agreement between **Iran** and the **Patriotic Union of Kurdistan (PUK)** to counter the developing understanding between **Turkey** and the **Kurdistan Democratic Party (KDP)**. This event was part of the KDP–PUK civil war that dragged on from 1994 until 1998. When it appeared likely that the **United States** would attack Iraq in February 2003, elements of the Badr Force were again deployed into northern Iraq. Some viewed the SCIRI and its Badr Force as a mere pawn of Iran, while others saw it as a legitimate Iraqi opposition group.

BADR KHAN BEG (c. 1802–47). *Mir* of the **emirate** of **Botan** (capital **Cizre**) around 1821, in what is today southeastern **Turkey**. Badr Khan has been described as brave, charming, pious, ambitious, and reckless and is still considered by many Kurds today to be one of their first nationalists.

Under his guidance, Botan grew to encompass much of what is today southeastern Turkey and even the **Bahdinan** part of northern **Iraq**. His strict rule made the emirate a noted place of security. The weakness of the **Ottoman Empire** at that time helped lead Badr Khan to strike for what some would argue was to be an independent Kurdistan. After he committed bloody massacres of the local Christians—who were being abetted by the European powers—**Great Britain** and **France** forced the Ottomans to move against Badr Khan. In 1847, Badr Khan was defeated and exiled to Crete, where he died soon afterward. Botan ceased to exist as a semi-independent emirate.

His descendants continued to play an important role in Ottoman and Kurdish affairs. Two grandsons, Thurayya Badrkhani (1883–1938) and Djaladat Badrkhani (1893–1951), dedicated their lives to the Kurdish national cause. Thurayya, who spent several years in prison for his nationalist activities, started a newspaper called *Kurdistan* in Constantinople after the **Young Turk** coup in 1908 and was an early member of the transnational Kurdish party, **Khoybun**. His brother, Djaladat, was elected the first president of Khoybun. Subsequently, Djaladat devoted himself to literary work and helped to develop a Kurdish alphabet in Latin characters.

BAGHDAD PACT. Formally known as the Middle East Treaty Organization, this cold war, anti-**Soviet** alliance was created in 1955, with

Great Britain, Iraq, Iran, Turkey, and Pakistan as members. Although it was not an official member, the **United States** also, in effect, participated. The Pact's significance for the Kurds was that it also implicitly obligated Iran, Iraq, and Turkey to cooperate on the Kurdish issue, as did the earlier **Saadabad Treaty** in 1937. The Baghdad Pact became increasingly unpopular in the Arab world because it was seen as an agent of Western imperialism. After Iraq withdrew in 1958, the pact's name was changed to the Central Treaty Organization (CENTO). Increasingly ineffective, CENTO was finally disbanded in 1979, after the **shah** of **Iran** was overthrown.

BAHDINAN. Former Kurdish **emirate** in what is now the **Kurmanji**-speaking area under the sway of the **Kurdistan Democratic Party (KDP)** in the northwestern part of **Iraq.** The area is still unofficially referred to as Bahdinan. With the hilltop city of Amadiya as its capital, Bahdinan lasted as a semi-independent emirate into the 1830s. The term "Bahdinan" comes from the eponymous Baha al-Din family, which originated from **Shamdinan** (now Turkicized as Semdinli) to the north in what is presently the Turkish province of **Hakkari.**

BAKHTIYARIS. The some 400,000 Bakhtiyaris are an Iranian-speaking ethnic group, or **tribe,** with their own dialect and living in a mountainous region of southwestern **Iran.** They are closely related to the Kurds. The Bakhtiyaris are divided into two main groups: the Haft–Lang consists of 55 tribes, while the Cahar–Lang number 24. Oil was discovered in their region early in the 20th century.

Apparently, the Bakhtiyaris migrated from northern Afghanistan or southern Tajikistan—ancient Bactria (whence the term Bakhtiyaris)—some 1,000 years ago. They settled first in **Syria** and then in the southern **Zagros** area just south of the Kurdish areas in Iran and close to the **Lurs,** with whom they also are closely associated. Indeed, up to the 15th century, the Bakhtiyaris were known as the Great Lurs.

Historically, the Bakhtiyaris journeyed great distances semiannually in search of grass for their animals, but today most of them have become settled. They are Shiite and famous for their courage and independence. The Bakhtiyaris have many interesting customs regarding birth, marriage, and death, as well as their own special games, poems, folk stories, love songs, and funeral hymns. Their women go unveiled and enjoy a high position. Soraya, the daughter of a Bakhtiyari chieftain, was married to **Muhammad Reza Shah Pahlavi** from 1951 to 1958. The tribe has also produced some of the most influential political leaders in the modern history of Iran. Shapour Bakhtiar, for example, was the last prime minister under Muhammad Reza Shah Pahlavi, in 1979.

BARADUST. The name of two Kurdish districts. The one in the south lies between the towns of Ushnu, Reyat, and Rawanduz and has Kani Resh—perched on a mountain at an altitude of more than 4,000 feet—as its chief town. The famous Urartu stele of Kel-i Shin is also located here. The other Baradust, called Sumay Baradust, is situated further to the north, between Targavar and Kotur, and has Cehrik Kala as its main town. The Bab (Sayyid Ali Muhammad of Shiraz) was imprisoned at Cehrik Kala before he was executed at Tabriz in 1850.

Some claim that the **Hasanwayhid** Kurdish dynasty (959–1095) first established Baradust. The army of Shah Abbas the Great of **Persia** besieged Khan Yakdas, a Baradust *mir,* in the mountain fortress of **Dimdim** in 1609–10, an event that became famous in Kurdish folklore. The Kurdish expression "Baradust, friend of a month," refers to how a former Baradust chieftain treacherously killed one of his allies.

In more recent times, the Baradust have been known as a Kurdish **tribe** in northern **Iraq** that is traditionally progovernment and opposed to the **Barzanis.** During the 1920s, Sheikh Rashid of Lolan led the Baradust Kurds against **Sheikh Ahmad Barzani,** whom Sheikh Rashid accused of heresy. The eccentric Sheikh Ahmad had apparently told his followers to eat pork to symbolize the synthesis of his **Naqshbandi Sufi** beliefs with Christianity. Eventually, Sheikh Ahmad and his younger brother **Mulla Mustafa Barzani** drove Sheikh Rashid into **Iran.**

In the mid-1940s, however, Sheikh Rashid's Baradust helped drive the **Barzanis** into Iran, where Mulla Mustafa joined the **Mahabad Republic of Kurdistan.** After Mulla Mustafa returned from exile in

1958, he eventually repaid the Baradust in kind. As allies of the Iraqi government, the Baradust continued to battle the Kurdish nationalist movement, now led by the Barzanis. However, in 1991, the Baradust joined the Kurdish uprising against the government. Karim Khan Baradust is currently a prominent Baradust leader.

BARAN, DOCTOR. Nom de guerre of Muslum Durgun, a longtime commander of the **Kurdistan Peoples Liberation Army (ARGK)** of the **Kurdistan Workers Party (PKK)**. He was active in the **Dersim** or Tunceli area of **Turkey**. In 1993 or 1994, however, Dr. Baran was apparently executed by the PKK for "passivism," or failing to launch attacks on Turkish targets. The PKK incredulously announced that he had committed suicide.

***BARIS DUNYASI* (WORLD OF PEACE).** An important intellectual journal published by a liberal Turk, Ahmet Hamdi Bashar, for a brief period in the early 1960s. The journal encouraged debate between state officials and Kurdish intellectuals such as **Musa Anter** and thus played a major role in reopening the Kurdish question in Turkey after a long hiatus following the crushing of the **Dersim** revolt (1936–38).

BARZAN. The eponymous home of the **Barzanis**, a remote old mountainous and economically marginal village in the upper regions of what is today northern **Iraq**, just south of the present Turkish border and on the left (eastern) bank of the Great Zab River. In his famous *Sharafnama,* **Sharaf Khan Bitlisi** called it Baziran and listed it as a possession of the *mirs* of **Bahdinan**. During the 1840s, Sheikh Abdul Rahman—sometimes called Tajuddin—(a disciple of the **Naqshbandi Sufi** order established in Kurdistan by **Maulana Khalid**) settled in Barzan and thus became the first Barzani of today's famous family and **tribe**. Barzan then served as a sort of utopian society in which refugees were welcomed.

Since Barzan was located next to the powerful **Zibari** tribe's territory, much fighting took place between the two. The **sheikhs** of Barzan became noted for their religious authority and martial prowess. The village itself was destroyed by the government during the fighting between it and the Barzanis, but it has been rebuilt since 1991.

BARZANI, AHMAD (SHEIKH) (1884–1969). The elder brother of **Mulla Mustafa Barzani** and the last Barzani to bear the title "**sheikh** of Barzan." During the 1920s, Sheikh Ahmad earned a reputation among some for religious eccentricity involving his claims of semi-divinity and his unorthodox religious practices. Along with his younger brother, Mulla Mustafa, he also rebelled against the government and was eventually imprisoned. In later years, Sheikh Ahmad attempted unsuccessfully to play a mediating role between the government and Mulla Mustafa.

BARZANI, IDRIS (1944–87). Idris Barzani was one of the many sons of **Mulla Mustafa Barzani**. After the elder Barzani's defeat in 1975 and death in 1979, Idris and his half brother **Massoud Barzani** emerged as coleaders of the revamped **Kurdistan Democratic Party**. Idris had a reputation as being scholarly, thoughtful, and traditional. He died suddenly of a heart attack in 1987, leaving Massoud as the undisputed leader of the family and party.

BARZANI, MASSOUD (1946–). The current leader of the **Barzani** family and president of the **Kurdistan Democratic Party (KDP)** was born in Mahabad, **Iran**, on 16 August 1946, the same day his father and others founded the KDP. Until his father, **Mulla Mustafa Barzani**, returned from the **Soviet Union** in 1958, Massoud lived with his wealthy grandfather, a **Zibari**. The political situation forced Massoud to complete his high school studies privately.

From 1976 to 1979, he lived in the **United States** with his exiled father. With the fall of **Muhammad Reza Shah Pahlavi** and the death of Massoud's father in 1979, the younger Barzani returned to Iran. These early years probably predisposed him to take a more cautious and conservative position. They also probably led him not to trust the United States and to assume that privilege and wealth were his rightful inheritance, as well as burdens that imposed duties toward his people.

Jalal Talabani, the longtime leader of the **Patriotic Union of Kurdistan**, has been the main rival of Massoud for many years. Since the establishment of the **Kurdistan Regional Government (KRG)** in 1992, Barzani and Talabani have had a complex partner–rival relationship. At first, they seemed to work together closely, but from 1994 to 1998, the two fought a bitter civil war against each other. In September 1996, Barzani even allied briefly with the hated **Saddam Hussein** and then **Turkey** to stave off defeat at the hands of Talabani. In September 1998, however, the United States finally brokered a truce between the two contending Kurdish leaders. Since then, Barzani and Talabani have made impressive strides to achieve unity for the welfare of their people. In the fall of 2002, the two were finally able to reunify the parliament of the KRG in order better to present their case for a federal Kurdish state in a post-Saddam Iraq. Amid U.S. threats to invade **Iraq** and eliminate Saddam Hussein, both Barzani and Talabani also played important roles in the Iraqi opposition conference held in London on 14–17 December 2002. In February 2003, Barzani warned both the United States and Turkey that the Iraqi Kurds would oppose any Turkish attempt to occupy Iraqi Kurdistan as part of an agreement with the United States to attack Iraq. The warning became moot, however, when Turkey decided not to join the U.S. war effort.

BARZANI, MULLA MUSTAFA (1903–79). Mulla Mustafa Barzani was the most famous Kurdish leader of the 20th century. His name became virtually synonymous with the Kurdish **nationalist** movement in **Iraq**, while his fame made him a legendary hero for Kurds everywhere. He was a natural leader, inspired emotional loyalty, and was physically strong and brave. Because of the stunted development of Kurdish nationalism, however, in some ways Barzani never exceeded the bounds of **tribal** chieftain. Some of his Kurdish opponents called him feudal and reactionary. Nevertheless, his career helped mightily to foster a nascent Kurdish national consciousness that continues to grow in the 21st century.

Mulla Mustafa and his mother were imprisoned by the **Ottomans** when he was an infant, and his elder brother **Sheikh Abdul Salam II** was executed by the **Ottomans** for disloyalty in World War I. Barzani eventually had three wives, 10 sons, and several daughters. Hamayl, his third wife, was a member of the **Barzani** tribe's hereditary **Zibari** enemy. She came to wield considerable power behind the scenes and is the mother of **Massoud Barzani**, the current Barzani and **Kurdistan Democratic Party** leader.

Mulla Mustafa emerged in the early 1930s, when with his elder brother, **Sheikh Ahmad Barzani**, he opposed a plan to settle **Assyrians** in Barzani tribal land. Fighting erupted, but eventually the Barzani brothers surrendered and were imprisoned. During World War II, Barzani escaped from house arrest and soon renewed his opposition to the government and various progovernment tribes. Despite early successes, Barzani was eventually forced across the Iranian frontier, where he became a general in the short-lived **Mahabad Republic of Kurdistan.** He also became the leader of the new Kurdish (later Kurdistan) Democratic Party (KDP), founded in **Iraq** on 16 August 1946.

With the fall of the Mahabad Republic in late 1946, Barzani was forced into an epic retreat with some of his best fighters to the **Soviet Union**, where he became known by some as the "Red Mulla." However, he did not become a communist. With the fall of the Iraqi monarchy in 1958, Barzani returned to Iraq, where he quickly regained his former tribal prominence.

By 1961, Barzani was in full revolt against the government. Given the weakness of the Iraqi government in those days, Barzani was able to achieve considerable success and maintain a de facto independence for many years. During his long period of ascendancy, Barzani mastered the art of guerrilla warfare in his mountainous homeland. Barzani also battled against and defeated the forces of the **KDP Politburo**, led by two former associates, **Ibrahim Ahmad** and his son-in-law, **Jalal Talabani**. By the late 1960s, Barzani was the undisputed leader of the Iraqi Kurds.

The **March Manifesto** of 1970, reached with the Iraqi government, now led by the **Baath Party** and increasingly by **Saddam Hussein**, held out the promise of real autonomy for the Kurds. In the end, however, neither side really wanted a compromise. The growing strength of the Baathist government and the treachery of the **United States** and **Iran** in withdrawing their support, which Barzani had naively come to rely on, finally enabled the Iraqi government to quickly win the new round of fighting that began in 1974 and ended in March 1975 with Barzani's total defeat.

Broken and in ill health, Barzani eventually went into exile in the United States, where he died in March 1979. He was initially buried in Iran, but in 1993 he was reinterred in his Kurdish homeland (the town of **Barzan**) amid emotional demonstrations on the part of all Iraqi Kurds.

BARZANI, NECHIRVAN IDRIS (1966–). The son of the late **Idris Barzani** and thus the nephew of the current **Kurdistan Democratic Party (KDP)** and **Barzani** leader, **Massoud Barzani.** Nechirvan Idris Barzani has risen quickly in the hierarchy to become, in the opinion of many, Massoud's heir apparent. Among various positions, Nechirvan Idris has headed the KDP intelligence organization and served as the deputy prime minister of the **Kurdistan Regional Government** in **Irbil.** Currently, he is the prime minister of that administration.

BARZANIS. Sometime in the 1840s, the **Naqshbandi sheikh** Seyyid Taha of **Nehri** apparently sent one of his *khalifas,* or disciples, Sheikh Abdul Rahman (also known as Tajuddin, an Arabic honorific that means "Crown of Religion"), to the remote village of **Barzan** to spread his order's *tariqa,* or school of thought. Despite its obscurity, Barzan was probably a good place for a sheikh to establish himself as a mediator, because it was situated between various disputing tribes at the very time that the last Kurdish **emirates** were being terminated. Sheikh Abdul Rahman thus became the first Barzani of the famous modern family and what eventually emerged as a new tribe out of the various refugees the family welcomed. The sheikh's arrival also set off a lengthy struggle between the Barzanis and the powerful **Zibari tribe,** near whose territory Barzan lay.

Although the Barzanis' power was originally founded on their religious authority as Naqshbandi sheikhs, they also developed into a tribe noted for its fighting abilities. Barzani tribal members still wear a distinctive turban with red stripes. Some Barzani sheikhs (such as **Sheikh Ahmad Barzani**) also gained a reputation for their religious eccentricity. Since Barzan served as a sort of utopian society in which refugees were welcomed, the Barzanis (despite their inherent conservatism and tribal allegiances) also became a center of emerging Kurdish **nationalism.**

Mulla Mustafa Barzani, arguably the most famous Kurd of the 20th century, was an excellent example of this development. His elder brother, father, and grandfather were all hanged by the **Ot-**

tomans for various political offenses. His son, **Massoud Barzani**, is the current Barzani and **Kurdistan Democratic Party** leader. The KDP is very closely associated with the fortunes of the Barzani family. In 1980, **Saddam Hussein**'s regime rounded up several thousand Barzani men and apparently executed them for their perceived disloyalty.

BARZINJI, MAHMUD (SHEIKH) (1881–1956). Descendant of an old and respected family of **Qadiri sheikhs** dating back several centuries. **Great Britain** appointed him their governor of the territory around **Sulaymaniya** in 1918. He promptly revolted and declared himself king of Kurdistan. His support proved limited, and using air warfare the British put down several of the sheikh's uprisings. After his final revolt in 1931, the sheikh lived out his long life under house arrest in the south of **Iraq**. Subsequently, his rebellions came to be seen as an early symbol of Kurdish nationalism.

BAYIK, CEMIL (CUMA). One of the original founders of the **Kurdistan Workers Party (PKK)** and presently the only one still alive and free. He was long identified as the number two man in the PKK after its longtime leader, **Abdullah Ocalan**. For many years, Bayik was also the head of the **Kurdistan Peoples Liberation Army**, the professional army of the PKK. Following Ocalan's capture in 1999, Bayik became just one of some 8–10 members of the party's presidential council to replace Ocalan as the daily leader.

BEG. Originally a feudal title given to the main chief of a tribe and simply added to his name. The title "khan" was similarly used. With the demise of feudalism, these titles have fallen out of use. The term *beg* was also used by the **Ottoman Empire** for a military commander of a district who was appointed by the sultan. Over the years, the precise meaning of this honorific changed, leading to difficulties in defining its precise meaning.

BEKAA VALLEY. Valley in Lebanon (but under the control of **Syria**) that was for many years used by terrorist and guerrilla organizations of many different descriptions for their headquarters and training camps. The **Kurdistan Workers Party**'s **Mazlum** (Mahsun) **Korkmaz Camp** was located here, until it was finally closed down in 1992 as a sop to **Turkey**. Following a Turkish ultimatum in October 1998, Syria finally expelled the PKK and its leader, **Abdullah Ocalan**, from its remaining bases in this valley.

BEKAS, SHERKO (1940–). One of the most famous contemporary Kurdish poets. Much of his work is **nationalistic** and patriotic: "If from inside of all my poetry . . . you take out the freedom, my year will die and I will die also."

Born in **Sulaymaniya** province in Iraqi Kurdistan, Sherko Bekas has published poetry in Kurdish newspapers and magazines all over Kurdistan. His work also has been translated into many different languages, including Arabic, Italian, Swedish, French, and English. In 1990, he was even awarded a prize for his poetry in a **literature** competition in Europe. He also briefly served as minister of information from 1992 to 1993 in the first unified **Kurdistan Regional Government** in Iraqi Kurdistan.

BESIKCI, ISMAIL (1939–). Turkish sociologist who since 1971 has spent many years off and on in Turkish prisons for his academic writings on the Kurds. Since he has never advocated violence, **Amnesty International** has adopted him as a prisoner of conscience. He has also become a *cause célèbre* among the many cases dealing with the legal suppression of the Kurds in **Turkey**.

BIRDAL, AKIN (1948–). Akin Birdal is an ethnic Kurdish citizen of **Turkey** who has become one of Turkey's best-known advocates of international **human rights**. For several years, he chaired Turkey's Human Rights Association. On 12 May 1998, he miraculously survived an assassination attempt by shadowy right-wing forces in his office, but has never fully recovered. Shortly afterwards, Birdal was sentenced to prison for referring to the rights of the Kurdish people in a public speech he had made in September 1996. He was sentenced under the provisions of Article 312(2) of the Turkish Penal Code for inciting people to hatred and enmity on the basis of class, race, or regional differences. **Amnesty International** has adopted him as a prisoner of conscience.

BITLIS (Bidlis). Prominent Kurdish **emirate** during the 16th and 17th centuries in what is now southeastern **Turkey.** Bitlis is the name of the province and its chief city. Although a scenic city long admired by visitors, it has very hot summers and rigorous winters. An ancient legend claims that the city was established by one of Alexander the Great's generals as an impregnable citadel.

One of its *mirs,* **Sharaf Khan Bitlisi,** was the author of the famous Kurdish history, the *Sharafnama.* This history contains a great deal of data on the emirate's history. **Evliya Chelebi,** the famous Turkish traveler and author of the *Seyahatname,* also spent much time here in 1655. Many of the emirate's inhabitants were **Armenians,** and the city played an important part in Armenian history. Until the problems at the end of the 19th century, the Armenians lived in relative harmony with the neighboring Kurds, Turks, and Jacobites (Christians).

BITLISI, IDRIS (?–1520). Highborn Kurdish scholar and diplomat who helped broker important agreements between the **Ottoman Empire** and Kurdish **emirates** when the Ottomans first expanded into Kurdistan in the early 16th century. Possessed with a great deal of political acumen, he was trusted by both sides.

Sultan Selim I (1512–20) authorized Idris Bitlisi to grant the former ruling Kurdish families prominent positions in the newly conquered territories of parts of Kurdistan and establish their administrative framework. In return, the Kurds recognized nominal Ottoman suzerainty. Thus over the years some 16 semiautonomous *Kurd hukumeti,* or Kurdish **emirates,** were recognized, covering approximately 30 percent of Kurdistan. Some of these emirates lasted into the middle of the 19th century.

The remaining territory was organized into some 20 *sanjaqs,* or provincial districts, some under hereditary Kurdish rulers and others directly administered by centrally appointed officials. Most of these Kurdish emirates and some of the hereditary *sanjaqs* were usually, but not always, exempt from taxes or other Ottoman interference. Specifics reflected the balance of forces at any given time. Although neither the central government nor the Kurdish rulers were completely satisfied, Idris Bitlisi's organizational policies proved largely successful.

In 1515, Idris Bitlisi also proved successful in defending **Diyarbakir** after a siege of one and a half years by the **Persians**. Subsequently, he captured **Mardin** and other towns in what is now largely southeastern **Turkey**. He used substantial numbers of Kurdish forces in these campaigns. His history, the *Hasht Bihisht* (Eight paradises), covers the reigns of the eight Ottoman sultans from Othman to Bayezid II and was written in the most elaborate style of Persian.

BITLISI, SHARAF KHAN (1543–1603). The Kurdish author of the *Sharafnama,* a very erudite history of the ruling families of the Kurdish **emirates**. The book was written in Persian, completed in 1596, and is arguably the single most important source for Kurdish history up to that time.

The *Sharafnama* divides its history into four parts. The first deals with five Kurdish dynasties that have enjoyed status as royalty *(saltanat):* the **Marwanids** of **Diyarbakir** and **Jazire**, the **Hasanwayhids** of Dinawar and Shahrizur, the Fadluyids of the Great **Lur**, the princes of little Lur, and the **Ayyubids**. The second part lists dynasties that have had coins struck and the *khutba* recited in their names. (The *khutba* is a religious invocation pronounced at the Friday prayer meeting that mentions the Prophet, the first four caliphs, and the current ruler.) The third part numbers the families of hereditary governors *(hukkam),* while the fourth details the history of the *mirs* of **Bitlis**.

Sharaf Khan Bitlisi, the former ruler of the emirate of Bitlis, had abdicated in favor of his son when he wrote the *Sharafnama*. He apparently spent much of his life gathering the information for his history.

BOTAN. Kurdish **emirate** in what is now southeastern **Turkey** that for many centuries was ruled by a family claiming descent from Khalid ibn Walid, one of the Prophet Muhammad's most famous generals. Cizre was its capital. The emirate reached its greatest period of expansion and final demise under **Badr Khan Beg** in the 1840s. Kurdish nationalists today often refer to much of southeastern Turkey as Botan.

BRITAIN. *See* GREAT BRITAIN.

BUCAK, FAIK (?–1966). Turkish Kurdish lawyer from Urfa who headed the **Kurdistan Democratic Party of Turkey**. Faik Bucak was murdered in 1966 (probably by police agents) and his party split into two hostile factions. Both fled to Iraqi Kurdistan, where under circumstances that remain obscure, both of the new leaders (**Dr. Shivan** [Sait Kirmizitoprak] and **Sait Elci**) were killed and their organizations eliminated. Some say that **Mulla Mustafa Barzani** executed Shivan for killing Elci, while others say that Elci's death was the work of the **Milli Istihbarat Teskilati**, or Turkish National Intelligence Organization.

BUCAKS. An influential progovernment Kurdish tribe or clan in the area around Siverek, **Turkey**. They are seen by the **Kurdistan Workers Party (PKK)** as a leading example of the Kurdish exploitative landlord class. To announce its establishment, the PKK in 1979 unsuccessfully attempted to assassinate Mehmet Celal Bucak, who was then leader of the tribe. Sedat Bucak, the present Bucak leader and True Path Party member of the Turkish parliament, was one of the principles involved in the notorious **Susurluk** incident involving the highest level connections between Turkey's intelligence community and organized crime. Sedat Bucak headed a 2,000-strong militia, which was deputized as **village guards** and received more than $1 million a month to battle Kurdish separatists. *See also ASHIRET.*

BURKAY, KEMAL (1937–). Turkish **Alevi** Kurd who established the relatively moderate, nonviolent (Turkish) **Kurdistan Socialist Party (PSK)** in 1974. Since then, he has served as the party's general secretary. The PSK calls for a Turkish–Kurdish federation. Burkay has lived in exile in Sweden since 1980, when the new Turkish government established by the military coup withdrew his Turkish citizenship. He declined to join the **Kurdistan Parliament in Exile** set up largely by the **Kurdistan Workers Party** in 1995. **Mehdi Zana**, the former mayor of **Diyarbakir**, is a close associate. Burkay is interested in **literature** and has written a number of short stories, novels, and poems.

BUSH, GEORGE H. W. (1924–). President of the **United States** during the **Gulf War** in 1991. After the defeat of **Iraq**, Bush called upon the Kurds and Shiites to rise up. When they did, however, the United States did nothing to prevent **Saddam Hussein**'s still relatively formidable forces from crushing them. The resulting Kurdish **refugee** exodus to the mountains caused Bush to reconsider his opposition to helping the Kurds. The United States established **Operation Provide Comfort (OPC)** to provide a **safe haven** and **no-fly zone** to protect the Kurds' return and establishment of a de facto state of Kurdistan. Subsequently, Bush gave only very lukewarm support to the Iraqi opposition to Saddam Hussein. He left office in January 1993, after he was defeated for reelection by **Bill Clinton**. His son, **George W. Bush**, was later elected president of the United States and assumed the office in 2001.

BUSH, GEORGE W. (1946–). The son of President **George H. W. Bush**, elected president of the **United States** in a controversial election in November 2000. At first, the younger Bush seemed somewhat overwhelmed in the position, but he quickly gained wide support in the United States when he responded forcefully to the al-Qaida terrorist attacks on September 11, 2001.

His administration publicly promised to continue to maintain the **no-fly zone** protecting the Iraqi Kurds. In the fall of 2002, President Bush demanded that **Saddam Hussein** disarm and threatened that the United States would lead a war to disarm him if he did not. The implications for the Iraqi Kurds of such a war were obviously important, as they had declared their intent to form a federal state in a post-Saddam Iraq. In February 2003, however, the United States seemed to be reneging on its promise to defend the Iraqi Kurds, when the United States agreed to allow Turkish troops to enter Iraqi Kurdistan if Turkey would permit U.S. troops to be stationed in Turkey as part of the U.S. war effort in the **Gulf War II**. Turkey, however, rejected the offer. As of this writing, therefore, Bush's policies toward Iraq held major implications for the future of the Iraqi Kurds.

BUWAYHIDS (BUYIDS). Generally considered a **Persian** dynasty, famous for having captured Baghdad and the Abbasid caliphate in 945 C.E. and remaining in power until 1055. Some Kurdish scholars argue, however, that the Buwayhids actually were descended from the Kurdish **Dailamites**, or Dilami, who had established a number of different kingdoms. Several other Buwayhid dynasties also ruled other parts of what are now **Iraq** and **Iran**. The name Buwayhid derives from Buwayh or Buyeh, the father of the three brothers who founded the dynasty. The Buwayhids were Twelve-Imam Shiites who practiced tolerance toward other Islamic groups. The dynasty ruled during the period between the ascendancy of the Arabs early in Islamic history and the subsequent Turkish conquest in the 11th century, a period termed by some the Iranian intermezzo. *See also* ANNAZIDS.

– C –

CARPETS. *See* RUGS.

CAYAN, MAHIR (1946–72). Famous leader of the Turkish revolutionary left in the 1960s and early 1970s who served as a model for the **Kurdistan Workers Party** leader **Abdullah (Apo) Ocalan**. An ethnic Kurd, Cayan led the Turkiye Halk Kurtulus Partisi ve Cephesi, or Turkish Peoples Liberation Party and Front, which had grown out of **Dev Genc**. Cayan was also associated with **Deniz Gezmis**, another famous leader of the Turkish revolutionary left. After he helped to kidnap the **Israeli** ambassador to Turkey, Cayan was killed by Turkish security forces during a shootout at the village of Kizildere on 30 March 1972.

CEGERXWIN, SEXMUS HESEN (1903–84). Much beloved Kurdish poet who advocated Kurdish union and radical social reform. His rhymes were particularly rich. He also exhibited an ability to write both in a classical and more modern form. *Diwane Cegerxwin* (Cegerxwin's poems) and *Sewra Azadi* (The revolt of liberty) were two of his most famous works. *See also* LITERATURE.

CENTRAL INTELLIGENCE AGENCY (CIA). U.S. agency involved in the covert U.S.–Iranian support and betrayal of **Mulla Mustafa Barzani** during the 1970s, U.S. incitement of the Iraqi Kurds to rise against **Saddam Hussein** following the **Gulf War** in 1991, and subsequent unsuccessful plots involving the Kurds against the regime in the mid-1990s. *See also* PIKE COMMITTEE RE-PORT.

CENTRAL TREATY ORGANIZATION (CENTO). *See* BAGH-DAD PACT.

CHALABI, AHMAD (1945–). Exiled Iraqi Shia banker who became the leader of the opposition **Iraqi National Congress (INC)** at its creation in 1992. He remains probably the most important person in that organization. He was educated in the **United States,** where he earned a Ph.D. in mathematics from the University of Chicago in 1969, and he is fluent in English; his sympathies toward the Kurds date to the time of **Mulla Mustafa Barzani**, whom he helped obtain arms.

He has had only limited success as the leader of the INC and his following within Iraq seems minimal. Due in part to reputed financial irregularities, even U.S. support has been lukewarm. His enemies have accused him of financial irregularities dating back to the collapse in 1990 of his Petra Bank, which he had established in Jordan in 1977. Despite these problems, Chalabi remained a leading member of the Iraqi opposition, but his future seemed uncertain following the removal of Saddam Hussein in April 2003.

CHALDEANS. Christians whom the **French** converted to Catholicism beginning in the 16th century. The Chaldeans suffered greatly in World War I and their numbers have been further reduced due to emigration. Along with the **Assyrians**, they remain part of the small Christian minority in northern **Iraq**.

CHALDIRAN, BATTLE OF (1514). At this important battle northeast of Lake Van, the **Ottomans** inflicted a crushing defeat upon the Safavid **Persians**. The resulting boundary established between the two was formalized by the Treaty of **Zuhab** in 1639 and has persisted into modern times. As a result, most Kurds lived within the boundaries of the Ottoman Empire, while the remainder lived within Persia. After the battle, pastoral nomadic Kurds increasingly began to join and even replace the indigenous **Armenian** agriculturist population on the plateau situated there.

CHELEBI, EVLIYA (c. 1611–85). Ottoman traveler and author who wrote the *Seyahatname,* or *Book of Travels,* one of the most useful sources on the social, political, economic, and cultural life of the **Ottoman Empire** in the 17th century. In 1655 and 1656, Chelebi traveled to many different parts of Kurdistan (in particular **Bitlis**) and took extensive notes on almost everything he saw.

CHEMICAL WEAPONS. During the **Iran–Iraq War (1980–88),** **Iraq** used chemical weapons against **Iran.** Usage of such weapons was clearly illegal under existing international law. At the end of the war, Iraq also turned these weapons against the Iraqi Kurds because they had supported Iran in the war. General **Ali Hassan Majid,** a first cousin of **Saddam Hussein** and governor in the north of Iraq, became known by the Kurds as Ali Chemical for his ruthless usage of chemical weapons against them during the **Anfal** campaigns and the notorious attack against **Halabja,** which killed some 5,000 Kurds on 16 March 1988.

Chemical weapons used by the Iraqi government included mustard, nerve, and cyanide gas, among others. There was very little international response to this clear violation of international law. This usage of chemical weapons illustrated Kurdish vulnerability and even **genocide** as defined by international law.

CHOKHSOR. *See* SHILLET.

CHRISTIANS. Indigenous Christian minorities remain living among the Kurds, who historically dominated most of them. At times, these Christians have also come into conflict with their Muslim neighbors, and in modern times they have been used as a fifth column offering an entry into local politics to Western imperialists. During World War I, these Christians suffered heavily and their numbers were greatly reduced.

Before the Europeans began their proselytizing activities in modern times, there were three Christian groups living among the Kurds. The Suryani belonged to the Syrian Orthodox, or Jacobite, Church and lived mainly in the Tor Abdin and **Jazire** areas of northwestern Kurdistan. They spoke Aramaic or Arabic dialects. The **Assyrians** belonged to the very different Nestorian Church, whose members also spoke Aramaic dialects and lived in central Kurdistan in **Bahdinan**, in **Hakkari**, and in Urumiya in present-day Iranian Kurdistan. The **Armenians**, with their own ancient church and language, constituted by far the largest group of ethnic Christians.

CILLER, TANSU (1946–). **Suleyman Demirel**'s successor as the leader of the right-wing True Path Party; also, **Turkey's** first female prime minister, from 1993 to 1995. At first, Ciller appeared to take a conciliatory approach to the Kurdish issue in Turkey, but soon she reversed herself and pursued an increasingly hard line. In 1994, she banned the pro-Kurdish **Demokrasi Partisi** (Democracy Party) and imprisoned several of its members of parliament, including **Leyla Zana**. Evidence indicates that she also was willing to use the so-called **Hizbullah–Contras** and other criminal actors to murder even peaceful Kurdish supporters. Despite previous promises not to, she opportunistically joined the short-lived **Islamist Refah** coalition of **Necmettin Erbakan** in 1996. She left the government when the coalition resigned in June 1997. Despite charges of corruption, however, she remained one of the leading Turkish politicians until her party failed to win enough votes even to remain in parliament in the landslide victory of the **AK Partisi** of 3 November 2002. She then resigned from her party's leadership.

CIZRE. Also called Jazire bin Omar, a frontier town in southeastern **Turkey** close to both the Syrian and Iraqi borders. Although ancient settlements existed on the site, it is said to have been founded and named after al-Hasan bin Omar, who died in 865. The town became an island (whence its Arabic name *jazire*) when a canal joining the two ends of the Tigris River at its bend was dug. Subsequently, however, the original riverbed dried up. Just downstream from Cizre are the ruins of a once magnificent bridge, still standing, having a single arch of 28 meters and carvings of the zodiac.

Cizre became a prosperous river port in the Middle Ages. For a long time, it also was under the control of various Kurdish *mirs*. During the 12th century, the city was famous for its scholars, writers, and imams. Early in the 19th century, Cizre was the capital of **Badr Khan Beg**, the *mir* of **Botan**. Following his defeat by the **Ottomans**, however, the town stagnated.

CIZRI, MELAYE (c. 1570–c. 1640). Also known as Sheikh Ahmed Nisani, considered by some the most famous early Kurdish poet. Melaye Cizri's *Diwan* (collected works) of more than 2,000 verses is an example of Persian **Sufism** and remains much admired by **sheikhs** and **mullas**. Mir Mihemed of Mukis, surnamed Feqiye Teyran, was a disciple of Melaye Cizri. He wrote an elegy on the death of his mentor, as well as several other works, such as the *History of Sheikh Sanan. See also* LITERATURE.

CLINTON, BILL (1946–). President of the **United States** from 1993 to 2001. His continuing support of the **no-fly zone** over northern **Iraq** allowed the de facto state of Iraqi Kurdistan to continue to exist and gradually prosper. However, Clinton hesitated to give more support to the Iraqi Kurds because of Turkish concerns that an Iraqi Kurdish state would destabilize the Kurdish situation in **Turkey**. Clinton also feared that too much support for the Iraqi Kurds might lead to a breakup of Iraq and instability in the geostrategically important Middle East.

Fighting between the **Kurdistan Democratic Party** and the **Patriotic Union of Kurdistan** also created difficulties for Clinton. Thus Clinton gave only lukewarm support to the Iraqi opposition against **Saddam Hussein**. Clinton's dual containment policy against Iraq and **Iran** also proved increasingly difficult to sustain. In general, Clinton supported the Iraqi Kurds much more than the Turkish Kurds because the United States was allied to Turkey but strongly opposed Iraq.

COPENHAGEN CRITERIA. Term referring to minority rights and **human rights** criteria to which modern European states are expected to conform. The term has become well known in **Turkey** as the standard Turkey must achieve for its Kurdish population before Turkey can be admitted into the **European Union**. The term comes from the "Document of the Copenhagen Meeting of the Conference on the Human Dimension of the CSCE" (Conference on Security and Cooperation in Europe, renamed in 1995 the Organization for Security and Cooperation in Europe, or OSCE), which was adopted on 29 June 1990.

COUNTERGUERRILLAS. One tactic that helped **Turkey** win the war against the **Kurdistan Workers Party (PKK)** in the 1990s was to use military special forces, *ozel tim* (the gendarmerie's special forces) and *ozel hareket tim* (police special forces). These were military units trained to use deadly covert, antiguerrilla tactics to defeat and destroy the PKK and also dry up civilian support for the PKK by destroying civilian villages, among numerous other tactics. Usage of these counterguerrillas called upon traditions dating back to the 1960s and earlier in which Turkey employed right-wing groups to defeat the states' internal enemies. *See also* JITEM.

COX, SIR PERCY (1864–1937). One of several important political officers of **Great Britain** in Iraqi Kurdistan in the years immediately following World War I. Succeeding **Arnold Wilson** in October 1920, Cox successfully worked to incorporate Iraqi Kurdistan and its rich oil deposits into the new state of Iraq that the British were creating.

CULT OF ANGELS. Called *Yazdani* in Kurdish, consists of several ancient, indigenous, non-Muslim, Kurdish **religions**, including the **Alevis**, **Ahl-i Haqq**, and **Yezidis**. These religions clearly include syncretic elements of shamanism, Zoroastrianism, Judaism, **Christianity**, and **Islam**.

Creation is often explained by a type of cosmic egg in which the Universal Spirit once lived. Adherents of the cult believe in seven luminous angelic beings of ether who protect the universe from an equal number of dark forces of matter. The cult also believes in the transmigration of souls with repeated reincarnations of the Deity through major and minor avatars or *Babs*. Both good and evil are important to the creation and continuation of the material world.

Although the numbers of followers of the cult are declining, some observers claim that as many as 30 percent of the Kurds still adhere to it. This figure, however, is almost certainly a gross exaggeration, as most Kurds now adhere to Sunni Islam. Elements of the cult arguably survive today in the radicalism, economic and social egalitarianism, and martyr syndrome of the Shiites. The cult's attempts to absorb Shiism through claims of a shared identity and willingness to use *taquiya* (religious dissimulation to survive) often confuse outside observers. *See also* GHULAT.

CURUKKAYA, SELIM (TILKI). Nicknamed "Tilki" ("fox"), former leader of the **Kurdistan Workers Party (PKK)** in Europe who fell out with the party over charges that he had made enormous amounts of money in drug dealing and who was sentenced to death. Curukkaya fled to Germany, where he published a book entitled *Verses of Apo,* which was denounced by the PKK. In his book, Curukkaya called **Abdullah (Apo) Ocalan,** the leader of the PKK, a "murderer" and "dictator" and referred to him as being "the biggest betrayer of the already betrayed Kurdish revolution." Curukkaya's wife, Aysel (Medya) Curukkaya, had earlier been a leading PKK militant in the province of Amed (**Diyarbakir**).

– D –

DAILAMITES. People traditionally thought to have originated in the Alburz mountains just south of the Caspian Sea, from where they launched several important military conquests in early Islamic times.

The Dailamites apparently were precursors of some of today's Kurdish populations, such as possibly the *guran,* nontribal farming peasants in the **Sulaymaniya** area of today's **Iraq**. However, the Dailamites apparently originated in the upper Tigris River area of Anatolia, the home of possibly their modern descendants, the **Dimili** or Zaza Kurds. Most of the Dailamites were originally adherents of the Kurdish **Cult of Angels** religions, although there was some Shiite influence among them. This may help to explain why the Dailamites were usually known for their religious tolerance of peoples they subjected.

Historic Dailamite dynasties included the Bavandis of the southern Caspian Sea area (665–1349); the Ziyarids of Tabaristan and Gurgan (927–1090); the Kangarids (also known as the Musafirids or Sallarids) of Azerbaijan (916–1090); the Jastanids of Gilan, Ruyan, and Talishan (c. 6th–12th centuries); the Shabankaras of Fars and Kirman; and the Kakuyids of central and southern Iran (1008–1119). The famous **Buwayhid** dynasty, which conquered Baghdad and the Abbasid caliphate in 945, was also of Dailamite origin. Daylaman in the Alburz Mountains was the site of the castle of Alamut, the legendary home of the Old Man of the Mountain. Alamut means "eagle's nest" in the Kurdish language of Dimili.

DARBANDIKHAN DAM. Constructed in the 1950s on the Sirwan and Diyala Rivers near **Halabja**, which is close to the Iranian frontier in Iraqi Kurdistan. There is now a large lake behind the dam that provides substantial irrigation and power resources. *See also* DUKAN DAM; WATER.

DAUD KHAN (?–1912). Ruthless Iranian Kurd of humble birth who usurped the leadership of the **Kalhur tribe** in the **Kirmanshah** area about 1900. For more than a decade, Daud Kahn played an important role until he gradually alienated so many other Kurdish tribes and the government that he lost his support. He was killed during an ill-conceived march on Tehran.

DEMIREL, SULEYMAN (1920–). Trained as a hydraulic engineer, a moderate right-wing prime minister of **Turkey** on several occasions from 1965 to 1993, and then president from 1993 to 2000, upon the death of **Turgut Ozal**. The military removed Demirel from leadership on two separate occasions (1971 and 1980), which probably made him very cautious about opposing it on the Kurdish issue.

Upon becoming prime minister again in 1991, Demirel offered great hope that Turkey might try to solve its Kurdish problem successfully when he recognized what he called "the Kurdish reality." The precedence of the national security mentality over the concept of basic **human rights**, however, helped cause Demirel's modest proposals to fail. Although he was an accomplished politician and public speaker, Demirel became symbolic of Turkey's inability to change and reform. His attempt to remain in the presidency failed, and he was succeeded in 2000 by a novice reformer, **Ahmet Necdet Sezer**.

DEMOCRATIC MASS PARTY (DMK). *See* ELCI, SEREFETTIN.

DEMOKRASI PARTISI (DEP). Or the Democracy Party, a Kurdish party in **Turkey** that succeeded the **Halkin Emek Partisi**, or Peoples Labor Party, when it was closed down by the government in 1993.

DEP was itself closed down by the government in 1994 and was succeeded by the **Halkin Demokrasi Partisi**, or Peoples Democracy Party.

In March 1994, the Turkish government lifted the immunity of six DEP members of parliament, including **Leyla Zana**, and eventually sentenced them to prison on charges that they were trying to destroy the unity of the Turkish state. DEP denied the charges, and those imprisoned became noted objects of extended **human rights** campaigns in the West. Other DEP parliament members escaped to the West, where they eventually joined the **Kurdistan Parliament in Exile**.

DEMOKRATIK HALKIN PARTISI (DEHAP). Or the Democratic Peoples Party, ran in the Turkish parliamentary elections held on 3 November 2002 as a thinly disguised version of the pro-Kurdish **Halkin Demokrasi Partisi (HADEP)**. DEHAP had previously been created as a hedge against the banning of HADEP, which itself had succeeded the previously banned pro-Kurdish parties. Formally, DEHAP was an alliance of HADEP and two much smaller leftist parties. DEHAP received 6.22 percent of the national vote, an increase of 1.49 percent over HADEP's total in the previous election of 1998, but this was not enough to meet the 10 percent requirement to enter the Turkish parliament. DEHAP did obtain more than 40 percent of the vote in several southeastern provinces that contained large ethnic Kurdish populations. *See also* AK PARTISI.

DENG **(VOICE).** Important bilingual journal published briefly by Yasha Kayar and Meded Serhat in the liberal period of **Turkey** during the early 1960s. The journal was closed down after only its third issue and Serhat was charged with separatism, the standard charge against those who suggested that Kurds lived in Turkey.

DEP. *See* DEMOKRASI PARTISI.

DERSIM. Former Kurdish name for the mountainous, isolated, present-day Turkish province of Tunceli. It is located farther west and nearer to the center of Anatolia than most of the other ethnic Kurdish provinces of **Turkey**. The province has a strong **Alevi** and **Zaza**-speaking population of ethnic Kurds who in the past have not necessarily supported Sunni Kurdish revolts, such as those of **Sheikh Said** in 1925.

Dersim became notorious in the history of the Republic of Turkey for the third and final major Kurdish uprising before World War II. Led by the septuagenarian Alevi cleric Sayyid Riza, the Dersim revolt lasted from 1936 to 1938 and was defeated only with the utmost in scorched-earth tactics. The name Dersim was then changed to Tunceli to help wipe out the memory.

However, the province again played an important role in the **Kurdistan Workers Party (PKK)** uprising during the 1980s and 1990s. "**Dr. Baran**" (Muslum Durgun) led the PKK forces in the province until his reported suicide in 1994. Some believe that Dr. Baran was executed on orders of the PKK leader **Abdullah (Apo) Ocalan** for "passivism," that is, failing to launch attacks on Turkish targets. His eventual successor was "**Parmaksiz Zeki**" (**Semdin Sakik**), who also had a falling out with Ocalan in 1998.

DEV GENC. Or Revolutionary Youth, an important radical, militant, student-based organization founded in **Turkey** in 1969. Its membership was largely Turkish, but Kurds also belonged. In time, it helped give birth to a number of other important radical leftist movements, including the **Kurdistan Workers Party**. Dev Genc was formally closed down by the state after the military coup by memorandum in March 1971.

DEV SOL. Or Revolutionary Left, a violent leftist movement established in **Turkey** in 1978 due to various disputes and splits in the original **Dev Genc** movement. Dev Sol terrorists assassinated former Turkish prime minister Nihat Erim in July 1980, one of the events that helped lead to the military coup of September 1980. A faction of Dev Sol still exists as a violent terrorist organization in Turkey, calling itself the Revolutionary Peoples Liberation Party-Front (Devrimci Halk Kurtulus Partisi-Cephesi). Over the years, it has been active in some urban areas and has also attempted to cooperate with the **Kurdistan Workers Party**.

DEV YOL. Or Revolutionary Way, a radical leftist movement established in **Turkey** in 1976 due to various disputes and splits in the original **Dev Genc** movement. The state eventually eliminated Dev Yol following the military coup in September 1980.

DEVRIMCI DEMOKRATIK KULTUR DERNEKLERI (DDKD). Or Revolutionary Democratic Cultural Associations, established in **Turkey** in 1975. The DDKD was one of a dizzying series of leftist Kurdish groups formed during the fervor of the 1960s and 1970s that eventually resulted in the creation of the **Kurdistan Workers Party (PKK).** In its early years, the PKK opposed the DDKD, branding its members as "social chauvinists" and "national reformists."

DEVRIMCI DOGU KULTUR OCAKLARI (DDKO). Or Revolutionary Eastern Cultural Hearths, an important network of cultural clubs established across Turkish Kurdistan beginning in 1969. The DDKO advocated political, civil, and economic rights for the people in the East (Turkish Kurdistan). This, of course, meant implicit development and recognition of the Kurdish national movement in **Turkey.** The state responded with a strong military crackdown reminiscent of its earlier excesses against its Kurdish population before World War II.

In October 1970, many DDKO leaders were arrested and trials were held in Istanbul and **Diyarbakir. Musa Anter**, **Sait Elci**, and **Ismail Besikci** were among those imprisoned. The DDKO was closed down, but not before it had played an important role in reviving the modern Kurdish movement in Turkey.

DEVRIMCI ISCI SENDIKALARI KONFEDERASYONU (DISK). Or the Revolutionary Workers Unions Confederation, a radical labor union established in **Turkey** in 1967 by leftists who broke away from Turk Is, the government-controlled union. DISK played an important role in the anarchy, intellectual fervor, and terrorism that helped lead to the creation of the **Kurdistan Workers Party** and the September 1980 military coup in Turkey. For example, DISK organized the notorious May Day rally in 1977 in Taksim Square, Istanbul, that resulted in the deaths of 37 people when persons unknown started shooting into the crowd. After it came to power in 1980, the military government of General **Kenan Evren** closed DISK down.

DIASPORA (KURDISH). One might argue that there is both an internal Kurdish diaspora, consisting of those who have migrated out of historically Kurdish areas but remain in their countries of origin, and an external Kurdish diaspora, those who have emigrated to Europe and other foreign locations such as North America and Australia. Although statistics are poor, many believe, for example, that more ethnic Kurds now live in central and western Anatolia than in the historical Kurdish provinces of **Turkey**, due to the forced deportations and violence associated with the **Kurdistan Workers Party (PKK)** and earlier uprisings. In this vein, Istanbul is sometimes referred to as the largest Kurdish city in the world, with estimates of the number of Kurds as high as 3 million.

The consequences of this internal Kurdish diaspora in Turkey are enormous but unclear. For one thing, it probably makes it physically impossible to give the Kurds in Turkey autonomy now that more of them may live outside of their traditional homeland than in it. This internal diaspora may also make assimilation into the larger Turkish population more likely. At the same time, this Kurdish migration to other parts of Turkey might also nationalize a Kurdish problem that was once just regional.

Externally, more than 1 million Kurds may now live in the West, with by far the largest number (more than 500,000) residing in Germany. Much smaller but significant numbers also live in **France**, **Great Britain**, Sweden, Belgium, and the Netherlands, among others. An undetermined number of Kurds also live in **Russia** and several other former Soviet republics, such as **Armenia**, site of the former **Red Kurdistan**. More than 20,000 Kurds also live in the **United States** and still others in Canada.

Already, this external diaspora is carrying out an important lobbying role both in the West and in the Kurdish homeland itself. It is also increasingly facilitating the transfer of needed human and technical resources back to the homeland. One may also speculate that the democratically socialized diaspora will even begin to further the democratization process in Kurdistan. Freed from the struggles that divide greater Kurdistan, the next generation of this new Kurdish diaspora may gradually become more pan-Kurdish in outlook. However, this external Kurdish diaspora may also be increasingly assimilated into its new homelands. *See also* REFUGEES.

DICLE–FIRAT (TIGRIS–EUPHRATES). Important bilingual monthly that appeared for eight issues in the brief liberal period of Turkish politics during the early 1960s. Before it was closed down for separatism, the journal helped to awaken and express long suppressed Kurdish awareness.

DIMDIM. In Kurdish history and heroic folklore, a place (in Persian, Dumdum) that has become a sort of Kurdish Masada. It was at this mountain fortress (elevation c. 2,000 meters) near the western shore of Lake Urmia that Hatem Beg, the grand vizier of the Safavid Persian shah Abbas the Great, besieged the **Baradust** *mir* Khan Yakdas from November 1609 to the summer of 1610. When Dimdim was finally captured, the Persians massacred all the defenders. Remains of the walls and piles of building stones are still visible to this day.

Bayti Dimdim treats the siege of Dimdim as a Kurdish struggle against foreign domination and is considered by many as a national epic, second only to **Ahmad-i Khani**'s *Mem u Zin*. Numerous modern poets and historians have also written about the revolt. In the **United States**, taped recitations of *Bayti Dimdim* are held in the ethnomusicological archive at the University of Illinois at Urbana.

DIMILI. More polite term for the Kurdish dialect (some would even call it a **language**) also known by the more popular, but somewhat derogatory, term Zaza (literally, stutterer, for the frequency of the *z* sound in the speech). Dimili is spoken in the northwestern provinces of **Turkey** (in particular the former **Dersim**, now Tunceli) by both **Alevi** and Sunni Kurds and also by Alevi Turks. Dimili is related to the Kurdish **Gurani** dialect (which some would call a language) spoken in some of the southeastern Kurdish areas in **Iran** and neighboring areas in **Iraq**. Dimili and Gurani are probably older Kurdish dialects, but most Kurds now speak **Kurmanji** or **Sorani**. The term Dimili is possibly associated with the **Dailamites**, a people from the Alburz Mountains just south of the Caspian Sea, and who were probably precursors of some of today's Kurds.

Some would consider the Dimili to be a separate ethnic group from the Kurds. Turkish authorities certainly encourage such a view as a divide-and-rule tactic. Dimili are more frequently known as sedentary farmers than are most other Kurds. There may be some 3–4 million Dimili at the present time.

DIWAN. Or guest house, a special room or house that the **agha** or landlord maintained for travelers to rest, be entertained, given tea or a meal, or a place to spend the night. Until recently, all male villagers came and sat there in the evenings to discuss daily matters. The agha settled minor disputes, and decisions affecting the village were made there. Also, the young learned traditions at the *diwan* and the older men would furnish examples of what a man should be like. Thus the *diwan* provided a powerful mechanism of social control. In recent years, the institution of the *diwan* has declined due to rapid economic changes among aghas and villagers.

Diwan also means a poet's collection of writings. The connection between these two different meanings is that in the sense of a guest house, a diwan is also a place where a magistrate and his staff discuss policy and write it down. These similar meanings of *diwan* also appear in Arabic, Persian, and Turkish.

DIYARBAKIR. Often called the unofficial capital of Turkish Kurdistan. Its Kurdish name is Amed. The city boasts an ancient Byzantine wall of black basalt constructed by the Emperor Constantius in 349 and still well preserved. In January 2000, **Mesut Yilmaz**, a former Turkish prime minister and at that time a member of the coalition government, famously declared that "the road to the EU [**European Union**] passes through Diyarbakir." By this, he meant that Turkey would only be admitted into the EU if it successfully solved its Kurdish problem in a democratic manner. In recent years, the city's population has swelled to well over 1 million due to the dislocations from the war against the **Kurdistan Workers Party**.

DOGUCULUK. Or "Eastism," the Turkish euphemism for a campaign in the relatively liberal 1960s to develop Turkey's badly neglected eastern (Kurdish) provinces without mentioning the forbidden words Kurds or Kurdistan. The campaign lasted for almost a decade and constituted in effect the first serious Kurdish self-expression permitted since the **Dersim** revolt in the late 1930s. **Musa Anter's** publications played an important role. In retrospect, it is evident that Doguculuk helped serve as an intellectual spawning ground for the birth of the **Kurdistan Workers Party** in the 1970s.

DOHUK. City of some 50,000 in the far northwestern, **Barzani**-controlled corner of Iraqi Kurdistan, some 80 kilometers from the Turkish border crossing used since 1991 for trade between **Turkey** and the de facto state of Kurdistan in northern **Iraq**. Dohuk has one of the three universities and medical schools in Iraqi Kurdistan. Dohuk is also the name of the surrounding province, one of three constituting Iraqi Kurdistan.

DROGHEDA PEACE PROPOSALS. Rather incongruous site (a suburb of Dublin, Ireland) where the **United States** persuaded the warring **Kurdistan Democratic Party (KDP)** and **Patriotic Union of Kurdistan (PUK)** factions to meet and try to reach a settlement of their internal conflict that raged off and on from 1994 to 1998. The Drogheda peace talks were held 9–11 August 1995 and September 12–15, 1995.

At first, the talks seemed to have a chance for success, but they eventually foundered, in part because of Turkish security interests. When it appeared that as part of the deal that the KDP would prevent the **Kurdistan Workers Party (PKK)** from attacking Turkey from PKK bases across the border in Iraqi Kurdistan, the PKK attacked the KDP. For their own ulterior motives, **Iran**, **Syria**, and the PUK supported the PKK, while Turkey aided the KDP. In addition, the KDP and PUK could not agree on the demilitarization of **Irbil** and the collection of customs revenues. However, the Drogheda talks probably helped lay the groundwork for the United States to finally broker a cease-fire deal three years later in Washington, D.C.

DUKAN DAM. Dam constructed in the 1950s on the Lesser Zab River in north-central Iraqi Kurdistan. There is a large lake behind the dam, which provides important irrigation and hydroelectric power. *See also* DARBANDIKHAN DAM; WATER.

– E –

EAGLETON, WILLIAM (1926–). One of the U.S. State Department's very few Kurdish specialists. Many Kurds admire him for writing what remains the definitive history in English of the **Mahabad Republic of Kurdistan**, *The Kurdish Republic of 1946* (1963). He also produced an illustrated study of Kurdish **rugs**. He began his career as a member of the U.S. Foreign Service in the Middle East in 1951. He served as the U.S. consul in Tabriz, **Iran**, in 1959–61 and as the head of the U.S. Interests Section in Baghdad in 1980–84. He was the U.S. ambassador to **Syria** in 1984.

ECEVIT, BULENT (1925–). Leftist, but strong Turkish nationalist, who was prime minister of **Turkey** twice in the 1970s and again as the head of a three-party coalition from April 1999 until his smashing defeat in the 3 November 2002 national elections.

Ecevit gained great popularity by his successful intervention in Cyprus in 1974. The moderate rightist **Suleyman Demirel** was Ecevit's longtime bitter rival, and their frequent alternating in power was seen by some as symbolizing Turkey's often unsuccessful domestic politics. Although both were banned from politics after the military coup of 1980, they eventually staged triumphal and popular returns. Ironically, they then worked together as president and prime minister. Ecevit has long argued that there is no Kurdish ethnic problem in Turkey, only an economic problem.

EDMONDS, CECIL JOHN (1889–1979). British political official in Iraq and an expert on Kurdistan and the Kurdish **language**. Edmonds entered the Foreign Service of **Great Britain** in 1912 and retired with the rank of minister in 1950. During his military career, he was honored by being mentioned in the dispatches three times. He was one of several British political officers posted to northern **Iraq** in the 1920s, and he served in the civil administration of Iraq from 1922 to 1945. In this role, he acquired a profound knowledge of Kurdistan and wrote one of the best analyses available in English: *Kurds, Turks, and Arabs: Travel and Research in North-Eastern Iraq, 1919–1925* (1957). He became a lecturer in Kurdish at the University of London in 1951 and also compiled with Tawfiq Wahby an early Kurdish–English dictionary.

ELCI, SAIT (?–1971). Conservative Kurdish nationalist and activist from Bingol, **Turkey**, active during the intellectual fervor of the rather liberal 1960s. Elci succeeded **Faik Bucak** as the leader of the **Kurdistan Democratic Party of Turkey (KDPT)** in 1966, but was imprisoned in 1968. In prison, he became friends with Sait Kirmizitoprak, a leftist **Dersim** Kurd whose nom de guerre became **Dr. Shivan.** However, when both left for Iraqi Kurdistan they had a falling out. Dr. Shivan apparently executed Elci, but was himself executed by **Mulla Mustafa Barzani.** This effectively brought an end to the KDPT, although Dr. Shivan's branch briefly reemerged as the Kurdistan Pesheng Karkaren Partiya (PPKK), or **Kurdistan Vanguard Workers Party**—or simply **Pesheng** (Vanguard).

ELCI, SERAFETTIN (1938–). Turkish ethnic Kurd who was the minister of public works under Prime Minister **Bulent Ecevit** in the late 1970s, when he became notorious in **Turkey** for stating: "I am a Kurd. There are Kurds in Turkey." For this outburst, he was sentenced to two years and three months in prison. In 1997, Elci became the chair of the new Demokratik Kitle Partisi (DKP), or Democratic Mass Party, which was an attempt to establish a more moderate pro-Kurdish party than the banned **Halkin Emek Partisi**, or Peoples Labor Party, and **Demokrasi Partisi**, or Democracy Party, pro-Kurdish parties that Elci termed Marxist. Elci called for the recognition of the Kurdish identity and reorganization of the strongly centralized Turkish state, but without changing Turkey's borders. The DKP failed to make any significant impact and was itself banned in February 1999.

EMERGENCY RULE (OHAL). Since the inception of the Republic of **Turkey** in 1923, the Kurdish provinces in the southeast have mostly been ruled by various special regimes such as martial law, states of siege, and since the summer of 1987, a state of emergency complete with a supragovernor. Moreover, until 1950 the region was under an inspector general for the eastern provinces.

The current emergency rule was instituted in the summer of 1987 by President **Turgut Ozal** when martial law was lifted in the last four of Turkey's southeastern provinces, where martial law had been implemented during the sectarian killing that had broken out in the southeastern city of Kahramanmaras in late December 1978. Emergency rule was a response to the **Kurdistan Workers Party (PKK)** insurgency then gathering steam. Headquartered in **Diyarbakir**, Hayri Kozakcioglu was appointed as the first supra- or regional governor with broad authority for eight (later as many as 11) provinces where the PKK threat seemed most serious. Kozakcioglu already had been the provincial governor in Diyarbakir and a former **Milli Istihbarat Teshilati (MIT)** ([Turkish] National Intelligence Organization) official.

Some of Kozakcioglu's most important powers included command over the special and general security forces; control over the MIT as detailed by a special decree; authorization to move around public employees and raise their salaries; power to evacuate or merge villages and pasture areas; supervision over civil trial procedures carried out against security forces; and authority over provincial governors. Emergency rule amounted to martial law in all but name. Over the years, it was periodically extended for fewer and fewer provinces, until it was finally ended in December 2002.

Along with the system of **village guards** instituted in the summer of 1985, the emergency rule system has long been considered a prime example of official state repression by many supporters of **human rights**. Both the village guards and emergency rule have been used by the state to help legalize the scorched-earth tactics that destroyed as many as 3,000 villages and carried out some 1,000 extrajudicial killings of those perceived to be enemies of the state. Despite Ankara's adamant refusal to grant some type of autonomy to the region, emergency rule and its various predecessors ironically amount to a tacit admission that a strict unitary state is too difficult to maintain.

Early in 2002, Gokhan Aydiner was the regional governor for OHAL and emergency rule continued in two Turkish provinces, **Diyarbakir** and **Sirnak**. Emergency rule was formally ended in December 2002 because of the military defeat of the **Kurdistan Workers Party** and also as part of the reforms Turkey began to implement in an attempt to enter the **European Union**.

EMIRATES. Kurdish principalities that possessed many of the characteristics of a state. They existed as early as the 1300s, with the last ones abolished only in the middle of the 19th century. At various times, their rulers bore such titles as *mirs* (emirs), *meliks* (kings), or *begs*. Famous examples of the many Kurdish emirates included

Ardalan, Baban, Bitlis, Botan, Hakkari, and **Hasankeyf.** The *Sharafnama,* written by **Sharaf Khan Bitlisi,** the former *mir* of the emirate of Bitlis, is an erudite history of the ruling families of these emirates up to the end of the 1500s.

In an era before the rise of the nation–states, the existence of the Kurdish emirates puts the lie to the claim that there never were any independent Kurdish states. With the demise of the last emirates in the 19th century, religious **sheikhs** increasingly began to exercise some of the political power of the former *mirs.*

ENIYE RIZGARIYE NAVATA KURDISTAN (ERNK). See KURDISTAN NATIONAL LIBERATION FRONT.

ERBAKAN, NECMETTIN (1926–). Member of the **Naqshbandi Sufi** order, the leader of various **Islamist** parties in **Turkey** since 1970. In July 1996, Necmettin Erbakan finally became secular Turkey's first Islamist prime minister in a coalition with **Tansu Ciller's** Dogru Yol Partisi, or True Path Party.

Before becoming prime minister, Erbakan had declared that he would replace the Turkish–Kurdish conflict with Islamic unity, a position that harkened back to the days of the **Ottoman Empire.** Despite considerable Kurdish electoral support from the southeast, however, Erbakan was unable to make any headway on the Kurdish issue. During an official state visit to Libya in October 1996, Erbakan was greatly embarrassed when Libyan leader **Muammar Qaddafi** told him that Turkey's Kurds should have independence.

Erbakan proved unable to reorient Turkish politics because of military and secular opposition. The Turkish military forced him to resign in June 1997 and banned him and his Refah Party in January 1998. However, Erbakan continued to exercise influence behind the scenes. Early in 2003, the ban was lifted against him, but by this time it appeared that the rise to power of the **AK Partisi** and its new leaders, as well as Erbakan's age, would prevent him from returning to power.

EUROPEAN UNION (EU). European intergovernmental organization that has influenced the Kurdish problem, especially in **Turkey.** This is because of Turkey's longtime goal, set by **Ataturk** himself, to achieve the level of contemporary civilization. In recent years, of course, this has come to mean membership in what has become the EU. To meet the EU criteria for membership, however, Turkey must in effect solve its Kurdish problem in a democratic manner.

In recent years, the European Court of Human Rights (ECHR) has handed down numerous judgments ordering Turkey (a party to the court) to make compensation for crimes committed by its official agents against ethnic Kurds who are (or were before they were murdered) citizens of Turkey. Turkey also suspended its death sentence against **Abdullah Ocalan** in November 1999 when the ECHR issued interim measures asking Turkey to do so until the court could rule on Ocalan's appeal. Much **Kurdistan Workers Party (PKK)** strategy since it abandoned its armed struggle following Ocalan's capture revolves around solving Turkey's Kurdish problem through Turkey's EU candidacy.

EVREN, KENAN (1918–). The Turkish military's chief of staff who presided over the military coup of 12 September 1980. He acted because the state seemed in imminent danger of collapse due to violence between leftist and rightist groups, including the Kurds.

Evren took harsh, but under the circumstances not unreasonable, steps to reinstitute order. A new constitution was adopted in 1982 and Evren was president from 1983 to 1989. The new constitution represented a reversal of the more liberal constitution the military had drawn up following its coup in May 1960. Evren's 1982 constitution contained a number of specific provisions that sought to limit even speaking or writing in Kurdish. Although Evren's rule ended the left–right sectarian violence in **Turkey**, the **Kurdistan Workers Party (PKK)** uprising was eventually renewed with much greater fervor during his tenure.

– F –

FADLAWAYH. Kurdish dynasty that eliminated the last **Buwayhid** in 1055 and then ruled in Shabankara from 1056 to 1318. They were named for their founder. The dynasty came to an end at the hands of the Muzaffarid dynasty.

FAILI KURDS. Group of some 150,000 Kurds originally from the **Kirmanshah** region in **Iran** who had lived in **Iraq** (many in Baghdad) since **Ottoman** times, but without Iraqi citizenship. In the late 1970s, the Iraqi government expelled at least 50,000 of them on the grounds that they were not citizens.

During the time of the **March Manifesto** of 1970, the Iraqi government refused to approve the **Kurdistan Democratic Party (KDP)** nominee, Habib Karim, as vice president of Iraq under terms of Article 12 of the Manifesto, on the grounds that Karim, a Faili Kurd, was of Iranian origin. The Faili Kurds were thus one specific element of the Iraqi policy of Arabization that sought to reduce Kurdish numbers, and thus influence, in Iraq in favor of the Arabs. The Faili Kurds joined many other Kurds as **refugees** in Iran.

FOURTEEN POINTS. An idealistic, but extremely influential set of peace proposals formulated by U.S. president Woodrow Wilson in January 1918 to end World War I on a just basis. Thus they were also meant as propaganda for the Allied cause.

Wilson's 12th point declared that the non-Turkish minorities of the **Ottoman Empire** should be granted the right of "autonomous self-development." This, of course, would have been a blueprint for Kurdish autonomy or even eventual independence. The **Sykes–Picot Agreement** between **Great Britain** and **France**, however, had made other provisions for these minorities, and Kurdish autonomy failed to develop.

FRANCE. Over the years, France has become more influential with regard to the Kurds than any other European power besides **Great Britain** and **Russia**. Under the provisions of the **Sykes–Picot Agreement**, France took over **Syria** following World War I and thus influenced the Kurdish situation in that state. Before the **Gulf War** in 1991, France gained a reputation as possibly **Iraq's** most important Western supplier of arms. At the same time, **Danielle Mitterrand**, the wife of former French president François Mitterrand, has been a longtime and ardent defender of the Kurdish cause. She also helped establish the influential **Institut Kurde de Paris** in 1982. After the Gulf War in 1991, France was a leading supporter of **Operation Provide Comfort**, which maintained the **no-fly zone** over northern Iraq.

In 1997, however, France pulled out of this operation and increasingly supported the removal of the sanctions against Iraq.

Although France banned the **Kurdistan Workers Party (PKK)** in 1993, the PKK continued to operate there through various front organizations. More than 60,000 Kurds currently live in France.

FURSAN SALAH AL-DIN. Or the Saladin Knights or Light Brigades, Kurdish **tribal** troops that supported the Iraqi government against their tribal enemy **Mulla Mustafa Barzani**, who referred to them by the better known term *josh,* or little donkeys. Thus the Fursan played a role similar to that of the **Hamidiye** in the **Ottoman Empire** and the **village guards** during **Turkey's** war against the **Kurdistan Workers Party** in the 1980s and 1990s.

– G –

GALBRAITH, PETER (1950–). Son of the famous economist John Kenneth Galbraith and an American diplomat who became one of the best American friends of the Iraqi Kurds when he alerted his country and the world to the impending Kurdish **refugee** crisis at the end of the **Gulf War** in 1991. He then helped convince the reluctant administration of **George H. W. Bush** to implement the **no-fly zone** to protect the Kurds upon their return. In 1987, as a staff member of the U.S. Senate Foreign Relations Committee, he had documented the destruction of rural life in northern **Iraq** while on an official visit there.

GECEKONDUS. Shantytowns in **Turkey** thrown up overnight (whence the Turkish term) on the edge of major cities. Many Kurdish immigrants were politicized here in the 1960s and 1970s. When they returned to the East, some of them became catalysts for various Kurdish movements, including the **Kurdistan Workers Party**.

GENOCIDE. Literally, the murder of an entire race. Raphael Lemkin coined the term in reference to the **Ottoman** Turkish massacres of the **Armenians** during World War I.

Following the Nazi atrocities against the Jews in World War II, the 1948 Convention on the Prevention and Punishment of Genocide legally defined genocide as any act "committed with intent to destroy, in whole or in part, a national, ethnical, racial or religious group, as such." It is particularly relevant for the Kurdish question that the international legal definition of genocide involves the destruction of a group "in whole or in part." This phrase has been interpreted as meaning "a reasonably significant number, relative to the total of the group as a whole, or else a significant section of a group such as its leadership."

The Iraqi **Anfal** campaign, which killed as many as 180,000 Kurds at the end of the **Iran–Iraq War** in the 1980s; the Iraqi **chemical** attack on **Halabja**, which killed some 5,000 Kurds in March 1988; and Turkish attempts to assimilate forcibly the Kurdish ethnic population in Turkey are all actions that might well qualify as genocide under the Genocide Convention.

Iraq acceded to the Genocide Convention without any reservation in 1959 and, therefore, theoretically may be brought before the International Court of Justice by any other contracting state that has not made a reservation to Article IX of the convention detailing the procedure to do so. The risks and associated problems entailed in bringing a case to the world court, however, have prevented any case from being considered to date. This lack of determination is specifically illustrated by the **United States**, which refused to ratify the convention for more than 40 years because of its own domestic racial problems and fear of international interference in its internal affairs. Turkey has never acceded to the Genocide Convention.

Other possible examples of genocide in recent times include the Khmer Rouge massacres in Cambodia during the 1970s, the Tutsi–Hutu massacres in Burundi in the 1970s and 1990s, and the Serb massacres in the former Yugoslavia during the 1990s. Subsequently, international tribunals have been created and are currently functioning to hear cases dealing with these atrocities in Burundi and the former Yugoslavia. The trial of the former Serb leader Slobodan Milosevic for war crimes and crimes against humanity by the international tribunal would signify that a similar indictment against **Saddam Hussein** might be in order for his actions against the Kurds over the years. *See also* HUMAN RIGHTS.

GEORGE, MARGARET (?–1966). Female **Assyrian** *peshmerga* in the 1960s who became famous as the leader of an all-male unit. Other *peshmergas* began to carry her portrait into battle as a kind of talisman, and she became a sort of Kurdish Joan of Arc. **Mulla Mustafa Barzani** apparently had her executed after she began to demand a position in the leadership.

GERMANY. Home to by far the largest part of the Kurdish **diaspora** in Europe. Probably more than 500,000 Kurds now live in Germany. Over the years, therefore, the Kurds have carried many of their internal and international struggles to Germany. In 1993, Germany banned the **Kurdistan Workers Party (PKK)**, but it continues to operate there.

GEZMIS, DENIZ (?–1972). Radical leftist Turkish Kurd who led the violent Turkiye Halk Kurtulus Ordusu, or Turkish Peoples Liberation Army. He was executed in 1972 for murder. Along with **Mahir Cayan**, Gezmis served as an early role model for **Abdullah (Apo) Ocalan**, the leader of the **Kurdistan Workers Party**.

GHASSEMLOU, ABDUL RAHMAN (1930–89). Leftist Iranian Kurdish intellectual who earned a Ph.D. in economics from the University of Prague and authored *Kurdistan and the Kurds* (1965). In 1971, he was elected the leader of the **Kurdistan Democratic Party of Iran (KDPI)**. He proved to be a major strategist, diplomat, and organizer. Under his sway, the KDPI adopted the slogan "autonomy for Kurdistan, democracy for **Iran**." He often came into opposition to the Iraqi Kurds, who supported Iran because he supported Iran's foe, **Iraq**. While attempting to negotiate peace in July 1989, he was treacherously assassinated by Iranian agents in Vienna. Many Kurds consider him to be one of their main leaders of the 20th century.

GHULAT. Kurdish Shiites so extremist in their views that many would not even call them Islamic. *See also* AHL-I HAQQ; ALEVIS; CULT OF ANGELS; KAKAIS; SARLIYYA; SHABAK; YEZIDIS.

GLADIO. Secret guerrilla group created and armed by the Turkish government with the help of the **United States** and the North Atlantic

Treaty Organization (NATO) during the height of the Cold War. It was to be activated behind enemy lines if the **Soviet Union** ever occupied **Turkey**. Similar units were apparently created in some Western European states that also were members of NATO. Some have speculated that elements of the Gladio were used by the Turkish government in the early 1990s in the extrajudicial murders of reputed **Kurdistan Workers Party** sympathizers.

GOKALP, ZIYA (1876–1924). Ethnic Kurdish intellectual born in **Diyarbakir**. He considered himself a Turk and ironically became one of the founders of modern Turkish nationalism. His seminal study, *The Principles of Turkism* (1920), defined a nation as being based on upbringing, not ethnicity. According to Gokalp, a nation was not a racial, ethnic, geographical, political, or voluntary group, but a group of people who had gone through the same education and received the same acquisitions in language, religion, morality, and aesthetics. His work probably helped influence **Mustafa Kemal Ataturk** to try to assimilate the Kurds into what was then the still aborning Turkish nation.

GORAN, ABDULLA SULAYMAN (1904–1962). One of the outstanding Kurdish poets of the 20th century. Abdulla Sulayman was born in **Halabja** in what is now **Iraqi** Kurdistan; Goran became his nom de plume. He wrote in **Sorani**.

Goran's innovative use of **language** and meter, as well as his harmonious combining of form and subject, represented a turning point in the development of contemporary Kurdish poetry. His work broke with tradition by introducing stress rhythms, which were closer to oral folk styles. He also sought to combat social injustice and thus helped to introduce Kurdish realism. During the early 1950s, he became known as the editor of *Jin,* a weekly that became a powerful voice for the dispossessed of Kurdish society. He was dismissed as editor and jailed until the revolution in 1958.

Guli Hiwenawi (Bloody rose)—the story of tragic love in an unjust world—became a modern Kurdish classic. Another classic, *Bukeki Nakam* (An unhappy bride), emphasized social themes as two lovers from different classes tried to overcome strong family prejudices. Many of Goran's poetic pieces were put to music. He also was an accomplished essayist who sought to create a single unified Kurdish language. *See also* LITERATURE.

GREAT BRITAIN. Leading Western power until well into the 20th century, long played an important role in the affairs of the **Ottoman Empire** and thus had occasion to influence Kurdish affairs. The **Sykes–Picot Agreement** between Britain and **France** divided up the Middle East after World War I. Britain artificially created and then ruled **Iraq** as a mandate of the **League of Nations** until 1932, and indeed continued to hold great influence in Iraq until the monarchy was overthrown in 1958.

During the 1920s and 1930s, Britain used its air force and other assets to put down several Kurdish revolts led by Sheikh **Mahmud Barzinji** and later by the **Barzanis**. After the **Gulf War** in 1991, Britain soon became the only ally of the **United States** enforcing the **no-fly zone**, which protected the de facto Kurdish state from intervention at the hands of **Saddam Hussein**. Britain also associated itself with U.S. attempts to implement numerous peace plans involving the Iraqi Kurds and their internal fighting during the 1990s. More than 20,000 Kurds presently live in Britain.

GULEN, FETHULLAH (1938–). *See* NURCULUK.

GULF WAR (1991). War that resulted in a quick victory for the coalition led by the **United States** against **Saddam Hussein**'s **Iraq** after he had invaded Kuwait in the summer of 1990. The Iraqi Kurdish **refugee** exodus following the unsuccessful Kurdish uprising encouraged by the United States after the war brought the Kurds to an international prominence they had never before known, and it led to the creation of a de facto Kurdish state in northern Iraq that continues today.

The Gulf War also proved a major watershed for the Kurdish problem in **Turkey** because the de facto Kurdish state in northern Iraq served as a powerful inspiration for Turkey's Kurds and provided a vacuum of authority in which the **Kurdistan Workers Party** found a new safe house. **Turkey** also housed **Operation Provide Comfort**, which enforced the U.S. **no-fly zone** over northern Iraq.

GULF WAR II (2003). As of March 2003, the **United States** and **Great Britain** launched a war against **Iraq** and removed **Saddam Hussein's Baathist** government from power. Although it might take months or even years before the full implications and final results of this war become clear, it was obvious that the war would strongly affect the Iraqi Kurds and the **Kurdistan Regional Government (KRG)** they had enjoyed since shortly after the first **Gulf War** in 1991.

At the start of the second Gulf War in 2003, most Iraqi Kurds were eager to eliminate Saddam Hussein and the threat he represented to them. The Iraqi Kurds also looked forward to a post-Saddam democratic, parliamentary, and federal Iraq in which their rights would be guaranteed. Given Iraq's historical divisions and lack of a democratic ethos, however, it was not likely to emerge easily as the democratic and federal model hoped for by the Kurds. Ironically, therefore, Saddam Hussein might have been the Iraqi Kurds' "best friend," because as long as he remained in power, the United States protected the Iraqi Kurds from Baghdad with a **no-fly zone**. Once Saddam Hussein was eliminated, this U.S. protection would be lifted and the Iraqi Kurds would again have to deal with the central government in Iraq.

What is more, **Turkey** feared that federalism for the Iraqi Kurds might be the first step toward independence and serve as an unwanted model for the Turkish Kurds. Only Turkey's inability to reach an agreement with the United States over allowing U.S. troops to use Turkey as a base from which to attack Iraq prevented the United States and Turkey from reaching a deal that would have allowed Turkish troops into northern Iraq. Nevertheless, the real possibility of Turkish intervention remained a threat to the Iraqi Kurds.

GUNEY, YILMAZ (1937–84). Internationally known filmmaker whose work was banned in **Turkey** during the 1980s, in part because it dealt with the Kurdish issue. A Turkish Kurd, Guney fled from Turkey after being accused of murdering a Turkish judge in 1974. He died in exile in Paris.

GUNEYDOGU ANADOLU PROJESI (GAP). Or the Southeast Anatolia Project, Turkey's massive, $32 billion, multidam project to harness the **waters** of the Euphrates and Tigris Rivers in southeast Anatolia in order to economically develop the area and help solve the Kurdish problem.

Critics argue that the project will really benefit western Turkey's energy needs, while the Kurds in the southeast lack the education or landownership to be helped. In addition, the creation of large lakes behind the project's dams will flood and destroy significant Kurdish cultural remains, such as has been claimed concerning the proposed **Ilisu Dam** near **Hasankeyf**. **Syria** and **Iraq** have also complained bitterly that GAP is already robbing them of their downstream water rights.

GURAN. Word that has referred to nontribal, farming peasants (or *misken*) in the **Sulaymaniya** area, as distinguished from **tribal** Kurds who are soldiers and seldom farm. In the 19th century, the guran were clearly distinguishable by their facial features and their dialect from the more prominent Kurdish tribes to the north and were often subjected by the tribal Kurds.

The evidence seems to indicate that the guran originally came from north-central **Iran** south of the Caspian Sea, were possibly a subgroup of the **Dailamites**, spoke a northwestern Iranian language, and have at least since the 14th century lived in southern Kurdistan, where in time they became considered to be Kurds. Usage of the term guran, however, varies according to the time context and is more complex than can be fully explained here. The Guran tribal confederation southeast of Sulaymaniya, for example, and the nontribal guran peasants should not be confused. Furthermore, **Gurani** is a Kurdish dialect or **language** associated with but not necessarily congruent with the guran. *See also* RAYAT.

GURANI. Or Hawrami, Kurdish dialect or **language** that belongs to the northwestern branch of Iranian languages, like the **Dimili** (Zaza) dialects of northern Kurdistan in **Turkey**, but unlike the Kurdish dialects or languages of **Kurmanji** or **Sorani**, which are southwestern Iranian languages and prevail in most of Kurdistan. A few scholars would even argue that Gurani is not a Kurdish dialect.

In the past, Gurani had a much wider geographical distribution. For example, it was the literary language of the brilliant court of the

Ardalan emirate, whose borders extended far beyond those of the current Iranian province of **Kordestan**. As a result, many outstanding poets wrote in Gurani. Examples run from Mulla Pareshan in the 15th century to Mulla Abdul Rahim Mawlawi in the 19th. Gurani only ceased as a court literary language with the downfall of the Ardalan emirate in the mid-19th century. Its former literary ascendancy is possibly still reflected by the fact that the term *gorani* is the common word for song in Sorani.

Presently, Gurani dialects persist only in the Hawraman region on the Iran–Iraq border, in the mountainous district west of **Kirmanshah**, and in a number of pockets in the eastern part of Iraqi Kurdistan. Gurani is often but not always associated with the **Ahl-i Haqq religion**, as Dimili (Zaza) is often associated with the **Alevi** religion.

– H –

HABUR. Border crossing between **Turkey** and the de facto Kurdish state of Kurdistan in northern **Iraq** and the only legal entry point for commerce and customs revenues between those two countries, because of the continuing **United Nations** sanctions against Iraq. Thus Habur has become a very important location.

The **Kurdistan Democratic Party** controls the Kurdish side and thus collects perhaps $150,000 (some say as much as $1 million) per day, while the **Patriotic Union of Kurdistan** collects nothing. Thus these revenue collections have become a major bone of contention between the two rival Iraqi Kurdish parties. The Habur border crossing point traverses a small river and is located just north of Zakho on the Iraqi side and just south of Silopi on the Turkish side. It is sometimes called the Ibrahim al-Khalil border crossing point, as there is a small town by this name just south of Zakho.

HAKKARI. Prominent mountainous Kurdish **emirate** for more than 500 years, until its last *mir* was deposed in the middle of the 19th century. For much of its history, it was a frontier area between the **Ottoman** and Iranian Empires. After 1534, however, Hakkari nominally belonged to the Ottomans.

At its height, Hakkari covered the present Turkish provinces of

Hakkari and Van and even stretched into what is now northern **Iraq**. Hakkari's ruling family claimed descent from the Abbasid caliphs, and at times coined its own money and had its names read in the Islamic ceremony of the *khutba,* acts signifying full independence. The *mirs* resided in the towns of Van and Colemerik (which is now called Hakkari).

However, Hakkari has had a checkered history. Until World War I, a large Nestorian **Christian** or **Assyrian** minority lived in Hakkari. Half of these Christians were peasants subservient to the Kurds, but the other half were organized into **tribes** and were noted fighters. Presently, Hakkari is the most sparsely populated province of **Turkey** and is very poor economically.

HALABJA. Strategic Iraqi Kurdish city of some 70,000 located close to the Iranian border. In March 1988, as the **Iran–Iraq War** was coming to its final climax, Iranian and **Patriotic Union of Kurdistan** forces managed to capture the town. On 16 March 1988, **Iraq** retaliated with the largest **chemical warfare** attack since World War I. Some 5,000 Kurds died. The very name Halabja became notorious for chemical warfare and the refusal of the international community to help end Kurdish suffering. **Saddam Hussein** soon stepped up his notorious **Anfal** campaign upon the war's conclusion. Before this notoriety, Halabja was noted among Kurds for its bookstores. More recently, it has become a center of **Islamic fundamentalist** activity.

HALKIN DEMOKRASI PARTISI (HADEP). Or the Peoples Democracy Party, was created in 1994 as the legal pro-Kurdish successor to the banned **Halkin Emek Partisi** and **Demokrasi Partisi** parties in **Turkey**. Although HADEP did rather well in local elections, it was unable to come anywhere near the required 10 percent of the vote to enter parliament. In part, this was because of government harassment, the **Islamist** appeal, and the failure of ethnic Kurds in the west of Turkey to support the party.

HADEP won 4.17 percent of the vote in the 1995 national elections and 4.75 percent in the 1999 elections. In the 1999 elections, HADEP did manage to elect the mayors of more than 30 southeastern cities or towns, including **Diyarbakir**. During the most recent national elections, held on 3 November 2002, HADEP formed an alliance with two other minor leftist parties as a hedge against being banned from participating in the elections. This alliance was called Demokratik Halkin Partisi (DEHAP) and it managed to win 6.22 percent of the vote. In the eyes of many Turks, however, HADEP was simply a front for the rebels of the **Kurdistan Workers Party**. Thus HADEP was harassed and its leaders off and on imprisoned. One of its leaders, Murat Bozlak, served three years in prison for his political activities. In March 2003, the Turkish Constitutional Court finally banned HADEP.

HALKIN EMEK PARTISI (HEP). In **Turkey**, in the fall of 1989, a number of parliamentary members of Erdal Inonu's Sosyal Demokrat Halkci Partisi (SHP), or Social Democratic Peoples Party, who were of Kurdish ancestry were expelled for attending a conference on "Kurdish National Identity and Human Rights" in Paris. These former SHP members became the seeds of the HEP, or the Peoples Labor Party, which was created in June 1990 and became the first legal Kurdish party to win representation in the Turkish parliament in modern times.

Since HEP's founding congress could not be held in time for it to qualify for the national elections in 1991, 22 HEP members rejoined the SHP and were elected to the new parliament. **Leyla Zana** and Hatip Dicle, two of these HEP members, caused an uproar in Turkey when they refused to take the traditional oath of office for parliament. Instead, Zana, wearing Kurdish national colors on her headband, declared "I take this oath for the brotherhood of the Turkish and Kurdish peoples."

Most Turks saw HEP as simply a front for the **Kurdistan Workers Party**. HEP was banned in June 1993, but was succeeded by the **Demokrasi Partisi** (DEP) or Democracy Party, which itself was banned in 1994, only to be succeeded by the **Halkin Demokrasi Partisi**, or Peoples Democracy Party, which was still in existence in early 2003. **Mehmet Sincar**, a former HEP member and then a DEP member of parliament, was murdered in September 1993, probably by state security officers. Leyla Zana and seven other members of HEP's successor, DEP, had their parliamentary immunity lifted in March 1994 and were put in prison, where Zana remains as an international *cause célèbre* as of early 2003.

HAMAWAND. Small Kurdish **tribe** presently living in the Chamchamal and Bazyan districts west of **Sulaymaniya** in **Iraq**. The tribe supported the **Baban** *mirs* until their final demise in 1850. Subsequently, the Hamawand became notorious for their brigandage against both the **Ottomans** and the **Persians**.

The tribe is noted for being deported in 1889 by the Ottomans, half to Adana and half to Tripoli in Libya. Seven years later, the half sent to Libya fought its way back to Bazyan, and the entire tribe was then permitted to reunite. During the 1920s, the Hamawand were staunch supporters of Sheikh **Mahmud Barzinji**.

HAMIDIYE. In 1891, the **Ottoman** sultan Abdul Hamid II established an irregular cavalry of Kurds modeled on the **Russian** Cossacks and named after himself. The purpose of the Hamidiye was to police eastern Anatolia by divide-and-rule policies that would reward loyal Kurdish **tribes** and make revolt against the government more difficult.

The Hamidiye were also notoriously used against the **Armenians**. By the end of the 19th century, there were probably more than 50,000 of these irregulars. Some of the Hamidiye also used their power in lawless assaults on their Kurdish tribal enemies. When the Committee of Union and Progress overthrew the sultan in 1908, it abolished the Hamidiye. However, it was soon reconstituted as Tribal Light Cavalry Regiments and used during wars up through the Turkish War of Independence following World War I. Today's **village guards** (in Turkey) and *josh* (in **Iraq**) are reminiscent of the Hamidiye.

HAMILTON ROAD. Road originally built by the **British** in the 1920s and 1930s as a strategic military highway to help facilitate the pacification of the Kurdish tribes. It runs from **Irbil** all the way to the Iranian frontier. Archibald M. Hamilton, for whom the highway is named, was a New Zealand engineer and author of *Road through Kurdistan* (1937).

HANEFI. The largest of the four recognized schools of law in Sunni **Islam**. The Hanefi school of jurisprudence was established in **Iraq** under Abbasid patronage and drew heavily on consensus and judicial reasoning, as well as on the Koran and the sunna. Since the establishment of the **Ottoman Empire**'s authority in eastern Anatolia and Mesopotamia in the 16th century, most Sunni Muslim Turks have been of the Hanefite school, while Kurds who were Sunni Muslim remained adherents of the Shafii jurisprudence, which had been predominant in the region earlier.

The Shafii school was established during the ninth century in Egypt as a synthesis of the Hanefi and Maliki schools, but with greater stress on analogy. In Kurdistan, the Shafii school has been less deferential to state authority than the Hanefi school. Most observers, however, conclude that this dichotomy between the Hanefi and Shafii schools is not very important in understanding the Kurdish issue.

HAQQA. Heterodox **Naqshbandi** sect in Iraqi Kurdistan established by Sheikh Abdulkarim of Sergelu early in the 20th century. Their wildly extravagant practices included sharing everything equally, including their women. Men and women were seen bathing together in the water tank of the village mosque and even taking dogs with them into the water! In 1944, the sect's new leader, Mame Riza, was arrested and exiled to the south of Iraq by the British, but he eventually was allowed to return to **Sulaymaniya** under house arrest. The sect still existed as late as 1975, when its then 70-year-old leader Hama Sur was said to have claimed the right of enjoying the first night with all the village girls. Clearly, the Haqqa are so different from the Naqshbandi as to warrant being considered a totally separate sect.

HARIRI, FRANCIS (FRANSO) (1937–2001). Important member of the politburo of the **Kurdistan Democratic Party** and a **Christian** who was assassinated by the Tawhid, an extremist **Islamist** group in northern **Iraq**, on 18 February 2001. Hariri also served as the governor of **Irbil** (Arbil) and as a minister in the **Kurdistan Regional Government** in Irbil.

HARKIS (HERKIS). Major Kurdish **tribe** that historically crossed the borders with their flocks between the **Ottoman** and **Persian** Empires and also were notorious for raiding and looting. According to certain old Nestorian accounts, the Harkis had once been **Christians** and still carried with them the head of one of the several Saint Georges of Eastern Christianity as a palladium in a chest.

In more recent times, the Harkis were considered *josh*, since they opposed **Mulla Mustafa Barzani.** In 1994, a portion of the Harkis helped ignite the civil war between the **Kurdistan Democratic Party (KDP)** and the **Patriotic Union of Kurdistan (PUK)** in northern **Iraq** when it switched its allegiance from the KDP to the PUK in return for support regarding territorial claims. In March 2003, Jawhad Harki, the Harki chief and long a *josh*, defected to the **Kurdistan Regional Government** on the eve of the U.S. attack against Iraq.

HASANKEYF. Ancient city with a fortress on the Tigris River. It is situated between **Diyarbakir** and **Cizre** in **Turkey.** Hasankeyf's ruler bore the title of *melik*, or king. The ruling family was descended from the famous **Saladin** and thus Hassankeyf was an **Ayyubid** successor state. The *Sharafnama* mentions this family as one of the five that without actually founding an independent state had at one time or another had money coined and the *khutba* read in its name. In the late 1990s, Hasankeyf became an issue because the proposed **Ilisu Dam** (part of the gigantic **Guneydogu Anadolu Projesi** project) sought to flood and destroy the city and its Kurdish relics.

HASANWAYHIDS. Kurdish dynasty who dominated the **Zagros** between Shahrizur and Khuzistan on the east side of the Shatt al-Arab River from c. 959 to 1014, during the period when the power of the Abbasid caliphate was declining. Their eponymous founder was Hasanwayh bin Husayn, who belonged to a branch of the Barzikani Kurdish tribe. He was able to gain some of his power by assisting the **Buwayhids (Buyids)** in their struggles against the Samanids.

After Hasanwayh's death in 979, his son, Abu al-Nadjm (later Nasir al-Dawla), achieved such notable successes as imposing order, developing a strong financial administration, building mountain roads and markets, securing the safety of the pilgrims who crossed his territory, and even striking his own coins, a symbol of sovereignty. Indeed, **Sharaf Khan Bitlisi** in the *Sharafnama* mentions the Hasanwayhids as one of the five Kurdish dynasties that enjoyed royalty. The last Hasanwayhid heir died in the family's old fortress of Sarmadj in 1047, just as the Selcuk Turks under Ibrahim Inal began to enter the region.

HASHEMITES. Royal Arabian family that supported **Great Britain** in World War I and were rewarded by being placed on the throne of several newly created Arab states carved out of the ruins of the **Ottoman Empire.** Faisal I eventually became king of **Iraq** and thus ruled over the Iraqi Kurds. The Hashemites in Iraq were overthrown in a bloody coup led by General **Abdul Karim Kassem** on 14 July 1958.

HAWRAMI. *See* GURANI.

HAY, W. R. (1893–1962). British political officer who served for two years in **Irbil** after World War I. His book *Two Years in Kurdistan* (1921) remains a useful study of former Kurdish tribes and customs.

HAZEN RIZGARIYA KURDISTAN (HRK). The **Kurdistan Workers Party (PKK)** created this group, the Kurdistan Freedom Brigades in English, in 1984 as a forerunner of the **Kurdistan National Liberation Front (ERNK)**—a popular front that also had a military function—and the **Kurdistan Peoples Liberation Army (ARGK)**, a professional guerrilla army.

The PKK announced the establishment of the HRK on 15 August 1984 by making two well-coordinated attacks on Eruh and Semdinli, villages in southeastern Turkey separated by more than 330 kilometers of rugged, mountainous terrain. Both **Turkey** and the PKK usually give this date for the beginning of the PKK armed rebellion.

Duran (Abbas) Kalkan was named the head of the HRK. He later broke with **Abdullah Ocalan**, the PKK leader, over the use of violence against Kurdish villages, which Kalkan believed hurt the party's recruitment efforts. Subsequently, however, Kalkan and Ocalan reunited. The HRK was abolished in 1986 after the creation of the ERNK in 1985 and the ARGK in 1986. At that time, the PKK announced that public relations and support had been inadequate. Thus the creation and abolishment of the HRK may be seen as an early attempt by the PKK to find a successful way to implement its involved long-term strategy.

HELSINKI COMMISSION. Independent U.S. government agency established to monitor the implementation of the **human rights** standards listed in the Final Act of the Helsinki Conference on Security and Cooperation, held in 1975 (subsequently the Organization for Security and Cooperation in Europe, OSCE), and its later initiatives. Since **Turkey** is a member of the OSCE, the Helsinki Commission also has served as a platform for public and private criticism of Turkey's Kurdish policy by sponsoring hearings and distributing information.

HEVERKAN. Large confederation of more than 20 **tribes** who formally belonged to the **Botan emirate** until it was taken over by the **Ottoman Empire** in 1847. Struggles for the leadership then broke out.

The unity of the confederation collapsed with the murder of its paramount leader in 1919. Hajo eventually emerged as the new leader. In March 1926, Hajo seized police and frontier posts in **Turkey**, but the Turkish army then forced him to retreat into **Syria**. There, he became one of the main leaders of the **Khoybun**, which did much of the planning for the **Ararat revolt** in 1927–30. In current times, the leadership of the Heverkan is not institutionalized and moves from one family to another.

HIWA (HEVA). In English, Hope, an Iraqi Kurdish nationalist party composed largely of urban intellectuals embracing the political spectrum from left to right and established in 1941. Thus Hiwa indicated the social shift gradually beginning in the Kurdish nationalist movement away from the stereotyped exclusive mountain and tribal identity. Rafiq Hilmi was the party's leader. Hiwa was weakened by the absence of peasant membership and was unable to exploit the **Barzani** rebellion in the early and mid-1940s. Although in March 1945 Hiwa presented a memorandum to the U.S. ambassador in **Iraq**, Loy Henderson, reminding him of U.S. president Woodrow Wilson's 12th point, concerning Kurdish self-determination, and requesting U.S. support for Kurdish autonomy, the party ceased to exist by the end of the year. Elements of Hiwa participated in the establishment of the **Kurdistan Democratic Party** in 1946.

HIZBULLAH–CONTRAS. Also called simply "Hizbullah," apparent right-wing hit squads supported by the Turkish government during the war against the **Kurdistan Workers Party (PKK)** in the 1990s.

More than 1,000 assassinations were carried out against various civilians perceived to be supportive of the Kurdish cause. Well-known victims included the intellectual **Musa Anter** and the **Demokrasi Partisi** member of parliament **Mehmet Sincar**. Although the government denied any involvement, Prime Minister **Tansu Ciller** apparently played a leading role in these events. Evidence that emerged from the **Susurluk** scandal in 1996 indicated how the state supported criminal right-wing gangs against perceived enemies. Further evidence emerged early in 2000, when the police found several hundred gruesomely tortured bodies of some of the disappeared buried at hideouts used by the group.

Several different groups were involved. "Hizbullah" (Party of God) referred to how the group's actions were supposedly seeking to protect the unity of the Muslim Turkish state, which the PKK threatened. "Contra" was in reference to its supposed official but covert support for the Contras against the Sandinista government in Nicaragua during the 1980s. The Hizbullah–Contras in Turkey were not related to other groups called "Hizbullah" in the Middle East (including Kurdish **Islamists** in northern **Iraq**).

HONOR KILLING. The murder of **women**, usually by their own male family members, because the women are deemed to have violated traditional codes of sexual mores and thus to have dishonored the family. Men frequently commit honor killing as a tool of repression against women. Until recently, the courts largely tolerated honor killing, but it has become an important issue in women's rights and **human rights**. *See also* SAHINDAL, FADIME.

HUMAN RIGHTS. Human rights are international legal liberties and privileges possessed by individuals simply by virtue of their being persons or human beings. Although many cultures and civilizations have developed ideas about the intrinsic worth and dignity of human beings, the modern concept of human rights finds its immediate origin in such Western documents as the Declaration of the Rights of Man and of the Citizen in **France** in 1789 and the Bill of Rights in the **United States** in 1791. **Great Britain** began to suppress the slave trade in 1815. The peace treaties ending World War I sought to provide certain protections for the inhabitants of mandates of the **League**

of **Nations** and various minorities in eastern and central Europe, while the International Labor Organization promoted international standards in working conditions.

The Charter of the **United Nations** opened an entirely new chapter for human rights that has potential relevance for the Kurds. Article I includes as a purpose of the world organization, "promoting and encouraging respect for human rights and for fundamental freedoms for all without distinction as to race, sex, language, or religion." Article 55 repeats this statement, while Article 56 declares that "all Members pledge themselves to take joint and separate action in cooperation with the Organization for the achievement of the purposes set forth in Article 55." Despite the domestic jurisdiction clause of Article 2(7), the progressive development of the UN Charter has been interpreted as not preventing the United Nations from addressing human rights violations in member states.

Also worth mention is the Universal Declaration of Human Rights, which was passed unanimously by the UN General Assembly on 10 December 1948. Although originally only a resolution, the International Covenants on Civil and Political Rights, and on Economic, Social and Cultural Rights, enacted into international law most of the provisions of the Universal Declaration of Human Rights, when the covenants went into effect in 1976 for those states that had ratified them.

Since the end of World War II, a number of other international human rights treaties have become part of international law. These include the 1948 Convention on the Prevention and Punishment of **Genocide**, the 1965 International Convention on the Elimination of All Forms of Racial Discrimination, the 1979 Convention on the Elimination of All Forms of Discrimination against Women, and the 1984 Convention against Torture and Other Cruel, Inhuman or Degrading Treatment or Punishment. Each of the international treaties has obvious relevance for the Kurdish question.

In 1999, Slobodan Milosevic was indicted for war crimes and crimes against humanity by an international tribunal established by the UN Security Council to look into the events in the territory of the former Yugoslavia since 1991. This would seem to indicate that a similar indictment against **Saddam Hussein** would be legally, if not politically, possible for his actions against the Kurds over the years, such as in the **Anfal** campaign and the **chemical** bombing of **Halabja**. Given the current difficulties in enforcing the international law of human rights in the diverse, multicultural world, human rights conventions may be easier to reach and implement on a regional level. The Council of Europe, for example, currently consists of 41 different states, including **Turkey**. Early in its history, the council drafted the European Convention for the Protection of Human Rights and Fundamental Freedoms, which entered into force in 1953. A number of protocols or supplementary agreements have been added over the years, with the result that regional international law regarding basic human rights covered in the Universal Declaration of Human Rights is now legally binding on members of the Council of Europe. A European Commission of Human Rights enforces these human rights, hears complaints against states party to the European Convention, and refers them to the European Court of Human Rights. In addition to states, individuals, groups of individuals, and nongovernmental organizations may also refer complaints to the commission. The court's decision is binding and may be enforced by the Committee of Ministers of the Council of Europe. In 1999, the court blocked the death penalty for treason **Turkey** had handed down earlier that year to **Abdullah Ocalan**, and early in 2003 it called for Turkey to give Ocalan a new trial.

The **Kurdish Human Rights Project** in **Great Britain** has listed the following articles of the European Convention on Human Rights as relevant to the Kurdish issue in Turkey: right to life, prohibition of torture, prohibition of slavery and forced labor, right to liberty and security, right to a fair trial, no punishment without law, right to respect for private and family life, freedom of thought, conscience, and religion, freedom of expression, freedom of assembly and association, right to marry, right to an effective remedy, prohibition of discrimination, application of restrictions under the convention only for prescribed purposes, examination of the case and friendly settlement proceedings, just satisfaction to an injured party in the event of breach of convention, protection of property, right to education, right to free elections, prohibition of imprisonment for debt, freedom of movement, prohibition of expulsion of nationals, prohibition of collective expulsion of aliens, abolition of the death penalty, procedural safeguards relating to the expulsion of aliens, right to appeal in criminal matters, compensation for wrongful conviction, right not to be tried or punished twice, and equality between spouses. Already, the European court has handed down numerous decisions involving Kurds against Turkey, while several thousand more cases are working their way through the legal system. Clearly, the legal process for enforcing human rights established by the Council of Europe system offers tangible opportunities for pursuing the Kurdish cause in Turkey.

In addition to these human rights developments in international and regional law, a great deal of what modern international law has to say that is relevant to the Kurdish question is what falls under the rubric of "soft" law or *de lege ferenda* (the law as it may be, or should be, in the future), as distinguished from *de lege lata* (the law as it currently stands). "Soft" law refers to guidelines of conduct, resolutions, or declarations, such as those currently being developed for international environmental and economic regulations that are not yet formally binding, but that do have important political and legal relevance as guides for political action and as beginning points for the future development of obligatory international norms in the form of subsequent treaties or customary laws. Specific examples of "soft" international law in regard to the Kurdish question include such concepts as self-determination, rights of minorities and indigenous peoples, the non–legally binding obligations imposed by the Helsinki Final Act of 1975 and its follow-up declarations, and humanitarian intervention.

Humanitarian intervention concerns the developing right of third parties to intervene even with armed force when severe human rights violations occur in a given state. The U.S.-led allied intervention into northern **Iraq** on behalf of the Iraqi Kurds after the failure of the Kurdish uprising and their subsequent **refugee** flight to the mountains in April 1991 may be seen as an example of humanitarian intervention. The unprecedented UN Security Council Resolution 688 of 5 April 1991 condemned "the repression of the Iraqi civilian population . . . in Kurdish populated areas, the consequences of which threaten international peace and security in the region," and demanded "that Iraq . . . immediately end this repression." The resolution also insisted "that Iraq allow immediate access by international humanitarian organizations to all those in need of assistance in all parts of Iraq" and requested that "the Secretary-General . . . use all the resources at his disposal, including those of the relevant United Nations agencies, to address urgently the critical needs of the refugees." It was the first time in its history that the United Nations so explicitly addressed the Kurdish question.

Using U.N. Security Council Resolution 688 as their legal basis, the **United States** and its allies initiated **Operation Provide Comfort** (OPC) and a **no-fly zone** to encourage the Kurds to return to their homes and to provide continuing protection for the Kurds from Saddam Hussein. OPC (renamed **Operation Northern Watch** in 1997) has continued as of this writing (March 2003) in the form of some 80 combat and support aircraft stationed at the Incirlik Air Base in Turkey's southern Adana province, from where they made almost daily flights over Iraqi Kurdistan to deter incursions from Baghdad.

Early human rights treaties concentrated on first generation individual rights, such as freedom of speech and assembly. Second generation rights concerned economic, social, and cultural rights indispensable for human dignity. Third generation rights concern the collective rights of peoples to, for example, freely dispose of their wealth and natural resources. Moderate Kurds and their supporters find that advocating human rights can be a more effective strategy than armed struggle to achieve their aims.

Finally, one should note that the Kurds themselves at times have been guilty of human rights violations against other Kurds and peoples. During the civil war between the **Kurdistan Democratic Party** and the **Patriotic Union of Kurdistan** in 1994–98, for example, numerous human rights violations occurred. At the height of the 1991 uprising against Saddam Hussein, 400–700 **Baathist** intelligence agents were summarily executed when they were captured in **Sulaymaniya**. Some fear more revenge killings will occur following the overthrow of Saddam Hussein. Honor killings also remain a problem. *See also* AMNESTY INTERNATIONAL; HUMAN RIGHTS WATCH.

HUMAN RIGHTS WATCH. Formerly Helsinki Watch, created in 1978 as an international nongovernmental organization to conduct regular systematic investigations of **human rights** abuses all over the world, both by governments and by rebel groups. The organization defends freedom of thought and expression, as well as due process and equal protection of the law, and documents and denounces murders, disappearances, torture, arbitrary imprisonment, and exile, among other abuses of internationally recognized human rights.

As such, Human Rights Watch has long played a very important role in publicizing human rights abuses against the Kurds, especially in **Turkey** and **Iraq**. Human Rights Watch specifically played an important role in translating the tons of captured **Anfal** documents that clearly demonstrate **Saddam Hussein**'s **genocide** against the Kurds as defined by the 1948 United Nations Convention on the Prevention and Punishment of the Crime of Genocide. This convention defined genocide as the "intent to destroy, in whole or in part, a national, ethnical, racial or religious group." Other important sources that have documented human rights abuses against the Kurds include **Amnesty International** and the U.S. State Department's annual country reports on human rights.

HUSSEIN, SADDAM (1937–). Baghdad strongman who officially became president of **Iraq** on 16 July 1979, when he succeeded Ahmad Hassan al-Bakr. He reached this position by employing ruthless, Stalin-like tactics against his associates in the **Baath Party** and Iraq. Later, he demonstrated these characteristics against the Kurds and others when he attacked **Iran** in 1980 and Kuwait in 1990.

At first, however, Saddam Hussein seemed more reasonable toward the Kurds when he negotiated the 1970 **March Manifesto** with **Mulla Mustafa Barzani**. Saddam Hussein's main purpose, however, was to secure his own power base. He was also alarmed by the Iraqi Kurds' international connections, which seemed to threaten Iraq's territorial integrity. In 1975, Saddam Hussein negotiated the **Algiers Agreement** with Iran, which allowed Iraq to launch a successful assault against the Kurds. During the **Iran–Iraq War** of the 1980s, Saddam Hussein used **chemical weapons** and the genocidal **Anfal** campaign in attempts to punish and defeat the Kurds for their support of Iran.

Because of his egregious **human rights** abuses against the Kurds, many Kurds (especially those living in Iraq) would consider Saddam Hussein to be their most deadly enemy. Early in 2003, most Iraqi

Kurds were giving strong support to the **United States** campaign to disarm and remove Saddam Hussein from power in **Gulf War II.**

HUSSEINI, SHEIKH IZZIDDIN (1921–). As a religious liberal and a leftist more comfortable with the Marxist **Komala** than with the moderate **Kurdistan Democratic Party of Iran (KDPI)**, this Iranian Kurd, whose name means Glory of Religion, made a most unconventional Sunni cleric. His exemplary personal conduct and secular Kurdish **nationalism**, however, made him respected and accepted by almost all political factions in the Iranian Kurdish movement when the Pahlavi regime collapsed in 1979.

Izziddin Husseini believed in the separation of state and religion and thus criticized **Ayatollah Ruhollah Khomeini**'s doctrine of the *vilayat-i faqih* (supreme arbiter of secular power) for interfering with government affairs when, as a clergyman, he ought to have been concerned only with religious affairs. However, Sheikh Izziddin himself became the head of the Council of Kurdish People and for some time acted as the representative of the Iranian Kurds in negotiations with the Islamic Republic. Khomeini came to view both Izziddin Husseini and **Abdul Rahman Ghassemlou**, the leader of the KDPI, as seditious and denounced Sheikh Izziddin as antireligious.

Sheikh Izziddin Husseini went into exile in Sweden in 1980. His career as a Kurdish nationalist leader, mediator, and unifying force illustrates how the Kurdish national movement in Iran has not been a religious movement, even when led by religious figures.

– I –

IBRAHIM PASHA OF THE MILAN (?–c. 1908). Chief of the **Milan** confederation beginning in 1863 who quickly rebuilt the confederation into a formidable force in what is now southeastern **Turkey.** Not to be confused with the famous Egyptian general of the same name who threatened the **Ottoman Empire** in the early 19th century. Ibrahim Pasha's loyalty to the sultan led to his being appointed as a **Hamidiye** commander.

When the **Young Turks** overthrew the sultan in July 1908, Ibrahim Pasha revolted and was defeated. Soon afterward, he died.

Turkish and other authors spread his fame as the uncrowned king of Kurdistan. His son Mahmud was also influential.

***IKIBINE DOGRU* (TOWARD 2000).** Influential pro-Kurdish journal in **Turkey** that was banned early in 1992. A series of successors promptly met a similar fate: *Gundem* (Agenda) 1992–93, *Ozgur Gundem* (Free agenda) 1993–94, *Ozgur Ulke* (Free land) 1994–95, and *Yeni Politika* (New policy) 1995, among others. Ironically, Turkish law allowed thinly disguised retreads to reappear, but only ephemerally. What is more, these journals were subject to regular confiscations, while their workers and buildings were targeted for fatal attacks at the hands of the shadowy **Hizbullah–Contras**.

***ILERI YURT* (FORWARD COUNTRY).** Pro-Kurdish journal that **Musa Anter** and others began to publish early in 1958 in **Diyarbakir, Turkey.** In many ways this heralded the start of almost a decade of Kurdish publications in the relatively liberal climate of **Doguculuk** in the 1960s. The journal, however, was closed down in 1959 following the arrest of a number of leading Kurdish intellectuals.

ILISU DAM. The proposal for this dam in **Turkey** became a highly charged **human rights** issue throughout western Europe in the late 1990s and into the early 2000s, until it was apparently scrapped in November 2001. The Turkish government sought to construct the dam as part of its far-reaching **Guneydogu Anadolu Projesi (GAP)** for the southeast of Turkey. The Ilisu Dam on the Tigris River (just upstream from the **Syrian** and **Iraqi** borders) was to be almost two kilometers long, more than 100 meters high, and cost some $2 billion. Its reservoir would have covered about 121 square miles of countryside and farmland, including the ancient city of **Hasankeyf**.

Turkish authorities maintained that the dam would bring many economic and social benefits to the surrounding population, which was mainly Kurdish. Opponents argued that the dam would destroy ancient and culturally significant Kurdish archeological sites forever and also have a negative environmental impact. In addition, Syria and Iraq protested that the dam would severely limit their water resources downstream. An internationally organized campaign against the Ilisu Dam finally convinced the British construction giant Balfour Beauty to withdraw its offer of funding. This apparently terminated the project.

IMSET, ISMET G. (1959–). Turkish journalist who became well known for his relatively unbiased, detailed analyses of the **Kurdistan Workers Party (PKK)** in the 1980s and into the mid-1990s, when he retired because of governmental pressure. His reports appeared in the English-language *Briefing* and *Turkish Daily News*. He also published his reports as a book, *The PKK: A Report on Separatist Violence in Turkey (1973–1992)* (1992).

INAN, KAMRAN (1929–). Kamran Inan is a prominent Turkish politician who is an ethnic Kurd. His father was an exiled **Naqshbandi sheikh** and his mother a survivor of the **Armenian** massacres in World War I. Inan graduated from the University of Geneva, and has been a diplomat, longtime member of the Turkish parliament, and even a presidential candidate against **Suleyman Demirel** in 1993. He has also been an ardent proponent of the **Guneydogu Anadolu Projesi** project. Thus, Inan is often held up by the Turkish establishment as an example of how high ethnic Kurds can rise in Turkey.

INDEPENDENCE TRIBUNALS. During the early years of the Turkish Republic established by **Mustafa Kemal Ataturk** in 1923, independence tribunals were established to deal swiftly and severely with opponents. Two independence tribunals were reestablished in 1925 to deal with the Kurdish uprising led by **Sheikh Said**, one for the provinces in the Kurdish areas and the other for the remainder of the country. Sheikh Said was sentenced to death along with his top lieutenants.

By the time the independence tribunals were disbanded two years later, more than 7,400 Kurds had been arrested, 660 had been executed, hundreds of villages had been destroyed, and thousands of other Kurds had been killed or exiled. Modern-day **State security courts** in Turkey are toned-down versions of the earlier independence tribunals. *See also* INONU, ISMET.

INONU, ISMET (1884–1973). Mustafa Kemal Ataturk's chief lieutenant and in 1938 his successor as president of **Turkey**. Some claimed that Inonu was of Kurdish ancestry.

At first, Inonu took a conciliatory position on the Kurdish issue, declaring that modern Turkey was a homeland of the Kurds and Turks. As Turkey's chief negotiator at the Treaty of **Lausanne** in July 1923, however, Inonu made no special mention of the Kurds. Following the **Sheikh Said** rebellion in 1925, Inonu is reputed to have declared that only the Turkish nation is entitled to claim ethnic and national rights in this country. No other element had any such right. As Ataturk's first prime minister, Inonu announced draconian measures in the form of the **independence tribunals** to hand down swift capital punishment for the rebels and their supporters.

In 1950, Inonu allowed Turkey's first competitive elections, which resulted in his defeat and removal from power. He returned to power in 1961–65, following the military coup of 1960. His eldest son, Erdal Inonu, was a prominent leftist Turkish politician in the 1980s and early 1990s, serving briefly as interim prime minister before his retirement.

INSTITUT KURDE DE PARIS. The Kurdish Institute in Paris was established in February 1983 and is arguably the oldest and most important such organization currently in existence. It is an independent, nonpolitical, secular organization embracing Kurdish intellectuals and artists from many different countries, as well as Western specialists on Kurdish studies. The objectives of the institute are to maintain a knowledge of the Kurds' language, history, and culture within their community, facilitate the integration of Kurdish immigrants to Europe, and present the Kurdish cause to the general public.

During its first 10 years, the Kurdish Institute was a nonprofit association. It became a foundation under French law in 1993. The income from this arrangement helps with financial activities. The institute also receives funds from the French government's Social Action Fund and Ministry of Culture, as well as subsidies from the **European Union**, the Swedish Agency for International Development, the Norwegian Foreign Ministry, the International Olof Palme Centre, the Norwegian Labour Movement, the Generalitat of Catalonia, and several Italian municipalities.

Kendal Nezan, an exiled ethnic Kurd from **Turkey** and a physicist, is the institute's longtime director. The institute has owned its own premises since 1987, contains a library, and issues a number of publications. It is located on 106, rue la Fayette, 75010 Paris, France. Its telephone number is 01-48 24 64 64 and its fax number is 01-48 24 64 66. Its web site is at www.fikp.org. Other important Kurdish institutes exist in Brussels, Belgium, and Washington, D.C.

IRAN. As one of the four main states (**Turkey, Iraq,** and **Syria** are the other three) in which historical Kurdistan lies, Iran and its predecessor, the **Persian Empire,** have always played a most prominent role in Kurdish affairs. Much of the competition between the **Ottoman Empire** and the Persian Safavid dynasty (1502–1736) took place on their Kurdish frontier. Turkish–Iranian rivalry in Kurdistan continues today in the de facto state of Kurdistan in northern Iraq.

In 1880, **Sheikh Ubeydullah of Nehri** led possibly the most significant Kurdish revolt of the 19th century, in the area along the Ottoman–Persian border. Although it was a **tribal** uprising, Sheikh Ubeydullah employed ideas of Kurdish national consciousness. From 1918 until 1922, **Ismail Agha Simko** led another significant Kurdish tribal revolt in Iranian Kurdistan and even established an autonomous government until he was defeated and eventually assassinated by the government.

The short-lived **Mahabad Republic of Kurdistan** (1946), under its famous leader **Qazi Muhammad,** also occurred in Iran. During the 1960s and the first half of the 1970s, Iran supported **Mulla Mustafa Barzani**'s rebellions in northern Iraq. Iraq finally prevailed in 1975, when Iran ceased its support for the Iraqi Kurds in return for border concessions from Iraq.

In the 1920s, the Iranian government began new policies that ended the traditional tribal nomadic economy based on herding. This was largely accomplished by dislocating and resettling Kurdish tribes and exiling their leaders. As the Kurdish society became part of Iran's developing market economy, further changes occurred in the social and political structure. The **shah**'s land reform in 1966 proved very significant in this process.

The Kurdish national movement in Iran lost most of its impetus following the defeat of the Mahabad Republic in 1946. Since then, Iraq and Turkey have seen much more Kurdish national activity. Nevertheless, a lesser Kurdish movement has repeatedly risen up in Iran. During the late 1940s and the early 1950s, the **Kurdistan**

Democratic Party of Iran (KDPI) cooperated closely with the Tudeh, or Iranian Communist Party. When the shah returned to power in 1953, however, he was able to close down most of this activity.

In the 1960s, the Iranian Kurds at first tended to cooperate with the much more successful Kurdish movement in Iraq headed by Mulla Mustafa Barzani. In the late 1960s, some young KDPI members launched a guerrilla war against Tehran, but completely failed. Relations between the Iraqi and Iranian Kurds soured because Barzani apparently aided Iran in suppressing the Iranian Kurds, even to the extent of handing some over for execution. In return, Barzani received aid from Iran.

During the late 1970s period of the Islamic revolution, there were two main Iranian Kurdish parties, the more moderate and flexible KDPI and the more radical, Marxist **Komala**. Both had explicitly secular programs and for a while they controlled most of Iranian Kurdistan. The KDPI goal was "autonomy for Kurdistan, democracy for Iran." **Sheikh Izziddin Husseini**, an unconventional Sunni cleric, also played an important role as a mediator and unifying force. In the end, however, the Iranian Kurds were not united, and their attempt at armed rebellion had completely failed by 1983. Fighting broke out between the KDPI and Komala in 1985 and hundreds died.

During the **Iran–Iraq War** (1980–88), the Iranian Kurds received logistical aid from Iraq, but never cooperated militarily with the Iraqi army. Iran assassinated the much-admired KDPI leader, **Abdul Rahman Ghassemlou**, in 1989 and his successor, Sadiq Sharafkindi, in 1992. These assassinations, along with the military defeats in the early 1980s, greatly demoralized the Kurdish nationalists in Iran, guerrilla elements of which now live in exile across the border in the de facto state of Kurdistan in northern Iraq.

During the **Kurdistan Workers Party (PKK)** rebellion in Turkey (1984–99), Turkey at times accused Iran of giving aid and sanctuary to the PKK. In 1996, Iran overtly supported the **Patriotic Union of Kurdistan** in its struggle with the **Kurdistan Democratic Party (KDP)** for supremacy in northern Iraq, while Turkey supported the KDP. Since then, Turkey and Iran have varied their support, but always with the purpose of preventing the creation of an actual Kurdish state, which might act as a powerful magnet to their own Kurds.

Iran has received large numbers of Kurdish **refugees** from Iraq, especially after the failed Iraqi Kurdish revolts in 1975 and 1991. Unlike the Arabs and the Turks, the Persians are closely related to the Kurds. This ethnic affinity has probably served to moderate Kurdish national demands in Iran. Still, with a few exceptions, Kurds (unlike Azeris) have been barred from high levels of power in Iran, which today contains the northwestern province of **Kordestan**, the only province in historical Kurdistan that bears this name. Iranian Kurds, however, also live in four other Iranian provinces—Western Azerbaijan, **Kirmanshah**, Hamadin, and Ilam. Currently, Iran contains some 6.5 million Kurds, which accounts for approximately 11 percent of its entire population. *See also* PERSIA.

IRAN–IRAQ WAR (1980–88). In September 1980, **Saddam Hussein**'s **Iraq** invaded **Iran** in the mistaken belief that Iran had been fatally weakened by its Islamic revolution. After initial Iraqi successes, the war bogged down into a long stalemate and thus created potential opportunities and dangers for the Kurdish national movements in both Iraq and Iran.

Both Iraq and Iran attempted to use each other's Kurds as fifth columns against the other. For their part, the Kurds of each nation attempted to win their national rights by supporting the enemy of the state in which they lived. Thus the war set loose forces that enabled the Kurds to become more important international actors than they previously had been.

In Iraq, the **Kurdistan Democratic Party (KDP)** supported Iran from the very beginning. The **Patriotic Union of Kurdistan (PUK)**, however, played a much more careful role, for a while even seeking to reach an understanding with Baghdad through the good offices of the **Kurdistan Democratic Party of Iran**. It was not until 1987 that the KDP and PUK were able to bury the hatchet and—with Iran's help—announce in principle the creation of the **Iraqi Kurdistan Front**. This front became the seed of the de facto state of Kurdistan in northern Iraq following the **Gulf War** in 1991.

The Iraqi Kurdish support for Iran, however, helped lead to Iraq's use of **chemical weapons** against the Kurds in **Halabja** in March 1988 and the genocidal **Anfal** campaign to punish the Kurds. As many as 1 million people died in the Iran–Iraq War. At the war's end, the Kurds were much worse off than they had been before the start of the war. The Gulf War three years later altered this situation for the Iraqi Kurds, but the Iranian Kurds remained in a weakened position.

IRAQ. Following World War I, **Great Britain** created the artificial state of Iraq out of the former **Ottoman** *vilayets* of Mosul, Baghdad, and Basra. The new state became a British mandate under the **League of Nations.** Faisal I, a **Hashemite** ally of the British, was made king. It was understood that the Kurds were to negotiate their future position in the **oil**-rich state.

From the beginning, however, the Kurds were in an almost constant state of revolt because their supposed rights were not implemented. The British established **Sheikh Mahmud Barzinji** of **Sulaymaniya** as their governor in 1918, for example, but he immediately began the first of several rebellions, even proclaiming himself king of Kurdistan. The British Royal Air Force successfully bombed the sheikh's forces and put down his repeated uprisings. With the final defeat of Sheikh Mahmud in 1931, **Mulla Mustafa Barzani** began to emerge as the leader almost synonymous with the Kurdish movement in Iraq.

Although Iraq technically became sovereign in 1932, it was not until the Hashemite monarchy was overthrown by a bloody coup on 14 July 1958 that the state really became independent. Article 23 of the new provisional constitution of Iraq gave the Kurds a recognition they had never before received in any state when it declared: "The Kurds and the Arabs are partners within this nation. The Constitution guarantees their rights within the framework of the Iraqi Republic." Despite earlier hopes for reconciliation, however, hostilities between the government and the Kurds again commenced in September 1961 and raged intermittently throughout the 1960s.

General **Abdul Karim Kassem** ruled from 1958 until he himself was overthrown and killed on 8 February 1963. The **Baath Party** briefly came to power for nine months and then permanently achieved power by two separate coups in July 1968. **Saddam Hussein** in 1970 negotiated the **March Manifesto** with Mulla Mustafa Barzani, which would have allowed a considerable amount of Kurdish autonomy. In the end, however, neither side was able to trust the other's ultimate intentions and the fighting resumed in 1974. The status of the oil-rich city and area of **Kirkuk** was one of the major disagreements. Under the terms of the **Algiers Agreement** between **Iran** and Iraq, Iran ceased its support for Barzani, and by March 1975 he had collapsed. The Iraqi government then attempted to solve the Kurdish problem by destroying more than 3,000 Kurdish villages, exiling some 500,000 Kurds to the south, and establishing a Kurd-free buffer zone on the borders of northern Iraq. Guerrilla warfare, however, resumed by the late 1970s.

The **Iran–Iraq War** during the 1980s offered new opportunities and dangers for the Iraqi Kurds, who ended up supporting Iran. The **Iraqi Kurdistan Front**, formed from the **Kurdistan Democratic Party (KDP)** and the **Patriotic Union of Kurdistan (PUK)**, along with most of the other smaller Kurdish parties, held out the hope for Kurdish unity. In retribution for the Kurdish support for Iran, however, **Saddam Hussein** unleashed **chemical weapons** against the Kurds at **Halabja** and during his genocidal **Anfal** campaign.

Saddam Hussein's annexation of Kuwait in August 1990 led to the first **Gulf War** in 1991. Iraq's quick defeat, the failed Kurdish and Shiite uprisings at the end of the war, and the horrific Kurdish **refugee** flight to the borders ultimately led to intervention by the **United States**, which imposed a **no-fly zone** over the north of Iraq. This response allowed the Kurds to establish a precariously situated, unrecognized de facto state that increasingly prospered, despite vicious Kurdish infighting between **Massoud Barzani**'s KDP and **Jalal Talabani**'s PUK during the mid-1990s.

By 2002, Saddam Hussein's Iraq increasingly appeared to be a failed, pariah, and rogue state. Despite adamant Turkish, Iranian, and Syrian opposition to Kurdish statehood, however, the U.S.-enforced no-fly zone and **United Nations** money from Iraq's share of renewed Iraqi oil sales allowed the Iraqi Kurds to prosper and construct a civil society. The Kurds presently number some 3.5 to 4 million of Iraq's 20 million people, or approximately 17 to 20 percent of the population of Iraq. The Kurdish percentage and total Iraqi population are somewhat less than that given by many others. Given the lack of precise population figures, of course, these numbers can only be approximations. *See also* GULF WAR II.

IRAQI COMMUNIST PARTY (ICP). Party founded in 1935 and for many years the most successful communist party in the Middle East. The absence of a Kurdish communist party for most of the time led what few Kurdish intellectuals there were to join or cooperate with the ICP, which generally took a favorable attitude toward the Kurdish movement. At times, a number of the party's senior members were Kurds.

Aziz Muhammad, a Kurd, led the ICP from 1963 until the early 1990s. The ICP also maintained a Kurdish Section or Branch, which became a member of the Iraqi Kurdistan Front when it was created in the late 1980s. Moreover, in 1943, a small Kurdish communist party called **Shoresh** (Revolution) was established. It joined the ICP in 1946, however.

The heyday of the ICP was from the 1940s until the 1960s. The ICP supported the peasants, took on the **aghas**, and also supported the **oil** workers of **Irbil**, **Kirkuk**, and **Sulaymaniya**. During the mid-1950s, the ICP cooperated with the **Kurdistan Democratic Party (KDP)**, which was led by **Ibrahim Ahmad**'s followers. For a while, the KDP even recognized this unity by calling itself the United KDP. Gradually, however, the ICP became marginalized both in Iraqi and Kurdish politics. The ICP still exists as a minor player and maintains a web site at www.iraqcp.org/.

IRAQI KURDISTAN FRONT (IKF). The Iraqi Kurdistan Front (IKF) was a noteworthy attempt to achieve a much-needed unity among the Iraqi Kurds who historically have been notoriously divided. It was announced in principle in July 1987 and formally in May 1988 as the **Iran–Iraq War** was nearing its climax. **Iran** played an important role in bringing the two main Kurdish parties—the **Kurdistan Democratic Party** and the **Patriotic Union of Kurdistan**—together. Six other smaller parties also eventually joined: the Socialist Party of Kurdistan in Iraq, led by **Rasul Mamand**, with **Mahmud Osman** as a prominent member; the **Kurdistan Popular Democratic Party**, led by **Muhammad "Sami" Abdurrahman**; the Kurdish Socialist Party (PASOK), headed by a collective leadership; the Kurdish Branch or Section of the **Iraqi Communist Party**, led by **Aziz Muhammad**; the Assyrian Democratic Movement; and the **Kurdistan Toilers Party**, led by Kadir Jabari. The various **Islamic**

groups (who taken together probably represented the third strongest force among the Iraqi Kurds) did not join the IKF. The **Turkoman** groups also remained aloof.

Upon its creation, the IKF declared that its main goals were to overthrow the **Baathist** regime of **Saddam Hussein**, establish a genuinely democratic government in Iraq, and develop a federal status for the Kurds in Iraq. **Jalal Talabani** and **Massoud Barzani** became the Front's copresidents.

Although crushed in September 1988 at the end of the **Iran–Iraq War** and again in April 1991 following the aborted uprising that ensued after Saddam Hussein's defeat in the **Gulf War**, the IKF subsequently came to power when the victorious allies instituted a **safe haven** and **no-fly zone** to protect the Kurds. Behind this protection, the IKF held regional elections in May 1992 that led to the formation of a parliament in June and a government in July that represented a higher form of Kurdish unity and thus replaced the IKF.

IRAQI NATIONAL CONGRESS (INC). Opposition organization to the regime of **Saddam Hussein** formally created in October 1991 following the **Gulf War**. Financed in part by the U.S. **Central Intelligence Agency (CIA),** INC attempted to represent all the elements of Iraqi society.

As such, both the **Kurdistan Democratic Party (KDP)** and the **Patriotic Union of Kurdistan (PUK)**—as well as Kurdish **Islamists**—officially played prominent roles in INC. **Massoud Barzani** joined Mohammad Bahr al-Ulum, a senior Shiite religious scholar, and Major General Hassan Mustafa Naquib, a Sunni Arab and former Iraqi army officer, on a three-man presidential council. **Ahmad Chalabi**, a Shiite banker and Ph.D. in mathematics, was chosen as the president of the executive council and thus ran INC on a daily basis.

INC's official goal is to overthrow the regime of Saddam Hussein and institute federalism and democracy in Iraq. If achieved, both the KDP and the PUK have agreed that this would solve the Kurdish problem in Iraq.

In 1995, INC attempted (with CIA encouragement) an offensive against Baghdad. The attempt failed when the CIA withdrew its support. In September 1996, at the invitation of the KDP, Saddam

Hussein's forces briefly intervened in the KDP–PUK struggle and took the opportunity to roll up the INC operatives in northern Iraq and execute some 96 of them. Despite continuing halfhearted U.S. support, INC has never fully recovered from this blow. Internal divisions also have reduced the effectiveness of INC. Nevertheless, the United States sought to breathe new life into INC after the September 11, 2001, terrorists attacks forced Washington to declare a war against terrorism, usually defined as including Saddam Hussein's Iraq.

IRBIL (ARBIL, ERBIL). Largest city and the capital of the de facto state of Kurdistan in northern Iraq. Irbil was already an ancient city in 331 B.C.E., when Alexander the Great defeated the Persian king Darius some 120 kilometers northwest of there.

Irbil was a bone of contention between the **Kurdistan Democratic Party (KDP)** and the **Patriotic Union of Kurdistan (PUK)** during their civil war from 1994 to 1998. Since 1996, the city has been held by the KDP and has been the site of its regional administration. Irbil contains the Salah al-Din University and shares its name with one of the three governorates constituting northern Iraq. The Kurds refer to Irbil as *Hawlar*.

ISLAM. Meaning "submission to God," the most recently established of the three main monotheistic **religions** in the world. The Prophet Muhammad (570–632), an Arab, began having visions when he was approximately 40 years old. The first pillar or duty of the new religion was to bear witness that there is no god but God (in Arabic, Allah) and that Muhammad is God's messenger. This simple, but profound principle probably helps explain Islam's quick success in supplanting **Christianity** (rent by esoteric theological debates)—as well as other older faiths—and becoming the main religion in the Middle East.

Most Kurds were Islamicized during the early periods of Islamic expansion after 640. Thus Islam has deeply affected Kurdish culture and society in all aspects, including national identity. Sunni Kurds, for example, adhere to the Shafii school of jurisprudence and therefore are distinguished from the Sunni Turks and Sunni Iraqi Arabs, who adhere to the **Hanefi** school. **Sufi** religious orders such as the **Naqhshbandi** and **Qadiri** also have played important religious and political roles among the Kurds. Indeed, almost all the major political leaders of the 20th century (**Sheikh Mahmud Barzinji, Sheikh Said, Mulla Mustafa Barzani** and his son **Massoud Barzani**, and **Jalal Talabani**, among many others) owe much of their early support to Sufi connections. **Sheikh Ubeydullah of Nehri** in the early 1880s also represented this pattern. **Abdullah (Apo) Ocalan**, the leader of the **Kurdistan Workers Party (PKK)**, was one of the very few exceptions. Even the distinctly secular PKK began to employ Islamic themes by the late 1980s, however, and established two Islamic affiliates, the Union of Religious Persons and the Union of Patriotic Imams.

Despite the importance of Islam to the Kurdish identity, earlier pre-Islamic faiths probably long continued (and still do), given the difficult geographic terrain of much of Kurdistan. Paradoxically, therefore, while most Kurds became strict adherents of Sunni orthodoxy, others became adherents of some of the most heterodox religious beliefs in the Middle East, such as the **Alevis** (Qizilbash), **Ahl-i Haqq** (Kakais), **Yezidis**, and others. Thus, although most Kurds tend to be rather moderate in their religious beliefs, some are wildly ecstatic. The well-known saying that "compared to the unbeliever, the Kurd is a good Muslim" partially reflects this situation.

Today, such major Kurdish parties as the **Kurdistan Democratic Party**, the **Patriotic Union of Kurdistan**, and the Kurdistan Workers Party are distinctly secular. After their own rivalries, however, their main opposition within Kurdistan has often been the **Islamists**. Some of these Islamist groups, such as the **Hizbullah–Contras** in Turkey and the **Ansar al-Islam** in Iraqi Kurdistan, have been extremely violent.

Although it is impossible to give precise figures, probably some 75 percent of the Kurds are Sunnis, while as many as 15 percent may be Shiites living in the Kurdish areas of **Iran**. The remainder belong largely to the various heterodox sects listed above. These figures are only approximations, and some authorities believe that the heterodox figures are actually appreciably larger. In the past, these heterodox sects certainly constituted larger portions of the Kurdish society. Some Shiite elements and elements that are more heterodox also overlap.

Given their location as a buffer zone between the Arab, Turkish, and Iranian heartlands of Islam, over the centuries educated Kurds have frequently acted as a bridge connecting the various intellectual schools of the Islamic world. Kurdish *ulama* (Muslim scholars and jurists) have made important contributions to Islamic scholarship. Examples are legion. For example, the famous Molla Gurani (d. 1488) was a Kurdish scholar born in what is now Iraqi Kurdistan. He studied in Baghdad, Damascus, Jerusalem, and Cairo. Eventually, he became the first *mufti* of Istanbul, the highest religious figure in the **Ottoman Empire**. Sheikh **Maulana Khalid** brought the highly influential Naqshbandi Sufi order to Iraqi Kurdistan early in the 19th century, while **Said Nursi** was the founder of the inspired **Nurculuk** movement in modern **Turkey**.

Finally, it should be noted how the *madrasahs* (Muslim schools) offered Kurdish students a place to meet and cultivate the idea of a Kurdish identity. The first Kurdish poets, whose work extolled the Kurdish heritage, were largely products of these Islamic schools, which also helped to spread their **literature**. In addition to the state *madrasahs* and those supported by the Kurdish **emirates**, there were also independent *madrasahs* attached to village mosques. These more modest religious schools produced **mullas** to serve the village and surrounding population. In so doing, they helped serve as a catalyst for the emergence of Kurdish **nationalism**.

ISLAMIC FUNDAMENTALISM (ISLAMISTS). With the perceived failure of modern secular nationalism in the Middle East (Gamal Abdul Nasser in Egypt during the 1960s is a good example), Muslim nationalists have increasingly fallen back upon their Islamic roots for inspiration and guidance. Islamic fundamentalists, or Islamists, have encouraged an idealized vision of their Islamic past and manifested a new global assertiveness that is challenging contemporary regimes and calling for a rebirth of ancient Islamic society. In extreme examples, Islamic fundamentalists have called for a jihad, or holy war, against Western imperialism.

To the initial surprise of modernists, Islamic fundamentalism has achieved some striking successes, **Iran** being a noteworthy example. The Muslim Brotherhood in Egypt, Hizbullah in Lebanon, the Palestinian Hamas, and Osama bin Laden provide further examples. Even secularists such as **Saddam Hussein** have felt it necessary to acknowledge Islam in their appeals for support. In **Turkey**, the only

Muslim state that is officially secular, Islamists also have become stronger, even electing **Necmettin Erbakan** briefly as Turkey's first Islamist prime minister in 1996.

Despite the strength of **Sufi** orders among some Kurds, however, a Kurdish proverb explains that "compared to an infidel, a Kurd is a good Muslim." In other words, Kurds respect Islam, but for the most part have not been fanatical in their allegiance. Islamic fundamentalism has not been a strong force among Kurdish **nationalists** in Turkey, **Iraq**, Iran, or **Syria**. In northern Iraq, for example, the **Islamic Movement of Kurdistan** ran a very distant third in the elections for a parliament in May 1992.

Recently, however, the Islamists have grown stronger and some extreme Islamists have turned to violence in northern Iraq. In Turkey, Islamists have begun to compete with such overtly Kurdish parties as the **Halkin Demokrasi Partisi (HADEP)** for the ethnic Kurdish vote. *See also* ANSAR AL-ISLAM; HIZBULLAH–CONTRA; SHEIKH.

ISLAMIC MOVEMENT OF KURDISTAN (IMK). Confederation of a number of small Kurdish Islamic groups in northern **Iraq** such as the Hizbullah of Kurdistan, led by Sheikh Muhammad Khalid Barzani (son of Sheikh **Ahmad Barzani** and thus the cousin of **Massoud Barzani**), and the Kurdistan Union of Clergy, led by Mulla Hamdi of Sirsank. The IMK was created to contest the elections for a Kurdistan parliament and government called for by the **Iraqi Kurdistan Front** in 1992.

In these unique elections, the IMK came in a distant third behind the **Kurdistan Democratic Party (KDP)** and the **Patriotic Union of Kurdistan (PUK)**. The IMK received only 5.1 percent of the vote for parliament and thus failed to meet the 7 percent required to receive any representation. Its leader, Sheikh Osman Abdul Aziz, also ran a very distant third to **Massoud Barzani** and **Jalal Talabani** for the position of supreme leader (president), receiving about 4 percent of the vote. The IMK was weakest in the more conservative and tribal areas of the **Dohuk** and **Irbil** governorates, where the conservative alternative KDP was dominant, and was strongest in the more developed **Sulaymaniya**, where the more progressive PUK prevailed.

In December 1993, fierce clashes broke out between the IMK and the PUK around Sheikh Osman Aziz's hometown of **Halabja**. This bloodshed proved to be a harbinger of the larger struggle between the KDP and the PUK that raged off and on between 1994 and 1998. During this larger struggle, the IMK acted at times as an ally of the KDP and solidified its position in a large area around the towns of Halabja, Panjwin, and Khurmal. **Iran** gave the IMK strong support. Aziz declared that his aim was to establish an Islamic state in northern Iraq similar to the one in Iran and then move on to create a pan-Kurdish Islamic state. He tended to benefit from the mistakes and corruption of the KDP and PUK. Aziz also was one of six Kurds chosen for membership on the executive council of the opposition **Iraqi National Congress** in its meeting in Salah al-Din in late October 1992. In the late 1990s, Aziz was succeeded by his brother, Mulla Ali Abdul Aziz, as the leader of the IMK. In 2000, **Islamists** won almost 20 percent of the seats on several student councils, in elections that were viewed as good predictors of relative party strength. Islamists also controlled the ministry of justice in both the KDP and PUK administrations.

On 18 February 2001, however, Tawhid, an Islamic extremist group that had split off from the more moderate IMK, assassinated **Francis Hariri**, a member of the KDP politburo and also a **Christian**. Several months later, Tawhid joined other Islamic extremists to form Jund al-Islam (Soldiers of Islam), an extremist Islamic group reputedly linked to elements of Osama bin Laden's al-Qaida. Heavy fighting took place around Halabja between the PUK and the Jund al-Islam, now called **Ansar al-Islam** (Supporters of Islam), in September 2001 and again in the fall of 2002. In April 2002, an agent of Ansar al-Islam narrowly missed assassinating **Barham Salih**, the prime minister of the PUK government in **Sulaymaniya**. Thus by early 2003 it was clear that Ansar al-Islam had grown into a serious problem for the PUK.

ISLAMISTS. *See* ISLAMIC FUNDAMENTALISM (ISLAMISTS).

ISRAEL. Because of its precarious position in the Arab world, and in particular the threat posed by **Iraq**, Israel has long taken an interest in the Kurdish problem as a possible way to siphon off some of the Arab threat posed to Israel. Even before the creation of the State of Israel, the Jewish Agency planted an operative in Baghdad. From there, under journalistic cover, Reuven Shiloah, who later became the founder of the Israeli intelligence community, trekked through the mountains of Kurdistan and, as early as 1931, worked with the Kurds in pursuit of a "peripheral concept" to promote Jewish and later Israeli security. Most Jewish Kurds immigrated to Israel after its establishment in 1948. Yitzhak Mordechai, the Israeli defense minister in one of the Likud governments of the mid-1990s, was one of them. During the 1960s, Israeli military advisers trained Kurdish guerrillas as a way to reduce the potential military threat Iraq presented to the Jewish state and also to help Iraqi Jews to escape to Israel. This training operation was code-named Marvad (Carpet). The important defection of an Iraqi air force MIG pilot with his plane to Israel in August 1966 was effected with Kurdish help, while Israeli officers apparently assisted **Mulla Mustafa Barzani** in his major victory over Baghdad at Mt. Hindarin in May 1966.

In September 1967, Barzani visited Israel and met with Moshe Dayan, the Israeli defense minister. Both the Israeli **Mossad** and the Iranian Savak helped Barzani establish a Kurdish intelligence apparatus called **Parastin** (Security). During the Middle East War in 1973, Barzani's Kurdish rebels in Iraq tied down Iraqi troops, which otherwise might have been used against Israel.

In 1996, Israel and **Turkey** began to develop a de facto alliance that has largely reversed the pro-Kurdish sympathies of Israel. Many Kurds believe that Israeli intelligence agents helped Turkey capture **Abdullah Ocalan**, the leader of the **Kurdistan Workers Party**, in February 1999.

– J –

JACOBITES. *See* ASSYRIANS.

JAF. Large and powerful Kurdish **tribe** historically located in the border area between the **Ottoman** and **Persian Empires** in what is now southern Iraqi Kurdistan and the Iranian province of Kordestan. The tribe claimed descent from **Saladin**. During the 1920s, the Jaf opposed **Sheikh Mahmud of Barzinji**, as well as **Great Britain**'s failure to grant Kurdish autonomy in **Iraq**. Such modernizing trends as a more defined border, effective government, and tribal settlement have decreased the Jaf's former importance. *See also* ASHIRET.

JAZIRE (JEZIRE). By far the largest both in area and population of the three discontinuous Kurdish districts in **Syria**. The term *jazire* (island) refers to the same geographical situation as does the ancient Greek Mesopotamia, which literally means "country between the two rivers" (the Tigris and Euphrates). Upper Mesopotamia became the Jazire, while lower Mesopotamia was called **Iraq** (which some say means "well rooted," but is probably simply of ancient eponymous origin). Since World War I, parts of Jazire have lain in **Turkey**, Syria, and Iraq.

Most Kurds living now in Syrian Jazire are considered foreigners by the Syrian government and lacking in the rights of citizenship. The rationale for this disenfranchisement is that many of these Syrian Kurds originally came from Turkey following the failure of the **Sheikh Said** rebellion in 1925 and subsequent Kurdish uprisings. Syria officially calls Jazire by the name Hasaka.

The present border was drawn by the French and Turks following World War I. This demarcation allotted to Syria what the French call *le Bec de Canard,* or the duck's beak, a large gash of territory pointed toward the main part of central Kurdistan that is now in Iraq.

JEWS (KURDISH). Kurdish Jewish communities existed from time immemorial until Jewish Kurds immigrated to **Israel** following the creation of that state in 1948. Traditionally, these communities and much larger Jewish communities in Iraq are dated from the 10 lost Jewish tribes, which according to the Bible were exiled to Assyria after the ancient Assyrians conquered ancient Israel in 722 B.C.E. Other traditions attributed these Jewish communities to the Babylonian captivity, following the fall of Jerusalem in 586 B.C.E.

Estimates show that just before the establishment of the modern state of Israel in 1948 there were approximately 187 Jewish Kurdish communities: 146 in **Iraq**, 19 in **Iran**, 11 in **Turkey**, and 11 in **Syria** and other places. These estimates also indicate that there were perhaps 25,000–30,000 Jewish Kurds, some 22,000 of them in Iraqi Kurdistan. The much larger Jewish community in Iraq numbered up to 125,000.

It seems that the Jewish Kurds got along fairly well with the other Kurds. Muslim Kurds attended Jewish Kurdish folk and religious rites and often participated in them. At times, Muslim Kurds did inflict indignities, exploitations, and even atrocities upon their Jewish relatives, but largely the Jewish Kurds managed to hold their own. Studies indicate that, like their Muslim Kurdish brothers and sisters, the Jewish Kurds were rather coarse, violent, and given to brigandage. The Jewish Kurds were also brave and physically strong. Their humor tended toward the sexual and scatological. Most of these traits probably derived from the much larger Muslim cultural environment. It is particularly interesting, therefore, that the Jewish Kurds managed to maintain so many Jewish characteristics, such as literacy, that were not typical of Kurdish society. The Jewish Kurds spoke **neo-Aramaic (Targum)**.

The establishment of the state of Israel brought an end to this more than 2,500-year-long existence of these Jewish communities. Early in the 1950s, virtually all of them—including, of course, the much larger Jewish Iraqi communities—were airlifted to Israel, where they quickly began to assimilate. Nevertheless, as recently as 1994 the present author, in company with several Muslim Kurds from Iraq, visited a Jewish Kurdish cooperative near Jerusalem. The two Kurdish groups greeted each other like long lost brothers. In the late 1990s, Yitzhak Mordechai, a Jewish Kurd from Iraq, rose to be the Israeli defense minister in one of the Likud governments.

JITEM. Or the Gendarmerie Intelligence and Counter Terrorist Service, reportedly the intelligence service of the Turkish gendarmerie, although this has been officially denied. During the war against the **Kurdistan Workers Party (PKK)**, JITEM became involved in such extralegal activities as arms and drug smuggling. It was also greatly feared for its **counterguerrilla** activities and its role in extrajudicial killings.

JOSH (JASH). Meaning little donkey, a derisive term Iraqi Kurdish nationalists began to use in the 1960s for the Kurdish militia who supported the government of **Iraq**. The Iraqi government called these auxiliaries **Fursan Salah al-Din** (Saladin Knights). Many, but not all, *josh* were the **tribal** enemies of **Mulla Mustafa Barzani**. Over the years, the term *josh* also has come to be used to refer derisively to any civilian Kurd who supported the Iraqi government. Because of their complex vulnerable positions, both **Massoud Barzani** and **Jalal Talabani** at times have been accused by their enemies of being *josh*. By the summer of 1986, there may have been as many as 150,000 to 250,000 *josh,* poorly organized and unequipped to handle mundane activities such as conducting road blocks so that regular troops would be free for the war against **Iran**. Sometimes these *josh* would engage in heated battles with Kurdish **nationalists**, but often the two sides simply had an unwritten understanding to avoid each other. During the Iraqi Kurdish uprising in 1991, most *josh* deserted the government and supported the rebels, which helps explain how the Kurdish nationalists initially captured so much territory and enemy troops. No organized *josh* have operated as progovernment militia in Iraqi Kurdistan since the creation of the de facto state of Kurdistan in the early 1990s. The term is still used, however, as an insult among Kurds.

JUMBLATS. Famous family of Druze chieftains in Lebanon. The Jumblats are of Kurdish origin, their name meaning in Kurdish "soul of steel." Tradition claims that the Jumblats are descended from the famous **Ayyubids** established by **Saladin** 1171. In modern times, Kemal Jumblat and now his son Walid Jumblat have played major roles in Lebanese politics. The Kurdish population in Lebanon today has been estimated at between 75,000 and 100,000.

JUND AL-ISLAM. *See* ANSAR AL-ISLAM.

– K –

KAKAIS. Name given by many in **Iraq** to members of the **Ahl-i Haqq religion**. *See also* GHULAT.

KALHUR. One of the largest Kurdish **tribes** or tribal confederations in the **Kirmanshah** area of **Iran** and along the **Ottoman–Persian** border. In the 1830s, the Kalhur were still largely **Ahl-i Haqq**, but by the early 1900s—when they played an important role—they had become at least outwardly Shia. The rapacious **Daud Khan** was the paramount leader of the Kalhur during the first decade of the 20th century. After his death, his eldest surviving son and grandson competed for the leadership and tribal fortunes declined. *See also* ASHIRET.

KALKAN, DURAN (ABBAS). Important leader of the **Kurdistan Workers Party (PKK)**. In the mid-1980s, he served as the head of the **Hazen Rizgariya Kurdistan**, or Kurdistan Freedom Brigades, a forerunner of the **Kurdistan National Liberation Front** and the **Kurdistan Peoples Liberation Army**. In 1988, Kalkan reportedly broke with **Abdullah Ocalan**, the leader of the PKK, over the party's use of violence against Kurdish villages, which Kalkan believed hurt its recruitment efforts. After being imprisoned in **Germany** in 1989, he was reinstated into the PKK. In the mid-1990s, Kalkin served on the PKK's leadership council (politburo) and was also chosen to be on the PKK's presidential council, which was created to act for Ocalan after his capture in 1999.

KARA KOYUNLU. *See* AK KOYUNLU.

KARASU, MUSTAFA (HUSEYIN ALI). Long one of the main leaders of the **Kurdistan Workers Party** (PKK). Karasu was imprisoned for a number of years after the military coup of 1980 in **Turkey**. In the 1990s, he was a member of the leadership council (politburo) of the PKK. After the capture of the PKK's leader, **Abdullah Ocalan**, in February 1999, Karasu was chosen as one of members of the presidential council assembled to act for Ocalan.

KARAYILAN, MURAT (CEMAL). Important leader of the **Kurdistan Workers Party** (PKK) for many years. In the 1990s, Karayilan served as a member of the PKK leadership council (politburo) and also commanded **Kurdistan Peoples Liberation Army** forces in the **Botan** and **Diyarbakir** (Amed) regions. After the capture of **Abdullah Ocalan** in 1999, Karayilan was chosen to sit on the presidential council that acted for Ocalan.

KARDOUCHOI. As recorded by the Greek historian Xenophon in his *Anabasis,* an independent people living in the **Zagros Mountains**

who gave the Greeks a terrible beating during their retreat from **Persia** in 401 B.C.E. Many scholars believe that the Kardouchoi were the ancestors of today's Kurds.

KARIM KHAN (1705–79). Founder of the Kurdish **Zand** dynasty, which ruled most of **Persia** from 1751 until 1794. The Zands belonged to the **Laks**, who had returned to their homeland in western Persia, from where they had been deported to northern Khurasan.

Having no claim to the title of shah, Karim Khan assumed that of *wakil al-dawla,* or regent. For the most part, he brought a period of sorely needed peace to Persia. Eventually, he established his capital in Shiraz, enriching it with magnificent buildings, some of which still stand. He also developed commerce, handicrafts, and agriculture and encouraged foreign trade. His paternal monarchy was based on tribal traditions common among the Lak and Lur nomads. His bodily strength, skill in arms, sense of humor, and concern for his peoples' welfare have become the stuff of folk tales. He died of tuberculosis.

KARIM, NAJMALDIN O. (1949–). Prominent spokesman for the Kurdish cause in the **United States** and the former longtime president of the **Kurdish National Congress of North America**. In 1996, Dr. Karim helped establish the **Washington Kurdish Institute** in Washington, D.C., and he continues to serve as its president.

As a young man, Karim served as the personal physician of the elderly **Mulla Mustafa Barzani**. Later, he became a prominent neurosurgeon living in Washington, D.C. Because of his knowledge of and connections with both the **Kurdistan Democratic Party (KDP)** and the **Patriotic Union of Kurdistan (PUK)**, as well as contacts he has made with officials in the United States, Karim has played an important, behind-the-scenes role in current Iraqi Kurdish politics. In December 2002, he was selected as one of the approximately 65 members of the Leadership Committee chosen by the Iraqi opposition meeting held in London.

KASSEM, ABDUL KARIM (1914–63). Organizer of the military coup that overthrew the **Hashemite** monarchy in **Iraq** on 14 July 1958. General Kassem (Qasim) invited **Mulla Mustafa Barzani** to return from exile in the **Soviet Union** and was at first very friendly toward him and the Kurds in general. Kassem, however, lacked a party to back him and grew increasingly unsure of his position. By 1961, Barzani had launched a rebellion, which in time further weakened Kassem. On 8 February 1963, Kassem was overthrown by the **Baathists** and executed. Kassem may be seen as a much more reasonable leader of Iraq than those who followed him. Some claim that one of Kassem's parents was Kurdish.

KAWA. Violent, anti-Soviet, Maoist Kurdish party in southeastern **Turkey** during the 1970s and 1980s that for a few years seemed to rival the **Kurdistan Workers Party** (PKK) for notoriety and violence. KAWA was named after a legendary Kurdish folk hero who rebelled against a tyrant during the time of the ancient **Persian Empire** and is also associated with the Kurdish New Year's holiday **Newroz**.

KAWA was established in 1976, but split two years later over arguments concerning China's "Three World" theory. The party ceased to exist after the Turkish military coup of 1980.

KAYPAKKAYA, IBRAHIM. Violent leftist **Alevi** Kurdish revolutionary spawned by **Dev Genc** in the late 1960s. Kaypakkaya headed an armed body called the Turkiye Isci Koylu Kurtulus Ordusu (TIKKO), or Turkish Workers–Peasants Liberation Army, which then established a political organization called the Turkish Communist Party–Marxist Leninist. Although Kaypakkaya was killed in the early 1970s, TIKKO went on to play a major role in the terrorist violence that plagued **Turkey** before the military coup in 1980. Supposedly destroyed by the new military government, TIKKO returned to the scene in the late 1980s, operating mainly in the Turkish province of Tunceli.

KAYTAN, ALI HAYDAR (FUAT). One of the original members and leaders of the **Kurdistan Workers Party (PKK)**. Kaytan was imprisoned for some time in **Germany**. During the 1990s, he served on the PKK's leadership council (politburo) and was also chosen to serve on the PKK's presidential council, appointed to act for **Abdullah Ocalan** after his capture in 1999. In 1996, Kaytan headed the **Kurdistan Peoples Liberation Army**'s central military command headquarters, which had been moved to northern **Iraq**.

KDP POLITBURO. Faction of the **Kurdistan Democratic Party (KDP)** led by **Ibrahim Ahmad** and his son-in-law, **Jalal Talabani**, against **Mulla Mustafa Barzani**, the president of the KDP. Ahmad and Talabani represented the more intellectual and socialist wing of the emerging Kurdish **nationalist** movement in **Iraq**, while Barzani headed the more **tribally** oriented, conservative forces. The relationship between these two factions varied considerably between unity and outright armed struggle. Eventually, Barzani won by driving the KDP Politburo over the Iranian frontier. Contritely, Ahmad and Talabani finally rejoined Barzani, who had become the undisputed leader of the Kurdish nationalist movement in Iraq by the mid-1960s.

After Barzani's defeat by the Iraqi government in 1975, however, the KDP Politburo in effect reemerged when Talabani created his **Patriotic Union of Kurdistan (PUK)** on 1 June 1975. Since then, the KDP and the PUK have been the two, virtually equal contenders for power among the Iraqi Kurds.

KEMAL, YASAR (1923–). Of Kurdish ethnic heritage, one of modern **Turkey**'s greatest living novelists. His most famous work, *Mehmet, My Hawk,* is the story of a Robin Hood–like bandit in the Taurus Mountains. Kemal has written more than 35 other books that have been translated into some 30 different languages, and he has won numerous prestigious awards. He also has been a perennial candidate for the Nobel Prize in literature.

In 1995, Kemal ran afoul of the Turkish authorities for his criticism of Turkey's policy toward its ethnic Kurdish population and he was tried under Article 8 of the **Anti-Terrorist Law**. Due to international publicity, he received only a suspended sentence.

KEMALISM. The official Turkish state doctrine, named for the founder of the modern Republic of **Turkey, Mustafa Kemal Ataturk**. The main principles, or "six arrows," of Kemalism are said to be republicanism, secularism, nationalism, populism, statism, and revolutionism. More than 60 years after his death, Ataturk remains a revered father figure, his portrait or bust are virtually omnipresent, and his mausoleum in Ankara is the sacred symbol of the Turkish Republic. No other political figure of the 20th century remains so honored. This has much to do with Ataturk's greatness and the flexibility of Kemalism.

In practice, Kemalism is a modernizing doctrine that holds that Turkey is a unitary state with a uniform national identity, and thus it has no place for a Kurdish national or even cultural identity. The much-abused and criticized appellation **Mountain Turks** for Turkish Kurds served as a code term for these beliefs. To the increasing detriment of modern **human rights** and Turkey's possible admission into the **European Union (EU)**, most of the ethnic Turkish population and the ever vigilant Turkish military see it as their duty to support and protect Kemalism.

However, as a modernizing and supposedly democratizing doctrine, Kemalism has as one of its ultimate aims the achievement of the level of contemporary civilization, which today means membership in the EU and thus adherence to its principles of human rights and democracy. Given the relative flexibility and even moderation of Kemalism over the years, there is no inherent reason why the so-called Kemalist consensus cannot eventually evolve to a position where it will be able to accept the EU's conditions.

KHALID BEG OF THE JIBRAN (?–1925). Jibran **tribe** member who was a key leader of **Azadi**, the clandestine Kurdish organization in **Turkey** that planned the **Sheikh Said** uprising in 1925. Although the son of a tribal chief, Khalid Beg was a Kurdish **nationalist**, probably due to his urban education in the military school for the **Hamidiye**. He was a colonel in the regular army and held the respect of most of the tribal militia commanders. He was arrested at the start of the uprising and executed along with his colleague, **Yusuf Ziya Beg**, in his prison cell.

KHALID, MAULANA (c. 1778–1826). Kurd who brought the highly influential **Naqshbandi Sufi** order to Iraqi Kurdistan early in the 19th century. He belonged to the **Jaf** tribe in Shahrizur and was a **mulla** in **Sulaymaniya**. Sheikh Abdullah of **Nehri** instructed him into the **Qadiri** order. When he was about 30 years old, however, Maulana Khalid traveled to India (a highly unusual action), where he studied in Delhi under Sheikh Abdullah Dihlawi, also known as Shah Ghulam Ali. It proved to be an extremely profound experience.

After Maulana received the *ijaza,* or authorization to transmit the Naqshbandi *tariqa* or school, he returned home and initiated an extraordinary number of *khalifas*. These disciples quickly spread the Naqshbandi order at the expense of the **Qadiri** order. Maulana claimed knowledge of the future, an ability to protect the living from harm, and the capacity to contact the spirits of the dead. These claims surpassed anything possessed by the Qadiris. Indeed, many Qadiris, including Sheikh Abdullah of Nehri, Maulana's original Qadiri instructor, converted to the Naqshbandi order. Maulana remains one of the most revered Kurdish holy men.

KHALKHALI, SADIQ (AYATOLLAH). Called "the hanging judge" because of his use of summary and mass executions in helping to crush the Kurdish uprising in **Iran**, which began in 1979 against the new Islamic Republic. It is estimated that some 10,000 Kurds had died either in battle or from execution by February 1981. *See also* KHOMEINI, RUHOLLAH (AYATOLLAH).

KHAN. *See* BEG.

KHANAQA. Also *tekiye,* a religious meeting place for a **Sufi** or dervish ritual gathering *(majlis).* The inside looks like a simple mosque with a *mihrab* (prayer niche), but no *minbar* (pulpit where Friday prayers are said). Portraits of **sheikhs**, flags, and the *silsila,* the spiritual pedigree or chain of transmission that links a Sufi master with the founder of his particular *tariqa* (mystical path), and sharp objects used during ceremonies distinguish a *khanaqa* from a regular mosque. Either a sheikh or his *khalifa* (deputy) leads the ceremony. During the *zikr,* or recitation of the divine name, the dervishes recite the *shahada* (confession of faith), "la illaha illa llah" ("there is no god but God") hundreds of times, thus inducing trances and even self-mutilation. *See also* NAQSHBANDI; QADIRI; SUFI.

KHANI, AHMAD-I (1650–1706). Author of *Mem u Zin,* the Kurdish national epic, who may thus be seen as an early advocate of Kurdish **nationalism**. Khani lamented Kurdish divisions. He argued that only a strong king would be able to bring unity, free the Kurds from foreign domination, and bring progress and prosperity. Despite his fame, Khani's ideas did little to achieve Kurdish unity.

KHOMEINI, RUHOLLAH (AYATOLLAH) (1900–89). Famous Iranian cleric who led the Shiite **Islamist** movement that overthrew the **shah** of Iran in 1979 and then established an Islamic republic. Initially, the Iranian Kurds welcomed Khomeini because he had ended the shah's rule. Soon, however, deadly combat broke out between the Iranian Kurds and the new Islamic government because Khomeini saw the Kurdish wish for autonomy as a challenge to his concept of the unity of Islam. Despite initial successes, the Iranian Kurdish guerrillas were defeated by 1983. *See also* GHASSEMLOU, ABDUL RAHMAN; KHALKHALI, SADIQ (AYATOLLAH); KURDISTAN DEMOCRATIC PARTY OF IRAN.

KHOYBUN. Or Independence, a pan-Kurdish party formed in Bhamdoun, Lebanon, in October 1927 by Kurdish intellectuals of aristocratic background and living in exile. Khoybun had the close cooperation of the **Armenian** Dashnak Party and also enjoyed some initial support from **France** and **Great Britain**. Jaladat Badr Khan served as the first president and the **Heverkan** confederation paramount, Hajo, also was a leader. Khoybun's permanent headquarters were established in Aleppo, **Syria**, then under French authority.

Khoybun sought to establish a strong Kurdish national liberation movement with a trained fighting force that would not depend on the traditional **tribal** leaders. It instigated the unsuccessful **Ararat** uprising of the Kurds in **Turkey** in 1927–30.

In 1928, France, responding to Turkish pressure, banned Khoybun's activities in Aleppo. The party also was singularly unsuccessful in promoting itself among the Kurds in northern **Iraq**. Nevertheless, Khoybun lingered on for many years, and in some ways may still be seen as one of the main organizational successes of pan-Kurdism in the 20th century.

KHUTBA. Religious ceremony read on Fridays. The *khutba* used to consist of prayers for the Prophet, the first four (*Rashidun* or rightly guided) caliphs, the current caliph, and the ruler who was regarded as sovereign. Thus having one's name pronounced in the *khutba* was the equivalent of proclaiming full independence. The *Sharafnama,* for example, mentions various Kurdish rulers who had their names read in the *khutba* and thus could be considered to be sovereign and independent.

KIRKUK. Large city with well over 500,000 people and in an **oil**-rich, ethnically diverse province (governorate) of **Iraq**. Kirkuk is situated along the line where the Kurdish and Arab populations of Iraq meet. Thus the Iraqi government and the Kurds have never been able to agree on whether or not it should be included in a Kurdish autonomous region. Kirkuk voted against Faisal becoming king of Iraq during the referendum of 1921. **Turkey** also claimed it until the **League of Nations** finally handed it over to Iraq, as part of the former **Ottoman** *vilayet* of **Mosul**, in 1926.

During the 1960s and 1970s, Kirkuk was perhaps the most important point of disagreement between **Mulla Mustafa Barzani** and the Iraqi government. Showing his ultimately poor judgment, Barzani refused to compromise on Kirkuk and even declared that he would allow the **United States** to exploit its oil fields. The Iraqi government believed that—given the Kurdish links to the West and **Iran**—handing Kirkuk to the Kurds, in effect, would be giving the area and its rich oil reserves back to the West.

Historically, most of the Kurds arrived rather recently to the city and its oil fields. The census in 1947 indicated that the Kurds constituted only 25 percent of the city's population and 53 percent of the surrounding province. As recently as 1958, the city of Kirkuk had a larger **Turkoman** than Kurdish population. The census in 1965, however, listed 71,000 Kurds, 55,000 Turkomans, and 41,000 Arabs. In July 1959, communist elements aided by bands of Kurds tragically massacred more than 100 Turkomans in Kirkuk.

After it crushed Barzani in 1975, the Iraqi government began to Arabize Kirkuk by forcibly expelling Kurds and replacing them with Arabs, as well as making it difficult for the remaining Kurds to hold property. The Iraqi government even officially renamed Kirkuk as Tamim (Nationalization), supposedly in honor of the nationalization of the oil fields in 1972. The government also gerrymandered towns with heavy Kurdish populations in Kirkuk province into **Sulaymaniya** province. These towns included Kalar, Kifri, Chamchamal, and Tuz Khurmatu. More recently, as **Saddam Hussein** turned to

genocide, more forcible methods were used. As a result, Kirkuk province today no longer has a clear Kurdish majority.

KIRMANSHAH. City in **Iran** and also the name of one of the two Iranian provinces containing a Kurdish majority. The province's population of more than 1.5 million people is approximately equally divided among Shia, Sunni, and **Ahl-i Haqq** Kurds. **Gurani** and various southeastern Kurdish dialects often called Kirmanshani are spoken in Kirmanshah. Principal **tribes** include the Guran, **Kalhur**, Jawanrud, and Sanjabi. The famous Behistun inscriptions—a cuneiform text, the decipherment of which was the key to all cuneiform script in ancient Mesopotamia—are near the city of Kirmanshah.

KIRMIZITOPRAK, SAIT. *See* SHIVAN, DOCTOR.

KISSINGER, HENRY (1923–). U.S. president **Richard Nixon**'s national security adviser and later secretary of state when the **United States** abandoned its support for **Mulla Mustafa Barzani** and the Iraqi Kurds in 1975. The support of **Iran** and the United States had become crucial for the Iraqi Kurds, and when it was lifted, **Saddam Hussein** and the Iraqi government were able quickly to crush the Kurds. Thus, the Kurds see Kissinger and the United States as having cynically betrayed them. This attitude influences the Iraqi Kurds—especially Barzani's son **Massoud Barzani**—to this day.

Kissinger justified his actions at the time by arguing that the initial support the United States and Iran had given the Kurds had enabled the Kurds to tie down several Iraqi divisions that otherwise might have been used against **Israel** during the October 1973 Middle East War. When further support for the Kurds was no longer feasible, Kissinger cynically justified its termination by declaring that "covert action should not be confused with missionary work." Many years later, he elaborated on how there had been no practical way for Washington to continue to support the Kurds in such "inhospitable mountains" and added that "the **Shah** had made the decision." Kissinger did grant, however, that "for the Kurdish people, perennial victims of history, this is, of course, no consolation." *See also* PIKE COMMITTEE REPORT.

KOMALA (1942–45). Or "Committee," a political party Iranian Kurds formed in September 1942 in Mahabad, **Iran**. Abdal Rahman Zabihi was appointed party secretary. Some Iraqi and Turkish Kurds were also represented in Komala. The party's activities eventually led to the short-lived **Mahabad Republic of Kurdistan** in 1946. Komala looked to the **Soviet Union** for guidance and emphasized language and social rights. In April 1945, **Qazi Muhammad**, a highly respected cleric and the unquestioned Kurdish leader in the city of Mahabad, was invited to become Komala's new president. In September 1945, Qazi Muhammad dissolved Komala and absorbed its membership in the new Kurdish Democratic Party, later called the **Kurdistan Democratic Party of Iran**. This new party was apparently created on Soviet advice.

A quarter of a century later, a completely new and different Iranian Kurdish party also, and therefore confusingly, called **Komala** was formed. See KOMALA (1969–).

KOMALA (1969–). Short name for the Revolutionary Organization of Toilers, the party that claims that it was originally established by extreme left-wing students in Tehran, **Iran**, in 1969. It only announced itself publicly at the end of 1978, however, when the **shah** was collapsing. The group was inspired by the Chinese communist revolution and sought the support of the rural and urban masses. Many of Komala's founders, however, were from notable families. Abdullah Muhtadi, one of its founders, has been Komala's leader for many years.

Along with the more moderate **Kurdistan Democratic Party of Iran** (KDPI), Komala became one of the two main Iranian Kurdish parties fighting for Kurdish autonomy against the Islamic Republic. Although both Kurdish parties were staunchly secular, Komala was more radical and Marxist. Komala, for example, viewed mere Kurdish **nationalism** as parochial.

Komala was strongly established around the city of Sanandaj, while the KDPI controlled the area around **Mahabad**, to the north. For a while, the writ of the two prevailed over much of Iranian Kurdistan, but by 1983 they had been defeated and reduced to waging guerrilla warfare from exile in northern **Iraq**. Komala reconstituted itself as part of the Communist Party of Iran, although it continued to be known as Komala in Kurdistan. In so doing, Komala, to its detriment, misjudged the depth of Kurdish nationalist feeling. In 1985, fighting began between Komala and the KDPI, resulting in hundreds of deaths. Shortly after the assassination of KDPI leader **Abdul Rahman Ghassemlou** in Vienna by Iranian agents in July 1989, a senior leader of Komala was assassinated in Larnaca, Cyprus. By the time it had resumed its Kurdish identity in 1991, Komala had become marginalized and the Kurdish national movement in Iran was for the time being suppressed.

KON–KURD (CONFEDERATION OF KURDISH COMMUNITY ASSOCIATIONS IN EUROPE). The umbrella organization for some 129 Kurdish community associations across western Europe. The nine country federations making up KON–KURD are: YEK–KOM in **Germany**, FEY–KOM in Austria, FEK–BEL in Belgium, FEY–KURD in Denmark, FEYKA–KURDISTAN in **France**, FED–KOM in the Netherlands, FED–BRI in **Great Britain**, KURDISTAN RADET in Sweden, and FEKAR in Switzerland.

KORDESTAN. One of the provinces of **Iran** and the only province in historical Kurdistan that bears this name, which means land of the Kurds. However, Kordestan covers only part of the historical Kurdish area in Iran. Kurds also live in **Kirmanshah**, Western Azerbaijan, Ilam, and Hamadin.

Sanandaj (Sinna) is the capital of Kordestan and the general name of the district around that city. The population of Kordestan is largely Sunni Kurdish. **Sheikhs** of the **Naqshbandi Sufi** order have traditionally been influential, although earlier the *mirs* of **Ardalan** were Shiite, possibly because of their former connections to the **Ahl-i Haqq**. Most Kurds in the region speak the so-called southeastern dialects of Kurdish, which are closer to modern Persian than to **Sorani**. Just to the west, however, are **Gurani** speakers.

KORKMAZ, MAZLUM (MAHSUN) (?–1986). First commander of the Eniye Rizgariye Nevata Kurdistan, or **Kurdistan National Liberation Front**, which was created in March 1985 as a popular front and propaganda division of the **Kurdistan Workers Party (PKK)**. At the time, Korkmaz was described by many as being second in command to **Abdullah Ocalan**, the leader of the PKK. Following Korkmaz's death in action in 1986, the PKK's main training camp in the **Bekaa Valley** in Lebanon was named for him.

KORUCULAR. *See* VILLAGE GUARDS.

KOYI, HAJI QADIR (1817–97). Poet and early advocate of modern Kurdish **nationalism**. Reacting against the traditional Kurdish tribal and religious leaders — although he himself was a **mulla** — Koyi argued that the Kurds could achieve a state only if they used the pen and the sword, that is, gain both a written language and state power. Accordingly, he called for Kurds to write down their great oral ballads and launch newspapers and magazines. His patriotic poems still arouse enthusiasm in many young people. *See also* LITERATURE.

KRAK DES CHEVALIERS. Or the Knights Krak, a huge fortress between Homs and Tartus in the Alawite mountains of **Syria**. The Frankish Crusaders who greatly enlarged and used the fortress as their headquarters for their knightly order Les Hospitaliers gave it its name.

Its Arabic name, Hisn al-Akrad, means "castle of the Kurds." The term "Krak" is probably a corruption of the Arabic word **Akrad**, or Kurds. The name may well testify to the Kurds' ancient presence in the area.

KUCHGIRI REBELLION. Rebellion of the **Alevi** Kuchgiri Kurdish **tribe** in western **Dersim** in **Turkey** that broke out in November 1920, while the **Kemalists** were desperately trying to head off **Armenian** attacks in the east and Greek attacks in the west. The rebellion was led by Alishan Beg, the son of Mustafa Pasha, chief of the Kuchgiri.

Sunnis Kurds did not join the rebellion because they still supported the Kemalists and also suspected Alevi connections with the Armenians. Even Alevi Kurds to the south did not join the Kuchgiri. The Kemalists played for time until they could bring their forces to bear, and by April 1921 the brief rebellion had been crushed. More serious Kurdish revolts subsequently broke out, such as the **Sheikh Said** rebellion in 1925, the **Ararat revolt** from 1927 to 1930, and the Dersim Rebellion from 1936 to 1938.

KURD ALI, MUHAMMAD FARID (1876–1953). One of the most important Syrian authors in history. Kurd Ali's father was a Kurd, while his mother was Cerkes. Fluent in Turkish and Arabic, he also learned French from the Lazarist fathers in Damascus. Kurd Ali enjoyed playing with words and joking and was a noted conversationalist. His literary style reflected all of these qualities.

In 1905, he founded in Cairo the review, *al-Muktabas*. After returning to Damascus in 1908, he continued to publish *al-Muktabas* until the **Ottoman** authorities closed it down in 1914. In 1908, he traveled to **France**, where he became especially interested in the Academie Française. On a trip to Italy in 1913, he spent time in the library of Prince Leone Caetani, whose *Annali dell Islam* gave him insights into methodologies not yet used in the Middle East. It was here that Kurd Ali also collected much of the documentation for his definitive history of Syria, *Khitat al-Sham*.

Following World War I, Kurd Ali was appointed general secretary of the Committee for Public Education. From this position, he helped to establish an Arab Academy. He headed it for much of the remainder of his life, with the exception of two terms of office as minister of public education. *See also* LITERATURE.

KURD DAGH. Kurd Dagh, or Turkish for "Kurds' Mountain," is one of the three main discontinuous Kurdish areas in **Syria**. The only mountainous Kurdish area in Syria, Kurd Dagh begins some 60 kilometers northwest of Aleppo, and is also only some 60 kilometers east of the Mediterranean Sea. **Turkey** borders on the immediate north. As many as 300,000 Kurds live in the area, whose main city is Afrin. Kurd Dagh is well irrigated by the Afrin River and also has abundant rainfall.

KURDAYETI. The coherent system of modern pan-Kurdish **nationalism** that was developed by Kurdish intellectual nationalists by the 1960s. The suffix *-ayeti* is used for forming abstract nouns.

Kurdayeti connotes the idea of and struggle for freeing the Kurds from national oppression by uniting all parts of Kurdistan under the rule of an independent Kurdish state. It is basically secular nationalism and has been influenced by Marxism–Leninism. The sedentarization of the rural population, the growth of urbanization, the rise of a middle and intellectual class, the development of a modern leadership, and the unique international attention following the **Gulf War** in 1991 all contributed to Kurdayeti. Given Kurdistan's division among the states of **Turkey, Iran, Iraq**, and **Syria**, as well as divisions among the Kurds themselves, however, Kurdayeti remains only a dream.

KURDISH HUMAN RIGHTS PROJECT (KHRP). Kurdish advocacy organization based in London. The KHRP monitors **human rights** abuses against Kurds within the Kurdish regions of **Turkey, Iran, Iraq, Syria**, and the Caucasus. It also is a frequent participant in cases brought to the European Court of Human Rights, the judicial arm of the **European Union**.

Established in December 1992, the KHRP is registered as a company limited by guarantee and is also a registered charity. Kerim Yildiz is its executive director. It maintains a web site at www.khrp.org.

KURDISH NATIONAL CONGRESS OF NORTH AMERICA (KNC). Kurdish advocacy group of Kurdish professionals living mainly in the **United States**, but also in Canada. It was created in 1989. The KNC seeks peacefully to achieve a united free Kurdistan and holds an annual conference. Since its creation, the KNC has played an important role in publicizing and promoting the Kurdish cause in the United States. It has particularly close relations with the **Kurdistan Regional Government** in Iraqi Kurdistan. Its president in 2003 is Hikmat Kikrat. Past presidents have been Fouad Darweesh, **Najmaldin Karim**, and Asad Khailany. The KNC maintains a web site at www.kurdishnationalcongress.org.

KURDISTAN DEMOCRATIC PARTY (KDP). The preeminent Kurdish party in **Iraq** and originally named the Kurdish Democratic Party (it was renamed *Kurdistan* Democratic Party in 1953 to indicate that it represented all the people in Iraqi Kurdistan, not just the Kurds), essentially a **nationalist** and traditionalist party that has been dominated by the **Barzanis**.

The KDP was founded at a meeting in Baghdad on 16 August 1946 in response to **Mulla Mustafa Barzani's** wishes to create financial and political independence from **Qazi Muhammad** and the **Ma-**

habad Republic of Kurdistan. Taking part in the proceedings were the remnants of at least four different political groups: **Hiwa, Shoresh** (revolution; a Kurdish communist group), Rizgari (liberation; a popular front group that sought freedom and unity for Kurdistan), and the Iraqi branch of the **Kurdistan Democratic Party of Iran** (KDPI). Barzani was elected president in exile, **Hamza Abdullah** secretary general, and two landlords, Sheikh Latif (son of Sheikh Mahmud of Sulaymaniya) and Sheikh Ziad Agha, vice presidents.

The KDP's program was vague, speaking of the Kurds' national goals and their desire to live in a state of their own choice. The program lacked any progressive social or economic substance due to the dominance held by the traditional **tribal** leaders. The new party did decide to publish a monthly called *Rizgari* (liberation), which later changed its name to *Khebat* (struggle). Because of Barzani's long exile in the **Soviet Union** and the dominant position of traditional tribal views, however, the KDP played only a minor role for some time.

Ibrahim Ahmad, a progressive socialist, joined the KDP following the collapse of the Mahabad Republic at the end of 1946. The KDPI's representative in **Sulaymaniya**, Ahmad had originally opposed the KDP's creation because it seemed to contradict the idea of pan-Kurdish unity. Now Ahmad began to lead the leftists who were opposed to the KDP's sole stress on mere Kurdish **nationalism.** An intraparty struggle broke out between Ahmad and Hamza Abdullah, apparently Barzani's representative. Eventually, Ahmad won, but without Barzani's enthusiastic approval. For a while in the late 1950s, the KDP called itself the United KDP to indicate Ahmad and Abdullah's temporary reunion and the addition of the Kurdish section of the **Iraqi Communist Party.** The fall of the **Hashemite** monarchy in Iraq and Barzani's return from exile in 1958, however, hastened renewed conflict within the KDP.

Thus began the struggle between the more conservative and traditional, **Kurmanji**-speaking, tribal wing of the KDP associated with Barzani and the leftist, intellectual, **Sorani**-speaking, Marxist wing (the so-called **KDP Politburo**) led by Ahmad and his son-in-law, **Jalal Talabani.**

In 1964, Barzani signed a cease-fire accord with Baghdad without even informing the KDP Politburo. Both KDP factions expelled each other, but Barzani won the day by driving the KDP Politburo over the

Iranian frontier. Although Ahmad and Talabani rejoined Barzani, they soon broke away again. Barzani remained allied with **Iran**, while Ahmad and Talabani developed ties with the **Baathists**. Although this intra-KDP split was basic, because of Barzani's predominance, eventually Ahmad and Talabani again contritely returned to the KDP, which had become Barzani's virtual fiefdom.

After Barzani's collapse in March 1975, his unified KDP broke into several factions. One even joined a KDP splinter already cooperating with Baghdad. Dr. **Mahmud Osman**, once Barzani's leading aide, broke with him and formed the KDP/Preparatory Committee. The real heirs of Barzani's KDP, however, proved to be his two sons, the half brothers **Idris Barzani** and **Massoud Barzani**. They joined a former associate of their father, **Muhammad (Sami) Abdurrahman**, to form the KDP/Provisional Command. In 1979, this Barzani-led faction resumed the old name of KDP. In time, this new KDP grew to be the strongest Kurdish party in Iraq. Following the death of Idris Barzani in 1987, Massoud Barzani became the KDP's undisputed leader. In June 1975, Talabani founded his **Patriotic Union of Kurdistan (PUK)**. Barzani's KDP and Talabani's PUK became the two main rivals for power in Iraqi Kurdistan, a situation that continues into the 21st century.

At the present time, Massoud Barzani remains the undisputed president of the KDP and Ali Abdullah continues to serve as the vice president. The political bureau (politburo) consists of **Muhammad (Sami) Abdurrahman**, Azad Barwari, Masrour Barzani, **Nechirvan Idris Barzani**, Fadhil Merani, Zaim Ali Osman, Jawhar Namiq Salem, Dr. Rojh Shaways, and **Hoshyar Zibari**. There is also a central committee with some 22 members and nine other substitutes.

KURDISTAN DEMOCRATIC PARTY OF IRAN (KDPI). Originally called the Kurdish Democratic Party, established by **Qazi Muhammad** in September 1945 as he moved toward proclaiming the short-lived **Mahabad Republic of Kurdistan** on 22 January 1946. This led to the dissolution of **Komala (1942–45)** and the absorption of its membership into the KDPI. The new KDPI listed as its goals autonomy for the Iranian Kurds within Iran; the use of Kurdish in education and administration; the election of a provincial council for Kurdistan; state officials all of local origin; unity with the Azeri people; and the establishment of a single law for both peasants and notables.

Although a few leaders, such as Aziz Yusufi, went underground, the KDPI in effect ceased to exist with the collapse of the Mahabad Republic in December 1946 and the execution of Qazi Muhammad three months later. During the populist rule of Muhammad Musaddiq from May 1951 until the **shah**'s coup in August 1953, the KDPI briefly reemerged. It began to recruit members and enjoy outward sympathy in Mahabad. The shah, however, quickly crushed this brief spring for the party when he returned to power.

The remnants of the KDPI fell under the powerful influence of **Mulla Mustafa Barzani** when he returned to **Iraq** in 1958 and rebelled against the Iraqi government in 1961. Under its new leader, Abd Allah Ishaqi (Ahmad Tawfiq)—who was close to Barzani—the KDPI abandoned its leftist position and even condemned Qazi Muhammad. Barzani went further by agreeing to restrain KDPI activities against Iran in return for Iranian aid, and he even handed over KDPI members to Iran for execution.

Thus a new Revolutionary Committee of the KDPI denounced Barzani and Ishaqi and then unsuccessfully tried to renew the struggle against Tehran. After this new failure, the progressive **Abdul Rahman Ghassemlou** was eventually elected the new secretary general in a meeting held in Baghdad in June 1971. Under Ghassemlou's leadership, the KDPI adopted the slogan "Democracy for Iran, autonomy for Kurdistan" and proclaimed a new armed struggle. The KDPI received aid from Iraq, but never supported Iraq against Iran or Kurds in other states.

Although the KDPI achieved little success until the fall of the shah in 1979, socioeconomic changes during this period were beginning to lead many Iranian Kurds to abandon their old village and **tribal** identities in favor of their Kurdish ethnic identity. Thus the KDPI and its rival, **Komala** (not to be confused with the earlier organization of the same name), presented a real challenge to the new Islamic Republic when they launched their rebellion in 1979. Eventual defeat, however, led to bitter in-fighting between the KDPI and Komala, as well as divisions within the KDPI, now exiled in northern Iraq. Jalil Ghadani led a faction called KDPI–Revolutionary Leadership, which accused Ghassemlou of abandoning socialism and using undemocratic methods.

Iranian agents assassinated Ghassemlou in August 1989 and his successor, Sadiq Sharafkindi, three years later. Mustafa Hijri became the new leader of the KDPI, but the party had obviously come on evil days. Somewhat confusingly, political parties with the name **Kurdistan Democratic Party (KDP)** also have existed in Iraq and, in the past, in **Turkey** and **Syria**. Indeed, the Barzani-led KDP in Iraq has been much better known over the years than its slightly older counterpart, the KDPI. The Iraqi government also sponsors a progovernment KDP.

KURDISTAN DEMOCRATIC PARTY OF TURKEY (KDPT). Party created in 1965 by **Faik Bucak** (a lawyer from Urfa, Turkey) on the conservative, nationalist model of **Mulla Mustafa Barzani's Kurdistan Democratic Party** (KDP) in **Iraq**. Thus the KDPT was under the influence of the KDP and Barzani. After Bucak's murder in 1966, **Sait Elci** became the leader. Splits within the KDPT led to its demise by the early 1970s, although a more radical branch briefly emerged in the 1970s as the **Kurdistan Vanguard Workers Party**, or **Pesheng** (Vanguard).

KURDISTAN FREEDOM AND DEMOCRACY CONGRESS (KADEK). New name of the **Kurdistan Workers Party (PKK)** as of February 2002. The name change represents the PKK's declared intention to become a legal Kurdish party in **Turkey** seeking to promote democracy and cultural rights for Kurds. The imprisoned **Abdullah Ocalan** was elected KADEK's honorary president, while a Council of Leaders provides daily direction.

Turkey continues to argue, however, that a mere name change does not justify the legalization of KADEK. As of late 2002, it appears that democratic reforms are slowly occurring in Turkey in response to Turkey's desire to join the **European Union**.

KURDISTAN NATIONAL CONGRESS. In Kurdish, Kongra Netewiya Kurdistan (KNK), formally established in May 1999 in an unsuccessful attempt to create an organization more representative of all the Kurds than the **Kurdistan Parliament in Exile**, which dissolved itself into the KNK, had been. The aged Kurdish scholar **Ismet Cheriff Vanly** was chosen as the president of the KNK. An executive council consisting of Abdurrahman Cadirci, Zubeyir Aydar,

Nadir Nadirov, Fikri Aho, Haci Ahmedi, and Nebil Hasan was also named. Brussels served as the headquarters of the KNK.

Like its immediate predecessor, the Kurdistan Parliament in Exile, the new KNK suffered from an inability to attract a full range of Kurdish participation and an image of being little more than an extension of the **Kurdistan Workers Party** (PKK). Indeed, Yasar Kaya, the president of the Kurdistan Parliament in Exile, apparently opposed the dissolution of that earlier organization and distanced himself from the new KNK.

KURDISTAN NATIONAL LIBERATION FRONT (ERNK). Or Eniye Rizgariye Navata Kurdistan, established in March 1985 as the popular front and propaganda division of the **Kurdistan Workers Party (PKK).** As such, the ERNK was mainly in charge of urban activities such as producing local recruits for the PKK and its professional army, the **Kurdistan Peoples Liberation Army (ARGK)**; organizing PKK activities such as mass riots; collecting money and information; liaison; carrying out Islamic activities and propaganda for the PKK; maintaining the logistical supply lines to ARGK guerrillas in the mountains; and organizing rural settlements.

In Europe, the ERNK liaised with the PKK membership abroad, carried on propaganda activities and staged demonstrations to attract attention to the PKK cause, found new recruits for the ARGK, and camouflaged ARGK militants. In the **United States**, the **American Kurdish Information Network** to some extent carried out the function of the ERNK on a much smaller level.

Although ERNK members were able to fight and sometimes did, they did not wear uniforms, as did the ARGK. During the day, ERNK members were waiters, students, shopkeepers, and peasants. During its heyday from the late 1980s to the mid-1990s, the ERNK may have had as many as 50,000 formal members and an additional 315,000 sympathizers. After the capture of PKK leader **Abdullah Ocalan** in 1999, the ERNK was dissolved. A more decentralized successor organization was established called Yekitiya Demokratia Gele Kurd, or the Democratic Union of the Kurdish People.

KURDISTAN NATIONAL LIBERATIONISTS. Or Kurdistan Ulusal Kurtulusculari (KUK), a leftist Kurdish party formed in

Turkey around 1979. The party often carried out violent fights with the **Kurdistan Workers Party** (PPK). The KUK eventually became marginalized, although as late as April 1988 it sent representatives to the PKK's first conference in Lazkiye, Syria.

KURDISTAN PARLIAMENT IN EXILE. In Kurdish, Parlamana Kurdistane Li Derveyi Welat (PKDW), established by the **Kurdistan Workers Party** (PKK) and other interested Kurdish bodies and personalities in 1995. The PKDW held its first plenary session in the Hague, the Netherlands, on 12–16 April 1995. With the PKDW headquartered in Brussels, subsequent plenary sessions of the peripatetic parliament were held in a number of European cities, including Vienna, Moscow, Copenhagen, and Rome.

The idea of such a body had been bandied about since at least 1993. **Abdullah Ocalan** (the PKK leader) envisioned such a structure evolving into something analogous to the African National Congress in South Africa or the Indian Congress Party. **Kemal Burkay**, the nonviolent leader of the **Kurdistan Socialist Party (PSK)** of Turkey and a longtime opponent of Ocalan, had been mentioned as a possible leader, but in the end he declined.

According to its founding bylaws, the parliament consisted of 65 members elected from the exiled Kurdish MPs from the **Demokrasi Partisi (DEP)** in Turkey, mayors, Kurdish personalities, **Assyrians**, **women**, and representatives from national institutions, youth organizations, and trade associations. Thus it represented "the will of people both inside and outside of Kurdistan" and would "constitute the first step of the new Kurdistan National Congress." Ocalan himself declared that the parliament was the first necessary step toward creating federative districts for the entire Kurdish population living in **Turkey, Iraq, Iran**, and **Syria**. As the oldest member, **Ismet Cheriff Vanly** served as the body's temporary chair until Yasar Kaya, the first chair of the DEP, was elected the permanent speaker. Virtually all the members were sympathetic to the PKK.

The parliament's first session elected a 15-person executive council chaired by Zubeyir Aydar, a former DEP member of the Turkish parliament. Seven committees also were chosen: judiciary; international affairs; education, culture, and the arts; ethnic and religious communities; public relations and information; finance; and women and youth.

A list of some of the more important aspects of the parliament's 35-point program gives an idea of the range of functions the parliament envisioned for itself: establishing a national parliament of a free Kurdistan; entering into voluntary agreements with the neighboring peoples; strengthening the national liberation struggle to end the foreign occupation of Kurdistan; undertaking programs to safeguard the political, cultural, and social rights of the Kurds; implementing the rules of war that relate to the Geneva Conventions of 1949 and those of 1977 to bring about a mutual cease-fire; taking the question of Kurdistan to the **United Nations**, the Organization of Security and Cooperation in Europe, the European Council, the European Parliament, and other international institutions; securing an observer status for the Kurds in these international bodies; pressuring the international community to initiate military, economic, and political embargoes against Turkey; working to establish unity among Kurdish political parties, organizations, institutions, and influential personalities; ending the fratricidal war then going on between the Kurdish parties in Iraqi Kurdistan; preparing draft resolutions concerning a constitution, laws on citizenship, conscription, and civil, penal, and environmental matters; ending oppression against women; improving the Kurdish **language**; laying the foundations for a national library and honoring **Ahmad-i Khani**; establishing schools and universities; dissuading the Kurdish youth from serving in "enemy" armies, rather than in the Kurdish national army; and building friendships with other peoples, including the democratic public of Turkey.

From its inception, the Kurdish Parliament in Exile was handicapped by its image as an organ of the PKK. As a result, such major states as the **United States, Great Britain, France**, and **Germany** refused to recognize it. In addition, most other important Kurdish parties, such as the **Kurdistan Democratic Party**, led by **Massoud Barzani**, and the **Patriotic Union of Kurdistan**, led by **Jalal Talabani**, remained aloof, thus inhibiting the parliament's attempt to represent all Kurds. Turkey, of course, put great pressure on foreign states not to cooperate with the parliament.

In an attempt to broaden its constituency, the Kurdistan Parliament in Exile dissolved itself into the supposedly more inclusive **Kurdistan National Congress** in May 1999, now chaired by the aged Kurdish scholar Ismet Cheriff Vanly. If anything, however, this new body is even more marginalized than its predecessor.

KURDISTAN PEOPLES LIBERATION ARMY (ARGK). Or Artes-i Rizgariye Geli Kurdistan, established by the third congress of the **Kurdistan Workers Party (PKK)** in October 1986 as the party's professional guerrilla army active in the mountains and rural areas, and thus distinct from the **Kurdistan National Liberation Front (ERNK)**, the party's civilian and propaganda front, based more in urban areas.

The ARGK never numbered more than some 10,000 members. Its members were always supposed to be party members, wear military uniforms, and operate under stricter codes of discipline than other party members. Following **Abdullah Ocalan**'s capture by **Turkey** in February 1999 and the defeat of the PKK's military struggle, the ARGK was withdrawn from Turkey into Iraqi Kurdistan and its named was changed to Peoples Defense Force to emphasize the PKK's new strategy of peaceful struggle for Kurdish rights within a democratic Turkey.

KURDISTAN POPULAR DEMOCRATIC PARTY (KPDP). Iraqi Kurdish party created by **Muhammad (Sami) Abdurrahman** in 1981 when he broke with the **Barzanis**. The KPDP did very poorly in the Iraqi Kurdish elections held in 1992. The KPDP joined with two other small Kurdish parties (the Socialist Party of Kurdistan in Iraq and **PASOK**, the Kurdish Socialist Party) that also had made very poor showings to form the **Kurdistan Unity Party**. In the summer of 1993, Abdurrahman led most of this new party into the **Kurdistan Democratic Party**, headed by **Massoud Barzani**.

KURDISTAN REGIONAL GOVERNMENT (KRG). Or Kurdistan Regional Administration, refers to the Kurdish self-government that has administered the de facto state of Kurdistan in northern **Iraq** since 1992.

After the **Gulf War** of 1991 and the failure of the ensuing Kurdish uprising in March 1991, the mass flight of Kurdish **refugees** to the mountains and borders of **Iran** and **Turkey** forced the **United States** to launch **Operation Provide Comfort (OPC)**. OPC created a **safe**

haven and maintained a **no-fly zone**, protecting the area from further attacks by the Iraqi government and thus encouraging the refugees to return to their homes. In addition, the unprecedented **United Nations Security Council Resolution 688** of 5 April 1991 gave the fledgling KRG support by condemning "the repression of the Iraqi civilian population . . . in Kurdish populated areas" and demanding "that Iraq . . . immediately end this repression."

On 19 May 1992, elections in the protected Kurdish region resulted in a virtual dead heat between **Massoud Barzani**'s **Kurdistan Democratic Party (KDP)** and **Jalal Talabani**'s **Patriotic Union of Kurdistan (PUK)**, both for the position of supreme leader (president) and parliament. A number of other parties also competed, but none of them met the qualification of receiving 7 percent of the vote to enter parliament. The KDP and PUK decided not to pursue the selection of a president and to share power equally in parliament. Parliament met for the first time in **Irbil** on 4 June 1992, and an executive with **Fuad Masum** as the prime minister was established on 4 July 1992.

From its inception, the KRG was crippled by the refusal of the surrounding states of Turkey, Iran, and **Syria** (not to mention Iraq) to countenance the concept of any type of Kurdish administration or state. Each feared the precedent it would set for their own restless Kurds. In addition, the KRG suffered from immense economic problems and a seeming paralysis of decision making due to power being shared equally between the KDP and the PUK, as well as Barzani's and Talabani's decisions not to participate in the administration.

In December 1993, fighting first broke out between the PUK and the **Islamic Movement of Kurdistan**. Then on 1 May 1994 the PUK and the KDP began a bloody on-again, off-again civil war that took more than 3,000 lives, caused untold suffering and destruction, and threatened the very existence of the KRG. The KDP–PUK fighting led to the creation of two rump governments or administrations: the KDP's in Irbil and the PUK's in **Sulaymaniya**. Only one parliament continues to meet in Irbil. After repeated attempts by the United States—as well as on other occasions **Great Britain**, **Iran**, and Turkey—the United States finally managed to broker a cease-fire in September 1998.

Some 3.4 million people live under the KRG, including 100,000–200,000 **Turkomans** and perhaps 50,000 **Assyrians**. Given recent developments, approximately 75 percent of the population is now urban and only 25 percent is rural. Irbil has some 750,000 people and Sulaymaniya has perhaps a little less. The KDP administration controls about two-thirds of the de facto state's territory and contains some 2.2 million people, while the PUK administration controls the remaining 1.2 million people who inhabit some one-third of the territory. As many as 900,000 people are internally displaced, while each month about 200 people are maimed or killed by land mines strewn over the landscape from generations of past wars. **Honor killing** of **women** remains a problem, but attempts are being made to control it.

Over the past several years, the economic situation in the KRG has improved dramatically, with the Kurds receiving 13 percent of Iraq's allotted funds from the **oil** the United Nations now allows Iraq to sell under UN Security Council Resolution 986 of 14 April 1995. From 1997 to 2001, the United Nations oil-for-food program pumped some $4.6 billion into the KRG. Despite some serious inefficiencies on the part of the Food and Agriculture Organization and the World Health Organization, most Kurds are now better off than are Iraqis under Baghdad's administration. Trade over the border with Turkey in particular has also been profitable, but since only the KDP benefits financially from this trade, the situation continues to exasperate relations with the PUK.

New roads are being built, refugees are being resettled, food supplies are adequate, **water** and electricity are available, and shops are full of refrigerators from Turkey, soaps from Syria, and even potato chips from Europe. Nongovernmental organizations contribute approximately $20 million more to all this with programs in the areas of literacy and community building, areas not addressed by the United Nations.

A civil society is also emerging, with dozens of newspapers, magazines, and television and radio stations representing a broad spectrum of opinion. People have freedoms impossible to imagine in the rest of Iraq. In addition to the KDP and PUK, there are numerous other much smaller political parties and criticism of both administrations is tolerated. During 2001, municipal elections were successfully held in both the KDP and PUK administrations. **Islamists** control **Halabja** within the PUK area and recently won almost 20 percent of the seats on several student councils. On a much less encouraging note, however, heavy fighting between extremist Islamists and the PUK broke out around Halabja in September 2001. A year earlier, fighting also took place between the PUK and the **Kurdistan Workers Party** (PKK), which uses parts of northern Iraq as a safe house from Turkey.

The entire region under the KRG has 10 hospitals. Better medical training, however, is needed, and medical specialties such as neurosurgery and plastic surgery are lacking. The electricity is often turned off, but hospitals have their own generators. The incidence of cancer is high, probably because of the use of **chemical weapons** in the past and the current lack of chemotherapy. Most services require only a nominal fee.

There are three separate universities (Salahaddin in Irbil, Sulaymaniya, and **Dohuk**), each of which has a medical school. At Salahaddin University, approximately 5,000 students in 12 colleges study subjects including education, agriculture, arts, sciences, economics, law, pharmacology, and dentistry. The universities have cell phones and even Internet access on some computers.

The future of the KRG is, of course, very uncertain. Protection from Baghdad is the ultimate concern, and this security must continue to be provided by the United States. Given the withdrawal of U.S. support in 1975 and the lack of it during the uprising in 1991, continuing U.S. protection cannot be assumed. The events of 11 September 2001 and the resulting U.S. commitment to uprooting international terrorism and its sources of support, however, will probably lead Washington to continue its support for the foreseeable future. Following the fall of Saddam Hussein in April 2003, the KRG officially continued to declare that it sought to be a part of a future democratic and federal Iraq. The KRG maintains a web site at www.krg.org.

KURDISTAN SOCIALIST PARTY (PSK). In Kurdish, Partiya Sosyalist a Kurdistan, originally established in 1974 as the Socialist Party of Turkish Kurdistan (SPTK) by **Kemal Burkay** as a nonviolent Marxist party. It was also known as Riya Azadi (Road to Freedom) in Kurdish and as Ozgurluk Yolu in Turkish, after its monthly journal, published from 1975 until its suppression early in 1979. The

PSK adopted its present name in 1992, when it reorganized itself at its third congress.

During the 1970s, the PSK had a small urban following of workers and intellectuals, possessed some influence in trade and teachers' unions, and was known for its pro-Soviet stance. The party also claimed to work through a legal youth front in **Turkey**, the Devrimci Halk Kultur Dernegi, or Revolutionary Popular Cultural Association, a descendant of the earlier **Devrimci Dogu Kultur Ocaklari**, or Revolutionary Eastern Cultural Hearths.

For most of its existence, the PSK has denounced the armed struggle of the **Kurdistan Workers Party** (PKK) as premature, counterrevolutionary, and terrorist. Instead, the PSK supported a nonviolent, two-stage strategy that would first lead to autonomy for the Kurds in a federation in Turkey and later achieve a unified socialist Kurdistan.

After the Turkish military coup in 1980, the PKK marginalized the PSK. PSK leader Kemal Burkay and his associates lived in exile. Ironically, however, the PKK eventually came around to adopting the nonviolent strategy long advocated by its rival, the PSK, after the capture of the PKK's leader, **Abdullah Ocalan**, in 1999.

KURDISTAN TOILERS PARTY. Small Iraqi Kurdish party that was led by Kadir Jabari and was one of the eight members of the **Iraqi Kurdistan Front** established in 1988. It joined the list of the **Patriotic Union of Kurdistan** in the elections for the **Kurdistan Regional Government** parliament in May 1992.

KURDISTAN UNITY PARTY. Short-lived attempt led by **Muhammad (Sami) Abdurrahman** to join his **Kurdistan Popular Democratic Party (KPDP)**, the Socialist Party of Kurdistan in Iraq, and **PASOK** (the Kurdish Socialist Party) after their poor showings in the Iraqi Kurdish elections held in May 1992. In the summer of 1993, Abdurrahman led most of his Kurdistan Unity Party into **Massoud Barzani**'s **Kurdistan Democratic Party (KDP)**.

KURDISTAN VANGUARD WORKERS PARTY (PPKK). Or Kurdistan Pesheng Karkaren Partiya, a minor Kurdish party in **Turkey** that eventually emerged from the split in the **Kurdistan Democratic Party of Turkey** (KDPT) in 1969 and was generally known as Pesheng (Vanguard). **Dr. Shivan**'s faction of the KDPT formed Pesheng in the early 1970s. After Dr. Shivan's death, Serhad Dicle led the PPKK.

Pesheng called for an independent republic of Kurdistan, saw itself as struggling for the social and economic rights of the workers and peasants, and tended to be pro-Soviet. Reduced by the arrests that followed the military coup of 1980 in Turkey, as well as splits within its own ranks, Pesheng became increasingly marginalized in the 1980s and passed out of existence.

KURDISTAN WORKERS PARTY (PKK). Kurdish party in **Turkey** that was formally established on 27 November 1978 by **Abdullah (Apo) Ocalan**, who became its leader. The PKK grew out of two separate but related sources: the older Kurdish nationalist movement that had seemingly been crushed in the 1920s and 1930s and the new leftist, Marxist movement that had formed in Turkey during the 1960s.

It was within this milieu that Ocalan (a former student at Ankara University) first formed the Ankara Higher Education Association at a **Dev Genc** meeting of some 7–11 persons in 1974. Ocalan told this initial meeting that since the necessary conditions then existed for a Kurdish **nationalist** movement in Turkey, the group should break its relations with leftist movements that refused to recognize Kurdish national rights.

Because of Ocalan's preeminence, the group initially began to be called **Apocular**, or followers of Apo. Most of the Apocular came from the lowest social classes, people who felt excluded from the country's social and economic development. Ocalan himself was the only contemporary Kurdish national leader who did not come from the traditional elite classes. In time, however, many other ethnic Kurds from all classes came to support and even identify with the PKK.

In 1975, the group departed from Ankara and began its operations in the Kurdish areas of southeastern Turkey. This entailed recruitment and indoctrination activities that by the late 1970s had spilled over into violence against leftist Turkish groups termed "social chauvinists" and various Kurdish groups called "primitive nationalists." These actions helped give the group its reputation for violence.

The PKK eventually came to consist of a number of different divisions or related organizations, themselves subdivided, which operated at various levels of command in Turkey, the Middle East, Europe, and even, on a lesser scale, other continents. Although there were at its best only several thousand hard-core members, tens of thousands and even several hundred thousand Kurds came to be associated with various PKK organizations and fronts.

At its peak, the PKK resembled the traditional model of a communist party with its undisputed leader (at various times called general secretary, chairman, or president), leadership council (in effect, politburo), and central committee. The PKK also held several congresses and conferences where major policy decisions were announced.

The PKK established a professional guerrilla army of some 10,000 fighters, the **Kurdistan Peoples Liberation Army**. The **Kurdistan National Liberation Front** was a much larger popular front that supposedly carried out political work, but also sometimes used violence. Furthermore, there was a variety of other suborgans for **women**, youth, and so forth. In addition, the PKK became adept at propaganda and journalism, publishing numerous journals and establishing the influential **MED-TV** to broadcast throughout the Middle East, including Turkey. Finally, the PKK established a **Kurdistan Parliament in Exile**, which later became the **Kurdistan National Congress**.

Shortly after the PKK was formally established in 1978, Ocalan moved to **Syria**, from where he led the party until he was finally expelled from that country in October 1998. In the intervening 20 years, the PKK had launched an increasingly virulent insurgency against Turkey that by the end of the 20th century had led to more than 37,000 deaths and the destruction of some 3,000 villages in southeastern Turkey.

The original aims of the PKK were to establish a pan-Kurdish, Marxist state through violent revolution. Pursuing guerrilla war tactics and appealing to Kurdish nationalism, the PKK grew throughout the 1980s. For a short while in the early 1990s, it seemed that the PKK might actually achieve a certain amount of military success. In the end, however, the party overextended itself, while the Turkish military spared no excesses in containing the threat. Slowly but surely, the PKK was marginalized, and Ocalan himself was finally forced out of Syria and captured in February 1999. The PKK created a presidential council of some 10 senior figures to act in his place.

By this time, however, the PKK had so ignited a sense of Kurdish nationalism in Turkey that it would be impossible for Turkey to return to the old days, in which the very existence of Kurds could be denied. In addition, the PKK's position had evolved over the years so that by the early 1990s it was only asking for Kurdish political and cultural rights within the preexisting Turkish borders. Turkey, however, saw this change in the PKK as insincere and felt that, if it relented even slightly in its anti-Kurdish stance, the situation would lead to the eventual breakup of Turkey itself.

After a Turkish court sentenced Ocalan to death in June 1999, the European Court of Human Rights asked Turkey to stay the execution, and the whole question became wrapped up in Turkey's candidacy for membership in the **European Union (EU)**. Responding to Ocalan's call to suspend military actions and pursue a peaceful political course, the PKK's eighth Congress changed the party's name to the **Kurdistan Freedom and Democracy Congress (KADEK)** in February 2002. Although it still maintains military forces in northern **Iraq**, the PKK/KADEK seems to be transforming itself into a peaceful political party to promote meaningful Kurdish cultural rights in a truly democratic Turkey that will join the EU.

KURMANJI. Or **Bahdinani**, one of the two main Kurdish dialects or **languages**, the other being **Sorani**. There are also many different variations or dialects of each of these main versions of the Kurdish language. Major dialects of Kurmanji include Buhtani, Bayazidi, Hakkari, Urfi, and Bahdinani proper.

Kurmanji predominates among the Kurds in **Turkey**, **Syria**, the areas of Iraqi Kurdistan controlled by **Masoud Barzani**'s **Kurdistan Democratic Party**, and the former **Soviet Union**. It is spoken by some 15 million, or half of all the Kurds. Sorani is spoken by some 6 million Kurds. It predominates in the areas of Iraqi Kurdistan controlled by the **Patriotic Union of Kurdistan**, led by **Jalal Talabani**, and is also spoken by a plurality of Kurds in **Iran**.

Dimili (Zaza) and **Gurani** are two other important dialects or languages and are spoken by a much smaller number of Kurds. Approximately 4.5 million Kurds speak Dimili, while some 1.5 million speak Gurani. These latter two versions of Kurdish are spoken mainly on the extreme northwestern and southeastern fringes of Kurdistan, respectively. Kurmanji and Sorani belong to the southwestern group of Iranian languages, while Dimili and Gurani belong to the northwestern group of Iranian languages. With some difficulty, Kurmanji and Sorani speakers can understand each other, as the two were separated only in relatively recent times. While Kurmanji differs from Sorani, for example, in retaining an old gender distinction that Sorani has lost, both possess the ergative construction, with verbs agreeing with the object rather than the subject. Dimili and Gurani do not use this grammatical construction.

– L –

LACHIN. The capital of the so-called Red Kurdistan (Kurdistana Sor), established by the **Soviet Union** in Azerbaijan for a brief period in the 1920s. Lachin, or Red Kurdistan, covered some 5,200 square kilometers, beginning about 40 kilometers south of the ancient city of Ganja, subsequently Kirovabad, and extending southwest to the Araks River and the border with **Iran**, with Nagorny Karabakh to the east.

Organized as an autonomous region *(uyez)* within Azerbaijan, Red Kurdistan included, in addition to the city of Lachin, the principal towns of Kalbajar, Kubatli, and Zangelan, as well as the administrative subdivisions of Karakushlak, Koturli, Murad–Khanli, and Kurd–Haji. Its population was almost entirely Kurdish. During its heyday, Lachin had a Kurdish governing body headed initially by Gussi Gajev, schools where Kurdish was the medium of instruction and that were complete with books in Kurdish, a teachers' training college at Shusha, Kurdish-language broadcasting, and a political periodical, *Sovyetskii Kurdistan*. Arab Shamo was a prominent Soviet Kurdish novelist who also helped develop a Kurdish alphabet. Other noted Soviet Kurdish authors included Casime Celil, Mihail Resid, Etare Sero, Usive Beko, Qacaxe Murad, Wezire Nadiri, Emine Evdal, Haciye Cindi, and Sement Siyabend, who was a hero of the Soviet Union.

This Soviet experiment in Kurdish self-government came to an end in 1929, when Azerbaijan downgraded Lachin from an autonomous region to a mere district *(okrug)*. This, of course, was the period in which Joseph Stalin was beginning to consolidate his absolute rule in the Soviet Union. The rationale for abolishing Lachin was apparently a desire to maintain good relations with the much larger Azeri population within the Soviet Union and with **Turkey** itself. In 1937, even the Kurdish *okrug* was abolished. Many Kurds were deported in 1937 and again in 1944. Some Kurds had their internal Soviet passports altered to list them as Azeri. Those who retained Kurdish as their nationality suffered discrimination. However, the Kurdish department of the Institute of Oriental Studies at Baku, Azerbaijan, was not abolished until the 1960s, while Kurdish studies continued in institutions in Moscow, Leningrad, and Yerevan.

Because of the lack of accurate figures and assimilation, the total Kurdish population in the states of the former Soviet Union is unknown. Estimates range from less than 100,000 to more than a million. Azerbaijan probably contains the most, but Kurds also live in Armenia, Georgia, Kazakhstan, Kirghizia, Russia, Uzbekistan, Tajikistan, and Turkmenia, among others. Following the dissolution of the Soviet Union, Nadir Nadirov, a prominent Soviet Kurd, publicized the travails of the Kurds under Stalin.

LAK (LAKK). The most southern group of Kurdish **tribes in Iran**. Some explain their name by the **Persian** word *lak,* for 100,000, which is said to be the original number of Lak families. The Lak are sometimes confused with the **Lurs**, whom they resemble physically but are distinguished from linguistically.

Although the Lak presently live in northern Luristan, they earlier emigrated from lands further to the north. The *Sharafnama* mentions the Lak as a secondary group of Kurdish tribes who were subjects of Persia. The Lak currently adhere to the **Ahl-i Haqq religion**. The Lak are probably best known for producing **Karim Khan** and his **Zand** dynasty, which ruled much of Persia from 1751 to 1794.

LALISH. In the **Bahdinani** area of Iraqi Kurdistan, the site of the **Yezidi** Kurds' holiest shrine. Lalish contains a temple and the burial site of Sheikh Adi, the most important figure in the **Yezidi** religion.

LANGUAGES (KURDISH). The Kurdish languages or language belong to the Indo–European language family and are thus distantly related to English and most other European languages. Persian, however, is the major language most closely related to Kurdish. Arabic and Turkish, despite their close geographic and religious connections, belong to completely separate language families. Because of geographic and political divisions, there is also a wide variety of Kurdish dialects. To add to the confusion, there are no standard names for these different languages and dialects. In addition, the various Kurdish languages and dialects use three different alphabets: Latin (in **Turkey**), Arabic (in **Iraq, Iran**, and **Syria**), and to a much lesser extent, Cyrillic (in the former **Soviet Union**). Exceptions, of course, exist.

At the present time, some would argue there are only two main Kurdish languages, or branches of Kurdish. **Kurmanji** and **Sorani** may be considered major dialects of one language, belong to the southwestern branch of Iranian languages, and have by far the most speakers of any Kurdish dialects. (Some, however, consider these two to be separate languages.) **Gurani** and **Dimili** (Zaza) may be considered dialects of a second language, belong to the northwestern branch of the Iranian languages, and have far fewer speakers. As already noted, there are many different dialects of each one of what may be called the two main Kurdish languages. If one were to compare the Kurdish languages to the Romance languages, the relationship between the two main Kurdish languages might be somewhat analogous to that between French and Italian. To further complicate matters, some would consider the southeastern dialects of Kurdish spoken in Iran from Sanadaj to **Kirmanshah** to be yet another Kurdish language. These southeastern dialects are closer to modern Persian than to Sorani.

This lack of Kurdish language standardization is not unique. In China, for example, Mandarin (the official language) and Cantonese—along with numerous other dialects—continue to coexist. Although *Hochdeutsch* (High German) is recognized as standard German, two principal divisions of the language still persist: *Hochdeutsch* and *Plattdeutsch* (Low German). There are also two official forms of Norwegian, *bokmal* (book language), which is also called *riksmal* (national language), and *nynorsk* (New Norwegian), also known as *landsmal* (country language). Modern Greek, too, has two different versions, a demotic or popular literary style and a reformed classical style.

LAUSANNE, TREATY OF (1923). Treaty between **Turkey** and the victorious Allies of World War I that made no specific mention of any Kurdish rights. It replaced the stillborn Treaty of **Sevres** (1920), which had provided for Kurdish autonomy and even possible independence. This change occurred because of the success of **Mustafa Kemal Ataturk** in creating the modern Republic of **Turkey** out of the ashes of the defeated **Ottoman Empire**.

Under the Treaty of Lausanne, Turkey agreed to recognize minority rights only for non-Muslims, such as Greeks, **Armenians**, and Jews. Thus the old Ottoman principle that Islam took precedence over nationality among Muslims was recognized and the Kurds received no minority recognition. Article 39 of the Treaty of Lausanne did provide that "no restrictions shall be imposed on the free use by any Turkish national of any language in private intercourse, in commerce, religion, in the press, or in publications of any kind or at public meetings." This provision, however, did not prevent Turkey from trying to ban the Kurdish **language** and assimilate its ethnic Kurdish population.

The Treaty of Lausanne was not able to settle the **Mosul** question, over whether Turkey or **Great Britain** and its mandate **Iraq** owned what became Iraqi Kurdistan. **Ismet Inonu** for Turkey and Lord George Curzon for Great Britain were the two main negotiators at Lausanne.

LEAGUE OF NATIONS. International organization created after World War I to preserve the peace. Under the terms of the Covenant (Constitution) of the League of Nations, **Great Britain** was granted a mandate over **Iraq**, or the former **Ottoman** *vilayets* of **Mosul**, Baghdad, and Basra. Thus the British became responsible for Mosul, or what became Iraqi Kurdistan (northern Iraq).

In 1926, the Council of the League of Nations settled the dispute over Mosul between **Turkey** and Great Britain and formally recognized the incorporation of Mosul into Iraq. At the same time, the International Commission of Inquiry established by the League Council required that "the desire of the Kurds that the administrators, magistrates and teachers in their country be drawn from their own ranks, and adopt Kurdish as the official language in all their activities, will be taken into account." Although Iraq did issue a "Local Languages

Law," these pledges to the Iraqi Kurds were not included in the Anglo–Iraqi Treaty of 1930, which granted Iraq its independence in 1932. Upon independence, Iraq promptly joined the League of Nations and, in effect, became one of the first independent third world states.

LEBANON. The Kurdish presence in Lebanon dates to the 12th century, when the **Ayyubids** arrived. In the following centuries, several other Kurdish groups followed, often as a result of deportation policies pursued by such authorities as the **Ottomans**. In time, these Kurdish groups were completely assimilated. The **Jumblats**—who became Druze leaders—are a well-known example. Others include the Sayfa in Tripoli, the Mirbi in Akkar, the Imads of Mount Lebanon, and the Hamiyya in Baalbeck.

There are 75,000–100,000 Kurds presently living in Lebanon. Their presence is the result of several waves of immigration that occurred after World War I. The first group came from the **Mardin**/Tor Abdin area of **Turkey**, where they were fleeing the violence prevalent in the 1920s. A second wave of immigrants fled **Syria** following the severe repression that began there in 1958. More Turkish Kurds arrived after World War II. Taken as a whole, the Lebanese Kurds constitute the second largest non-Arab group in Lebanon. Only the **Armenians** are larger.

All of the Lebanese Kurds are Sunni Muslims, but they are divided into numerous **tribal** and communal groups linked to their villages or regions of origin. They also suffer from having most of their numbers denied Lebanese citizenship. Given their lack of any appreciable political power, most of the Kurds in Lebanon belong to the lower socioeconomic class and suffered considerably during the Lebanese civil war that waged from 1975 until 1991.

The Lebanese Kurds were often the victims of contempt, hatred, ridicule, and violence. As noncitizens, their property rights were restricted. They did not enjoy the equal protection of the laws, were denied the right of voting, and were excluded from public office. Recently, however, the Lebanese Kurds increasingly have begun to win citizenship and improve their status.

LITERATURE. Although no records exist of pre-Islamic Kurdish literature and much undoubtedly has been lost because of the ceaseless conflicts that have ravished Kurdistan, it is possible to mention a few important works and authors. In the first place, there have long been Kurdish authors who wrote in Arabic, Persian, and Turkish, while in modern times many Kurds use Western languages. Use of these languages obscures the Kurdish origins of this literature. Also, many early dates are uncertain, and the frequent employment of nom de plumes further complicates matters.

The 13th-century Kurdish historian and biographer Ibn al-Athir wrote in Arabic, while at the beginning of the 16th century **Idris Bitlisi's** *Hasht Behesht* (The eight paradises) traced the early history of the **Ottoman** sultans in Persian. **Sharaf Khan Bitlisi's** *Sharaf-nama*, a history of the Kurdish dynasties up to the end of the 16th century, was also written in Persian. **Melaye Cizri** was a famous **Sufi** poet in the early part of the 17th century who declared, "I am the rose of Eden of **Botan**; I am the torch of the knights of Kurdistan." His poems remain popular today. Other early Kurdish authors included the famous 14th-century Islamic historian and geographer, **Abu al-Fida**; the great poet of the Turkish language, Fuduli (d. 1556); Eli Heriri; Mele Ahmed of Bate; and Mir Mihemed of Mukis, surnamed Feqiye Teyran.

Under the patronage of the **Ardalan** court, a number of excellent Kurdish poets also wrote in the **Gurani** Kurdish language. This list covers the period from Mulla Muhammad Pareshan in the 15th century to Mulla Abdal Rahim Mawlawi in the 19th century, and also includes Ahmede Texti, Sheikh Mistefa Besarani, Khanay Qubadi, and Mahzuni.

In the 17th century, **Ahmad-I Khani** was the first author to broach the subject of Kurdish independence in his epic, *Mem u Zin*. Notable 18th-century poets included Serif Khan of Culamerg, from the family of the **Hakkari** *mirs,* and Murad Khan of Bayazid.

The 19th and 20th centuries saw so many noteworthy writers that it is impossible to list all of them. A partial roll would include the great patriotic poet, **Haji Qadir Koyi**; the much-adored patriotic journalist, **Haji** (Piremerd) **Tewfiq**; the incomparable Kurdish–Syrian scholar, **Muhammad Farid Kurd Ali**; the vibrant patriotic poet, **Sexmus Hesen Cegerxwin**; Faiq Abdallah Bakes; Abdallah Mihemed Ziwer; Ahmad Shawki, the Kurdish–Egyptian who was known as the prince of poets; the Kurdish–Egyptian brothers,

Muhammad and Mahmud Taymur; and Mihemed Sheikh Abdul Kerim Qani, among many others.

In 1898, *Kurdistan,* a journal published in Cairo by a group of Kurdish exiles, proved seminal in the development of Kurdish literature and modern Kurdish **nationalism**. Sheikh Rida Talabani (c. 1840–1910)—possessed with gifts of satire, improvisation, and an occasional obscene verve—is still remembered as one of the most popular poets of Iraqi Kurdistan. In the 20th century, **Abdulla Goran** experimented with stress rhythms, which imitated oral folk works. Tawfiq Wahby introduced the Latin alphabet, an endeavor such foreign authorities as **Vladimir Minorsky** and **C. J. Edmonds** also supported. Contemporary Kurdish is now written in Arabic, Latin, and even Cyrillic scripts.

Despite the obstacles put forward by the regimes under which the Kurds live, Kurdish literature continues to blossom. During the short days of the **Mahabad Republic of Kurdistan**, such poets as Abd al-Rahman Hezar and M. Hemin emerged, as did writers like Heseni Qizilji. Ibrahim Ahmad's *Zhani Gel* (The people's plight, 1972) and *Dirk u Gul* (The thorn and the flower, 1992) dealt with such social concerns as **women's** rights, education, the family, and the exploitation of the peasants. In **Turkey**, **Musa Anter** and Mehmet Emin Bozarslan published occasional magazines in Kurdish and Turkish.

In addition, a vigorous Kurdish literature exists in the **diaspora**. Sweden even allocates a generous budget to finance this development. The Kurdish author Mahmut Baksi became the first foreign member of the Swedish Writers Union's Board of Directors, and he was followed by Mehmet Uzun. The **Institut Kurde de Paris** was founded in 1983 to preserve and renew the language.

Joyce Blau, a professor of Kurdish **language**, literature, and civilization at the Institut National des Langues et Civilisations Orientales, Paris, has contributed a great deal to the knowledge and renaissance of Kurdish literature in the West. In the United States, Michael Chyet has translated *Mem u Zin* and gives Kurdish language classes at the **Washington Kurdish Institute**. Vera Saeedpour offered earlier support to these developments with her Kurdish Library in Brooklyn, New York. Mehrdad Izady and Amir Hassanpour (among numerous others space does not permit mentioning) have also made important contributions.

LURS. People closely related to the Kurds and living in Luristan, or the southern **Zagros Mountains** of **Iran**, south of the mainly Kurdish area of Iran. The Lurs apparently began to be distinguished from the Kurds some 1,000 years ago. It is interesting, however, that in the *Sharafnama,* completed in 1596, **Sharaf Khan Bitlisi** mentioned two Lur dynasties among the five Kurdish dynasties that had in the past enjoyed royalty, or the highest form of sovereignty or independence.

The vocabulary of the Lurs is still largely Kurdish, but their verbal system and syntax are Persian. Lur men can be very heavily bearded, and Iranians sometimes refer to Luristan as *madan-i rish,* or "mine of beards." The Lurs are probably more than 70 percent Shia. Up to 20 percent are **Ahl-i Haqq**, while no more than 8 percent are Sunni. At the beginning of the 19th century, the **religion** of the Lurs was so unorthodox—even from the Shiite point of view—that Muhammad Ali Mirza had to send for a *mujtahid* to convert them to Islam.

The **Bakhtiyaris** are another tribal group living mainly in Iran and closely related to the Kurds and Lurs. The Turkic Qashqais, too, are closely associated with these groups both geographically and culturally. Since the time of **Reza Shah Pahlavi** beginning in the 1920s, the modernizing central government has brought all of these groups into the main administrative framework.

– M –

MADRASAH. In **Turkey** and elsewhere, Muslim religious schools, especially for teaching the Shariah, or Islamic law, to the *ulama,* or Muslim scholars and jurists. *Madrasahs* were famously closed down in **Turkey** by **Mustafa Kemal Ataturk** in 1925 as a reaction to the rebellion of **Sheikh Said of Palu** and in an effort to promote secularization and modernity. In recent times, the Turkish government has permitted Imam Hatip secondary schools, which have a religious curriculum. Strict secularists have argued that these new religious schools present a danger to the future of secular Turkey.

MAHABAD REPUBLIC OF KURDISTAN. Rump Kurdish state in northwestern **Iran** that was proclaimed on 22 January 1946, received considerable aid from the **Soviet Union**, but collapsed by December

1946. Its much revered leader, **Qazi Muhammad**, was hanged on 31 March 1947, and the **Kurdistan Democratic Party of Iran (KDPI)**, which he headed, virtually ceased to exist.

During the republic's brief tenure, schools in the Mahabad Republic began to teach in Kurdish, while scholars also began to translate texts into that **language**. A printing press provided by the Soviet Union produced a daily newspaper and a monthly journal. Also, limited amounts of Soviet military aid arrived.

There is debate over whether Qazi Muhammad actually sought complete independence or simply autonomy. During its brief existence, the miniscule entity extended no further than the small cities of Mahabad, Bukan, Naqada, and Ushnaviya in a part of what is now the Iranian province of Western Azerbaijan. Thus not even all of Iranian Kurdistan, let alone the Kurds of other states, supported the experiment. However, the Mahabad Republic did attract such non-Iranian Kurds as **Mulla Mustafa Barzani**, who served as one of the republic's generals. There also can be no doubt that the Mahabad Republic became a symbol of forlorn Kurdish statehood in the 20th century. The Mahabad Republic collapsed due to Iran's vigorous response, the Soviet Union's unwillingness to offer more support, and the usual Kurdish divisions.

Mahabad acquired its current name during the 1920s in the time of **Reza Shah Pahlavi**. Previously, it was known as Sawadj or Sawdj-Bulak. The city has long boasted a purer Kurdish culture and more intense Kurdish **nationalism** than the larger cities of Urumiya (Rezaiya) to the north and Sanandadj to the south, both of which have important non-Kurdish minorities. Thus, Mahabad has earned the premier role in the development of Iranian Kurdish nationalism.

MAHDI. In messianic or folk Islam, a divinely guided, messiah-like leader expected to appear some time before the end of the world to restore true Islamic order. Although the entire concept of a Mahdi is rather vague, such a figure would usually be associated with a revolutionary movement. During the past century, a number of revolts in Kurdistan have occurred around some figure considered by his followers to be the Mahdi. Sheikh Abdul Salam I of **Barzan** and Muhammad Barzani in the 19th century were proclaimed Mahdi by some of their followers. More recently, **Sheikh Ahmad Barzani** was considered by some of his followers as semidivine. The rebellion of **Sheikh Said of Palu** in 1925 in **Turkey** had some aspects of Mahdism. Some conservative religious leaders in Turkey saw **Mustafa Kemal Ataturk** as the *Daijal*, or Fiend, whose coming was to precede that of the Mahdi.

MAJID, ALI HASSAN (1940–). Cousin of **Saddam Hussein** who was given unprecedented powers to act ruthlessly against the Kurds when he was appointed secretary general, or governor, of the **Baathist** Northern Bureau in northern **Iraq** on 3 March 1987. His appointment came during some of the darkest days of the **Iran–Iraq War** and at a time when the Iraqi Kurds were seen as a fifth column aiding the Iranian advance.

General Majid became known by the Kurds as Ali Chemical for his willingness to use **chemical warfare** against them beginning in 1987 in the Balisan valley and continuing into 1988 with the notorious chemical attacks on **Halabja** and during the **genocidal Anfal** campaign. Majid used a scorched-earth policy to destroy Kurdish villages, evacuate the Kurds from the frontier areas, and deport large numbers of them to their deaths. In crude Arabic slang, Majid bragged in a captured document how he butchered and bulldozed thousands of captured Kurds and cared nothing for international opinion.

MAM JALAL. *See* TALABANI, JALAL.

MAMAND, ABBAS AGHA. Chief of the Aku Kurdish tribe whose lands lay between Ranya and Rawanduz in northern **Iraq**. Although he was a traditional tribal leader seeking mainly to protect his landed interests, Mamand decided in 1961 to support **Mulla Mustafa Barzani**'s revolt against the government of **Abdul Karim Kassem**. Despite the failure of Mamand's forces, his support probably helped Barzani's emergence as a Kurdish **nationalist** leader.

During the mid-1960s, Barzani appointed Mamand the president of a consultative assembly to help administer Kurdish affairs. When he was an old man in 1991, some of Mamand's younger followers helped initiate the Kurdish uprising in Ranya that in turn helped lead to the de facto state of Kurdistan in northern Iraq that has existed since that year.

MAMAND, RASUL (?-1994). Iraqi Kurdish leader who first gained prominence as a member of the Socialist Movement of Kurdistan, which was headed by **Ali Askari**, and was one of the founding members of **Jalal Talabani**'s **Patriotic Union of Kurdistan (PUK).** After Askari was executed by the **Kurdistan Democratic Party** in 1978, Mamand led his followers in joining **Mahmud Osman**'s Kurdistan Democratic Party/Preparatory Committee to form the Socialist Party of Kurdistan in Iraq (SPKI).

The SPKI was a small party that was an original member of the **Iraqi Kurdistan Front**, which was formed in May 1988. After his SPKI did very poorly in the Iraqi Kurdish elections of May 1992, Mamand at first joined **Muhammad (Sami) Abdurrahman** to form the **Kurdistan Unity Party**. When this group soon failed, however, Mamand rejoined the PUK as a senior member of its politburo. Shortly afterward, he died suddenly of a heart attack while in **Great Britain**.

MARCH MANIFESTO (1970). Manifesto negotiated in 1970 by **Mulla Mustafa Barzani** and the **Baathist** Iraqi government in effect headed by **Saddam Hussein** that held out the promise of real autonomy for the Iraqi Kurds and thus an overall settlement of the Kurdish problem in Iraq. The March Manifesto consisted of 15 detailed articles. In the end, however, neither side trusted each other enough to implement the provisions, and fighting was renewed in 1974 that led to Barzani's final defeat. Over the years, the March Manifesto has been continually referred to as a background for a settlement by both sides. For example, it was declared as the basis of the negotiations that took place following the Kurdish uprising of 1991.

MARDIN. Small city and also the name of a province in southeastern **Turkey** bordering on **Syria** and thus in the northern part of the historic **Jazire**. The population is heavily ethnic Kurdish, and the province was under **emergency rule** for many years during the uprising staged by the **Kurdistan Workers Party**.

MARWANIDS. Kurdish dynasty that held sway from **Diyarbakir** southward into the northern parts of what are now **Syria** and **Iraq** from approximately 984 to 1083. **Islam** and family ties defined such dynasties more than the Kurdish ethnicity of its rulers. Indeed, it is likely that the Marwanids ruled a largely **Christian** population, at least in the city of **Diyarbakir.** The founder of the dynasty was a Kurdish chief named Badh. The Marwanids took their name, however, from Marwan, a miller who had married Badh's sister. Their third son, Nasr al-Dawla Ahmad, brought Marwanid power to its zenith. During his long rule (1011–61), Nasr al-Dawla skillfully balanced his buffer state among the three main powers of the **Buwayhid** sultan, the Fatimid caliph, and the Byzantine emperor. His court at Mayyafarikin was frequented by famous *ulama* (Islamic scholars and jurists) and poets. He also built bridges and citadels, as confirmed by inscriptions found on the walls of Diyarbakir.

Turkic invasions eventually overthrew the dynasty. The Marwanids are one of the five Kurdish dynasties mentioned by **Sharaf Khan Bitlisi** in the *Sharafnama* as enjoying royalty.

MASUM, FUAD. A senior member of the politburo of the **Patriotic Union of Kurdistan (PUK)** and an Islamic scholar, named the first prime minister of the **Kurdistan Regional Government** in northern **Iraq** upon its formal creation in June 1992. Basically a technocrat, Masum resigned in March 1993 in favor of a more dynamic leadership headed by **Kosrat Rasul,** also a senior member of the PUK. However, internal conflict between the **Kurdistan Democratic Party** and the PUK soon followed.

MAWAT. Iraqi Kurdish town some 30 kilometers northeast of **Sulaymaniya** and very close to the Iranian border. During the early 1960s, it served as the headquarters of the **KDP Politburo,** headed by **Ibrahim Ahmad** and **Jalal Talabani,** who were opposed to **Mulla Mustafa Barzani.** Barzani at times referred to the KDP politburo as the "Mawat Empire."

MAZLUM KORKMAZ CAMP. Important camp of the **Kurdistan Workers Party (PKK)** in the **Bekaa Valley** of Lebanon on the border with **Syria** that was finally closed down as a sop to **Turkey** in 1992. It was named for **Mazlum Korkmaz,** the first commander of the **Kurdistan National Liberation Front (ERNK),** which was the

PKK's popular front. After the closure, Syria continued to provide invaluable help to the PKK until October 1998, when Turkish pressure finally forced Syria to expel **Abdullah Ocalan**, the longtime leader of the PKK, and its fighters.

MED-TV. The **Kurdistan Workers Party (PKK)**–affiliated television station that began broadcasting from **Great Britain** and Belgium to Kurdistan and the Middle East, as well as Europe, in 1995. Its name was taken from the **Medes**, an ancient nation from whom many Kurds claim descent.

MED-TV broadcast in the various Kurdish dialects, in Turkish, and even a little in Syriac in order to reach as many sympathizers as possible. The TV station led to a great deal of pride and interest among many Kurds not accustomed to hearing the news and cultural events broadcast from their point of view and in their **languages**. Before Turkey captured him in February 1999, **Abdullah Ocalan**, the leader of the PKK, frequently participated in broadcasts by telephone. Due to Turkish pressure and the claim that it was inciting violence, MED-TV lost its broadcasting license and was shut down on 22 March 1999, but it soon, in effect, reopened under the new name MEDYA-TV.

MEDES. Ancient Indo–European people who spoke an Iranian language related to old Persian, but who have left no written records of their own. The Medes flourished from the eighth to the sixth centuries B.C.E. Under King Cyaxares, the Medes joined forces with the Babylonians and destroyed the Assyrian Empire in 612 B.C.E. The Medes then established a large but short-lived empire of their own over areas that are now in western **Iran** and northern **Iraq**. Cyrus the Great defeated Astyages, the last Median king, in approximately 550 B.C.E. and established the Persian Empire.

Many Kurds claim that their nation descended from the Medes. The early-20th-century authority on the Kurds, **Vladimir Minorsky**, agreed with this assessment on the basis of historical and linguistic evidence he had gathered. However, D. N. MacKenzie, a later authority on Kurdish **languages**, challenged this genealogy by showing that the Medes spoke a northwestern Iranian language, while the Kurds speak a southwestern one. Nevertheless, the Medes probably do constitute an important element from which the contemporary Kurds derive.

MEDYA-TV. *See* MED-TV.

MELA. *See* MULLA.

MELIK. Title meaning "king" that was used in the past, for example, by the *meliks* of **Hasankeyf.**

MEM U ZIN. Composed by the 17th-century poet **Ahmad-i Khani,** universally considered to be the Kurdish national epic because its introductory parts contain an obvious reference to Kurdish **nationalist** beliefs: "If only there were harmony among us, if we were to obey a single one of us, he would reduce to vassalage **Turks,** Arabs and **Persians,** all of them. We would perfect our religion, our state, and would educate ourselves in learning and wisdom." Since the epic was written at a time when nationalism was unknown in the Islamic Middle East, some have argued that Kurdish is the oldest nationalism in that area of the world.

The poem itself runs for more than 2,650 distichs, or couplets. Its plot concerns tragic lovers and has been called by some a Kurdish *Romeo and Juliet.* Mem and Zin are two lovers. Bakir's intrigues cause the death of Mem. Zin then dies of grief at her lover's grave. She is buried next to Mem's grave, while Bakir is killed there in revenge. A thornbush grows out of Bakir's blood and its roots separate the two lovers even in death. Recently, Michael Chyet, an American scholar of the Kurdish **language,** has written a contemporary analysis of the epic; Mehmet Emin Bozarslan, a Kurdish scholar living in Sweden, has translated it. *See also* LITERATURE.

MEZIN. Meaning a great or big man, title sometimes used for the head of a *bavik,* or subvillage unit. **Agha** is a similar, more frequently used title.

MILAN. Ancient Kurdish legend claims that all Kurdish **tribes** originated in the distant past from two primordial tribes, the Milan and the Zilan. Supposedly, the Milan came from the south, while the Zilan originated from the east. Many tribes still claim to belong to one of these two oppositional groups. Early in the 20th century, **Ibrahim Pasha** was the chief of the large Milan confederation in what is now southeastern **Turkey**.

MILLET. In **Ottoman** times, this term indicated what religious community one belonged to, and status as a *millet* guaranteed religious minorities considerable autonomy in cultural, religious, and educational affairs. In the 20th century, the term *millet* has come to mean nation.

MILLI GUVENLIK KURULU (MGK). Or National Security Council, which in **Turkey** often acts as the ultimate source of authority in that country. Over the years, the MGK has played a leading role in the suppression of Kurdish **nationalism** and, from the viewpoint of most Kurds, the prevention of many meaningful reforms that might have helped solve the Kurdish problem in Turkey.

The modern Republic of Turkey, of course, was founded by **Mustafa Kemal Ataturk**, whose power originally stemmed from his position in the military. Thus, from the beginning, the military played a very important and, it should be noted, very popular role in the defense and, therefore, the politics of Turkey. Following the military coup of May 1960, the new constitution, which went into effect in 1961, provided a constitutional role for the military for the first time by establishing the MGK. The MGK consists of 10 members to advise the government on internal and external security. Chaired by the president (or in his absence the prime minister), the MGK also consists of the chief of the general staff, four military service chiefs, and the defense, foreign affairs, and interior ministers.

Over the years, the MGK has gradually extended its power over governmental policy, at times replacing the civilian government as the ultimate center of power over issues of national security. After the "coup by memorandum" in March 1971, for example, the MGK was given the power to give binding, unsolicited advice to the cabinet. Subsequent to the military coup of September 1980, for a while all power was concentrated in the MGK, chaired by the chief of staff, General **Kenan Evren**, who later was president from 1982 to 1989. Although the MGK greatly reduced the rampant terrorism in Turkey, a major price was paid in terms of **human rights**.

During the 1990s, the MGK began to exercise virtually total authority over security matters dealing with the Kurdish problem. The "postmodern coup" in June 1997 toppled Turkey's first **Islamist** government and was sanctioned by an MGK edict issued a few months earlier. One of the requirements for Turkey's membership in the **European Union** is the reduction of the MGK's influence over civilian government.

MILLI ISTIHBARAT TESHILATI (MIT). Or National Intelligence Organization, agency operating in **Turkey** since the 1920s, although it was only officially established in 1965. It combines the functions of internal and external intelligence services. Although in theory the MIT reports to the prime minister, in practice it remains close to the military, which continues to wield considerable influence over Turkish civilian governments through the **Milli Guvenlik Kurulu**, or National Security Council.

The MIT has no police powers. It is only authorized to gather intelligence and carry out counterintelligence abroad. Internally, it is only permitted to investigate communists (extreme leftist groups), separatists (Kurdish groups), and extreme rightists. In practice, the MIT has been accused of using extreme rightists to infiltrate and destroy extreme leftist and Kurdish groups. For example, it appears that the MIT played a role in the notorious **Susurluk** scandal, which broke in November 1996 and involved official, but illegal actions to destroy the **Kurdistan Workers Party (PKK)**.

MINORSKY, VLADIMIR (1877–1966). Arguably the most prominent **Russian** authority on the Kurds. His writings are still highly respected more than 35 years after his death. Since most Western scholars know very little about the significant work Russian scholars have done in Kurdish studies, it is important to know about Minorsky's work.

Minorsky graduated from the University of Moscow in 1900 and then studied oriental languages at the famous Lazarev Institute of Oriental Languages in Moscow for three years. He entered the Russian Foreign Ministry in 1903 and eventually served in **Persia**, Turkistan, and the **Ottoman Empire**. Among other duties, he performed intelligence work in Persia in 1911 with Sir **Arnold Wilson**, the representative from **Great Britain**. The two also helped delineate the Ottoman–Persian frontier.

After the communists came to power in Russia, Minorsky eventually began working as an academic in **France** and then Great Britain. His association with the School of Oriental and African Studies at the University of London began in 1932. Several of Minorsky's publications are listed in the bibliography at the end of this historical dictionary.

MIR. One of the most frequently held titles by the rulers of the numerous Kurdish **emirates** that existed from the 14th century to the mid-19th century. Although in theory, and usually in practice, vassals of the **Ottoman Empire**, these Kurdish emirates sometimes possessed many of the characteristics of independent states.

MIRI KOR. *See* SORAN.

MISKEN. In southern (Iraqi) Kurdistan, landless, nontribal peasants tied to the land and dependent on a landlord. The term also can be used simply to mean "poor," "submissive," or "servile." However, some misken are not necessarily poor and even hold plots of land so big that they have to employ helpers. *See also* GURAN; RAYAT.

MITTERRAND, DANIELLE (1924–). Widow of former **French** president François Mitterrand and a longtime and effective spokesperson for the Kurdish cause. Danielle Mitterand helped persuade her husband to support the Iraqi Kurdish **refugees** fleeing from **Saddam Hussein** in 1991. Her backing has also proved invaluable for the **Institut Kurde de Paris**.

MOSSAD. The foreign intelligence agency of **Israel**. Over the years, the Mossad has sometimes surreptitiously aided the Kurds and other times worked against their interests.

MOSUL. City on the Tigris River in northern **Iraq** opposite the ruins of Nineveh, the capital of the ancient Assyrian Empire. With a population of more than 500,000, it is probably the third largest city in Iraq. Into the early years of the 20th century, most Kurds claimed the city as part of Kurdistan, but due to subsequent population changes, they no longer would. The surrounding area, however, remains largely Kurdish. After the **Gulf War** in 1991, Mosul remained under Iraqi control. In the past, the term Mosul has also been used to refer to northern, or Iraqi, Kurdistan, which constituted a *vilayet* in the **Ottoman Empire**. Thus the Mosul question involved a dispute between **Great Britain** and **Turkey** after World War I over who owned the former Ottoman *vilayet* of Mosul. The Council of the **League of Nations** finally decided in favor of Britain, and thus the former *vilayet* of Mosul and its Kurdish population became part of Iraq.

MOUNTAIN TURKS. Disparaging term given to the Kurds in **Turkey** by the Turkish government during the early years of the republic in an attempt to deny the very existence of the Kurds. In recent years, the term is no longer used, but official repression of Kurdish attempts to express their culture continues to occur because of fears of Kurdish separatism.

MUDROS, ARMISTICE OF. The Mudros Armistice between **Great Britain** and the **Ottoman Empire** on 30 October 1918 was in effect an Ottoman surrender at the end of World War I. It led to the subsequent end of the Ottoman Empire and the creation of the modern Republic of **Turkey**. After the armistice was signed, British troops continued to advance into the Ottoman *vilayet* (province) of **Mosul**, or what subsequently became northern **Iraq**. This situation led to the British–Turkish dispute over Mosul, which was finally resolved by the decision of the Council of the **League of Nations** in 1926 to award the *vilayet* and its mainly Kurdish population to Britain and thus Iraq.

MUHAMMAD, AZIZ (1933–). Born a Sunni Kurd in **Sulaymaniya**, Aziz Muhammad headed the **Iraqi Communist Party (ICP)** from late in 1963 until the early 1990s. By the time he retired, the once powerful ICP had been reduced to a very minor role. Muhammad joined the party in 1948 and served a term in prison from 1948 too 1958. He had only an elementary school education and was a tin worker. During the late 1990s, he played an important role as a mediator between the **Kurdistan Democratic Party** and the **Patriotic Union of Kurdistan** in an attempt to end their internal fighting.

MUHAMMAD REZA SHAH PAHLAVI (1919–79). Usually known during his lifetime as simply "the shah," Muhammad Reza Shah Pahlavi ascended to the throne in **Iran** in 1941, after his father, **Reza Shah Pahlavi**, was forced to abdicate because of reputed pro-**German** sentiments. The new shah continued his father's policies of centralization, which tended to reduce the power of the Kurdish **tribes**.

After crushing the **Mahabad Republic of Kurdistan** in December 1946, the shah hanged the republic's highly respected leader, **Qazi Muhammad**, in March 1947. In March 1975, the shah treacherously ended his support for **Mulla Mustafa Barzani** by making a deal with **Saddam Hussein**. Barzani's long-running revolt quickly collapsed, while Barzani himself went into exile and died in March 1979. The shah's collapse in 1979 helped lead to a new Kurdish revolt in Iran, but it, too, was crushed, by the new Islamic Republic of Iran, headed by the **Ayatollah Ruhollah Khomeini**.

MUKHABARAT. The intelligence agency of the **Baath Party** in **Iraq** and **Syria**. Over the years—especially in Iraq—it has ruthlessly dealt with the Kurds, as well as other opposition forces. The term *Mukhabarat* comes from an Arabic word that means "to tell on" or "news" and means "intelligence" in Arabic.

MUKRI. Powerful Kurdish **tribal** confederation that existed for hundreds of years south and west of Lake Urumiya in the **Persian Empire**. In 1623, the Mukri helped the Safavid Persians recapture Baghdad from the **Ottomans**, and they long provided the shah the best cavalry he could muster. By 1900, the Mukri were divided into two main tribes, the Dihbukri and the Mamash. *See also* ASHIRET.

MULLA. In Kurdish, *mela,* the only clerical office in Sunni **Islam**. The mulla leads religious services at the village level and instructs the children of the village in the Koran. In earlier times, the mulla was usually the most educated man in the village. More recently, however, some younger people have a better education. Among mullas, the *imam* is the leader of prayers, while the *khatib* repeats the *khutba,* or prayers for the Prophet, his immediate successors, and the current ruler. The *khatib* requires more education than other mullas. It should be noted that **Mulla Mustafa Barzani**, arguably the most famous Kurd of the 20th century, used the name "Mulla" without having any particular religious significance attached to it.

MUSTAFA PASHA OF THE MIRAN. Pasha of the **Hamidiye**, the Kurdish **tribal** militia formed by Sultan Abdul Hamid II. Achieving this post in the 1890s, Mustafa Pasha of the Miran was the only chieftain of the former **emirate** of **Botan** who received the title of pasha (general). At the height of his power, Mustafa Pasha was virtually independent of the **Ottoman** government in the area of what is now southeastern **Turkey** around the city of Cizre.

– N –

NAQSHBANDI. **Sufi** order, or **Islamic** mystical brotherhood, that rapidly became the most influential throughout Kurdistan in the 19th century and still holds that distinction despite the inroads of modernization. The Naqshbandi and the rival **Qadiri** order are the only organizations in Kurdistan that cut through **tribal** boundaries and are independent of the state.

The present orders came into existence only in the 14th century. The Naqshbandi *tariqa,* or school of thought, originated in central Asia, but the **sheikh** from whom it takes its name, Bah ad-Din Naqshband of Bukhara (1318–1389), was not its founder. He was, however, an important reformer of the order whose rules were apparently first established by Abd al-Khaliq Ghujdawani of Ghujdawan (near Bukhara), who died in 1220. Given these origins, it is not surprising that the Naqshbandi order is influenced by Buddhist mystical techniques. The order spread to India and Anatolia, where it flourished. **Maulana Khalid** (c. 1778–1826), a Kurd from what is now northern **Iraq**, journeyed to Delhi, India, in 1808 to study and receive the *ijaza,* or authorization to transmit the order.

Maulana Khalid returned home in 1811, an event that precipitated the order's quick proliferation throughout what is now northern Iraq, in part at the expense of the older, rival Qadiri order. This rapid success was partly due to the Naqshbandis' willingness to transmit the *ijaza* to any who was qualified, not just to relatives, as was done by the Qadiris. The Naqshbandi order also may have seemed to many to be spiritually superior in its rituals compared to the ecstatic excesses of the Qadiri order. In addition, the collapse of the Kurdish **emirates** during this period helped both Naqshbandi and Qadiri sheikhs to assume significant political powers.

The Naqshbandi *majlis* (also called *khatma*), or ritual, differs considerably from that of the Qadiri order. The *zikr*, or recitation of the divine name, is silent and ecstasy is not encouraged. There are usually one or two ritual meetings per week held in a **khanaqa** (also called *tekiye* or *zawiya*) or meeting house (oratory, convent, or retreat) of the sheikh. The sheikh or his *khalifa* (deputy) sits surrounded by his disciples *(murid)*. A **mulla** might recite prayers for the Prophet and verses from the Koran. Silent periods intervene in which the *murids* recite these verses to themselves several times. Meditative contemplations on death follow in which the *murids* imagine themselves in the grave and having to give an account of their misdeeds to an angel. Loud sighs indicate how vivid these thoughts must be. Then the mulla announces the *rabita bi'sh-sheikh,* or connection with the sheikh and through him ultimately with the Prophet. A silent *zikr* and then the first part of the *shahada,* or confession of faith, follows: "*la illaha illa llah*" ("there is no god but God"). The recitation of the *silsila,* or spiritual pedigree of the sheikh, concludes the ritual.

No self-mutilation occurs in Naqshbandi rituals. Although the terms "dervish" and "Sufi" largely overlap, in Kurdistan the Naqshbandi refer to themselves as Sufis and strongly resent being referred to as dervishes. This latter word is used instead for followers of the Qadiri order.

Since Maulana Khalid had no recognized successor and there is no acknowledged head of the Naqshbandis today, the Naqshbandi order is decentralized. Nevertheless, Naqshbandi connections certainly helped **Sheikh Said of Palu** to mobilize fighters in his rebellion in **Turkey** in 1925. As a result of this revolt, however, the Turkish authorities branded the Kurdish movement in Turkey as nothing more than religious reaction. In quick order, they closed the **madrasahs** (Islamic religious schools) and *tekiyes* (religious convents or oratories) and outlawed all Sufi and dervish orders, including the Naqshbandis.

Although greatly reduced, the Naqshbandis and other orders simply went underground. The greater freedoms allowed in Turkey after Adnan Menderes' Democratic Party came to power in 1950 allowed the religious orders to make somewhat of a comeback. In more recent times, the late Turkish president **Turgut Ozal** was known to be sympathetic to the Naqshbandis. Indeed, Ozal's brother Korkat was apparently a formal member. Today the Naqshbandis are tolerated in Turkey and have become the largest Sufi order in the southeast of Turkey.

NATIONAL PACT (TURKEY). From July to August 1919, under the leadership of **Mustafa Kemal (Ataturk)**, the Turkish nationalists held a congress in Erzurum in eastern **Turkey**. Here they drew up the National Pact *(Milli Misak)*, which basically established modern Turkey's existing borders. Although recognizing the loss of the Arab provinces, the National Pact showed that Turkey would not accept an independent Kurdistan in southeastern Anatolia.

Interestingly, the National Pact also claimed for modern Turkey the *vilayet* (province) of **Mosul** (northern Iraq), which was only grudgingly recognized as part of **Iraq** after the issue was settled by the **League of Nations**. The National Pact also pledged to maintain these borders even if the sultan's government in Istanbul were forced to abandon them under foreign pressure. Thus the National Pact was an important step in the creation of the modern Republic of Turkey and the denial of Kurdish ethnic rights.

NATIONALISM. Usually, the demand of a nation or large group of people to have its own independent state or at least to have the right to exercise its own cultural, social, and educational characteristics. Thus the nation becomes the supreme object of loyalty and the nation–state the ideal form of political organization. Modern nationalism is relatively new in international politics, as in the past most people owed their supreme loyalties to empires, religions, or parochial units such as cities, regions, or **tribes**. Although its roots reach much deeper into history, the French Revolution that began in 1789 is an important date for the beginning of modern nationalism. From there, modern nationalism spread first to the rest of Europe and then to the world.

In traditional **Islam**, however, the *ummah,* or community of believers, was the sole object of supreme political loyalty. Thus modern nationalism was foreign to the world of Islam. All Muslims were supposed to be brothers and sisters, regardless of race, nation, culture, or language. Therefore, modern nationalism came late to the land of Islam, where the multinational **Ottoman Empire** still held sway at the beginning of the 20th century.

Nevertheless, nationalism began to splinter the Ottoman Empire as, first, the Christian nations in southeastern Europe in the 19th century and, then, the Arabs in World War I sought their independence. **Armenian** nationalism had developed by the late 19th century. As a reaction, Turkish nationalism led to the creation of the modern Republic of **Turkey** from the ruins of the Ottoman Empire. The Zionist movement led to the creation of the state of **Israel** in 1948. Largely as a reaction to Western imperialism and the creation of Israel, Arab nationalism led to the creation of more than 20 Arab states in the 20th century and the seemingly intractable Arab–Israeli conflict.

In Islam, nationalism has become identified with the Islamic *ummah.* Thus there exists the seemingly paradoxical situation of a movement to unite in the name of nationalism the one Arab nation, at the same time that there is in the name of Arab nationalism a proliferation of Arab states. Thus nationalism has also been the result of more than a century of Westernization and modernization throughout the Islamic world. Modern armies, bureaucracies, schools, printing presses, transportation (roads, rails, and airplanes), and centralized state power—all are both among the causes and results of modern nationalism.

Modern nationalism came late to the Kurds, but for them, too, it has played a most important role in recent times. **Salah al Din (Saladin)**, for example, was an ethnic Kurd, but clearly his supreme loyalty was to Islam. Even today in modern Turkey, the idea of separate Islamic minorities seems difficult to accept. The seemingly obstinate refusal to admit that its citizens of Kurdish ethnic heritage constitute a minority can be understood partially in light of the old Ottoman and Islamic principle that Islam took precedence over nationality among Muslims and that only non-Muslims could hold some type of officially recognized minority status. Indeed, this very position was acknowledged by the Treaty of **Lausanne** (1923)—under which the

West recognized the new Republic of Turkey—as only non-Muslims such as Greeks, Armenians, and Jews were granted minority status in Turkey. Years later, when he became modern Turkey's first **Islamist** prime minister, **Necmettin Erbakan** argued that the solution to his country's Kurdish problem was to emphasize the unity among Islamic brothers and sisters.

The Kurds continue to suffer from a form of internal colonialism that has divided them into at least four other nations' nation–states, namely Turkey, **Iran**, **Iraq**, and **Syria**. This situation has inhibited the full development of Kurdish nationalism, or *Kurdayeti*. Unless this bondage ends soon, there is reason to argue that the artificial states that contain the Kurds may assimilate them, a process that is already occurring. Scholars, for example, have analyzed how the artificial states created by the colonial powers in Africa in time came to help mold new senses of ethnic self-definitions. Other scholars have shown how states in effect can create, invent, or even imagine nations.

In addition, Kurdish nationalism remains stunted by such primordial divisions as families, clans, tribes, **language**, and other types of parochial loyalties. *Kurdayeti* seems stuck in a time warp from which other nationalisms emerged more than a century ago. As a result, no Kurdish leader has proven able to make the transition from tribal warlord to true statesman.

Given this situation, a Kurdish state would probably only emerge if there were a major collapse of the existing state system in the Middle East. It took the seismic upheaval of World War I, for example, to shake loose a Polish state from the shackles of internal colonialism imposed by **Germany** (Prussia), Austria, and **Russia** from 1795 to 1919. And then it took the collapse of the **Soviet Union** in 1991 to win real Polish independence.

Although the **Gulf War** in 1991 did result in the halting, defective emergence of a rump proto-Kurdish state in northern Iraq, only a total rerolling of the international dice that would follow another world war would be likely to lead to the creation of an independent Kurdistan. What seems more likely for some success for Kurdish nationalism is the gradual development of full democracy in those states in which the Kurds now live. True democracy would allow the Kurds to enjoy many of the cultural, social, and educational rights usually associated with modern nationalism without destroying the territorial integrity of the preexisting states.

NEHRI. The *seyyids* (*sada,* or those who claim descent from the Prophet) of Nehri were a powerful family of **sheikhs** in what is now the Turkish province of **Hakkari** in the extreme southeastern tip of Turkey near the borders with **Iraq** and **Iran.** Thus the term Sadate of Nehri was sometimes used to refer to their domain. They claimed descent from Abdullah Qadir al-Jailani—known by many Kurds as the *ghawth,* or the highest saint in the spiritual hierarchy—and for whom the **Qadiri** order is named. The family therefore also was known by the name of Gailanizade (Jailanizade). The Nehris adhered to the Qadiri order until they were initiated into the **Naqshbandi** order by **Maulana Khalid** after 1811.

By the 1840s, Sheikh Sayyid Taha I of Nehri had become influential in the **emirate** of **Botan** by appealing to **religion** and inciting people against the local **Christians.** After the defeat of the powerful *mir* of Botan, **Badr Khan Beg,** in 1847, Sheikh Sayyid Taha fled to Nehri, the residence of the last *mir* of Shamdinan (now Turkicized as Semdinli). Nehri was the main village of the Shamdinan district and thus became the family home. At that time, Shamdinan was still a small emirate and the sheikhs of Nehri for a while exercised a sort of dual rule with the *mir* until they eventually replaced him as the sole authority. It was around this time that Sheikh Sayyid Taha I of Nehri also apparently initiated Tajuddin (also sometimes called Abdul Rahman) into the Naqshbandi order and sent him to **Barzan,** where Tajuddin established the line of **Barzani** sheikhs.

Calling upon both his spiritual and temporal authority, Taha's son, **Ubeydullah,** became one of the most powerful Kurdish leaders of the 19th century and led the famous, but ultimately unsuccessful, revolt of 1880, which in retrospect many see as a protonationalist Kurdish rebellion. Ubeydullah's two sons, Muhammad Siddiq and Abdul Qadir, also became very influential Kurdish leaders. The former was living in Nehri early in the 20th century and was considered the most influential sheikh in central Kurdistan.

After Muhammad Siddiq's death in 1911, his younger brother emerged as an important figure in **Ottoman** politics. Abdul Qadir played a role in practically all Kurdish nationalist activities in Istanbul and was also a member of the Ottoman Senate and president of the Council of State. Although he was probably not involved with **Sheikh Said's** great rebellion in 1925, Abdul Qadir was arrested and executed by the Turkish authorities.

Sayyid Taha II—the son of Muhammad Siddiq and thus the grandson of the great Ubeydullah—played an active role in politics during the 1920s. He joined the famous revolt of **Ismail Agha Simko** in **Iran**, and in 1922 began working with **Great Britain** against Turkish attempts to move into northern Iraq. The British eventually appointed him governor of the province around Rawanduz because of his influence over the local **tribes**. In 1932, however, Taha II accepted an invitation from **Reza Shah Pahlavi** of Iran to journey to Tehran and was apparently poisoned there. His two sons, Sheikh Abdullah Efendi and Muhammad Siddiq (Sheikh Puso), remained respected among the locals, but their sons apparently did not become sheikhs.

NEO-ARAMAIC (TARGUM). Purely oral **language** of the **Kurdish Jews**. Upon its Neo-Aramaic base, Targum also included aspects of the Kurdish language of **Kurmanji**, Arabic, Turkish, Old Aramaic, and Hebrew. Since Targum was a spoken language—not employed in writing—its vocabulary and pronunciation did not have a standard form and marked variations existed.

There were at least three overall categories of local dialects. The western category was spoken in Amadiya, Dohuk, Nirwa, and Zakho in **Iraq**, and in **Diyarbakir**, Urfa, **Mardin**, and **Cizre** in **Turkey**. The northwestern category was spoken in **Persian** Azerbaijan, while the southeastern category was used in the Persian areas of Kurdistan to the south, as well as in Rawanduz, **Irbil**, and **Sulaymaniya** in Iraq.

NESTORIANS. See ASSYRIANS.

NEWROZ. Meaning new sun, day, or year, a celebration of the beginning of the Kurdish New Year on 21 March, when spring begins. Other Iranic peoples also celebrate the occasion. It is the most important Kurdish national holiday of the year and, because of its association with freedom, has also become the most important Kurdish **nationalist** holiday. During its long running rebellion (1978–99), the

Kurdistan Workers Party (PKK) often began its spring offenses and other violent attacks against the Turkish state on Newroz. In a clumsy effort to preempt this Kurdish national holiday, the Turkish government suddenly announced in 1995 that the date—which it termed Nevroz—was in fact a Turkish holiday commemorating the day the Turks first left their ancestral Asian homeland, Ergenekon. Newroz celebrations can last for a week or more. People visit each other's houses for festive meals and sometimes give gifts. Bonfires are frequently lit and exuberant Kurds jump over them. These bonfires may possibly be associated with the Kurds' **Zoroastrian** past. Newroz is also associated with the legend of the blacksmith Kawa, who defeated the ruthless ruler Zohhak (or Dahak), who had been feeding the brains of young men to two giant serpents' heads growing from his shoulders. In other versions, however, Zohhak is a Kurdish hero.

There is considerable confusion among Kurds concerning their calendar because, in addition to their own Kurdish one, they have occasion to use the Muslim, Gregorian, and Iranian calendars. The Kurdish calendar is a solar one that consists of 365 days and a leap year every four years. It begins on Newroz. It is also identical to the Iranian calendar, except for the names of the months and the original beginning year. The Iranian calendar commences with the fall of the Assyrian Empire in 612 B.C.E. and the Kurdish calendar starts in 380 C.E., the year of the fall of the Kurdish Kavusakan dynasty (House of Kayus), and includes an unexplained seven extra years. Thus the year 2003 C.E. is 1616 in the Kurdish calendar.

NEZAN, KENDAL (1949–). Turkish Kurdish physicist who fled from Turkey in 1971 and has since become a major critic of the Turkish government's policies toward the Kurds. Over the years, he has developed close ties with the **French** government, in particular with **Danielle Mitterrand**, the wife of the late socialist president François Mitterrand (served 1981–95). For many years, Kendal Nezan has headed the **Institut Kurde de Paris,** which receives financial support from the French Foreign Ministry and the Fonds d'action social.

NIXON, RICHARD M. (1913–94). President of the **United States** who with his national security adviser, **Henry Kissinger**, offered the covert, and inevitably unkept, promises to **Mulla Mustafa Barzani** in the early 1970s that encouraged the Iraqi Kurds to rebel, but eventually led to their final defeat at the hands of the Iraqi government in 1975. Nixon and Kissinger were simply using the Iraqi Kurds as a pawn in their larger strategy to help **Israel** and oppose the **Soviet Union.** Later, Kissinger explained that "covert action should not be confused with missionary work." *See also* PIKE COMMITTEE REPORT.

NO-FLY ZONE. Following the abortive Kurdish uprising against **Saddam Hussein** in March 1991 and the horrific Kurdish **refugee** exodus that ensued, the **United States, Great Britain**, and **France** imposed a no-fly zone north of the 36th parallel in **Iraq** to allow the Kurds to return to their homes without fear of continued attack. The no-fly zone was enforced by allied aircraft based in southeastern **Turkey** and supposedly sanctioned by **United Nations** Security Council Resolution 688 of 5 April 1991, which condemned "the repression of the Iraqi civilian population . . . in Kurdish populated areas" and demanded "that Iraq . . . immediately end this repression."

Also called **Operation Provide Comfort** (and after 1 January 1997, **Operation Northern Watch**, without further French participation), the no-fly zone provided the protection and security that allowed a de facto Kurdish state that covered some 17,000 square miles in much of northern Iraq to form. The United States and Great Britain also maintained a much less successful no-fly zone over the southern part of Iraq in an attempt to offer some protection to the Iraqi **Shiites.**

NOEL, EDWARD (1886–1974). Political officer (intelligence agent) of **Great Britain** in **Sulaymaniya** in 1919. Major Noel supported the Kurds so strongly that he was disparagingly called the "Second Lawrence" by officials in the Colonial Office. Noel was convinced of the strength of Kurdish **nationalism** and worked for either an independent Kurdish state or some type of viable Kurdish autonomy, both under ultimate British control.

After a successful earlier career in the Caucasus and along the northwest frontier in India, Noel made extensive trips throughout Kurdistan during 1919. He played an important role in bringing **Sheikh Mahmud Barzinji** to power in the area around **Sulaymaniya.** His efforts in what is now southeastern **Turkey**, however, failed to win the support of his own government, probably because of Sheikh Mahmud's refusal to cooperate with Britain and because of the **Kemalist** revival in **Turkey**. Indeed, the Turks suspected Noel of trying to incite the Kurds to attack the aborning Kemalist government. Noel was replaced by Major **E. B. Soane**.

Noel wrote a 77-page report on his experiences among the Kurds entitled *Diary of Major Noel on Special Duty in Kurdistan, from June 14th to September 21st, 1919,* and available in the archives of the Public Record Office, Kew Gardens, as FO 371/5068. Noel also participated in the famous Cairo conference on the future role of Great Britain in the Middle East, held in March 1921.

NURCULUK. Followers of the Nur (Light) movement in **Turkey**, which grew out of the inspired Islamic teachings of **Said Nursi** (1873–1960), an ethnic Kurd born in what is now southeastern Turkey. Said Nursi's many writings are collectively referred to as *Risale-i Nur Kulliyati,* or *The Epistles on the (Divine) Light.* Most of them are available on the Internet at www.nesil.com.tr. These writings elaborate upon an interpretation of the Koran that is a synthesis of modern science and reformist Islamic learning seen through strongly mystical lenses. Thus the Nurculuk treat scientific discoveries as a way to further deepen the understanding of the Koran. Many of Said Nursi's interpretations are based on his dreams and visions and written in an obscure 19th-century **Ottoman** Turkish that few people can completely comprehend.

Basically, the Nurculuk seek to transform society by raising individual religious consciousness. The movement offers a conceptual framework for people undergoing the transformation from a confessional community *(gemeinschaft)* to a secular national society *(gesellschaft).* Folk Islamic concepts and practices are updated to provide practical strategies for dealing with modernity. To overcome the tension between desires and resources, Said Nursi sought to bring God back by raising Islamic consciousness. He argued that this would even alleviate the sources of many conflicts and wars.

In seeking to reconcile scientific reasoning with **Islam**, the Nurculuk treat freedom as an integral part of faith. Said Nursi identified poverty, ignorance, and internal enmity as the problems of the Muslim community. He called upon Islamic conceptualizations to provide a current vocabulary for constitutionalism, liberty, and elections. He argued that democracy and Islam are not opposite concepts, indeed that democracy and freedom are necessary conditions for a just society. In addition, he called upon the people in eastern Anatolia (the Kurds) to transcend their narrow **tribal** and religious loyalties to achieve a larger Islamic nation. In one of his earlier writings, Said Nursi identified the causes of the decline of the Islamic community as the end of truthfulness in sociopolitical life, enmity, despotism, and egoism. Despite Said Nursi's mysticism and earlier **Naqshbandi** contacts, he explicitly argued that the order was no longer appropriate for the current situation.

Over the years, the Nurculuk spread throughout Turkey, appealing to both ethnic Kurds and Turks and becoming probably the most influential religious movement in the entire country. The movement seems to appeal to different kinds of people for different reasons. Mystics are attracted by its visionary and mystical aspects, Islamic intellectuals for its acceptance of modern science, and Kurdish **nationalists** because of Said Nursi's ethnic heritage and earlier support of Kurdish national aims. Even secularists admire the movement's opposition to military rule that has appeared in modern Turkey on several occasions.

Fethullah Gulen (1938–) has become the leader of the modern Nurcu movement in Turkey. This new Nurcu movement has a powerful transnational *darshane* (originally, "reading circle") network of schools in Turkey, central Asia, and the Balkans, and also exercises a strong presence in the media. Gulen's writings and worldview seek to create a unity between **religion** and tradition, on the one hand, and science and modernity, on the other. Gulen's Nurcu community supposedly stresses state-centric Turkic nationalism, the free market, and education. Although Gulen has presented himself as a distinct, acceptable Islamic alternative to the other unacceptable political **Islamists** and has regularly met with high-level politicians, the Turkish government accused Gulen in 2001 of working clandestinely to overthrow the secular order. Thus, if Gulen is truly not a closet enemy of the Turkish state, these criminal accusations against him and the Nurculuk threaten the development of civil society in Turkey in a way analogous to the continuing refusal to accept the Kurdish people.

NURI, IHSAN (1892–1976). Famous military leader of the Kurdish revolt against **Turkey** around **Mt. Ararat** in 1929–30. In 1910, Ihsan Nuri graduated from the Military College in Istanbul and then served in the **Ottoman** army. After World War I, he became involved in the **Azadi** Kurdish nationalist movement and served as an informant for British intelligence. In August 1924, he was involved in the premature Kurdish uprising at Bayt Shabab, a small town in Turkey just north of the Iraqi border. This fiasco tipped the Kurds' hand to the Turks and helped lead to the ultimate failure of the **Sheikh Said** uprising in 1925.

In 1929, the **Khoybun**, a transnational Kurdish party based in **Syria**, sent Ihsan Nuri to organize and lead **tribal** chiefs already in rebellion on Ararat. At first, the Kurds achieved some notable successes, but after Turkey was able to convince **Iran** to cede a small piece of Iranian territory on the eastern side of Ararat in exchange for some Turkish territory, the Turks were able to surround Ararat and crush the rebellion. Ihsan Nuri lived out his life in exile in Iran.

NURSI, SAID (1873–1960). Highly respected Kurdish scholar, inspired interpreter of the Koran, and founder of the **Nurculuk**, or followers of Nur (Light) movement. To his followers, he was a great saint who could appear at different places at the same time and perform other miracles. Even his opponents testified to his courage, honesty, and character.

Said Nursi was born in the village of Nurs in the province of **Bitlis** in what is now southeastern **Turkey**. He was educated at various *madrasahs*, some of which were associated with the **Naqshbandi Sufi** order, although he himself always claimed that his movement was not a part of that order. At a young age, he began to refer to himself as Bediuzzaman, the unique of the age, and was known as a proponent of Kurdish identity without being a separatist. Indeed, throughout his life, being a Muslim was much more important to him than being Kurdish. In 1907, he moved to Istanbul, where he proposed that the government establish a university in Kurdistan attached to the famous **Islamic** university al-Azhar in Cairo. He also wanted to see a primary school for the Kurds in Istanbul.

Said Nursi distinguished himself in the Balkan Wars, and during World War I he saved some 1,500 **Armenians** whom he had been or-

dered to kill by instead sending them to safety across the **Russian**
lines. After the war, he initially supported **Mustafa Kemal
(Ataturk)**, but he quickly broke with him over the role of **religion** in
the new state. Although Said Nursi did not support **Sheikh Said**'s rebellion in 1925, he still was exiled to western Turkey in the subsequent crackdowns that led to the banning of the *madrasahs*, *tekiyes*,
and anything else that suggested a Kurdish identity.

From that time on, Said Nursi devoted himself exclusively to in-
terpreting and preaching the Koran. Nevertheless, he remained fond
of referring to himself as Saidi Kurdi, or Kurdish Said. In his remaining years, he developed his Nurcu philosophy, or movement,
which became and remains today the most influential religious movement among the Kurds in Turkey. The Kemalist press considered him
to be a dangerous reactionary, and he was arrested on numerous occasions. In the final years of his life, he and his followers enjoyed
somewhat greater freedom under the more religiously tolerant rule of
Adnan Menderes and the Democratic Party (1950–60). Neverthe-
lesss, when Said Nursi finally died a very old man in 1960, the government feared his continuing influence so much that it had his body
disinterred and reburied in an unknown location. More than 40 years
later, his mystical movement constitutes the most powerful Islamic
movement in modern Turkey.

– O –

OCALAN, ABDULLAH (APO) (1946–). Founder of the **Kurdistan
Workers Party (PKK)** on 27 November 1978 who, despite his capture and imprisonment by **Turkey** on 16 February 1999, has been its
leader *(serok)* ever since. To a large extent, therefore, the important
facts of Ocalan's biography are also those of the PKK's history.

Ocalan was born in the village of Omerli in the Hilvan–Severek region of the province of Urfa in southeastern Turkey. He was the first-
born in a family of poor farmers and apparently had six brothers and
sisters. (His younger brother **Osman Ocalan** also became and remains a top official in the PKK, while his ex-wife Kesire Yildirim
was also a high-ranking PKK member until their divorce in 1987.)
Abdullah Ocalan has long been known by his nickname, "Apo," or

uncle. In the earlier years, his followers were even called the **Apocular**, or "followers of Apo." His surname means "revenger."

Ocalan claims that as a young boy he could not speak Turkish and that he learned to do so only gradually in elementary school. When he was an adult, however, Turkish became his working language and he had to study Kurdish in an effort to begin using it even occasionally. When he first visited Ankara in 1966 to take the university entrance examinations, he thought of himself as a Turk.

After failing to gain admission to the Turkish War Academy, Ocalan studied political science at Ankara University, where he particularly enjoyed classes in economic history. He also spent seven months in prison in 1970 for participating in an illegal student demonstration, an experience that apparently was a turning point. At this time, he became a Marxist. Many years later, Ocalan specifically testified that he had been affected by the careers of **Deniz Gezmis** and **Mahir Cayan**, two radical leftist leaders of the 1970s in Turkey who were both ethnic Kurds and died fighting for their causes.

At a **Dev Genc** meeting in Ankara in 1974, Ocalan and a few other students first formed the Ankara Higher Education Association. Ocalan told this first meeting that since the necessary conditions then existed for a Kurdish nationalist movement in Turkey, the group should break its relations with the other (Turkish) leftist movements that refused to recognize Kurdish national rights.

In 1975, the group left Ankara and began its operations in the Kurdish areas from where they had originally come. This entailed recruitment and indoctrination activities that by the late 1970s had spilled over into violence against other leftist and Kurdish groups. What separated the Apocular from these other groups was their appeal to members almost exclusively drawn from the lowest social classes and their willingness to use violence. Sensing the military coup that finally did occur in September 1980, Ocalan fled to **Syria** in May 1979, and from there he led the PKK until Syria—under intense Turkish pressure—expelled him in October 1998.

Originally, Ocalan called for an independent pan-Kurdish state based on Marxist principles. Over the years, he gradually altered these positions and began to argue for some type of Kurdish autonomy or federalism within Turkey's preexisting boundaries. For a short period in the early 1990s, Ocalan seemed close to achieving a certain degree of military success. In the end, however, he overextended himself, while the Turkish military spared no excesses in containing him.

Despite his earlier reputation as a Stalin-like, murderous terrorist, Ocalan became seen in the eyes of many Kurds as having done more to reestablish a sense of Kurdish self-esteem and **nationalism** in Turkey than any other Kurdish leader in recent years. This was aptly illustrated by the dismay most Kurds and their supporters throughout the world showed upon hearing that he had been apprehended by the Turkish authorities in Kenya on 16 February 1999. In the process, Ocalan once again illustrated how one person's freedom fighter can be another's terrorist.

During his trial in 1999, Ocalan offered to end the PKK insurgency in return for real and complete democracy that, if Turkey spared his life, he argued he could then accomplish. From his prison cell on the island of Imrali in the Sea of Marmara, Ocalan issued a remarkable statement that called for the implementation of true democracy to solve the Kurdish problem within the existing borders of a unitary Turkey, and thus fulfilled **Ataturk's** ultimate hopes for a strong, united, and democratic Turkey that could join what is now the **European Union (EU)**. Indeed, the PKK withdrew most of its fighters from Turkey, while practically all PKK violence against Turkey stopped. Nevertheless, Ocalan was sentenced to death for treason on 29 June 1999.

On 25 November 1999, the Turkish Court of Appeals rejected Ocalan's appeal, but the European Court of Human Rights (ECHR)—to which Turkey belonged—quickly issued interim measures asking Turkey to suspend the execution until it could rule on his appeal, a process that might have taken two years or more. At this point, Turkey was admitted to the EU as a candidate member. Turkey's membership, however, hinged on its acceptance of the **Copenhagen Criteria** of recognizing minority rights and abolishing the death penalty.

As part of this process, Turkey finally abolished the death penalty in 2002, and early in 2003 the ECHR called for Turkey to give Ocalan a new trial. As of this writing, Ocalan's (and the Turkish Kurds') future seemed to be wrapped up with the future of Turkey's EU membership application and the whole issue of democratization in Turkey.

OCALAN, OSMAN (FERHAT). Osman Ocalan is the younger brother of **Abdullah Ocalan**, the longtime leader of the **Kurdistan Workers Party (PKK)**. One of six siblings, the younger Ocalan has also long been a leading member of the PKK, particularly its professional guerrilla army, the **Kurdistan Peoples Liberation Army**, now termed the Peoples Defense Force.

For many years, Osman Ocalan was active in northern **Iraq** and **Iran**. He had a reputation of being a tough guerrilla leader without the sophistication of his elder brother. Reportedly, he fell into temporary eclipse after his forces were deemed to have performed poorly when attacked by the Iraqi Kurds and then the Turks in northern Iraq in October 1992. Subsequently, he was for some time the PKK commander at the **Zaleh** camp in northeastern Iraqi Kurdistan, where his forces were supposedly being interned by those of **Jalal Talabani**'s **Patriotic Union of Kurdistan**. During the summer of 1996, Osman Ocalan attended the 50th anniversary celebrations of **Massoud Barzani**'s **Kurdistan Democratic Party**.

Following the capture and imprisonment of Abdullah Ocalan in February 1999, Osman Ocalan became one of the main leaders of the PKK's presidential council, named to act on a daily tactical basis for the now imprisoned Abdullah Ocalan. Osman Ocalan at first called for a violent reaction to his elder's brother's capture, but soon fell into line with the new policy of promoting peace. Osman Ocalan remains one of the main leaders of the now renamed **Kurdistan Freedom and Democracy Congress (KADEK)**.

OHAL. *See* EMERGENCY RULE.

OIL. Kurdistan possesses some of the largest oil reserves in the world. **Kirkuk**, long a bone of contention between the Iraqi Kurds and the Iraqi government, holds by far the most productive resources, which largely explains why the area has been so hotly contested. **Mulla Mustafa Barzani** tried to solicit the support of the **United States** during his rebellion by declaring he would turn over the oil fields to the United States and make an independent Kurdistan a friend of the United States in the Organization of Petroleum Exporting Countries! An important oil pipeline carries the oil from Kirkuk through some of the Kurdish areas of **Turkey**, but skirts south of the Iraqi Kurdish area. Much of the present relative prosperity of the **Kurdistan Regional Government** (KRG) in northern **Iraq** stems from the 13 percent of Iraq's oil receipts it receives from the **United Nations**, as well as the fees the KRG collects from the surreptitious oil trade that traverses it from Iraq to Turkey. The little oil that Turkey produces comes from Kurdish areas centered around the town of Batman east of **Diyarbakir**. With the discovery of the huge new Rumailah oil fields in southern Iraq, the older Kirkuk sites have lost some of their earlier importance.

OPERATION NORTHERN WATCH. As a result of the heavy infighting between **Massoud Barzani's Kurdistan Democratic Party** and **Jalal Talabani's Patriotic Union of Kurdistan** that broke out again in August 1996, Barzani invited **Saddam Hussein** to intervene on his side. This allowed the Iraqi forces to capture some 96 local Kurds working for **Operation Provide Comfort (OPC)**, the allied relief program in northern **Iraq** that also gathered intelligence and enforced the **no-fly zone** that was supposed to protect the Iraqi Kurds from Iraqi incursion. As a result, OPC was scaled down (**France** dropped out) and renamed Operation Northern Watch as of 1 January 1997.

OPERATION PROVIDE COMFORT (OPC). Term that has been used to refer to both the U.S.–led humanitarian operations that enabled the Kurdish **refugees** to return to their homes in a **safe haven** in northern **Iraq** after their failed uprising in March 1991 and the allied (largely U.S.) planes that enforced the **no-fly zone** over northern Iraq. The operation is sometimes called Operation Poised Hammer in **Turkey**.

Following suggestions from Turkish president **Turgut Ozal**, French president François Mitterrand, and British prime minister John Major, OPC was begun on 5 April 1991. Its original mission was to provide immediate humanitarian assistance to Iraqi Kurdish refugees who had fled to the mountains of northern Iraq and across the border into southern Turkey to escape repression from **Saddam Hussein** at the end of the 1991 **Gulf War** and upon failure of the subsequent Kurdish uprising. At one time or another, coalition forces from 13 different states participated. At OPC's peak in May 1991, the

United States had more than 12,000 military personnel committed to relief efforts, and they themselves were part of an overall coalition force of nearly 22,000. U.S. general Richard M. Naab played a prominent role in the implementation of these humanitarian objectives.

OPC officially continued until the end of 1996 in the form of 80 combat and support aircraft stationed at the Incirlik Air Base in Turkey's southern Adana province. From there, they made frequent patrol flights over Iraqi Kurdistan to enforce the no-fly zone that protected the Iraqi Kurds from Iraqi incursions. Turkish permission was thus necessary for OPC's continuance and had to be renewed at frequent intervals. A small Military Coordination Center team was also stationed in Zakho in Iraqi Kurdistan near the Turkish border to monitor conditions. Several thousand local Kurds were employed in relief and intelligence operations. The United States, **Great Britain**, and **France** were the main Western participants.

The continuance of OPC became a major political issue in Turkey, because many Turks believed it was facilitating the vacuum of authority in northern Iraq that enabled the **Kurdistan Workers Party (PKK)** to enjoy sanctuary there. Some even argued that OPC was the opening salvo of a new Treaty of **Sevres** that would lead to the creation of a Kurdish state in northern Iraq. Thus, went the argument, Turkey was facilitating its own demise by housing OPC. However, to abandon support for OPC would simply lead it to regroup elsewhere and strip Turkey of influence over events. Indeed, OPC gave Turkey important intelligence information on PKK units in northern Iraq and also enabled Turkey to intervene in northern Iraq with relative impunity.

Following **Massoud Barzani**'s opportunistic alliance with Saddam Hussein in August 1996, the small military mission in Zakho was withdrawn to Turkey and OPC relief efforts in northern Iraq terminated. The French withdrew from the force, while a scaled-down **Operation Northern Watch** continued to enforce the no-fly zone after 1 January 1997.

OSMAN (OTHMAN, UTHMAN), MAHMUD (1938–). Physician and longtime Kurdish political figure in northern Iraq. During the 1960s and early 1970s, Osman was one of **Mulla Mustafa Barzani**'s top lieutenants and his personal physician. Osman played a key role in negotiating the **March Manifesto** of 1970, which supposedly provided for Kurdish autonomy within **Iraq**. Following Barzani's final defeat in 1975, Osman escaped to Europe, where he wrote a stinging critique of his former leader. Later, he established his own party, the Kurdistan Democratic Party/Preparatory Committee. At first based in Damascus, Osman moved back into northern Iraq in 1978. The following year he joined **Rasul Mamand** to form what eventually came to be called the Socialist Party of Kurdistan in Iraq.

Osman was one of the Kurdish leaders who negotiated with **Saddam Hussein** and his associates after the failed Kurdish uprising in 1991 had been alleviated by the **safe haven** and **no-fly zone** imposed by the **United States** and its allies. These negotiations eventually led to an impasse, and a de facto Kurdish state began to form in northern Iraq. Osman was a candidate for supreme leader (president) during the elections of 1992, but he came in a very distant fourth behind **Massoud Barzani**, **Jalal Talabani**, and even Sheikh Osman Abdul Aziz, the **Islamist** candidate. Essentially a leader without any following, Osman went into exile in **Great Britain**, where he has continued to play a prominent role as an elder statesman in Kurdish **diaspora** politics.

OTTOMAN EMPIRE. Tracing its origins to the end of the 13th century, the Ottoman Empire at its zenith was one of the greatest Islamic states in history. In 1453, the Ottomans finally captured Constantinople and ended the Byzantine Empire. In the following century, the Ottoman Empire grew to span parts of three continents—southeastern Europe, southwestern Asia (the Middle East), and northern Africa. During its period of growth, the Ottoman Empire confronted the Christian West as the champion of Islamic expansion. Europe's modernization, however, began to roll the Ottomans back, and by the 19th century they were seen as the "sick man of Europe." Nevertheless, the empire lasted into the 20th century, when defeat in World War I led to its final collapse. **Mustafa Kemal Ataturk** established the modern Republic of **Turkey** in 1923.

The Ottoman Empire first incorporated the Kurds in 1514, following its famous victory (with considerable Kurdish support, it should be noted) over Safavid **Persia** at the Battle of **Chaldiran**, northeast of Van. The border thus established basically lasted into the 20th century. Most Kurds lived within the boundaries of the Ottoman Empire, where they usually enjoyed a large amount of local autonomy, until the Ottoman centralization policies of the 19th century destroyed the semi-independent Kurdish **emirates**. The remainder of the Kurds lived within the **Persian Empire**. During the ensuing centuries, the Kurds inhabiting the frontier marches played a major role in the confrontations between the two empires.

Ottoman backwardness in the 19th century contributed to the stunted sense of Kurdish **nationalism** that failed to take advantage of its opportunities at the end of World War I. To this day, historians debate whether **Sheikh Said**'s famous rebellion against Turkey in 1925 was motivated by genuine Kurdish nationalism or simple longing for the abolished caliphate. Certainly the stunted sense of Kurdish nationalism helped prevent Sheikh Said from uniting most of the Kurdish **tribes** under his banner.

Historical memories of European imperialist schemes to weaken and divide the Ottoman Empire in the 19th and early 20th centuries continue to influence modern Turkey to oppose recognition of Kurdish rights that might snowball into demands for Kurdish independence. The seemingly stubborn refusal of modern Turkey to admit that its citizens of Kurdish ethnic heritage constitute a minority can be partially understood in light of the old Ottoman principle that **Islam** took precedence over nationality among Muslims and that only non-Muslims could hold some type of officially recognized minority status. Indeed, this very principle was recognized by the Treaty of **Lausanne** (1923), which made no provisions for the Kurds in Turkey, while overturning the stillborn Treaty of **Sevres** (1920), which had sought to provide for Kurdish autonomy or even independence.

What many remember as harsh Ottoman rule probably continues to influence successor Arab states such as **Iraq** and **Syria** to be wary of modern Turkey. The Ottomans hanged the elder brother of **Mulla Mustafa Barzani** in World War I for supposedly conspiring with the **Russian** enemy.

OZAL, TURGUT (1927–93). Prime minister of **Turkey** from 1983 to 1989, president until his sudden death from a heart attack on 17 April

1993, and possibly the most important Turkish leader since **Mustafa Kemal Ataturk**. Ozal's liberal economic policies, for example, reoriented Turkey's autarkic market and changed it forever.

Trained as an engineer and an economist, Ozal was seen by many as primarily a technocrat when he was brought in by the military government that seized power in Turkey in September 1980 to rescue the economy. However, Ozal proved skeptical of government-run businesses and had troubling links with the Islamic right through his connections with the **Naqshbandi** order. In the election of November 1983, Ozal's Anavatan Partisi, or Motherland Party, handily defeated the military's candidates and swept Ozal into power.

Although Ozal had originated the **village guards** system and **emergency rule**, two measures long considered prime examples of official state repression of the Kurds, he in time began to make some imaginative reforms in an attempt to help solve the Kurdish problem in Turkey. For one, he revealed that one of his grandparents had been an ethnic Kurd. In response to the 1991 **Gulf War** and its repercussions among the Kurds, Ozal introduced a draft bill into the Turkish parliament to repeal some of the longstanding obstacles to the legal usage of the Kurdish **language** in Turkey, except in broadcasts, publications, and education. He also broke Turkey's stringent policy against negotiating with any Kurdish group and invited **Jalal Talabani** and a representative of **Massoud Barzani**, the two main Iraqi Kurdish leaders, to Ankara.

By the following year, Ozal was arguing not only for an amnesty for the guerrillas of the **Kurdistan Workers Party (PKK)**, but also for its recognition as a participant in Turkey's political system. Shortly before his death, Ozal warned his prime minister, **Suleyman Demirel**, that the Kurdish issue was the gravest issue ever facing Turkey. These truly were radical ideas for a Turkish leader and they found some positive response from **Abdullah Ocalan**, the leader of the PKK. In March 1993, Ocalan announced a unilateral cease-fire on top of his already toned-down demands for Kurdish independence.

All of these promising initiatives came to an end with Ozal's sudden death from a heart attack. Under the new president, **Suleyman Demirel**, Turkey returned to its more traditional policy of smashing the Kurds. The rumor arose that Ozal had actually been murdered by those in the Turkish government who opposed his Kurdish initiatives.

Given his bad health, however, it is highly unlikely that this was the case.

OZEL HAREKET TIM. *See* COUNTERGUERRILLAS.

OZEL TIM. *See* COUNTERGUERRILLAS.

OZGURLUK YOLU. *See* KURDISTAN SOCIALIST PARTY (of Turkey).

– P –

PARASTIN (SECURITY). The original name of the effective intelligence organization the **Israeli Mossad** and Iranian Savak helped **Mulla Mustafa Barzani** establish in 1966. Both **Massoud Barzani** and his elder half brother, **Idris Barzani**, ran it at various times. The intelligence organization of the **Kurdistan Democratic Party** is still sometimes unofficially called by this name.

PARLIAMENT IN EXILE. *See* KURDISTAN PARLIAMENT IN EXILE.

PARMAKSIZ ZEKI. *See* SAKIK, SEMDIN.

PASOK. Or Kurdish Socialist Party, one of eight parties that joined the Iraqi Kurdistan Front in May 1988. PASOK, not to be confused with the Socialist Party of Kurdistan (in Iraq) (SPKI), led by **Rasul Mamand**, or the Socialist Party in Greece (PASOK), was a minor Iraqi Kurdish party with a collective leadership.

For a short period in 1992, PASOK was called the Kurdistan Democratic Independence Party. It reportedly united with the SPKI for the Iraqi Kurdish elections held in May 1992, but did very poorly. This new entity then joined **Muhammad (Sami) Abdurrahman**'s **Kurdistan Popular Democratic Party** to form the **Kurdistan Unity Party**, but the new party broke up in the summer of 1993. Most of its members followed Abdurrahman into the **Kurdistan Democratic**

Party, while a few led by Rasul Mamand joined the **Patriotic Union of Kurdistan.**

PATRIOTIC UNION OF KURDISTAN (PUK). Following the collapse of **Mulla Mustafa Barzani**'s revolt in March 1975, the Iraqi Kurdish movement Barzani had headed splintered and fell into disarray. On 1 June 1975, **Jalal Talabani** announced in Damascus, **Syria**, the creation of the Patriotic Union of Kurdistan (PUK), made up at the time of two major groups: Komala, a Marxist organization headed by **Noshirwan Mustafa Amin** and no relation to the Iranian organization of the same name, and the Socialist Movement of Kurdistan, led by **Ali Askari.**

Talabani himself had been Barzani's off-again, on-again associate in earlier years, and with his father-in-law, **Ibrahim Ahmad**, had led the **KDP Politburo** as a rival to Barzani's authority. Thus the new PUK was in many ways the successor of the earlier KDP Politburo, claiming to be progressive and socialist, while denouncing Barzani and his **Kurdistan Democratic Party (KDP)**—now led by Barzani's sons, **Massoud Barzani** and **Idris Barzani** (d. 1987)—as **tribal** and reactionary. In 1977, Talabani returned to Iraqi Kurdistan, establishing his headquarters just inside the **Iranian** border, west of Sardasht. Since then, the KDP and PUK have been the two most important Iraqi Kurdish parties. Indeed, their up-and-down fortunes have been largely those of the Iraqi Kurds and their **Kurdistan Regional Government** created in 1992.

At its first formal congress in 1992, the PUK merged its constituent groups within a unified political movement that affirmed its social democratic identity. Jalal Talabani continues to be the undisputed head of the PUK, holding the official title of secretary general. The party also has a Leadership Council (Central Committee) of 32 members and a politburo of 11 members. In addition, there are branches in all the major cities and towns of the area, which the PUK has ruled since the unfortunate civil war it fought against the KDP from 1994 to 1998. As of early 2003, the PUK continues to govern its portion of Iraqi Kurdistan from **Sulaymaniya**, but is on record (as is its rival the KDP) as advocating new elections that would lead to a reunited Kurdistan Regional Government.

The PUK's organizational structure includes several media outlets: the People of Kurdistan TV, based in Sulaymaniya, and other smaller television stations; the Voice of the People of Kurdistan, a radio station broadcasting in Kurdish and Arabic that can be received throughout the Middle East and Europe; *Kurdistan-i-Nwe*, a daily newspaper in Kurdish; the *Al-Itihad* weekly in Arabic; and *The Moniter*, a daily bulletin in Kurdish and Arabic monitoring international broadcasts on matters relating to Kurdish and Iraqi affairs. The PUK also maintains a web site at www.puk.org/. Presently, the PUK maintains permanent offices abroad in Washington, London, Paris, Berlin, Moscow, Rome, Stockholm, Brussels (the seat of the European Union), Tehran, Ankara, Damascus, and Cairo.

According to its program, the PUK strives for the right of self-determination for the Kurdish people within a unified, democratic **Iraq**. The party advocates a political settlement to the Kurdish problem that is based on the principles of democracy, **human rights**, and the recognition of national and cultural identity. In addition, the PUK program seeks the promotion of a civil society with democratic institutions. It advocates free and open elections and freedom of speech, press, and other fundamental human rights, including gender equality. Indeed, the PUK's program specifically declares that the "PUK struggles to implement the Universal Declaration of Human Rights." The PUK program also states that it believes in a combination of free-market forces and government policy to promote balanced economic and social development and welfare.

At present, there are as many as 30 newspapers and magazines, eight television stations, and numerous radio stations operated by various political and cultural groups within the area of Kurdistan governed by the PUK, along with the Toilers Party, the Social Democratic Party of Kurdistan, the Conservative Party, the Islamic Party, and independent personalities as junior coalition partners.

PERSIA. The old name for the country now called **Iran**. **Reza Shah Pahlavi** changed the name to Iran, the land of the Aryans, in 1935. The name "Persia" comes from the country's southern province, Fars, from where the Achaemenids came to establish the original Persian Empire of Cyrus the Great in 550 B.C.E. Persian, or Farsi, is the national language of Iran, but many of its people speak variants of

Turkish, Kurdish, and Arabic. Kurdish is related to Persian. Historically, Persia has been closely associated with the Kurds, who are ethnically related to the Persians, but ethnically distinct from the Arabs and Turks.

In 1514, the **Ottoman** sultan Selim Yavuz (the Grim) defeated Shah Ismail of the Safavid Persians at the famous Battle of **Chaldiran** northeast of Lake Van in what is now eastern **Turkey**. In the succeeding centuries, Kurdistan became a frontier between the two empires and suffered accordingly. In addition, both empires deported entire Kurdish **tribes**. The descendants of these tribes still live today in areas south of Ankara, Turkey, and in Iran, some 1,000 miles east of their original homeland in Khorasan and even farther east, in Afghanistan's Hindu Kush Mountains. The Treaty of **Zuhab** in 1639 established the basic boundary that still exists today between **Turkey** and Iran.

PERWER, SIVAN (1955–). Famous contemporary Kurdish singer born in **Turkey**, but exiled from there since 1976. Sivan Perwer travels extensively, and political songs constitute an important part of his repertoire. He is much admired by Kurds throughout the world, and his songs serve to unite otherwise divided Kurds and promote their sense of Kurdish **nationalism**. His dirge for the 5,000 Kurds who died from the **chemical weapons** used by **Saddam Hussein**'s forces at **Halabja** is particularly haunting. He is also famous for singing traditional epic and love songs.

PESHENG. *See* KURDISTAN VANGUARD WORKERS PARTY (PPKK).

PESHMERGAS. Or those who are willing to face death for their cause, the Iraqi Kurdish guerrillas who first fought under **Mulla Mustafa Barzani**. The term *peshmergas* has come to have a very patriotic connotation and is opposed to the term *josh*, or little donkeys, Kurds who fight on the side of the Iraqi government.

The Kurdish term *peshmerga* is similar in meaning to the Arabic word *fedayeen,* or fighters willing to sacrifice themselves for the cause. Originally, *peshmergas* referred to Iraqi Kurdish guerrillas, but the term later came to be used sometimes for Kurdish guerrillas elsewhere. With the institutionalization of the **Kurdistan Regional Government** in northern Iraq after 1992, *peshmergas* have become increasingly obsolete, as more regular soldiers have been employed.

PIKE COMMITTEE REPORT. U.S. Representative Otis Pike chaired a committee in the House of Representatives during the mid-1970s that investigated the **Central Intelligence Agency (CIA)**. Although the Pike Committee proved much less important in investigating the CIA than its contemporary, the U.S. Senate Church Committee, the Pike Committee did reveal the details of the U.S. and Iranian role in supporting the revolt of **Mulla Mustafa Barzani** during the 1970s. The details were revealed by the unauthorized publication of the Pike Committee Report by the *Village Voice* on 16 February 1976.

This document shows that, in May 1972, the shah of **Iran** (**Muhammad Reza Shah Pahlavi**), who already was supporting Barzani because Iran and **Iraq** "had long been bitter enemies," asked U.S. president **Richard M. Nixon** and soon-to-be secretary of state **Henry Kissinger**—who were returning from a Moscow summit meeting—to help him in this project. Although the U.S. aid was "largely symbolic," the **United States** in effect guaranteed that the Kurdish insurgent group would not be summarily dropped by the shah. The Pike Committee Report explained that "on numerous occasions the leader of the ethnic group [Barzani] expressed his distrust of our allies' [Iran's] intentions. He did, however, [naively] trust the United States."

The report concluded that "the project was initiated primarily as a favor to our ally [Iran], who had cooperated with United States intelligence agencies, and who had come to feel menaced by his neighbor [Iraq]." Other reasons for the U.S. action included the Cold War, in which Iraq was a **Soviet** ally; providing a means for tying down Iraqi troops during any Arab–**Israeli** war, and creating a potential way for the United States to obtain **oil** if the Kurds obtained independence.

Unfortunately for the Kurds, the U.S. and Iranian covert support for the Kurds helped lead to the breakdown of the **March Manifesto** of 1970, which held out the possibility of Kurdish autonomy. In addition, the U.S.–Iranian aid was never intended to be enough for the Kurds to triumph because, if Barzani were actually to win, the Kurds would no longer be able to play the enervating role against Iraq that the United Sates and Iran desired.

Thus the United States and Iran actually "hoped that our clients [the Kurds] would not prevail. They preferred instead that the insurgents simply continue a level of hostilities sufficient to sap the resources of our ally's [Iran's] neighboring country [Iraq]." Of course, "this policy was not imparted to our clients, who were encouraged to continue fighting. Even in the context of covert action, ours was a cynical enterprise."

On 6 March 1975, moreover, Iran and Iraq signed the **Algiers Agreement**, under which Iraq recognized the middle of the Shatt al-Arab River as the boundary between their two states, while Iran undertook to halt its aid to Barzani. "The cut-off of aid . . . came as a severe shock to its [the Kurds'] leadership" and caused the Kurdish rebellion to collapse. Barzani told the CIA that "there is confusion and dismay among our people and forces. Our people's fate [is] in unprecedented danger. Complete destruction [is] hanging over our head. . . . We appeal [to] you . . . [to] intervene according to your promises."

Despite these pleas, "the U.S. [even] refused to extend humanitarian assistance to the thousands of **refugees** created by the abrupt termination of military aid." As the Pike Committee Report explained, the United States had become such "junior partners of the Shah," that it "had no choice but to acquiesce" to his cutting off Barzani's support. Kissinger infamously added that "covert action should not be confused with missionary work."

– Q –

QADDAFI, MUAMMAR (1942–). Military officer who seized power in Libya in 1969 and has ruled there ever since as an eccentric, radical Arab leader. His support for international terrorism and isolation from most other world leaders because of his maverick reputation has made him an easy target for international sanctions from the **United States** acting through the **United Nations**. Despite these unsavory characteristics, Qaddafi is admired by some as a sincere, romantic Arab nationalist. He certainly is not the notorious killer and danger to world peace **Saddam Hussein** has been.

For the Kurds, Qaddafi has long held a unique place among Arab leaders as the only one who has called for Kurdish independence. In October 1996, for example, Qaddafi caused an uproar in **Turkey** when he told the visiting Turkish prime minister, **Necmettin Erbakan**, that Turkey's Kurds should have independence. Many, however, simply dismissed this position as simply another example of Qaddafi's eccentricity.

When Turkey finally captured **Abdullah Ocalan**, the leader of the **Kurdistan Workers Party**, in February 1999, Qaddafi released a lengthy statement comparing Ocalan's capture to earlier failed **Ottoman** attempts to stamp out Arab revolutionaries. The Libyan leader then declared: "To my Kurdish brothers . . . do not weaken or be sad for the more your enemy spills your blood the more he adds fuel to the fire of the Kurdish revolution. Denying the right of nations to independence constitutes an act of ignorance and shows superficiality, selfishness and ignorance of history."

QADIRI. One of the two main **Sufi** orders in Kurdistan, the other being the **Naqshbandi**. The Qadiris take their name from Sheikh Abd al-Qadir (1077–1166)—a most revered Islamic saint whose tomb in Baghdad remains a well-known shrine—but he had nothing to do with establishing the order. It is not unusual for groups to later claim descent from famous reputed progenitors in order to gain legitimacy from the association.

Two brothers—Sayyid Musa and Sayyid Isa—are said to have established the Qadiri order in what is now Iraqi Kurdistan around 1360, and until early in the 19th century, the Qadiris monopolized Sufism throughout the region. By the 19th century, the Barzinjis, Sadate **Nehris**, and Talabanis became the best-known Qadiri **sheikhs**. From these religious connections, all three families developed strong temporal authority, too. Indeed, **Sheikh Mahmud Barzinji** and **Jalal Talabani** are two of the best-known Iraqi Kurdish **nationalists** of the entire 20th century.

Due to the prodigious efforts of **Maulana Khalid**, however, the Naqshbandi order spread rapidly after its introduction early in the 19th century and replaced the Qadiris in many places, for a variety of reasons. The Sadate Nehris adopted the Naqshbandi order, and the sheikhs of **Barzan** were also Naqshbandi. But one of the main reasons Sheikh Mahmud Barzinji failed to unite more of the population behind him when he proclaimed himself king of Kurdistan in the 1920s was that most inhabitants of **Kirkuk** owed allegiance to the rival Qadiri Talabanis. It is also interesting to note that the two great contemporary rivals in Iraqi Kurdistan (**Massoud Barzani** and **Jalal Talabani**) are scions of the Naqshbandi and Qadiri orders, respectively.

The Qadiri order is noted for holding much more ecstatic rituals than its rivals, the Naqshbandis. Some, but not all, of the dervishes or participants can go into trances and inflict self-mutilation upon themselves. When participants recite the *shahada,* or confession of faith, *la illaha illa llah* (there is no god but God), drums can join in and bodily movements become ever wilder. When turbans are pulled off, the long hair adds a fierce look to the performance. Others actually cut themselves with skewers or other sharp objects. At times, glass is chewed and eaten, poisonous chemicals are swallowed, and bare electric wires are touched.

The dervishes believe that they are protected from harmful consequences by the *karama,* or special graces, of the very holy Abd al-Qadir (the Qadiris' reputed founder), which are transmitted to the present sheikh or his *khalifa,* or deputy. The ecstatic practices apparently demonstrate that **Islam** is the one true religion and that the Qadiri *tariqa,* or path, is particularly blessed with supernatural powers. In addition, the Qadiri dervish who performs these acts illustrates his trust in God and his *tariqa,* and thus proves his superior spirituality.

QAZI MUHAMMAD (1898–1947). Revered leader of the short-lived **Mahabad Republic of Kurdistan**, which was established with **Soviet** help in northwestern **Iran** soon after World War II. An erudite and very respected hereditary religious leader and judge *(qazi),* he was a popular member of Mahabad's leading family and de facto ruler of the area.

As president of the Kurdish republic, Qazi Muhammad instituted a functioning public administration and compulsory education. In addition, he encouraged news and cultural publications, as well as a state radio. He also was noted for his chivalry toward enemies and negotiated in good faith with the Iranian government. Unfortunately, he presided over only a miniscule area extending no more than 100 kilometers around the city of Mahabad. The usual Kurdish divisions shadowed his authority, and the economic situation was desperate. Once Soviet aid was lifted due to various international pressures and the forlorn promise of Iranian **oil** concessions, the Iranian government easily reasserted its authority, and it hanged Qazi Muhammad on 31 March 1947. His memory, however, remains inspirational to Kurds everywhere.

QIZILBASH. *See* ALEVIS.

– R –

RAFSANJANI, ALI AKBAR HASHEMI (1934–). President of the Islamic Republic of **Iran** from 1989 to 1997. Although Rafsanjani was a relative moderate, during his rule, Iran carried out two high-profile assassinations of prominent Iranian Kurdish leaders: **Abdul Rahman Ghassemlou** (Vienna in 1989) and Sadiq Sharafkindi (Berlin in 1992). **Kordestan** was the only Iranian province that did not give the majority of its vote to Rafsanjani when he was reelected in 1993.

However, Iran accepted more than 1.5 million Iraqi Kurdish **refugees** after the failure of their uprising in 1991. Rafsanjani criticized the West for its initial meager response to the refugee crisis. During Rafsanjani's term, Iran also continued to give covert support to the **Kurdistan Workers Party (PKK)** as a way to counterbalance **Turkey.** Iran also continued to compete with Turkey for influence within the **Kurdistan Regional Government** in northern Iraq after 1991. On several occasions, Iranian troops intervened in northern Iraq, most notably in the summer of 1996 to support the **Patriotic Union of Kurdistan** in its internecine struggle against the **Kurdistan Democratic Party.**

RASUL, KOSRAT. Senior member of the politburo of the **Patriotic Union of Kurdistan (PUK)** who distinguished himself in the fighting that occurred during the Kurdish uprising in 1991. In April 1993, Kosrat Rasul became the prime minister of the **Kurdistan Regional Government** in an attempt to introduce more political figures into the administration. He continued as the prime minister of the rump PUK administration in **Sulaymaniya** after internal fighting began in 1994 between the PUK and the **Kurdistan Democratic Party (KDP)**. The KDP maintained its rump administration in **Irbil**. In January 2001, Kosrat Rasul resigned and was replaced by **Barham Salih**.

RAWWADIDS (RAWAD). Minor dynasty of northwestern **Persia** that flourished from approximately 758 C.E. (when the governor of Azerbaijan appointed Al-Rawwad bin al-Muthanna to secure the area) until the Selcuk Turks took the region after 1071. The Rawwadids were originally Arabs, but gradually became Kurdicized by their environment. They began, for example, to use Kurdish forms in their genealogy, such as Mamlan for Muhammad and Ahmadil for Ahmad. Survivors of the dynasty can be traced up to Mongol Il-Khanid times in the early 14th century.

RAYAT. A somewhat derogatory Arabic term used throughout the Middle East and by the **Ottoman** administration for the peasantry. Indeed, the original meaning of the word was flock, as in a flock of sheep, which was a productive asset to be exploited. In Kurdistan, the rayat were often held up in contemptuous contrast to the **tribes**men because the rayat were deemed unfit to fight. Other terms used for the rayat in various parts of Kurdistan include **misken** and **guran**.

RED KURDISTAN. *See* LACHIN.

REFAH. Or the Welfare Party of **Necmettin Erbakan**, in 1996 became the first **Islamist** party to come to power through the ballot box in the entire Middle East. Many voters supported it because it was seen as an efficient, honest party in contrast to **Turkey**'s other main parties.

Because of its Islamic ideology, Refah was not as averse to admitting the existence of the Kurds in Turkey as were the other main parties. Indeed, Refah held out a forlorn hope that it could solve Turkey's Kurdish problem by emphasizing overall Islamic unity. However, it should be emphasized that Refah and the **Kurdistan Workers Party (PKK)** remained enemies competing for some of the same (ethnic Kurdish) clientele.

Refah advocated the elimination of **emergency rule** in the southeast of Turkey, favored the liberalization of restrictions on the Kurdish **language**, and emphasized a peaceful settlement. Because the Peoples Democracy Party, the overtly Kurdish party, had been severely restricted by the government, Refah was able to do quite well in the Kurdish southeast of Turkey during the national elections held in December 1995.

Refah's attempts to make headway with the Kurdish problem foundered, and its tenure in office proved short-lived because of the strong opposition expressed by Turkey's military. Erbakan was forced to resign in June 1997 and Refah itself was banned by the Constitutional Court in January 1998, the same fate ironically suffered by earlier Kurdish parties. *See also* AK PARTISI (AKP).

REFUGEES. In earlier times, both the **Ottoman** and **Persian Empires** deported large numbers of Kurds from their historic homelands in an attempt to control them better. More recently, the modern Republic of **Turkey** has also internally displaced many ethnic Kurds in an attempt to assimilate them. Thus more Kurds in Turkey may today live outside their historic homeland in eastern Anatolia than those who remain there. **Iraq** and **Syria** have also displaced hundreds of thousands of Kurds during the 20th century. This situation remained little known, however, until the aftermath of the **Gulf War** in 1991.

The tragic flight of more than 1.8 million Iraqi Kurdish refugees from **Saddam Hussein**'s vengeance following the **Gulf War** in April 1991 brought the longstanding Kurdish question to the forefront of international concern. Eventually, it led to the creation of a **Kurdistan Regional Government** behind the protection of the **no-fly zone** enforced by the **United States**. Because of continuing upheavals in Turkey and Iraq, however, Kurdish refugees remain a major problem both in the Middle East and in Europe. Indeed, a sizable Kurdish **diaspora** has now arisen in Europe in particular.

It is important to note that the term "refugee" has a much more precise and narrow definition in international law than its everyday reference to persons fleeing from their homes in times of war or because of political or religious persecution. The difference between the precise international legal meaning of "refugee" and its common usage no doubt helps explain frequent frustration with the inability to solve refugee problems more readily. Moreover, as with most difficulties involving international law, state sovereignty plays a major role in inhibiting the progressive development of the international law of refugees. Municipal (national) administrative and judicial decisions interpret and apply many of the international legal rules involving refugees on a daily basis.

The modern international legal definition of "refugee" stems from the Statute of the **United Nations** High Commissioner for Refugees (UNHCR) adopted by the United Nations General Assembly on 14 December 1950 and on the 1951 Convention Relating to the Status of Refugees, as modified by the 1967 Protocol Relating to the Status of Refugees. Thus under international law a refugee is any person who "owing to a well-founded fear of being persecuted for reasons of race, religion, nationality, membership of a particular social group or political opinion, is outside the country of his nationality and is unable or, owing to such fear, is unwilling to avail himself of the protection of that country; or who, not having a nationality and being outside the country of his former habitual residence, is unable or, owing to such fear, is unwilling to return to it."

This international legal definition accords important protections and economic and social benefits only to those narrowly defined as refugees and only in states party to the Refugee Convention and/or Protocol to which the refugee has been lawfully admitted under that state's municipal (national) laws. Most displaced Kurds have great difficulties in meeting these strict requirements for being classified as refugees. For example, Kurds who remain within the borders of their country of origin are simply internally displaced persons, not refugees with internationally recognized rights. Many displaced Kurds in Turkey, Iraq, and Syria suffer from this problem. Furthermore, even Kurds who cross international borders often fail to meet the strict legal requirements of being a refugee as interpreted by the host country where they have arrived, often because such host countries do not want to burden themselves with additional problems and expenses. Many Kurds who arrive in Europe are faced with this situation and are subject to being deported back to the country from which they originated.

Although it is a party to both the 1951 Refugee Convention and the 1967 Protocol, Turkey has made important reservations to them that severely limit the designation of refugees from the Middle East. This, of course, largely refers to the Kurds. In addition, neither Iraq nor Syria is even a party to either refugee treaty. **Iran**, by contrast, has often offered generous aid to Kurdish refugees and others.

Non-refoulement, or the right not to be expelled or returned to a territory where one's life would be threatened, remains one legal right that a Kurd or anybody else has who cannot meet the legal definition of "refugee." Unfortunately, the **United States** itself seriously challenged this right in 1993 when it intercepted Haitian refugees on the high seas who were fleeing their homeland and returned them to Haiti without first determining whether they might qualify as refugees under international law. In 1998, however, the U.S. Congress gave renewed life to the concept of *non-refoulement* when it enacted an appropriations rider forbidding the use of appropriated funds for extraterritorial *refoulement* of refugees and also establishing the policy of applying the *non-refoulement* requirements of the 1984 Convention against Torture without regard to geographical location.

RELIGION. Although most Kurds are Sunni Muslims, they are not as a rule overly religious. Indeed, an old Kurdish maxim has it that compared to an unbeliever, a Kurd is a good Muslim.

However, it must also be noted that there exists an incredible religious diversity among the Kurds, not only in **Islam**, but also in various pre-Islamic, heterodox, and syncretist beliefs. What is more, **sheikhs** still play not only an important religious role but also an important political role in rural areas. Finally, as with the rest of the Islamic world, **Islamist** forces have been gaining strength among a minority of Kurds. Indeed, within the sway of the **Kurdistan Regional Government** in Iraqi Kurdistan, the Islamists are clearly the third strongest force after the **Kurdistan Democratic Party** and the **Patriotic Union of Kurdistan**. Sunni Kurds distinguish themselves from their Sunni Turkish and Arab neighbors by adhering to the Shafii school of Islamic law, instead of the **Hanefi** school. In addition, at least 5 percent of the Kurds profess orthodox Shiite beliefs, with numbers in **Iran** particularly high.

Among Iraqi Kurds, adherents of what has been called the **Cult of Angels** still exist. **Alevis** (Qizilbash), **Ahl-i Haqq** followers, and **Yezidis** practice elements of pre-Islamic, syncretistic, and extreme

Islamic heterodox beliefs. Although some claim that as many as one-third of the Kurds still adhere to these sects, this is almost certainly an exaggeration. In **Turkey**, a sizable minority of the ethnic Kurds are Alevis, which serves to divide them from their orthodox Sunni cousins. **Naqshbandi** and **Qadiri Sufi** orders also continue to play an important role in the lives of some Kurds.

Finally, it should be noted that, historically, **Christians** and Jews were also present among the Kurds. Christian **Assyrians** still constitute an important minority within the Kurdistan Regional Government's sway in northern Iraq.

REZA SHAH PAHLAVI (1877–1944). Originally known as Reza Khan, the future shah of **Iran** began his career as an illiterate, but successful army officer and went on to end the decrepit Qajar dynasty and in 1925 establish himself as the head of the new Pahlavi dynasty.

Like **Mustafa Kemal Ataturk** in **Turkey**, Reza Shah was a great modernizer, changing the name of his country from **Persia** to Iran; reorganizing the army, government, and finances; and making his country truly independent. He sought to accomplish the latter by applying the ancient Persian technique of protecting his country's independence by balancing such powerful foreign enemies as **Great Britain** and the **Soviet Union** with a third force, **Germany**, a country he greatly admired. In the end, this proved his downfall, as the former two took over Iran at the start of World War II and forced Reza Shah to abdicate in favor of his son, **Muhammad Reza Shah Pahlavi**.

Reza Shah's centralization policies beat the Kurdish tribes of Iran into submission. His agents treacherously assassinated **Ismail Agha Simko**, the famous Iranian Kurdish rebel, in 1930, a time-honored Iranian tactic against Kurdish leaders. The shah's policies also included an attempt to impose the Persian language throughout the country, including on its Kurdish population. As one of its covert objectives, the **Saadabad Treaty** of 1937 (named for the Shah's palace of Saadabad) sought to harmonize the policies of Iran, Turkey, and **Iraq** on the Kurdish issue, instead of these three states trying to use the Kurds against each other.

RIYA AZADI. See KURDISTAN SOCIALIST PARTY (PSK).

RIZGARI. Small Kurdish Marxist party in **Turkey** that grew up in 1976 around the publishing house Komal and became known by the name of its journal, *Rizgari,* which was banned after only its second issue. *Rizgari* argued that as a colonized people, the Kurds could expect little from the Turks. Kurdish liberation would be won by a socialist revolution led by the Kurdish proletariat.

Ideological and personal conflicts led to a split in 1979, and a splinter group called **Ala Rizgari** (flag of Liberation) was created. Both parties were destroyed by the Turkish military coup that seized power in September 1980. The **Kurdistan Workers Party** eventually emerged as the main Kurdish revolutionary party in Turkey after 1980.

Rizgari was also the name of a short-lived Iraqi Kurdish party in 1945 that merged into the **Kurdistan Democratic Party** when the latter was created in 1946.

RUGS. As with many other elements of Kurdish history and culture, Kurdish rugs (carpets) and kilims are often subsumed in the popular culture under Turkish and Persian headings. This, of course, ignores the rich Kurdish contributions in yet another area.

Many travelers during the 19th century wrote about the beautiful colors and high quality of Kurdish rugs they saw. Most were woven by nomadic **women** from sheep wool. Kurdish rugs usually are woven on a rather narrow loom three to four feet across and are often twice as long as they are wide. They usually have only one or two borders, as compared to the three borders of Persian and Turkish rugs. Their multicolored side selvages, or edges, also distinguish them. The end finishes of Kurdish rugs contain excess warp length at their fringes that to some gives a wild, barbaric or rustic, bold appearance. The high pile of many Kurdish rugs and their shagginess may be the origin of the somewhat pejorative term "bear rugs" some have given them.

Typical designs in Kurdish rugs include the eight-pointed star, crab, turtle, fish and lotus, latch-hooked diamonds, squares or crossroads, roses and lotus, and pine cones. These designs are often stylized and talismanic. Older Kurdish rugs used strong natural dyes that improved with age.

With the decline of the nomadic tradition in Kurdistan, the quality of Kurdish rugs has also steadily declined. Cheap, synthetic dyes and an unwillingness to spend the necessary time to produce the finely knotted pieces of the past have also contributed to this situation. Nevertheless, their simplicity, multitude of colors and motifs, and even mistakes in design execution have all helped make Kurdish rugs popular. **William Eagleton**'s *An Introduction to Kurdish Rugs and Other Weavings* (1988) is a beautifully illustrated study of Kurdish rugs in English.

RUSSIA. In Tsarist times, Russia often tried to use the Kurds to stir up trouble in the **Ottoman Empire**. Indeed, the Ottomans created the **Hamidiye** cavalry of Kurdish irregulars in the 1890s, in part as a response to such Russian pressures. Despite their efforts, however, the Russians were never able to make significant claims upon Kurdish allegiances, largely because as **Christians** who supported the **Armenians** they were suspect. Russian depredations upon the Kurdish population were also infamous. To this day, some Kurdish mothers are said to stop their children from crying by warning them that the Russians will hear them and attack.

The **Soviet Union** also sought to use the Kurds as a fifth column during the Cold War, the **Mahabad Republic of Kurdistan** immediately after World War II being a prime example. Since the collapse of the Soviet Union in 1991, various Kurdish exile groups have been given a certain amount of sanctuary in Russia. The **Kurdistan Parliament in Exile**, for example, was allowed to meet in Russia in October 1995, and **Abdullah Ocalan**, the fugitive leader of the **Kurdistan Workers Party** unsuccessfully sought refuge there in 1998.

While the Russians sought to play the Kurdish card against **Turkey** in the 1990s, the Turks responded by supporting Chechnya in its rebellion against the Russian Federation. Eventually, however, both sides agreed that they lost more than they were gaining by pursuing such covert tactics. During the 1990s, Russia also opposed the continuance of **United Nations** sanctions against the regime of **Saddam Hussein**. This position was in opposition to the **United States** and taken because of Russian economic needs.

During Soviet days, the **Lachin** area of Soviet Armenia (Red Kurdistan) contained a sizable Kurdish minority, some of which retains its Kurdish identity today. Josef Stalin deported ethnic Kurds to central Asia, and some claim that as many as 1 million largely assimilated Kurds live in Russia today. Most experts, however, would put the figure at approximately 200,000. Historically, there is a strong tradition of Russian scholarship concerning the Kurds. Mikhail S. Lazarev, the director of the Division of Kurdology and Regional Issues of the Middle East Department of the Institute of Oriental Studies at the Russian Academy of Sciences in Moscow, for example, has published extensively on the Kurds, as has his colleague, Olga Jigalina.

– S –

SAADABAD, TREATY OF. Treaty concluded in 1937 between **Iran, Turkey,** and **Iraq.** Its main unstated purpose was to harmonize the policies of these three states on the potentially volatile Kurdish issue, which overlapped their borders and tempted each to use the Kurds against the others. In so doing, the Treaty of Saadabad adumbrated the **Baghdad Pact** of 1955. Neither, however, proved ultimately successful. Saadabad was the palace of **Reza Shah Pahlavi.**

SAFE HAVEN. Temporary, small area in northern **Iraq** around the city of Zakho just over the border from **Turkey** where Kurdish **refugees** could return and be protected from attack by **Saddam Hussein's** forces after the failure of the Kurdish uprising that followed the Gulf War in 1991. The **United States** and several of its **Gulf-War** allies established the safe haven.

The concept was first proposed by Turkish president **Turgut Ozal** and then advocated by British prime minister John Major. **United Nations** Security Council Resolution 688, of 5 April 1991, which condemned "the repression of the Iraqi civilian population . . . in Kurdish populated areas" and demanded "that Iraq . . . immediately end this repression," was used to legally justify the safe haven and the **no-fly zone** that helped to protect it. The safe haven was implemented by **Operation Provide Comfort,** and out of these concepts grew the **Kurdistan Regional Government,** which continues to hold sway over much of Iraqi Kurdistan.

SAHINDAL, FADIME (c. 1975–2002). Young Kurdish woman living in Sweden who became a noted victim of an **honor killing.** On

21 January 2002, Fadime Sahindal's father (Rahmi Sahindal, who had emigrated from Turkey in 1981) shot her to death while she was visiting her mother and two sisters in Uppsala. He told the police that Fadime had shamed her family by rejecting an arranged marriage and choosing her own partner.

Earlier, Fadime had brought a highly publicized court case against her father and brother because they had threatened to kill her. In this previous case, the court had given her father a suspended sentence and her brother a year's probation. Although Fadime had hidden from the male members of her family, she continued to publicize her situation up to her death. Her death has become a symbol of the evils of honor killing.

SAID, SHEIKH OF PALU (1865–1925). Charismatic **Naqshbandi sheikh** who in 1925 led the first great Kurdish revolt in the modern Republic of **Turkey**. After some spectacular initial successes, the revolt was crushed by the vastly superior Turkish military, and Sheikh Said himself was captured. He was convicted of treason and hanged.

To this date, debate rages over whether Sheikh Said led a Kurdish **nationalist** uprising or simply one of religious reaction. In truth, both are valid explanations for what occurred. The revolt was prepared by **Azadi**, a political organization that chose Sheikh Said to be the military leader because of his mass following, which Azadi itself lacked. The explicit goal of the revolt was to establish an independent Kurdish state in which Islamic principles, violated by a secular Turkey that had just abolished the caliphate, would be respected.

Unfortunately for the Kurds, Sheikh Said could rally only the **Zaza**-speaking Kurds. **Alevi** Kurds fought on the side of the Turkish government because they believed they would be better off in a secular Turkey than in a Sunni Kurdistan led by a Naqshbandi sheikh. Other Kurdish **tribes** simply remained neutral. Sheikh Said himself was apparently betrayed by one of them while trying to escape. The **Ararat** revolt, which came to a climax in 1930, can be seen as a continuation of Sheikh Said's uprising.

SAKIK, SEMDIN. Also known as Parmaksiz ("Fingerless") Zeki because of a finger he lost while firing a rocket, a hard-line commander of the **Kurdistan Workers Party (PKK)** in the **Diyarbakir** (Amed) area of southeastern **Turkey**. Sakik is often credited with sabotaging the PKK's unilateral cease-fire called in March 1993 by killing some 33 unarmed Turkish soldiers along the Bingol-Elazig highway in May 1993.

Early in 1998, Sakik formally broke away from the PKK amid accusations from its leader, **Abdullah Ocalan**. Shortly afterward, Sakik was captured in northern **Iraq** by a Turkish commando unit. He was tried in Turkey and sentenced to death, but for political reasons the sentence has not been carried out.

Sakik's brother, Sirri Sakik, was a member of the pro-Kurdish **Democracy Party** who sat in the Turkish parliament until expelled in 1994. He was sentenced to prison along with several other DEP members of parliament—including **Leyla Zana**—for treason.

SALADIN (SALAH AL DIN) (1137–93). Arguably the greatest and most famous Kurd who ever lived, although he thought of himself first as a Muslim. Born in Tikrit, Iraq (ironically the hometown of **Saddam Hussein**), Saladin was a tribal Kurd who earned fame as a Muslim warrior.

In 1171, he overthrew the Shiite Fatimid caliphate in Egypt and established the Sunni **Ayyubid** dynasty in Egypt, **Syria**, and **Iraq**. Saladin, of course, gained his greatest fame in the West as the chivalrous and generous Muslim leader who defeated the **Christian** Crusaders in the famous Battle of Hattin (near Tiberias) in modern **Israel** and regained the holy city of Jerusalem for **Islam**.

Saladin also constructed fine mosques, restored irrigation systems, patronized **literature** and learning, and was an able theological disputant. His descendants continued to rule Egypt until 1249 and Syria until 1260. In addition, the **meliks** of **Hasankeyf** in what is now **Turkey** descended from the Ayyubids.

SALIH, BARHAM (1960–). Articulate and moderate member of the politburo of the **Patriotic Union of Kurdistan (PUK)** who became the prime minister of the PUK administration in **Sulaymaniya** on 21 January 2001, succeeding **Kosrat Rasul**. He speaks flawless English.

Barham Salih joined the PUK in 1976 and was arrested on two separate occasions by Iraqi security agents, before leaving Iraq in 1979 for **Great Britain**. He received a Ph.D. in statistics and computer modeling from the University of Liverpool. In 1985, he became the PUK spokesman in Britain. He assumed a similar position in 1991 in the **United States**, where he served for 10 years. During this time, he also became a candidate member of the PUK politburo. In the spring of 2002, Barham Salih just missed being assassinated by agents of **Ansar al-Islam**, which was reputedly associated with Osama bin Laden.

SANANDAJ (SINNA). See KORDESTAN.

SARLIYYA. Small group of Kurdish **Ahl-i Haqq** followers (**Kakais**) living in northern **Iraq** in six villages close to where the Great Zab River meets the Tigris River and approximately 45 kilometers southeast of **Mosul**. Like the **Yezidis**, **Shabaks**, and **Badjwan**, the Sarliyya, or Sarlis, are very secretive about their **religion**. Therefore, some have accused them of scandalous rites and a sort of secret language. Actually, the Sarliyya speak a Gurani dialect. See also GHULAT.

SEROK. Kurdish word for "leader" that has sometimes been used as a title to refer to **Abdullah Ocalan**, the leader of the **Kurdistan Workers Party**.

SERXWEBUN. Meaning "Independence," for many years the rather sophisticated, official journal of the **Kurdistan Workers Party**, published in Cologne, **Germany**.

SEVRES, TREATY OF. On 10 August 1920, the defeated **Ottoman Empire** was forced to sign a treaty in a suburb of Paris called Sevres that would have reduced the former empire to only a small rump section of Anatolia. The Turkish War of Independence subsequently overturned the stillborn Treaty of Sevres and in 1923 a new Treaty of **Lausanne** recognized the modern Republic of **Turkey**. The very term "Treaty of Sevres" remains a byword in Turkey today for the West's desire to partition and destroy Turkey.

For the Kurds, however, the Treaty of Sevres represents a lost opportunity, because it specifically provided for "local autonomy for predominantly Kurdish areas" (Article 62), while Article 64 even looked forward to the possibility that "the Kurdish peoples" might be granted "independence from Turkey." One obvious flaw in all this was that the Treaty of Sevres did not demarcate the borders between a putative Kurdistan and an independent **Armenia**, which the treaty also tried to establish. The main problem was that the Kurds proved to be too divided to take advantage of their opportunity, while the Turks proved resurgent under **Mustafa Kemal (Ataturk)**.

SEYAHATNAME. *See* CHELEBI, EVLIYA.

SEZER, AHMET NECDET (1941–). Elected as the 10th president of the Republic of **Turkey** by the Turkish Grand National Assembly (Parliament) on 5 May 2000, succeeding **Suleyman Demirel**. Sezer had been serving on the Constitutional Court since 1988 and had been its chief justice since 1998.

Sezer burst onto the national scene during the spring of 1999 by openly criticizing the Turkish constitution for the restrictions it placed on basic freedoms. He specifically mentioned the necessity to defend freedom of speech and eliminate the use of what some have called "thought crimes" to imprison as terrorists those who call for Kurdish cultural rights. He also lashed out at the restrictions still existing against the use of the Kurdish **language**, insisted on the need to conform to the universal standards of **human rights**, and asked for the appropriate revisions of the Turkish constitution, among other points. One year later—and largely on the basis of these comments— Sezer was elected the new president of Turkey over Suleyman Demirel.

Sezer's election was a breath of fresh air for those in favor of reform in Turkey. His comments came at the same time the trial of **Abdullah Ocalan**, the captured leader of the **Kurdistan Workers Party**, was about to begin. As president, Sezer has enjoyed some modest success, but very serious economic and continuing political problems plague Turkey. It also should be noted that in Turkey's parliamentary democracy, the constitution gives the president rather limited powers. In addition, the Turkish military continues to hold ultimate power in the country.

SHABAK. Community living in several dozen villages east of **Mosul** whose religious beliefs are similar to the **Alevis** (Qizilbash) in

Turkey. Although they consider themselves to be Kurds, in recent years the Iraqi government has made strong efforts to Arabize the Shabak. Approximately 20 of their villages were destroyed in the government crackdown at the end of the **Iran–Iraq War** in 1988. Most Shabak are multilingual. Their religious rites are conducted in Turkish, but the mother tongue of most of them is a **Gurani** dialect. They are nontribal peasants who sharecrop on land that belongs to *sayyid* who live in urban areas and have strong moral authority over the Shabak due to the *sayyid* claim to have descended from the Prophet and Ali. Indeed, one of the basic Shabak beliefs is that Allah, Muhammad, and Ali constitute a trinity in which Ali is actually the dominant aspect of the divine. One of their invocations specifically refers to Haji Bektash and the Safawids as the founders of their religion. Some of the poems sung in their religious meetings are reputed to have been composed by Shah Ismail and the Anatolian saint Pir Sultan Abdal.

The Shabaks' sacred book is known as the *Kitab al-Manakib* or *Buyuruk*. It consists of two parts, the second of which resembles the texts of the Alevis in Turkey. Each adult Shabak has a *pir* as a spiritual elder. The *pir* holds regular religious meetings in his house. There are three major annual nocturnal celebrations in which both sexes participate. Termed in earlier literature the *laylat al-kafsha*, these gatherings led to charges of scandalous sexual behavior. Pilgrimages to several local shrines are also an important part of the Shabak ritual.

Their Alevi–Safawid connections help distinguish the Shabak from neighboring heterodox communities, such as the **Yezidis** and the **Sarliyya**, who profess the **Ahl-i Haqq religion**. The nearby **Badjwan** are sometimes said to be a section of the Shabak, but the former are tribally organized while the latter are not. Since all these groups, as well as the **Kakais** and Shiite **Turkomans**, intermarry freely, the boundaries between their religious communities have become somewhat blurred. *See also* GHULAT.

SHABANKARA. Kurdish **tribe** who played an important role for many years in the **Persian** provinces of **Kirmanshah** and Fars in medieval Islamic times. Shabankara was also the name of their country in southern Persia. Their capital was Ig, or Idj. Contemporaries mention the fortifications of Shabankara and the fertility of their country, its mills, and its bazaars.

Shabankara power reached its brief zenith in 1200–1201, when the two sibling *mirs* (Kutb al-Din Mubariz and Nizam al-Din Mahmud) conquered Kirmanshah. The latter brother became notorious for his debauchery and rapacity, however, and the Atabeg of Fars soon reasserted his authority. In 1260, the Mongol Hulegu destroyed Ig and killed the Shabankara *mir,* Muzaffar Muhammad. Muhammad bin Ali Shabankara (c. 1298–1358) was a noted Persian historian who wrote during the Mongol Il-Khanid period.

SHADDADIS. Kurdish dynasty who ruled the area in east Transcaucasia between the Kur and Araxes Rivers between 951 and 1074 C.E., during the decline of the Abbasid caliphate. They had a main line in Gandja and Dwin and a junior line in Ani that lasted long after the senior line ended.

It is not clear just how thoroughly Kurdish the Shaddadis were, as their ethnicity was complicated by their adoption of **Dailamite** names such as Lashkari and Marzuban, as well as **Armenian** ones such as Ashot. This mixture reflected the ethnic diversity of northwestern **Persia** at this time. Contemporary **Christian** sources testify to the fairness the Shaddadis showed their Christian Georgian and Armenian subjects. The Shaddadis were eventually overrun by Turkic incursions.

SHAFII. *See* HANEFI.

SHAH, THE. *See* MUHAMMAD REZA SHAH PAHLAVI.

SHAKAKI. *See* SHIKAK (SHAKAK).

SHAMDINAN (SEMDINLI). *See* NEHRI.

SHARAFNAMA. See BITLISI, SHARAF KHAN.

SHARIF PASHA, MUHAMMAD (1864–194?). Member of the **Baban** family in what is now northern **Iraq** and a cosmopolitan Kurdish leader during the final years of the **Ottoman Empire.** A former Ottoman envoy to Sweden and a member of the first Kurdish **nationalist** organization that appeared in Istanbul early in the 20th century, General Sharif Pasha lacked serious contacts in Kurdistan. He also was a supporter of the deposed sultan, Abdul Hamid II, and as a result had to flee the country after he was sentenced to death following the abortive countercoup of April 1909 against the Committee for Union and Progress. At the beginning of World War I, Sharif Pasha offered his services to **Great Britain** in Mesopotamia, but was turned down. He retired to his luxurious villa in southern **France**. In May 1919, he offered to become *mir* of an independent Kurdistan, but given his lack of a constituency there, the British again rejected his proposal.

Late in his career, however, Sharif Pasha headed the Kurdish delegation at the Paris Peace Conference ending World War I, where he briefly created a stir by cooperating with the **Armenian** delegation headed by Boghos Nubar Pasha. On 20 November 1919, the two presented a joint proposal for separate Kurdish and Armenian states whose exact borders remained to be determined. When the specifics of the agreement were announced, however, both Kurds and Armenians were outraged at how the compromise negated their nationalist positions. In addition, Sharif Pahsa's willingness to talk with the Ottomans left many distrustful of him. As a result, he was forced to resign, leaving the Kurds without representation. The **Kemalist** revival in **Turkey**, of course, further frustrated Kurdish hopes.

SHEIKH. Arabic word originally meaning simply "old man." In Kurdistan, sheikhs are holy men, recipients of popular devotion that at times borders on worship, and leaders of **Sufi** orders. Traditionally, they enjoyed wide respect and thus became ideal mediators in conflicts after the last Kurdish **emirates** were abolished in the 19th century. This political role was reinforced by the Sufi orders, which occasionally enabled sheikhs to mobilize large masses for political aims. Indeed, most of the main Kurdish nationalist leaders of the late 19th and early 20th centuries owed at least some of their power to their sheikhly connections. **Sheikh Ubeydullah of Nehri, Sheikh Mahmud Barzinji**, and **Sheikh Said of Palu** come readily to mind. **Mulla Mustafa Barzani** and **Jalal Talabani** also owed their initial power to their association with families of sheikhs.

In the 20th century, however, the power of sheikhs has greatly declined before the forces of modernization. Following the uprising of Sheikh Said in **Turkey** in 1925, the *tekiyes* (religious meeting places) were closed, and sheikhs were persecuted and exiled as reactionary opponents of the modern Republic of Turkey. Some sheikhs were even executed. Even more important in this decline of sheikhly influence were various socioeconomic developments. Mass migration to the cities, better education and communication networks, more effective governments, and improved agricultural techniques made the sheikh less important as a mediator and more likely to be seen as an exploiter or even a charlatan. Many sheikhs died without appointing a successor, the sheikh of **Barzan** being a noted example.

Nevertheless, sheikhs continue to exist, even in Turkey, where they had gone underground after 1925. Indeed, after the institution of competitive politics in Turkey in 1950, some sheikhs emerged as important vote-getters, especially for the Democratic Party of Adnan Menderes. Sheikh Salahaddin of Khizan, who became a member of the Turkish parliament, was a prime example. His son, **Kamran Inan**, remains an influential politician in Turkey.

SHIKAK (SHAKAK). Tribal confederation that became powerful in the second half of the 19th century on both sides of the **Ottoman–Persian** border in the mountainous regions west and northwest of Lake Urumiya. The Shikak are Sunni Muslim and speak **Kurmanji**. They obtained a reputation for attacking both the Kurdish and **Christian rayat** (peasants) and refusing to pay taxes. In some of the literature, they are confused with the Shakaki (a Turkish-speaking **Alevi tribe** of Kurdish origin), who live to the east and northeast of Tabriz and early in the 20th century provided four regiments for the Qajar shah's army. The relationship between the Shikak and Shakaki does seem to be more than a mere similarity of names.

The Shikak opposed **Sheikh Ubeydullah of Nehri** when he invaded Persia in 1880. In 1896, the Shikak ambushed some 800 **Armenian** revolutionaries retreating from Van in the Ottoman Empire, while two years later they were chasing Armenians on behalf of the Persians. Shikak tribesmen captured **Sheikh Abdul Salam II** of **Barzan**, the elder brother of **Mulla Mustafa Barzani**, and handed him over to the Ottomans for execution in 1914, when the sheikh tried to flee after being charged with conspiring with the **Russians**.

Ismail Agha Simko, the famous Iranian Kurdish rebel of the 1920s, was the leader of the Abdui section of the Shikak. During the days of the **Mahabad Republic of Kurdistan**, the Shikak played a cautiously opportunistic role and quickly deserted the cause. They acted similarly in 1979, when central authority was temporarily absent following the Islamic revolution. Likewise, the Tudeh (Iranian Communist Party) office in Urumiya in northwestern Iran was able only temporarily to enroll thousands of Shikaks in 1945.

SHILLET. The Shillet and Chokhsor were two powerful **tribal** confederations in the **emirate** of **Botan** in what is now southeastern **Turkey**. With the demise of Botan as an emirate in 1847, both confederations quickly fell apart. The Miran tribe from the Chokhsor confederation came to dominate the others for a period of time, **Mustafa Pasha of the Miran** in the 1890s providing a prime example of this dominance. The Shillet confederation was composed of the Batuan, Kichan, Teyyan, Kherikan, and Musereshan tribes.

SHIVAN, DOCTOR. Nom de guerre of Sait Kirmizitoprak, a leftist ethnic Kurd from Tunceli in **Turkey**. While in prison in the 1960s, Dr. Shivan became friends with **Sait Elci**, a conservative nationalist who headed the small **Kurdistan Democratic Party of Turkey (KDPT)**. After his release from prison in 1969, Dr. Shivan went to northern Iraq and set up his own leftist base of the KDPT in the Zakho area. In 1971, he captured and executed Elci when he, too, crossed over into northern **Iraq**. **Mulla Mustafa Barzani** then apparently apprehended Shivan and executed him. Shivan's group briefly reemerged as the small Kurdistan Vanguard Workers Party, or Pesheng.

SHORESH. In English, "Revolution," a small, short-lived Kurdish communist party formed in Iraqi Kurdistan in 1943 and named after its journal. Shoresh played an active role in Kurdish politics until the party finally dissolved itself in 1946, largely because of pressures caused by **Mulla Mustafa Barzani** and the new all-embracing **Kurdistan Democratic Party** (KDP), which was established on 16 August 1946.

Hamza Abdullah, the first secretary general of the KDP, had been an active member of Shoresh. For many years thereafter, there was a Kurdish section of the **Iraqi Communist Party**. In 1988, this Kurdish section was one of the smaller founding members of the **Iraqi Kurdistan Front**.

SIMKO, ISMAIL AGHA (1875–1930). While considered by many as a notorious Iranian Kurdish adventurer and **tribal** chief *par excellence,* for some others, he was a nascent Kurdish **nationalist** who established an autonomous Kurdish government in the area south and west of Lake Urumiya in northwestern **Iran** for much of the period from 1918 to 1922. To do so, he created a strong army, which for several years proved superior to government troops and on numerous occasions actually defeated them. For a short period, Simko even formed a cross-border alliance with Sheikh Taha of **Nehri** in Turkish Kurdistan and was in contact with other Kurdish nationalist leaders in **Iraq** and **Turkey**.

Simko exploited the instability of the frontier region at the end of World War I to build his power. At one time or another, he took aid from **Russia** and the **Soviet Union**, Turkey, **Great Britain**, and Iran. In March 1918, Simko also treacherously killed his guest, the **Assyrian** leader Mar Shimun. (The Assyrians had fled from their mountainous home in **Hakkari** in Turkey and settled in the region claimed by Simko.) By February 1920, however, Iranian government forces had temporarily defeated him and chased him into exile, but they then gave him clemency. Soon Simko was building an even greater force. He was at the height of his power in 1921 and even published a newspaper in Sawdj–Bulak (Mahabad).

Many Kurds feared and disliked Simko, however, and on 9 August 1922, he was dealt a sharp defeat by the Iranian government from which he never really recovered. He spent his remaining years trying to regain his former position, moving from Iraq to Turkey, while mending fences with Sheikh Taha of Nehri and **Sheikh Mahmud Barzinji**. In the spring of 1925, Simko returned to Iran and replaced Amr Khan, his rival, as the chief of the Abdui **Shikak** tribe. Soon he was again in open rebellion. When half of his troops defected to Amr Khan, however, the modern government troops of Reza Khan (later **Reza Shah Pahlavi**) easily defeated him. In 1930, the government tricked him into returning to Iran and killed him in an ambush.

Simko's main strength, and his main weakness, was the Kurdish tribal system. While he was in ascendance, the tribes gave him a great deal of support that, however, melted away as soon as he was defeated. Simko had neither clear nationalist goals nor any political party base to support him. He remained at heart a tribal leader who had little but disdain for urban livers and sedentary, nontribal peasants. In the end, Simko was defeated by the modernizing government of Reza Shah Pahlavi, which successfully sought to break tribal power and centralize the state. Nevertheless, after **Abdul Rahman Ghassemlou** and **Qazi Muhammad**, Simko was probably the best-known Iranian Kurdish leader during the 20th century. All three, however, ended up being killed by the Iranian government.

SINCAR, MEHMET (?–1993). Demokrasi Partisi (DEP) member of the Turkish parliament murdered in broad daylight while attending a political rally in the southeastern city of Batman on 4 September 1993. His assassination was one of many involving prominent nonviolent ethnic Kurdish leaders in **Turkey** that have been blamed on the **Hizbullah–Contras**, an apparently right-wing hit squad supported by the Turkish government during the war against the **Kurdistan Workers Party (PKK)**.

Sincar originally had been elected to parliament in 1991 as a member of the pro-Kurdish **Halkin Emek Partisi (HEP)**, or Peoples Labor Party, which had been formed in 1990 as a legal Kurdish party and had entered the Turkish parliament as members of Erdal Inonu's Social Democratic Party. When HEP was closed down by the Constitutional Court in July 1993, it simply reincarnated itself as DEP.

Sincar was not given the state funeral he was entitled to as a member of parliament, and DEP supporters were not allowed into Ankara for the funeral services. Just before his assassination, Sincar's heavy police protection had been pulled. Alaattin Kanat, a former member of the **Kurdistan Workers Party** who became a Turkish government agent carrying out assassinations of government foes, was supposedly seen in Batman the day Sincar was assassinated. Sincar's murderers have never been apprehended, and his case is an egregious example of **human rights** violations in Turkey.

SINDJABI. Kurdish **tribe** in the Iranian province of **Kirmanshah** who were loyal to the state and played an important role in the defense of its frontiers against the **Ottomans**. In part, this situation was probably due to the tribe's location on the plains, rather than in a mountainous locale where access to refuges would more likely exist. The tribe apparently only gained its name in 1838, when it sent a detachment to take part in the recapture of Herat, now in western Afghanistan. Since the lining of their tunics was made of squirrel fur, they were called Sindjabi, or those who dressed in the fur of squirrels. The Sindjabi chieftains were Shiite. The Sindjabi are noted, however, for being the only tribe that assimilated within itself, in a spirit of great tolerance, Sunnis, Shiites, and **Ahl-i Haqq**.

Shir Muhammad Khan Sandjabi continued to defend the state's frontiers into more modern times and was officially called Samsam al-Mamalik, or the Sharp Sword of the Kingdom. His grandson, Dr. Karim Bakhtiyar Sandjabi, was minister of national education under Muhammad Mussadegh in the 1950s and minister of foreign affairs at the beginning of the Islamic Revolution in the late 1970s. In contemporary times, the tribe has suffered economically because of the government's policies of settling the tribes.

SIRNAK. Small city in southeastern **Turkey** of some 25,000 ethnic Kurds. On the pretext that units of the **Kurdistan Workers Party (PKK)** were hiding there, the Turkish army virtually destroyed the city on 18 August 1992. Official reports put the death toll at 34, but at least another 500 were killed over the next 30 days. Sirnak thus became a byword for excessive brutality by the Turkish military in its struggle against the PKK. Similar military operations took place against such other ethnic Kurdish towns in Turkey as Cukurca, Dargecit, Yuksekova, and Lice, among others.

SOANE, ELY BANNISTER (1881–1923). Politically controversial writer, traveler, and from 1919 to 1921, political officer of **Great Britain** in northern **Iraq**. Although he considered **Sheikh Mahmud Barzinji** a rogue, Major Soane was deeply committed to Kurdish autonomy and eventually lost his post as a result.

Soane replaced Major **Edward Noel**, Sheikh Mahmud's supporter, as British political officer in **Sulaymaniya** in March 1919. After the Sheikh's first defeat in June 1919, Soane strictly administered the area, but also initiated public works projects and encouraged what was then considered the novel use of written Kurdish in newspapers and the schools. When the Cairo conference in March 1921 finally decided to abandon the idea of Kurdish autonomy as part of the overall policy of maintaining British control as cheaply as possible, Soane was summarily dismissed.

Soane was the author of *To Mesopotamia and Kurdistan in Disguise* (1912) and "A Short Anthology of Gurani Poetry" (1921). Following the death of Soane's widow, Lynette Lindfield–Soane, in 1994, the Soane Trust for Kurdistan was established to promote projects dealing with Kurdistan. The trust is administered by Sheri Laizer, a British/New Zealand author and friend of the Kurds.

SORAN. Kurdish **emirate** in what is now northern **Iraq** that was in decline before experiencing a brief revival early in the 19th century. Under Mir Muhammad Pasha of Rawanduz, or Soran (called Miri Kor, or the blind *mir,* because of an affliction of the eyes), the emirate of Soran ruthlessly conquered much of what is now northern Iraq after 1814, only to be extinguished by the **Ottomans** in 1834. These events involved much intrigue among the Ottomans, **Persians**, **Great Britain**, and **Russia**. Miri Kor was finally invited to Istanbul and given many honors, but he mysteriously disappeared on his way back to Kurdistan. His brother Rasul became governor of Rawanduz until the *wali,* or Ottoman governor, of Baghdad expelled him in 1847.

SORANI. One of the two major Kurdish dialects or **languages.** Sorani is spoken by some 6 million Kurds in southeastern Iraqi Kurdistan and **Iran**, while **Kurmanji** is spoken by some 15 million in **Turkey** and northwestern Iraqi Kurdistan. Both belong to the southwestern group of Iranian languages. It is said that grammatically the two differ from each other as much as English and German do. The differences in vocabulary are of perhaps the same degree as those between German and Dutch. Nevertheless, the speakers of the two languages are able to communicate with one another with some difficulty.

Major dialects of Sorani include **Mukri**, Ardalani, Garmiyani, Khushnow, Pizhdar, Warmawa, Kirmanshahi, and Arbili (or Sorani proper). The split between **Massoud Barzani's Kurdistan Democratic Party (KDP)** and **Jalal Talabani's Patriotic Union of**

Kurdistan (PUK) partly reflects the fact that the former speak Kurmanji, while the latter speak Sorani. During the time of **Mulla Mustafa Barzani** and the **KDP Politburo** of **Ibrahim Ahmad**, there was a tendency to view Sorani speakers as urban intellectuals and Kurmanji speakers as more backward, tribal people. This characterization, of course, was a gross oversimplification.

Dimili (Zaza) in the extreme northwest of Kurdistan and **Gurani** in the southeast are probably older Kurdish languages from the northwestern Iranian language group and were largely, but not completely, replaced beginning in the 18th century by Kurmanji and Sorani.

SOUTHEAST ANATOLIA PROJECT. *See* GUNEYDOGU ANADOLU PROJESI.

SOVIET UNION. Inheritor of tsarist **Russia**'s interest in and sometimes influence over Kurdistan. During the Cold War, many in the West believed that the Kurds offered a possible fifth column to facilitate Soviet expansion into the Middle East. In retrospect, however, this Soviet role was largely exaggerated because the Soviets usually calculated that supporting the regional governments in which the Kurds lived would prove more useful. Certainly among the great powers, **Great Britain** played a much more important historical role regarding the Kurds. In more recent years, the **United States** has inherited this position.

Early in its history, the Soviet Union signed a Treaty of Friendship with **Kemalist Turkey.** The resulting relationship gave invaluable aid to both fledgling states and certainly helped Turkey to suppress its Kurdish population. At one time or another, the Soviet Union also gave important support to **Iraq** and **Syria** to the detriment of their Kurdish populations.

However, the Soviet Union was the only foreign backer of the ill-fated **Mahabad Republic of Kurdistan** in 1946 and also offered a home to the exiled **Mulla Mustafa Barzani** from 1947 to 1958. Indeed, Barzani was for a time called the Red Mulla, a title that proved ludicrous, however, given his subsequent career. During the 1920s, the Soviet Union also housed a Red Kurdistan in **Lachin**, but this experiment was dropped by the end of the decade.

Joseph Stalin exiled many Kurds to central Asia during the 1930s and 1940s. Some claim that as many as 1 million largely assimilated

Kurds now live in various parts of the former Soviet Union. Although most experts list considerably smaller figures, probably at least 200,000 Kurds presently inhabit the area.

The Communist Party's organizational style has influenced that of the **Kurdistan Workers Party (PKK)**, the **Patriotic Union of Kurdistan (PUK)**, and even the more conservative **Kurdistan Democratic Party**, which use terms such as politburo and central committee. Although the PKK began life as an avowedly Marxist party, as to some extent did even the PUK, in the long run little should be assumed by such organizational titles other than that they were at the time the fad. *See also* RUSSIA.

STATE SECURITY COURTS (TURKEY). State Security Courts in **Turkey** were toned-down, modern-day versions of the earlier **independence tribunals** during the 1920s. Turkey's eight state security courts had jurisdiction over civilian cases involving the **Anti-Terrorist Law** of 1991, which contained the notorious Article 8, covering membership in illegal organizations and the propagation of ideas banned by law as damaging the indivisible unity of the state. Each court consisted of five members: two civilian judges, one military judge, and two prosecutors. In all, there were 18 such panels.

These courts took a leading role in trying to stifle violent and nonviolent Kurdish activists and in so doing provide a veneer of legality to the state's campaign against Kurdish **nationalist** demands. Thus these courts closed down newspapers and narrowly interpreted the right of free speech. Nurset Demiral, the former head of the Ankara State Security Court, became both the symbol and reality of the problem these courts presented to democratic freedoms. For example, Demiral demanded the death penalty for **Leyla Zana** and the other **Demokrasi Partisi** members of parliament who were finally imprisoned in 1994. Later, Demiral joined the ultraright Nationalist Action Party led by Alparslan Turkes.

Turkey eventually abolished the state security courts in an attempt to help meet the requirements for membership in the **European Union (EU)**.

SUFI. The Arabic word *suf* literally means wool, so a Sufi is a man of wool, or an ascetic, wool being a material worn by such people.

"Sufi" and "dervish" are terms used throughout the **Islamic** world for men who belong to mystical brotherhoods (*tariqa*, plural *turuq*) that emphasize the immanence of God rather than His transcendental aspect. The Sufi orders in the Muslim world rose during the 12th and 13th centuries and were somewhat analogous to the monastic orders of medieval Christendom.

In Kurdistan, there are only two basic Sufi orders, the **Naqshbandi** and the **Qadiri**. The term Sufi is used for the *murids,* or followers of the Naqshbandi order, while dervishes are followers of the Qadiri. To the Naqshbandi, the term "dervish" possesses pejorative connotations of backwardness and superstition involving ecstatic utterances, trances, fire-eating, and self-mutilation.

The Sufi orders serve both to strengthen and divide Kurdish society. Those who belong to the same *tariqa* order possess an obvious bond, regardless of their tribal affiliation. However, relations between different orders or even different *tariqa* networks are often tense. A well-known example was the conflict between the two Naqshbandi families—the Sadate **Nehri** and the **sheikhs** of **Barzan** in the latter half of the 19th century.

Mustafa Kemal Ataturk banned the Sufi orders in **Turkey** following the uprising of the Naqshbandi sheikh **Said** of Palu in 1925. The orders continued to exist underground, however, because they gave their adherents an identity and a way to deal with the changing world, especially after the abolition of the caliphate. When the Democrat Party came to power in Turkey in 1950, it allowed the revival of many traditional Islamic values. Thus there was ironically a certain amount of Sufi resurgence in Turkey, while in **Iraq**, **Iran**, and **Syria** the Sufi orders remained in decay.

SULAYMANIYA. Or "Slemani" in Kurdish, city with a population of some 750,000 and probably the second largest in the area ruled by the **Kurdistan Regional Government** of northern **Iraq**. Often called the cultural capital of Iraqi Kurdistan, Sulaymaniya is located in the **Sorani** area, or the southeastern area of northern Iraq. Compared to ancient **Irbil**, Sulaymaniya is a much newer city, as it was only founded in 1785, when it became the capital of the **Baban emirate**. The city was named for Buyuk Suleyman Pasha, who was the governor of Baghdad in 1780–1802. After the last Baban *mir* was deposed in 1850, the Barzinji family of **sheikhs** came to wield great power.

In more modern times, Sulaymaniya was the seat of **Sheikh Mahmud Barzinji**, who led several failed uprisings against **Great Britain** during the 1920s. More recently, the city has served as the capital of the regional administration of **Jalal Talabani**'s **Patriotic Union of Kurdistan**. It is the site of one of the three universities in Iraqi Kurdistan and in the past few years has shared amply in the relative prosperity brought on by de facto Iraqi Kurdish autonomy and the receipt of Iraqi **oil** revenues through the **United Nations**. Sulaymaniya is also the name of the surrounding governorate, one of three constituting northern Iraq.

SURCHI. An important Kurdish **tribe** in Iraqi Kurdistan who live near the **Barzanis** and have often been at odds with them. In the time of **Mulla Mustafa Barzani**, the Surchi were *josh* supporting the government of **Abdul Karim Kassem**. During the Kurdish uprising of 1991, however, the Surchi, under their leader Omar Surchi, joined the Kurdish nationalists.

The Surchi became one of the leaders of the tribally oriented Kurdistan Conservative Party (also known as the Kurdish Tribes Society or Mosul Vilayet Council), which was created in September 1991. On 16 June 1996, the Barzani-led **Kurdistan Democratic Party (KDP)** killed Hussein Agha Surchi, an important member of the Surchi family, during a squabble over the Surchis' ultimate allegiances in the KDP's civil war against the **Patriotic Union of Kurdistan**. The incident caused a great deal of ill will among the Kurds and illustrated their continuing tribal divisions.

SUSURLUK. Site of a notorious car accident in **Turkey** on 3 November 1996 in which in the same vehicle a well-known, right-wing terrorist and convicted drug dealer, supposedly a fugitive from justice, was killed along with a high-ranking police official, while a Kurdish **village guard** chieftain (Sedat **Bucak**) who also was a member of the Turkish parliament was seriously injured. The accident seemed to give credence to allegations of a state infiltrated at the highest levels by organized crime.

Among many other specific allegations, Susurluk indicated that

Turkey had probably created an illegal organization to extrajudicially kill several thousand ethnic Kurdish civilians who were perceived as supporters of the **Kurdistan Workers Party**. In return for their services, Turkey allowed gangsters to traffic in drugs, murder their opponents, and engage in a host of other illegal activities. Despite the widespread publicity, only the lightest sentences have been handed down very reluctantly in the Susurluk case.

SYKES–PICOT AGREEMENT. Originally a secret pact in 1916 among **Great Britain, France,** and **Russia** detailing their plans to partition the **Ottoman Empire**—and thus most of Kurdistan—at the end of World War I. Sir Mark Sykes for Britain, François Picot for France, and Sergei Sazanov for Russia drew the agreement up, but Russia dropped out following the Bolshevik revolution. The new **Soviet** government then revealed the agreement to the world.

Originally, the Sykes–Picot Agreement gave most of the Kurdish areas in what became **Turkey** and **Syria** to the French and gave the areas in Iraq and parts of Turkey to Russia. After Russia dropped out of the agreement, Britain took over the Russian portion of **Mosul** and attached it to its mandate, **Iraq**. The Sykes–Picot Agreement became a byword for British–French imperialist control of the Middle East and, with it, manipulation and control of the Kurds. With the quick rise of the **Kemalists** in Turkey, however, the new Republic of Turkey acquired much of what were originally to be French and Russian areas. These areas then became Turkish Kurdistan.

SYRIA. One of the four Middle Eastern states containing parts of historical Kurdistan. Approximately a million Kurds live in Syria, many of whose grandparents crossed the frontier to escape Turkish repression after the failure of the **Sheikh Said** rebellion in 1925. As a result, many Kurds in Syria have been denied Syrian citizenship and thus lack the most elementary rights. This lack of citizenship also makes it particularly difficult to estimate their numbers.

Although much larger Kurdish populations exist in **Turkey, Iran,** and **Iraq**, the Kurds in Syria constitute as much as 9 percent of the total population and thus represent the largest ethnic minority in Syria. They are concentrated in three noncontiguous parts of northern Syria: **Kurd Dagh** and Kobani (Ain al-Arab) in Aleppo province and the northern part of the province of Hasaka. The latter is part of **Jazire** and is contiguous to Turkish and Iraqi Kurdistan in the area the **French** called le Bec de Canard, or the "Duck's Beak." Qamishli is the largest city here and is situated just across the Turkish border from the city of Nisibin.

The repressive **Baathist Party** under Hafez Assad (and since 2000 his son, Bashar) has ruled Syria since 1970. Along with Turkey, Iran, and Iraq, Syria strongly opposes the establishment of any Kurdish state because it would be a threat to its existing territorial integrity. At times, all four states have worked together to prevent such an eventuality.

Nevertheless, as have Iran, Iraq, and Turkey, Syria has not hesitated to use the Kurds against the other three, Turkey especially. Indeed, for many years Syria and the **Kurdistan Workers Party (PKK)** conducted what might justifiably be called a strategic alliance. As early as 1979, Syria provided a haven for **Abdullah Ocalan**, the leader of the PKK. All through the 1980s and up to October 1998, the Syrians allowed the PKK to maintain military camps on their territory or territory Syria controlled in Lebanon. The **Mazlum Korkmaz Camp** in the **Bekaa Valley** was probably the most famous example. From Syrian territory, the PKK could raid into Turkey and then retreat to a safe house.

There were many reasons for Syria's position. **Water** was probably the main one, as Turkey controlled the flow of the Euphrates River into Syria. As Turkey's **Guneydogu Anadolu Projesi** (GAP), or Southeast Anatolia Project, of harnessing the rivers to the north neared completion, Syria used the PKK as a bargaining tool in an unsuccessful attempt to obtain a more favorable guaranteed annual water quota from Turkey. Smoldering animosities concerning the Turkish annexation of Hatay (Alexandretta) province in 1939 also led to the Syrian willingness to support the PKK. Some believe that the PKK kept the lid on Syria's Kurds in return for its Syrian bases. Whatever the reasons, a dialogue of the deaf occurred between Turkey and Syria over the situation for many years. With the collapse of Syria's **Soviet** mentor and because of Turkey's new strategic understanding with **Israel**, however, Turkey finally was able to force Syria to expel Ocalan in October 1998. This then led to Ocalan's capture in February 1999.

Over the years, Syria has also provided considerable logistical aid to the two main Iraqi Kurdish parties, the **Kurdistan Democratic Party** and the **Patriotic Union of Kurdistan**, both as a tool against Iraq and as a way to play the Iraqi Kurds off against each other so that they could not form an independent state.

– T –

TALABANI, HERO. Daughter of the late **Ibrahim Ahmad** and the wife of **Jalal Talabani**, the longtime leader of the **Patriotic Union of Kurdistan (PUK)**. Hero Talabani has played an important political role in her own right and is a member of the parliament in the **Kurdistan Regional Government**. She is an advocate for **women**'s rights and has probably influenced her husband to be, too. She and her husband have two sons, Bafel, a physical education instructor, and Qubad, who has studied automotive mechanics. Both sons are slowly beginning to play political roles.

TALABANI, JALAL (1933–). Jalal Talabani established the **Patriotic Union of Kurdistan (PUK)** in June 1975 and has been its secretary general ever since. Along with his rival, **Massoud Barzani**, the president of the **Kurdistan Democratic Party (KDP)**, Talabani has long been one of the two main leaders of the Iraqi Kurds. Among the Kurds, Talabani is universally known as Man (Uncle) Jalal. He is married to **Hero (Ahmad) Talabani**, the daughter of his political mentor, **Ibrahim Ahmad**, and a notable Kurdish figure in her own right.

Jalal Talabani was born in Kelkan, a village near Lake Dukan in the **Sorani** area of Iraqi Kurdistan. The Talabani family itself goes back at least some 300 years. The Talabani **sheikhs** belonged to the **Qadiri** order and played an important religious and political role that no doubt helped young Jalal Talabani get his start.

Talabani has been very active in politics all his life. When he was only 13 years old, he formed a secret Kurdish student association. The following year, he became a member of the KDP, and he was elected to its central committee when he was only 18 years old. A graduate of the Baghdad law school, Talabani served in the Iraqi military as a tank commander in 1959 and also practiced journalism.

As an associate of **Ibrahim Ahmad** in the **KDP Politburo**, Talabani had an off-again, on-again relationship with **Mulla Mustafa Barzani**. In time, Barzani came to characterize Talabani as "an agent for everybody"—that is, he would work for anyone—and thus Talabani played only a minor role during Barzani's last years. Following Barzani's final defeat in March 1975, Talabani founded the PUK, and by 1977 he had returned to Iraqi Kurdistan.

Talabani's life then became interwoven with the Kurdish struggle in Iraqi Kurdistan and the policies of the PUK. Along with Mulla Mustafa Barzani's son, Massoud Barzani, Talabani has long been one of the two main leaders of the Iraqi Kurds. The relationship between Talabani and the younger Barzani has been part of the KDP–PUK struggle for power among the Iraqi Kurds, which intertwined with cooperation between the two parties for the larger Iraqi Kurdish cause. Although the situation is, of course, more complicated, Talabani has been characterized as more modern and progressive than Barzani.

Compared to Massoud Barzani, Jalal Talabani has been much more the world traveler and international negotiator. After Iraq's defeat in 1991, for example, Talabani broke ancient taboos and journeyed to Ankara to meet Turkish president **Turgut Ozal**. During the drawn-out talks with the Iraqi government in 1991, **Saddam Hussein** planted a hypocritical kiss on Talabani's surprised face. Jalal Talabani speaks good English and has visited the **United States**, **Great Britain**, **Turkey**, **Syria**, and **Iran**, among others, on numerous occasions. Many of his family members have long lived in Great Britain.

Although Talabani holds a reputation as being mercurial and too clever for his own good, his championship of Kurdish **nationalism**, progressive development, and **human rights**, as well as his experience, cannot be gainsaid and are virtually unique among contemporary Kurdish leaders.

TARGUM. *See* NEO-ARAMAIC.

TATLISES, IBRAHIM (1952–). Very popular folk singer in **Turkey**, where he was born in Urfa as an ethnic Kurd. In the late 1980s, Tatlises was asked to sing in Kurdish at a cultural evening in Usak, Turkey. He declined by declaring: "I am a Kurd, but the laws ban me from singing in Kurdish." He was then prosecuted for "separatist propaganda." Even though he was not convicted, this incident illustrates the constant harassment ethnic Kurds have long suffered in Turkey because of their Kurdish culture.

TEWFIQ, HAJI (1863–1950). Writer whose nom de plume was Piremerd, or "the Old Man," and who was one of the most important figures of modern Kurdish **literature**. A journalist from **Sulaymaniya**, Tewfiq also was known as an original spirit and great traveler. He was much admired by the Kurdish public and his work illustrated the beauty of the Kurds' land, **language**, literature, and history.

TOBB REPORT. In August 1995, **Turkey**'s Chamber of Commerce and Commodity Exchange (TOBB)—the country's main business federation—issued a 168-page report on the Kurdish problem formally entitled *The Southeast Problem: Diagnoses and Observations.* The TOBB Report quickly became a controversial and sensational issue in Turkey, as it illustrated both the importance of the Kurdish problem to the future of Turkey and the country's bitter, almost paranoid fear of compromising its Turkish identity. Dogu Ergil, the head of the political science branch of the faculty of political sciences at Ankara University, was the main researcher, while Yalim Erez—the chairman of TOBB, a close political adviser of then–prime minister **Tansu Ciller**, and himself an ethnic Kurd—authorized it.

The TOBB Report was based on interviews with 1,267 people, all but 3.6 percent of whom were Turkish Kurds. Slightly more than 90 percent of them were male. All were either residents of the southeastern provinces of **Diyarbakir**, Batman, and **Mardin** or were recent immigrants from the southeast now living in the southern Mediterranean cities of Adana, Mersin, and Antalya.

The report analyzed the demographic, economic, religious, ethnic, linguistic, and political characteristics of the interviewees. Among its principal findings were that although 96 percent spoke Kurdish as their mother tongue, 75 percent did not believe that the state could defeat the **Kurdistan Workers Party (PKK)**, 43 percent backed some sort of a federation as the best solution, and 85 percent did not demand a separate Kurdish state. Professor Ergil concluded from these findings that most Turkish citizens of Kurdish ancestry would be satisfied by the legal and constitutional guarantee of their Kurdish cultural identity. The report also argued that the PKK would eventually move its struggle onto the political plane, a change that would cause Turkey considerable difficulties, since the state had pursued solely a military strategy. By late 2002, this prediction seemed to be coming true.

Despite its rather innocuous and even hopeful findings, much of the Turkish establishment effected outrage, lambasting Ergil as an opportunist, a left-wing extremist, an agent of the U.S. **Central Intelligence Agency**, and a PKK sympathizer. This unwillingness to read the report seriously, and instead resorting to ad hominem attacks on its author, illustrated well the inability of Turkey to come to grips with the Kurdish problem.

TRIBE. *See* ASHIRET.

TUNCELI. *See* DERSIM.

TURKEY. Slightly more than half of the Kurds in the entire world live in Turkey, where depending on how one counts them they make up some 12–15 million people, or as much as 18 to 23 percent of the total population.

There were three great Kurdish revolts during the early history of the modern Republic of Turkey: **Sheikh Said** in 1925, **Ararat** in 1927–30, and **Dersim** (now called Tunceli) in 1936–38. All were brutally crushed and attempts were made to erase the very name of the Kurds through assimilation and exile. Under **Mustafa Kemal Ataturk**, all Kurdish schools, organizations, and publications, as well as religious institutions such as *tekiyes* (**Sufi** fraternities) and *madrasahs* (religious schools) were closed. Use of the term **Mountain Turks** when referring to the Turkish Kurds served as a code for these actions.

Turkey also took a leading role in suppressing any manifestation of Kurdish **nationalism** in any other bordering state. To this day, for example, Turkey continues to take an almost schizophrenic attitude toward the **Kurdistan Regional Government** in northern **Iraq**. The fear is that any Kurdish state in northern Iraq would encourage Kurdish nationalism in Turkey. Some in Turkey also harbor hopes for reclaiming **Mosul**, or northern Iraq, which was lost to **Great Britain**, and subsequently Iraq, after World War I.

The modern Kurdish national movement in Turkey grew out of the intellectual ferment caused by the leftist, Marxist movement that formed during the 1960s. This in turn was largely a result of Turkey's halting attempts to democratize and join the West. In November 1978, **Abdullah (Apo) Ocalan** created the **Kurdistan Workers Party (PKK)**, which formally began its revolt in August 1984. Both sides employed ruthless tactics that began to polarize much of Turkey and that by the end of the century had led to more than 37,000 deaths.

Gradually, however, Turkey was able to militarily defeat the PKK and, in October 1998, they forced the expulsion of Ocalan from **Syria**, where he had lived since 1979. Following Ocalan's capture in February 1999, the PKK revolt quickly came to a practical end. Kurdish nationalism, however, had been bestirred in a way that could never again be denied. The question of Kurdish rights now had to be solved for Turkey to progress and even survive.

In December 1999, Turkey was accepted as a candidate member of the **European Union**. Eventual membership, however, in part is dependent on a satisfactory solution to the Kurdish problem. This has brought about a great constitutional debate in Turkey upon which the country's future depends. In August 2002, the Turkish parliament finally passed significant reform measures that, if implemented, may help solve the Kurdish problem by granting Kurdish **language**, cultural, and educational rights. These reforms, of course, would also help alleviate broader problems concerning **human rights**. It remains to be seen if this indeed will occur.

Meanwhile, the ethnic Kurdish population in Turkey is growing faster than is the ethnic Turkish population. In addition, younger people make up a considerably higher percentage of the Kurdish population than of the Turkish population. Furthermore, more than half the ethnic Kurdish population in Turkey now lives west of Ankara. Istanbul has arguably the largest Kurdish population of any city in the world. *See also* AK PARTISI (AKP); GULF WAR II; OTTOMAN EMPIRE.

TURKOMANS. The Turkomans first entered Kurdistan around 1000 C.E. as part of the wave of Turkic invasions of the Middle East. During the 14th century, two rival Turkoman dynasties—the **Ak Koyunlu** and the Kara Koyunlu—ruled much of Kurdistan. Many of these Turkomans were Qizilbash, or **Alevis**, who came to support the Safavid **Persians** against the **Ottomans**.

Although population statistics are inadequate, the Turkomans today number approximately 500,000 and constitute the second largest ethnic minority in **Iraq** after the Kurds. The Turkomans themselves and **Turkey** (which often uses the Turkomans to exercise influence in northern Iraq) claim as many as 2.5 or even 3 million, a number much too high. Many Turkomans still live under Iraqi government control. In 1920, ethnically diverse **Kirkuk** in northern Iraq still had a plurality of Turkomans. Indeed, as recently as 1958 there were more Turkomans in that city than Kurds, a factor that complicated **Mulla Mustafa Barzani**'s claim to it. In July 1959, riots in Kirkuk involving the Kurds and communists killed some 50 Turkomans; these riots still remain a divisive memory. During the 1920s, Turkomans also still constituted a majority along the high road between **Mosul** and Baghdad.

Unlike the **Christian Assyrians**, the Turkomans did not join the **Iraqi Kurdistan Front** when it was created in 1988 to bring unity to the Kurdish groups fighting against the Iraqi government in northern Iraq. This was probably because the Turkomans did not want to alienate their outside protector, Turkey, and also because many Turkomans still lived under Baghdad's control. The Turkomans also did not participate in the elections that created the **Kurdistan Regional Government (KRG)** in May 1992. In addition, the Iraqi Turkoman Front—an umbrella organization for several Iraqi Turkoman parties that was created and is funded by Turkey—is openly hostile to the KRG.

However, some Turkomans, such as Jawdat Najar, have participated in the regional administration in **Irbil** run by the **Kurdistan Democratic Party (KDP)**. Muzafar Arsalan, the leader of the National Turkoman Party of Iraq, also was appointed to the executive council of the opposition **Iraqi National Congress**. In recent years, the Turkomans have suffered as much as the Kurds at the hands of **Saddam Hussein**.

– U –

UBEYDULLAH OF NEHRI, SHEIKH (1831–?). Son of Sheikh Sayyid Taha I of Nehri and one of the most powerful Kurdish leaders of the 19th century. In 1880, Sheikh Ubeydullah led a famous but ultimately unsuccessful revolt that is sometimes said to have been the prototype for subsequent Kurdish **nationalist** revolts. Explaining his actions, Sheikh Ubeydullah famously wrote the consul general of **Great Britain** in Tabriz that "the Kurdish nation . . . is a people apart. . . . We want our affairs to be in our own hands."

After his two sons had already commenced attacks within the **Persian Empire**—apparently because of the way the Persian government had been treating local **tribal** leaders who acknowledged Sheikh Ubeydullah's religious authority without consulting the sheikh—Ubeydullah himself crossed the border from the **Ottoman Empire** into Persia. After initial success, however, Ubeydullah's tribal forces broke up before a determined Persian counterattack.

The Ottomans dealt rather leniently with Ubeydullah, simply exiling him first to Istanbul and then, after his escape in 1882, to the Hijaz, where he died in 1883. This is because Sheikh Ubeydullah probably had the sultan's tacit consent to prevent the emergence of any **Christian Armenian** state and prevent the encroachment of Western reforms into the sultan's eastern domains. Earlier, Sheikh Ubeydullah had been appointed commander of the Kurdish tribal forces in the Russo–Turkish War of 1877–78. As a **Naqshbandi**, he not only would defend Sunni **Islam** against the Christians and Shiite Persians, but also support the Ottoman Empire.

In retrospect, therefore, Sheikh Ubeydullah's revolt was more of a large Kurdish tribal revolt partially manipulated by the Ottomans to contain Western pressures for reform that might threaten their empire. However, Sheikh Ubeydullah clearly sought an autonomous domain similar to that enjoyed earlier by the Kurdish **emirates**. Thus his revolt did indeed bear some seeds of emerging Kurdish nationalism.

UNITED NATIONS. The United Nations is an international organization that was established at the end of World War II, according to UN Charter Article 1, to "maintain international peace and security." Since it is an international organization made up of sovereign independent states, however, the Kurds have no legal standing as members. Indeed the states in which the Kurds live (**Turkey**, **Iran**, **Iraq**, and **Syria**) have a vested interest in keeping the Kurdish question out of the United Nations in order to preserve their own respective territorial integrities. This they—and others who have similar interests in keeping the lid on their own minority problems—have largely done. Until the end of the first **Gulf War** in 1991, therefore, the United Nations had had almost nothing to do with the Kurdish question. Ironically, however, more than half the members of the United Nations—who by definition have legal standing in the world organization—have populations less than that of the Kurds.

Those who would seek an entry for the Kurdish issue onto the UN agenda might point out that UN Charter Article 1 also lists as its purposes "to develop friendly relations among nations based on respect for the principle of equal rights and self-determination of peoples" and "to achieve international co-operation in solving international problems of an economic, social, cultural, or humanitarian character, and in promoting and encouraging respect for **human rights** and for fundamental freedoms for all without distinction as to race, sex, language, or religion." In addition, Article 14 declares that "the General Assembly may recommend measures for the peaceful adjustment of any situation, regardless of origin, which it deems likely to impair the general welfare or friendly relations among nations."

One of very few early attempts to bring the Kurdish question to the United Nations occurred in January 1946, when Rizgari Kurd, an Iraqi Kurdish predecessor of the **Kurdistan Democratic Party**, unsuccessfully made a formal appeal to the world body for Kurdish self-determination and sovereignty. Following Iraq's use of **chemical weapons** during the **Iran–Iraq War** (1980–88) and against the Iraqi Kurds in **Halabja** in March 1988, UN Security Council Resolution 620, of 26 August 1988, finally condemned the use of such weapons. At the same time, **Massoud Barzani** appealed to the United Nations to stop Iraq's **Anfal** campaign, with its use of chemical warfare against the Kurds. The overall international response, however, was largely one of deafening silence, as few wanted to offend **Saddam Hussein** and Iraq in those days.

The first Gulf War, in 1991, partially changed this neglect. UN Security Council Resolution 688, of 5 April 1991, condemned "the repression of the Iraqi civilian population . . . in Kurdish populated areas" and demanded "that Iraq . . . immediately end this repression." This was by far the most important specific recognition of the Kurds by the United Nations ever. In the succeeding years, the **United**

States has used this Security Council resolution to justify, first, its temporary creation of a **safe haven** for the Kurds in northern Iraq and, second, its enforcement of a **no-fly zone** over the area. Under this protection, the **Kurdistan Regional Government** has developed since 1992. Also, the United Nations has maintained a number of humanitarian programs in the region.

UN Security Council Resolution 986, of 14 April 1995, authorized Iraq to sell a limited amount of **oil** for food and other humanitarian needs, thus partially lifting the economic sanctions that had been imposed since the first Gulf War. After a great deal of haggling, UN Security Council Resolution 1153, of 20 February 1998, dramatically increased the permitted amount of oil sales to $5.256 billion every six months. The Iraqi Kurdistan region received 13 percent of the funds from the sale of this oil.

Since then, these oil funds from the United Nations have helped immensely to develop economically the Kurdish area in northern Iraq to the point that the region is becoming a model for the entire Middle East. Many administrative problems regarding UN projects remain, however, since the United Nations continues to take the position that it is acting on behalf of the Iraqi government when it administers its programs in the Kurdish region. Compared to the past, however, the Kurdish issue in Iraq at least has had an entry into the United Nations. The **Gulf War II** will certainly affect the future relationship between the United Nations and the Iraqi Kurds.

UNITED STATES. In recent years, by far the most important outside state involved in the Kurdish problem. This is not only because of the United States' primary role in international politics, but also because **Turkey** was an important ally in the North Atlantic Treaty Organization (NATO) and the first **Gulf War** against **Iraq**.

U.S. involvement in Kurdistan dates back to World War I and President Woodrow Wilson's famous **Fourteen Points**, the 12th of which concerned a forlorn promise of "autonomy" for "the other nationalities, which are now under Turkish [**Ottoman**] rule." Resurgent **Kemalist** Turkey's successful struggle to regain its territorial integrity and **Great Britain**'s decision to maintain control over the **oil**-rich Kurdish region of northern Iraq, however, quashed nascent Kurdish hopes for independence or even some type of autonomy.

The first brief stage of U.S. foreign policy concern with the Kurds was over.

More than a half century later, the United States again became involved with the Kurds. The United States supported the Turkish position on the Kurdish issue because Turkey was an important member of NATO. Thus Kurds who supported the **Kurdistan Workers Party (PKK)** became "bad Kurds," or even officially terrorists, from the point of view of the United States. In February 1999, Washington went so far as to play a leading role in helping Turkey capture **Abdullah Ocalan**, the leader of the PKK.

In Iraq, however, the United States encouraged **Mulla Mustafa Barzani**'s revolt in the early 1970s, and thus the Iraqi Kurds became "good Kurds" from the point of view of the United States. The United States pursued this path for several reasons: as a favor to its then-ally **Iran**, which was an enemy of Iraq; as a gambit in the Cold War, as Iraq was an ally of the **Soviet Union**; as a means to relieve pressure on **Israel** so Iraq would not join some future Arab attack against the Jewish state; and as a possible means to satisfy its own need for Middle East oil if the Kurds came to control the oil in their land.

Accordingly, U.S. president **Richard Nixon** and his national security adviser, **Henry Kissinger**, first encouraged the Iraqi Kurds to revolt against Baghdad, but then with their ally Iran double-crossed the Kurds when the shah (**Muhammad Reza Shah Pahlavi**) decided to cut a deal with **Saddam Hussein**. To rationalize these actions, Kissinger argued that they helped prevent Iraq from participating in the October 1973 Middle East War against Israel. Cynically, he also explained that "covert action should not be confused with missionary work." **Mulla Mustafa Barzani** himself died as a broken man four years later in exile as an unwanted ward of the U.S. **Central Intelligence Agency**. As a result, his son and eventual successor, **Massoud Barzani**, never fully trusted the United States. Years later, Kissinger explained that to have saved the Kurds in 1975 would have required opening a new front in inhospitable mountains close to the Soviet border. In addition, the shah had made the decision, and the United States did not have any realistic means to dissuade him.

The third and current stage of U.S. foreign policy involvement with the Iraqi Kurds began with the first **Gulf War** in 1991 and the United States' continuing attempt to contain and remove **Saddam**

Hussein from power. At the end of the first Gulf War, the United States urged the Iraqi Kurds to rise against Baghdad, but when the uprising began to fail, the United States decided not to intervene because it feared that to do so could lead to an unwanted, protracted U.S. occupation that would be politically unpopular in the United States and destabilize Iraq, and thus possibly the entire Middle East. In addition, Kurdish success in Iraq might provoke Kurdish risings in Turkey, a U.S. NATO ally.

The ensuing mass Kurdish **refugee** exodus, however, caused the United States to reverse its position and institute **Operation Provide Comfort** and a **no-fly zone** under which the Iraqi Kurds were eventually able to construct a **Kurdistan Regional Government** in northern Iraq. When the Iraqi Kurds fell out among themselves in an enervating civil war from 1994 to 1998, Washington finally was able to broker a cease-fire, which has stuck. Since then, the United States has continued to play a most important role in Kurdish affairs. Early in 2003, the future of the Iraqi Kurds was uncertain as the United States prepared to overthrow Saddam Hussein in the **Gulf War II**.

– V –

VANLY, ISMET CHERIFF (1924–). Well-known, elderly Kurdish scholar and spokesman who was born in **Syria**. In the 1960s and 1970s, Professor Vanly worked for **Mulla Mustafa Barzani** in Europe and **Israel**. Iraqi agents unsuccessfully attempted to assassinate him in Switzerland during the 1970s. Although he was shot through the head at almost point blank range, Vanly somehow survived. In 1995, he was elected to the executive council of the **Kurdistan Parliament in Exile**, and in 1999 he was chosen as the president of its successor, the **Kurdistan National Congress**.

VEJIN. *See* YILDIRIM, HUSEYIN.

VILLAGE GUARDS. System of Kurdish **tribes** and villagers created by the Turkish government in April 1985 as a divide-and-rule tactic to combat the **Kurdistan Workers Party (PKK)**. Thus they were reminiscent of the **Hamidiye** during late **Ottoman** times and, more recently, the *josh* in northern **Iraq**.

Incentives to join the village guards included relatively good pay in an area that was chronically poor, a chance to pursue ancient blood feuds with impunity, and sheer state intimidation against those who refused to participate. The most notable tribes that participated in the system were identified with the political right or were already in conflict against tribes associated with the PKK. The government was also willing to use blatant criminal elements, such as Tahir Adiyaman, the chief of the Jirki tribe and, at the time he was recruited, still wanted for the 1975 killings of six gendarmes. Other tribes that participated in the village guards included the Pinyanish, Goyan, **Bucaks**, and Mamkhuran. At their height the village guards probably numbered more than 60,000.

The PKK quickly targeted the village guards, resulting in some of the worst examples of the terrorism that became endemic in the southeast of Turkey. At times, both sides killed entire families of the other. Although they helped the state eventually defeat the PKK, the village guards were also a throwback to the past in which the Turkish government placed itself in the ironic role of revitalizing feudalistic tribes contrary to **Ataturk**'s supposed policies, while supporting criminal elements, as illustrated by the **Susurluk** scandal, which broke in October 1996.

Over the years, the system of village guards became one of the most criticized policies pursued by the Turkish government in its struggle against the PKK and a strong symbol of official state repression. Abolition of the village guards was always one of the first demands the PKK and other Kurds made for ending their armed struggle against the government. The supporters of the system, of course, came to have a vested financial stake in its continuance. With the military defeat of the PKK, by the end of the 20th century the village guards began to be phased out.

– W –

WASHINGTON KURDISH INSTITUTE (WKI). Nonprofit, research, educational, and advocacy organization concerning the Kurds and created in 1996. It is located in Washington, D.C. **Najmaldin O. Karim** serves as its president, while Michael Amitay is its executive director.

Since its creation, the WKI has sponsored conferences on a variety of issues such as the long-term health effects of the **chemical weapons** attack on **Halabja**, promoted cultural initiatives such as Kurdish **language** classes, and lobbied the U.S. government on Kurdish issues, among others. The WKI has an Internet homepage at www.kurd.org and also maintains close relations with the **Institut Kurde de Paris** in **France**.

WATER. In sharp contrast to most of the Middle East, Kurdistan is blessed with water. Both the Tigris and Euphrates Rivers rise in the Kurdish areas of **Turkey** before flowing south into **Syria** and **Iraq**.

In recent years, Turkey has sought to harness this enormous resource by building an ambitious series of dams. The resulting **Guneydogu Anadolu Projesi**, or Southeast Anatolia Project, has led to bitter quarrels with Syria and Iraq and was probably one of the main reasons Syria provided sanctuary for **Abdullah Ocalan** and his **Kurdistan Workers Party** until October 1998. Also, the dams have flooded important Kurdish archeological sites, or may do so, as with the proposed **Ilisu Dam** at **Hasankeyf**. This has created much ill will among many Kurds and concerned foreigners.

Three large dams also exist in Iraqi Kurdistan: Bekhma on the Greater Zab, **Dukan** on the Lesser Zab, and **Darbandikhan** on the Sirwan and Diyala. In addition to these rivers, strong springs exist in many areas of Kurdistan. The names of numerous Kurdish towns and villages attest to this fact by including the prefix *Sarab-* or *Kani-* ("spring" in Kurdish).

In the coming years, these water resources can only become more important. Along with the **oil** resources, which are prevalent around the Iraqi Kurdish city of **Kirkuk**, water will make Kurdistan economically, as well as politically, important.

WILSON, ARNOLD (1884–1940). One of a number of important political officers of **Great Britain** stationed in **Iraq** after World War I who helped determine the policies that eventually led to the Kurds of the **Mosul** *vilayet* being incorporated into Iraq. Wilson based his policies on the belief that, given Britain's financial difficulties, Mesopotamia could be most economically defended from the Kurdish foothills. Following Wilson's failure to implement indirect British control through a pliant **Sheikh Mahmud of Barzinji**, Sir **Percy Cox** replaced Wilson in October 1920. Wilson wrote *Mesopotamia, 1917–1920: A Clash of Loyalties* (1931).

WILSON, WOODROW. *See* FOURTEEN POINTS.

WOMEN. Like most traditional and **Islamic** societies, men are given certain rights and responsibilities in Kurdish society that are denied to women. Men are supposed to govern, fight, and support their families, while women are supposed to bear and care for children, manage their households, and obey their husbands.

Nevertheless, compared to women in other Islamic societies around them, Kurdish women have often exercised more freedom. Indeed, travelers have long noted how Kurdish women usually went unveiled and were allowed greater freedom, while also performing most of the hard manual labor. In marriage, Kurdish women could sometimes be wooed and won, although arranged marriages also existed. Wives were treated more equally by their husbands than wives in most other Middle Eastern locales. Kurdish women have also held a more secure financial position than did their sisters in neighboring societies. Women, for example, could more easily succeed their husbands as the head of a family, even when there were male children.

Kurdish women have also occasionally played prominent roles in politics and the military. Lady Kara Fatima of Marash won fame as a female warrior who led hundreds of Kurds against the **Russians** in the Russo–Turkish War of 1877 and represented the Kurds in the **Ottoman** court in Constantinople. The last autonomous ruler of the **Hakkari** region was a woman. Also, the Ottoman army had to face Mama Pura Halima of Pizhdar, Mama Kara Nargiz of the Shwan tribes in what is now Iraqi Kurdistan, and Mama Persheng of the **Milan** tribe. Adila Khanem was a famous and cultured chief of the **Jaf** tribe until her death in 1924. Although actually an **Assyrian**, **Margaret George** was a more recent example of a Kurdish female warrior. **Hero Talabani**, the wife of **Jalal Talabani**, is a well-known personality in her own right. Despite these examples, women's rights, or the lack thereof, are increasingly an issue in Kurdistan. Kurdish women in **Turkey**, for example, have sometimes been subjected to various forms of state violence, including rape and sexual harassment, especially during the years of violence associated with the **Kurdistan Workers Party** in the 1980s and 1990s. The **Kurdistan Regional Government** in northern **Iraq** has recently sought to deal with **honor killing**, the murder of women by their own families because the women have somehow dishonored their families by infidelity or otherwise. Similar concern regarding honor killings has been expressed in Turkey. Female Kurdish **refugees** and widows suffer more than their male counterparts. Clearly, much remains to be done regarding women's rights in Kurdistan.

– X –

XENOPHON. *See* KARDOUCHOI.

XULAM, KANI. *See* AMERICAN KURDISH INFORMATION NETWORK.

– Y –

YEZIDIS (YAZIDIS). Religiously heterodox Kurdish group who have often, but incorrectly, been referred to pejoratively as devil worshippers. In reality, the Yezidis are a branch of the indigenous Kurdish religion of the **Cult of Angels**.

The Yezidis have two sacred books written, rather surprisingly, in Arabic. The *Mashaf-rash* (black, i.e., sacred book) is the much longer of the two and contains the fundamentals of the Yezidis' religion. The *Kitab al-Djilwa* is much shorter and is ascribed to the reputed founder of the religion, Sheikh Adi.

"Yezidi" refers to angels, and Lucifer (Malak Tawus, or the Peacock Angel) is the main angel worshipped. Malak Tawus, however, is not the prince of darkness, but the most powerful of all the archangels. Anzal, a sculptured bird icon, is the main relic of the Peacock Angel, who created the material world out of the pieces of the original cosmic egg in which the Spirit formerly resided. When Adam was driven out of paradise, he had no opening in his bowels and thus suffered great discomfort until God sent a bird to peck an orifice in him. The most important Yezidi celebration is the *Jam,* a seven-day feast during the second week of October in which the bird icon Anzal is presented to the faithful.

The Yezidis are prohibited from eating lettuce, fish, gazelles, the flesh of poultry, and gourds. The color dark blue is also forbidden, as are urinating in a standing position, dressing while sitting, using a closet, and washing in a bathroom.

Formerly a much larger group, the Yezidis have been decimated by persecution and massacres perpetrated by their Muslim neighbors, who look upon them as heretics. Today, the Yezidis constitute at the most 5 percent of the Kurdish population and probably a lot less. They were concentrated in several different pockets in the **Bahdinani** area of northern **Iraq**: southwest of **Mosul** and east of Mosul in **Lalish**, where their most important shrine, the tomb of Sheikh Ali, is located.

During the 1830s, many Yezidis left these areas due to persecutions carried out by such Kurdish leaders as Mir Muhammad of **Soran** (also known as Miri Kor, or the Blind Mir) and settled in the Tor Abdin mountains, between **Mardin** and Midyat in what is now **Turkey**, and near Batman in Turkey. Subsequently, most of them have migrated to **Germany** to escape continuing persecution. Yezidis also migrated to the Caucasus in **Russia** for similar reasons in the 19th century. Lately, however, the Yezidis have also suffered persecution in **Armenia**.

The Yezidis speak the Kurdish language **Kurmanji**. In recent years, there has been an Arab attempt to strip them of their Kurdish identity by declaring them Umayyad Arabs. This rewriting of ethnic history is attempted by falsely identifying the Yezidis with the Umayyad caliph Yezid, who reigned from 680 to 683 C.E.

YILDIRIM, HUSEYIN. Kurdish lawyer living in Sweden who for several years in the early 1980s served as the European spokesman for the **Kurdistan Workers Party (PKK)**. In the late 1980s, however, Yildirim broke with the PKK's leader, **Abdullah Ocalan**, over the party's policy of killing civilians who collaborated with the state. Yildirim helped established an alternative movement called PKK–Vejin (Resurrection), but this new organization failed to make much headway.

YILDIRIM, KESIRE. Former wife of **Abdullah Ocalan**, the leader of the **Kurdistan Workers Party (PKK)**. They were married in the late 1970s. Kesire Yildirim was also one of the founding members of the PKK. In 1987, she and Ocalan were divorced. Following a brief house arrest, she managed to escape to Sweden, where she became a member of Vejin (Resurrection), a PKK opposition group. Although Ocalan denounced her, he also credited her with making him sensitive to feminist demands. Kesire Yildirim was not related to **Huseyin Yildirim**.

YILMAZ, KANI. Figure sometimes said to have been the third highest-ranking member of the **Kurdistan Workers Party (PKK)** and in charge of all its European activities before his capture and imprisonment in **Great Britain** in October 1994. After he was finally released, Kani Yilmaz (whose real name is Faysal Dumlayici) returned to work for the PKK in Europe. He was blamed in part for failing to find a sanctuary for **Abdullah Ocalan** while Ocalan was in Europe before his capture in February 1999. Initial reports even indicated that Kani Yilmaz might have been executed for this failure, but this proved erroneous. Clearly, however, Yilmaz has been demoted in the organization.

YILMAZ, MESUT (1947–). One of the few important Turkish politicians in recent years who at times has seemed willing to recognize a certain amount of Kurdish rights, although he pulled back from this stance under political pressure. Yilmaz graduated from the political science faculty of Ankara University in 1971 and studied for a master's degree in Cologne, **Germany**. Following **Turgut Ozal**'s assumption of the Turkish presidency in 1987, Yilmaz became Ozal's ultimate successor as leader of the Motherland Party. He has been prime minister on three separate, but short occasions.

While prime minister in 1996, Yilmaz promised a political solution to the Kurdish problem in Turkey. He asserted he would lift the state of emergency and strengthen the individual cultural rights of the Kurdish citizens in **language** and education. He also talked about strengthening local administrative bodies in the southeast. However, Yilmaz called the reasonable **TOBB Report** on the Kurdish problem a "CIA report."

Most famously, when Turkey was admitted to candidate membership in the **European Union (EU)** in December 1999, Yilmaz—in reference to the need for Turkey to establish Kurdish rights to be admitted into the EU—declared that "the road to the EU passes through **Diyarbakir**," a city often called the unofficial capital of Turkish Kurdistan. Under political pressure, however, Yilmaz later pulled back from this statement. Yilmaz resigned his party's leadership after its smashing defeat in the landslide **AK Partisi** electoral victory on 3 November 2002.

YOUNG TURKS. The Young Turks began in the 1880s as an enlightened reform movement stirred by the rise of **nationalism** and the decay of the **Ottoman Empire**. Originally, they advocated constitutionalism and political freedom for all the inhabitants of the empire. Indeed, two Kurdish intellectuals (Abdullah Jevdet and Ishaq Sukuti) were part of its first 12-member leadership society.

As the multinational Ottoman Empire continued to fall apart, however, the Young Turks gradually adopted pan-Turkist positions. In 1908, the Young Turks came to power and led the Ottoman Empire into World War I on the side of **Germany**. Operating through the Committee of Unity and Progress, the Young Turks became an ultra-Turkish nationalist precursor of the **Kemalist** Republic of **Turkey**, which until very recently refused to recognize any Kurdish rights.

– Z –

ZAGROS MOUNTAINS. Range running from the northwest to the southeast of Kurdistan like a mighty spinal column. They are the epitome of the most prominent geological characteristic of the land, namely its mountainousness. As a result, the very term "Zagros" is often used as a patriotic term among the Kurds.

ZALEH. Camp in the mountains northeast of **Sulaymaniya** in northern **Iraq** near the Iranian border where some 1,700 fighters of the **Kurdistan Workers Party (PKK)** were supposedly interned by **Jalal Talabani**'s **Patriotic Union of Kurdistan (PUK)** following the bloody fighting that occurred between them in October 1992. **Turkey** had backed the PUK and the other Iraqi Kurdish party—the **Kurdistan Democratic Party**—against the PKK.

Soon, however, many Turkish commentators began to accuse Talabani of having provided a new base and safehouse for the PKK in the Zaleh camp. In January 1994, therefore, Turkish planes destroyed the camp, but the PKK successfully escaped before the blow fell. Instead, some Turkish bombs erroneously fell across the border in **Iran**, where they killed some 20 Iranians.

Ironically, the PKK and the PUK fell into conflict in 2000. In part, this was due to the PKK trying to establish themselves further in the Zaleh area, which seemed to threaten the PUK's base. The Turkish capture of **Abdullah Ocalan**, the leader of the PKK, had forced the PKK to withdraw further from the Turkish border into PUK territory.

ZANA, LEYLA (1961–). Female ethnic Kurd elected to the Turkish parliament as a member of **Halkin Emek Partisi (HEP)**, or Peoples Labor Party, in 1991. Leyla Zana caused a national sensation and scandal by wearing Kurdish national colors on her headband and declaring that "I take this oath for the brotherhood of the Turkish and Kurdish peoples," when she was sworn in as a member of the parliament.

In March 1994, Leyla Zana was one of six members of the **Demokrasi Partisi**—HEP's successor—who had their parliamentary immunity lifted and was arrested. She was then convicted of disseminating separatist propaganda and supporting or being a member of an armed band, and she was sentenced to 15 years in prison. Her case has become a *cause célèbre* for Kurdish **human rights** in Turkey. Leyla Zana is married to **Mehdi Zana**.

ZANA, MEHDI (1941–). Ethnic Kurdish citizen of **Turkey** associated with **Kemal Burkay** in the **Kurdistan Socialist Party** of Turkey and the former mayor of **Diyarbakir**. He was imprisoned in the early 1980s for separatist activities, but not accused of involvement in violence. As a result, **Amnesty International** worked for his release. He was freed in 1991 under the terms of an amnesty issued by President **Turgut Ozal**, imprisoned, and then again released. He is the husband of **Leyla Zana**.

ZAND. Kurdish Iranian tribe that established a dynasty that ruled western **Persia** in 1751–94. They belonged to the **Lak** group of **Lurs**, who had been deported from their central **Zagros** homeland in Deh Pari to northern Khurasan by Nadir Shah in 1732, but had then fought their way back home under **Karim Khan** after Nadir's assassination in 1747.

The Zand dynasty's reputation rests on its founder, Karim Khan. He was able to put together an army from the nomadic tribes of the Zagros and establish alliances with the bureaucrats and influentials of such important cities in western Persia as Isfahan, Shiraz, Tabriz, and Kirman. For a while, Karim Khan used the fiction of a Safavid revival and contented himself with the title of *wakil,* or regent. He rebuilt his capital, Shiraz, pursued intelligent economic policies, endorsed the majority Twelver Shiism while manifesting notable religious tolerance, and exhibited commendable humanity, as recorded in popular folklore. At one point, Karim Khan even temporarily took the port of Basra from the **Ottomans**.

At their height, however, the Zand ruled only over western Persia without completely subduing the Qajars at Astarabad on the Caspian littoral. Karim Khan was also content to allow Khurasan in the northeast to remain out of his control. Karim Khan's incompetent successors fell into internecine warfare and were soon overcome by the **Turkoman** Qajars from Astarabad. Luft Ali, the last Zand ruler, was defeated and tortured to death by the founder of the Qajar dynasty, Agha Muhammad Khan, who had spent his youth and received his education at the benevolent court of Karim Khan.

ZAZA. *See* DIMILI.

ZIBARI, HOSHYAR. Longtime member of the politburo of the **Kurdistan Democratic Party (KDP)** and often the major spokesman for the KDP on foreign affairs. Zibari is related to **Massoud Barzani**, the leader of the KDP, and also speaks excellent English.

ZIBARIS. Tribe that was a historic enemy of the **Barzanis**, whom the Zibaris saw as latecomers rivaling them for control of the area they both inhabited along the Greater Zab River in the northernmost regions of Iraqi Kurdistan. (Zibar is located just south of **Barzan**.) Thus the Zibaris were *josh* who usually supported the Iraqi government against **Mulla Mustafa Barzani**. To help end this feud, Barzani married Hamayl Zibari, who became his third wife and the mother of **Massoud Barzani**, the current president of the **Kurdistan Democratic Party**.

Symbolic of this new cooperation, **Hoshyar Zibari** is a high-ranking member of the KDP and spokesman for it on foreign affairs.

ZILAN. *See* MILAN.

ZIYA BEG, YUSUF (?–1925). One of the main leaders of **Azadi**, a clandestine Kurdish party founded in 1923 that helped foment the **Sheikh Said** uprising in **Turkey** in 1925. Yusuf Ziya Beg was a descendant of the *mirs* of **Bitlis** and commanded great influence there. Indeed, he was elected its deputy to the new Turkish parliament.

During the Sheikh Said rebellion, Yusuf Ziya Beg unsuccessfully attempted to establish contact with the **Kemalist** Turkish opposition. He was imprisoned with **Khalid Beg of the Jibran** (another key Azadi leader), and both were executed in their prison cells.

ZOROASTRIANISM. The dominant, pre-Islamic **religion** of both the Achaemenid (550–330 B.C.E.) and Sassanid (226–650 C.E.) **Persian Empires**. The religion undoubtedly exerted a powerful influence on the indigenous Kurdish religion of the **Cult of Angels**. Some have also speculated that the use of fire in the Kurdish **Newroz** celebration stems from the special veneration shown to fire as part of a purification ritual in Zoroastrianism.

ZOHHAK. *See* NEWROZ.

ZUHAB, TREATY OF. Treaty in 1639 between the **Ottoman** and **Persian** Empires formally establishing their border, which had been unofficially marked after the Ottoman victory at the Battle of **Chaldiran** in 1514. The importance for the Kurds is that this border divided them between these two great Middle Eastern empires and in effect still largely exists in the border between **Turkey** and **Iran**.

Bibliography

CONTENTS

INTRODUCTION

Although the Kurds have no independent state to record or encourage academic study of their situation, and although history is usually written by the victors, which the Kurds have not been, there is still a relatively large body of works on the Kurds in Western as well as Middle Eastern languages. Among the former, studies exist in English, French, German, and Russian, among others. Among the latter, work has been done in Turkish, Arabic, Kurdish, and Iranian.

Since this historical dictionary is intended for English readers, most (but not all) sources cited in this bibliography are in English. A few particularly important entries in other languages are also included. The choices made in these cases are of necessity arbitrary and subjective. Much important work on the Kurds exists in languages other than English, but has not been included here. In addition, the bibliography consists mainly of more recent materials, rather than older ones. Nevertheless, some older items have been included when they seemed particularly important. Also, a number of broader studies are omitted that include an individual chapter or two on the Kurds along with other groups.

Only a few primary or official sources are included here because for the most part there has been no independent Kurdish state to compile them. Of course, primary and official sources concerning the Kurds do exist in the government documents of Great Britain, France, Germany, Russia, and the United States, among others. In addition, of course, primary and government documents concerning the Kurds also exist in the archives of those Middle Eastern states in which the Kurds live, namely Turkey, Iran, Iraq, and Syria. Thus a few important official documents from the United States and Iraq are included here.

What is more, since its inception in 1992, the de facto state of Kurdistan in northern Iraq has produced a wealth of contemporary data. The Mahabad Republic of Kurdistan in Iran (1946) also produced documents. In earlier times, various Kurdish emirates and other entities also left records. Finally, different Kurdish organizations—often ephemeral—have produced innumerable documents. Clearly, one could compile a large additional bibliography from all those sources mentioned in this and the previous paragraph, but to do so is beyond the parameters of this bibliography.

The author is pleased to emphasize that his efforts in compiling this bibliography are dwarfed by the work of Lokman I. Meho, who has compiled two excellent bibliographies: *The Kurds and Kurdistan: A Selective and Annotated Bibliography* (1997), and (with Kelly L. Maglaughlin) *Kurdish Culture and Society: An Annotated Bibliography* (2001). Meho's first bibliography contains 814 mainly historical and political entries in English published largely after World War II. His second bibliography lists 931 entries in such areas as anthropology, archaeology, art, communication, demography, description and travel, economy, education, ethnicity, folklore, health conditions, journalism, language, literature, migration, music, religion, social structure and organization, urbanization, and women. In this second bibliography, 60 percent of the entries are in English, 15 percent are in Arabic, 15 percent are in French, 5 percent are in German, and the remaining 5 percent are in other languages, including Russian. Both bibliographies are annotated.

Although this author has gathered a considerable number of Kurdish sources since he first began seriously working on the subject in 1985, he is pleased to commend Meho's two bibliographies to his readers and to recognize his considerable debt to Meho in compiling the present bibliography. Meho also called the author's attention to the existence of several other bibliographies on the Kurds, which he has listed here.

Because of the general nature of many works on the Kurds, their classification into separate categories proved difficult and in the end sometimes arbitrary. Some of the best work on particular states or other topics appears in works listed here as general history. Thus readers should consult the works listed under the general categories as well as under any more specific heading in which they are interested.

Among others, particularly recommended are Martin van Bruinessen, *Agha, Shaikh and State: The Social and Political Structures of Kurdistan* (1992); David McDowall, *A Modern History of the Kurds* (1996); and Mehrdad Izady, *The Kurds: A Concise Handbook* (1992). Susan Meiselas, in *Kurdistan: In the Shadow of History* (1997), has compiled a most useful collection of often rare photographs with useful commentaries by Martin van Bruinessen. In a certain modest sense, Meiselas's compilation serves in lieu of a Kurdish national archival collection of photographic resources along with primary source material from oral histories, diaries, letters, newspapers, memoirs, and British and American government documents.

GENERAL

Bibliographies

Atroushi, Alex. *Old Books on Kurds and Kurdistan.* At www.kdp.pp.se/bookon.html, 1998. Accessed 25 September 2002.

Behn, Wolfgang. *The Kurds in Iran: A Selected and Annotated Bibliography.* London: Mansell, 1977.

Blau, Joyce. *Les Kurds et le Kurdistan: bibliographie critique, 1977–1986.* Paris: Institut français de recherché en Iran, 1989.

Bois, Thomas. *Bulletin raisonné d'études kurdes.* Beirut: Imprimerie Catholique, 1964.

Dzhalil, Dzhalile. *Kurdy Sovetskoi Armenii: Bibliografiia, 1920–1980.* Erevan: Izd-vo AN Armianskoi SSR, 1987.

Erdem, Engin I. *Research Guide: A Bibliography of the Kurdish Question in the Middle East.* At meria.idc.ac.il/research-g/kurds_biblio.html. Accessed 17 April 2002.

Ghafur, Abd Allah. *Bibliyughrafiyat Kurdistan.* Stockholm: Sara Distribution, 1994.

Gilet, M., and M. M. Beriel. *Les Kurdes et le Kurdistan: Bibliographie 1987–1996.* Paris: CNRS, 1996.

Hansen, Gerda. *Die Kurden und der Kurdenkonflikt: Literatur seit 1990: Eine Auswahlbibliographie.* Hamburg: Deutsches Übersee-Institut, 1994.

———. *Die Lage der Kurden: Literatur seit 1985.* Hamburg: Deutsches Übersee-Institut, 1991.

Institut Kurde de Paris. *Publications for Sale.* Paris: Institut Kurde de Paris, 2001.

Lytle, Elizabeth E. *A Bibliography of the Kurds, Kurdistan, and the Kurdish Question.* Monticello, Ill.: Council of Planning Librarians, 1977.

Meho, Lokman I. *The Kurds and Kurdistan: A Selective and Annotated Bibliography.* Westport, Conn.: Greenwood, 1997.

Meho, Lokman I., and Kelly L. Maglaughlin. *Kurdish Culture and Society: An Annotated Bibliography.* Westport, Conn.: Greenwood, 2001.

Mokri, Mohammad. "Kurdologie et enseignment de la langue kurde en URSS (avec une bibliographie concernant études kurdes." *L'Ethnographie* 57 (1963): 71–105.

Musaelian, Zh. S. *Bibliografiia po Kurdovedeniiu: Nachinaia s XVI Veka.* Saint Petersburg: Tsentr "Peterburgskoe Vostokovedenie," 1996.

Nariman, Mustafa. *Ma Asdahu al-Akrad ila al-Maktaba al-Arabiya, 1900–1981.* Baghdad: Matba'at Husam, 1983.

Rooy, Silvio van, and Kees Tamboer. *ISK's Kurdish bibliography.* 2 vols. Amsterdam: International Society for Kurdistan, 1968.

Biographies

Basri, Mir. *A'lam al-Kurd* (Biographies of famous Kurdish persons). London: Riad al-Rayyis lil-Kutub wa-al-Nashr, 1991.

Zaki, Muhammad Amin. *Mashahir al-Kurd wa-Kurdistan fi al-Dawr al-Islami* (Biographies of famous Kurdish persons from the rise of Muhammad to the late days of the Ottoman Empire). Vol. 1. Translated from Kurdish by Sanha Amin Zaki. Baghdad: n.p., 1945.

———. *Mashahir al-Kurd wa-Kurdistan fi al-Dawr al-Islami* (Biographies of famous Kurdish persons from the rise of Muhammad to the late days of the Ottoman Empire). Vol. 2. Translated from Kurdish by Muhammad Ali Awni. Cairo: Matba'at al-Sa'ada, 1947.

Dictionaries

Amindarov, Aziz. *Kurdish–English, English–Kurdish Dictionary.* New York: Hippocrene, 1994.

Blau, Joyce. *Le Kurde de Amadiya et de Djabal Sindjar: Analyse Linguistique, Textes, Folkloriques, Glossaires.* Paris: Klincksieck, 1975.

Chyet, Michael L. *Kurdish Dictionary: Kurmanji–English.* New Haven, Conn.: Yale University Press, 2002.

Gewrani, Ali Seydo al-. *Ferhenga Kurdi Nujen: KurdiErebi = al-Qamus al-Kurdi al-Hadith: Kurdi-Arabi.* (The modern Kurdish dictionary; Kurdish–Arabic). Amman, Lebanon: Sharikat al-Sharq al-Awsat lil-Tiba'a, 1985.

Gharib, Kamal Jalal. *Al-Qamus al-ilmi: Arabi, Inklizi, Kurdi.* Vol. 2. (A science dictionary: Arabic-English–Kurdish). Baghdad: al-Majma al-Ilmi al-Kurdi, 1979.

Hakim, Halkawt, and Gerard Gautier. *Dictionnaire Français–Kurde.* Paris: Klincksieck, 1993.

Jaba, Alexandre Auguste. *Dictionnaire Kurde–Français.* Osnabruck, Germany: Biblio–Verlag, 1975. Reprint of the 1879 edition published by the Commissionaire de l'Académie impériale des sciences, Saint Petersburg.

McCarus, Ernest Nasseph. *A Kurdish–English Dictionary: Dialect of Sulaimania, Iraq.* Ann Arbor: University of Michigan Press, 1967.

Omar, Feryad Fazil. *Kurdisch–Deutsches Wörterbuch (Kurmanci) Ferhenga Kurdi–Elmani.* Berlin: Kurdische Studien Berlin im VWB–Verlag für Wissenschaft und Bildung, 1992.

Rizgar, Baran. *Kurdish–English English–Kurdish Dictionary.* London: Onen, 1993.

Wahby, Taufiq, and Cecil John Edmonds. *A Kurdish–English Dictionary.* Oxford: Clarendon, 1966.

Travel

Bird, Isabella L. *Journeys in Persia and Kurdistan.* 2 vols. London: Murray, 1891.

Bruinessen, Martin van, and H. E. Boeschoten, eds. *Evliya Celebi in Diyarbekir: The Relevant Section of the Seyahatname.* Leiden, Netherlands: Brill, 1988.

Bruni, Mary Ann Smothers. *Journey through Kurdistan.* Austin: Texas Memorial Museum, 1995.

Dankoff, Robert, ed. *Evliya Celebi in Bitlis: The Relevant Section of the Seyahatname.* Leiden, Netherlands: Brill, 1990.

Douglas, William O. *Strange Lands and Friendly People.* New York: Harper, 1951.

Eriksson, Ann. *Kurdistan.* Stockholm: Sigma Reportage, Havregatan, 2001.

Hamilton, Archibald Milne. *Road through Kurdistan: The Narrative of an Engineer in Iraq.* London: Faber & Faber, 1937.

Hay, William Robert. *Two Years in Kurdistan: Experiences of a Political Officer, 1918–1920.* London: Sidgwick & Jackson, 1921.

Hitchens, Christopher. "Struggle of the Kurds." *National Geographic* 182 (August 1992): 32–61.

Kahn, Margaret. *Children of the Jinn: In Search of the Kurds and Their Country.* New York: Seaview, 1980.

Kashi, Ed. *When the Borders Bleed: The Struggle of the Kurds.* New York: Pantheon, 1994.

Kisraiyan Nasr Allah. *Kurdistan: Photos.* Ostersund, Sweden: Oriental Art, 1990.

Noel, Edward William Charles. *Diary of Major Noel on Special Duty in Kurdistan.* Baghdad: n.p., 1920.

Soane, Ely Bannister. *To Mesopotamia and Kurdistan in Disguise: Narrative of a Journey from Constantinople through Kurdistan to Baghdad, 1907–1909, with Historical and Ethnographical Notices of the Various Kurdish Tribes and of the Chaldaeans of Kurdistan and an Index.* London: Murray, 1912.

Sykes, Mark. *The Caliph's Last Heritage: A Short History of the Turkish Empire.* London: Macmillan, 1915.

Thornhill, Teresa. *Sweet Tea with Cardamom: A Journey through Iraqi Kurdistan.* London: Pandora, 1997.

HISTORY

Early

Blaum, Paul. "A History of the Kurdish Marwanid Dynasty." *International Journal of Kurdish Studies* 5 (Spring–Fall 1992): 54–68; 6 (Fall 1993): 40–65.

Diakonoff, I. M. "Media." In *The Cambridge History of Iran, Vol. 2: The Median and Achaemenian Periods,* 36–148. Cambridge: Cambridge University Press, 1985.

Izady, Mehrdad R. "Roots and Evolution of Some Aspects of Kurdish Cultural Identity in Late Classical and Early Medieval Periods." Ph.D. diss., Columbia University, 1992.

Medvedskaya, Inna N. "The Rise and Fall of the Medes." *International Journal of Kurdish Studies* 16, nos. 1–2 (2002): 29–44.

Minorsky, Vladimir F. "Kurds, Kurdistan: Origins and Pre-Islamic History"; and "The Islamic Period up to 1920." In *The Encyclopedia of Islam*, 447–64. New ed. Vol. 5. Leiden, Netherlands: Brill, 1981.

———. "Kurdistan." *The Encyclopaedia of Islam*, 1130–32. Vol. 2. Leiden, Netherlands: Brill, 1927.

———. "Kurds." *The Encyclopaedia of Islam*, 1132–55. Vol. 2. Leiden, Netherlands: Brill, 1927.

Reid, James J. "Hakkari Clan and Society: Kurdistan, 1502–1656." *Journal of Kurdish Studies* 2 (1996–1997): 13–30.

Saeedpour, Vera Beaudin. "A Tangled Web They Weave: The Mystery of Kurdish Roots." *International Journal of Kurdish Studies* 16, nos. 1–2 (2002): 1–28.

———, ed. *The Legacy of Saladin*. Published as a special issue of the *International Journal of Kurdish Studies* 13, no.1 (1999).

Solecki, Ralph S. *Shanidar: The First Flower People*. New York: Knopf, 1971.

Woods, John E. *The Aqquyunlu: Clan, Confederation, Empire*. Revised and expanded edition. Salt Lake City: University of Utah Press, 1999.

Xenophon. *The Persian Expedition*. Edited by E. V. Rieu. Translated by Rex Warner. Middlesex, England: Penguin, 1949.

Zaki, Muhammad Amin. "A Brief History of Kurds and Kurdistan, Part I: From the Advent of Islam to AD 1750." Translated by Nemat Sharif. *International Journal of Kurdish Studies* 10, nos. 1–2 (1996): 105–155. (This article consists of three chapters of a work originally published in Kurdish in 1931 as *A Brief History of Kurds and Kurdistan, from Antiquity to the Present*.)

Modern

General

Ahmad, Kamal Madhar. *Kurdistan during the First World War*. Translated from Kurdish by Muhammad Mulla Karim. Baghdad: Kurdish Academy Press, 1977.

Arfa, Hassan. *The Kurds: A Historical and Political Study*. London: Oxford University Press, 1966.

Blau, Joyce. *Le problème Kurde: Essai sociologique et historique*. Brussels: Centre pour l'étude des problemes du monde musulman contemporain, 1963.

Bois, Thomas. "The Kurds and Their Country: Kurdistan." *The Encyclopedia of Islam*. New ed. Vol. 5, 439–47. Leiden, Netherlands: Brill, 1981.

———. *The Kurds*. Translated from the French by M. W. M. Welland. Beirut: Khayats, 1966.

Bruinessen, Martin van. *Agha, Shaikh and State: The Social and Political Structure of Kurdistan.* London: Zed, 1992.

————. "Kurdish Society, Ethnicity, Nationalism and Refugee Problems." In *The Kurds,* ed. Philip G. Kreyenbroek and Stefan Sperl, 33–67. London: Routledge, 1992.

Bulloch, John, and Harvey Morris. *No Friends but the Mountains: The Tragic History of the Kurds.* New York: Oxford University Press, 1992.

Chaliand, Gerard. *The Kurdish Tragedy.* Translated from the French by Philip Black. London: Zed, 1994.

————, ed. *A People without a Country: The Kurds and Kurdistan.* New York: Olive Branch, 1993.

Cruickshank, A. A. "International Aspects of the Kurdish Question." *International Relations* 3 (October 1968): 411–30.

Dunn, Michael Collins. "The Kurdish 'Question': Is There an Answer? A Historical Overview." *Middle East Policy* 4 (September 1995): 72–87.

Edmonds, Cecil John. "Kurdish Nationalism." *Journal of Contemporary History* 6, no. 1 (1971): 87–107.

Elphinston, W. G. "The Kurdish Question." *International Affairs* 72 (January 1946): 91–103.

Emadi, Hafizullah. "Conflicts in the Middle East: The Kurdish National Question." *Contemporary Review* 261 (August 1992): 62–71.

Ghassemlou, Abdul Rahman. *Kurdistan and the Kurds.* Prague: Publishing House of the Czechoslovak Academy of Science, 1965.

Hakim, Halkawt, ed. *Les Kurdes par-délà l'éxode.* Paris: L'Harmattan, 1992.

Harris, George S. "Ethnic Conflict and the Kurds." *Annals of the American Academy of Political and Social Sciences,* no. 433 (September 1977): 112–24.

Hazen, William E. "Minorities in Revolt: The Kurds of Iran, Iraq, Syria and Turkey." In *The Political Role of Minority Groups in the Middle East,* ed. Ronald D. McLaurin, 49–75. New York: Praeger Special Studies, 1979.

Honigman, Gerald A. "British Petroleum Politics, Arab Nationalism and the Kurds." *Middle East Review* 15 (Fall–Winter 1982–1983): 33–39.

Hyman, Anthony. "Elusive Kurdistan: The Struggle for Recognition." *Conflict Studies,* no. 214 (September 1988): 1–25.

Izady, Mehrdad. *The Kurds: A Concise Handbook.* Washington, D.C.: Crane Russak, 1992.

Jwaideh, Wadie. "The Kurdish Nationalist Movement; Its Origins and Development." Ph.D. diss., Syracuse University, 1960.

Kaplan, Robert. "Kurdistan: Sons of Devils." *Atlantic* 265 (November 1987): 38–44.

Kinnane, Derk. *The Kurds and Kurdistan.* London: Oxford University Press, 1964.

Kreyenbroek, Philip G., and Stefan Sperl, eds. *The Kurds: A Contemporary Overview.* London: Routledge, 1992.

Laizer, Sheri J. *Martyrs, Traitors, and Patriots: Kurdistan after the Gulf War.* London: Zed, 1996.

———. *Into Kurdistan: Frontiers under Fire.* London: Zed, 1991.

McDowall, David. *The Kurds.* 7th ed. London: Minority Rights Group International, 1996.

———. *A Modern History of the Kurds.* London: Tauris, 1996.

———. "Addressing the Kurdish Issue." In *Powder Keg in the Middle East: The Struggle for Gulf Security,* ed. Geoffrey Kemp and Janice Gross Stein, 211–36. Lanham, Md.: Rowman & Littlefield, 1995.

———. "The Kurdish Question: A Historical Review." In *The Kurds: A Contemporary Review,* ed. Philip G. Kreyenbroek and Stefan Sperl, 10–32. London: Routledge, 1992.

———. *The Kurds: A Nation Denied.* London: Minority Rights Publications, 1992.

More, Christiane. *Les Kurdes aujourd'hui: mouvement national et partis politiques.* Paris: L'Harmattan, 1984.

Nash, Theodore Richard. "The Effect of International Oil Interests upon the Fate of an Autonomous Kurdish Territory: A Perspective on the Conference at Sevres, August 10, 1920." *International Problems* 15 (Spring 1976): 119–33.

Nikitine, Basile. *Les Kurdes: Étude sociologique et historique.* Paris: Klincksieck, 1956.

O'Ballance, Edgar. *The Kurdish Struggle, 1920–1994.* New York: St. Martin's, 1996.

Pelletiere, Stephen C. *The Kurds: An Unstable Element in the Gulf.* Boulder, Colo.: Westview, 1984.

Picard, Elizabeth, ed. *La Question Kurde.* Brussels: Editions Complexe, 1991.

Randal, Jonathan C. *After Such Knowledge, What Forgiveness? My Encounters with Kurdistan.* New York: Farrar, Straus and Giroux, 1997.

Safrastian, Arshak. *The Kurds and Kurdistan.* London: Harvill, 1948.

Sim Richard. "Kurdistan: The Search for Recognition." *Conflict Studies,* no. 124 (November 1980).

Sluglett, Peter, and Marion Farouk–Sluglett. "The Kurds." In *The Times Guide to the Middle East: The Arab World and Its Neighbours,* ed. Peter Sluglett and Marion Farouk–Sluglett, 51–67. London: Times Books, 1991.

Strohmeier, Martin. *Crucial Images in the Presentation of a Kurdish National Identity: Heroes and Patriots, Traitors and Foes.* Leiden, Netherlands: Brill, 2003.

Waheed, A. *The Kurds and Their Country: A History of the Kurdish People from Earliest Times to the Present.* 2d ed. Lahore, Pakistan: University Book Agency, 1958.

Yassin Borhanedin A. *Vision or Reality? The Kurds in the Policy of the Great Powers, 1941–1947.* Lund, Sweden: Lund University Press, 1995.

Zaza, Noureddine. *Ma vie de Kurde, ou, le cri du peuple kurde.* Lausanne: Favre, 1982.

Iran

Aristova, T. F. "The Kurds in Persia." *Central Asian Review* 7, no. 2 (1959): 175–201.

Bruinessen, Martin van. "Kurdish Tribes and the State of Iran: The Case of Simko's Revolt." In *The Conflict of Tribe and State in Iran and Afghanistan,* ed. Richard Tapper, 364–400. London: St. Martin's, 1983.

Coyle, James John. "Nationalism in Iranian Kurdistan." Ph.D. diss., George Washington University, 1993.

Eagleton, William. *The Kurdish Republic of 1946.* London: Oxford University Press, 1963.

Entessar, Nader. "Causal Factors in Kurdish Ethnonationalism." *International Review of History and Political Science* 22 (May 1985): 57–80.

Garthwaite, Gene R. *Khans and Shahs: A Documentary Analysis of the Bakhtiyari in Iran.* Cambridge: Cambridge University Press, 1983.

Ghassemlou, Abdul Rahman. "Kurdistan in Iran." In *A People without a Country: The Kurds and Kurdistan,* ed. Gerard Chaliand, 95–121. New York: Olive Branch, 1993.

Izady, Mehrdad, ed. *The Republic of Kurdistan: Fifty Years Later.* Published as a special issue of *International Journal of Kurdish Studies* 11, nos. 1–2 (1997).

Koohi–Kamali, Fereshteh. "The Development of Nationalism in Iranian Kurdistan." In *The Kurds: A Contemporary Overview,* ed. Philip G. Kreyenbroek and Stefan Sperl, 171–92. London: Routledge, 1992.

MacDonald, Charles G. "The Kurdish Challenge and Revolutionary Iran." *Journal of South Asian and Middle Eastern Studies* 13 (Fall–Winter 1989): 52–68.

Ramazani, Rouhollah K. "The Autonomous Republic of Azerbaijan and the Kurdish People's Republic: Their Rise and Fall." In *The Anatomy of Communist Takeovers,* ed. Thomas T. Hammond, 448–74. New Haven: Yale University Press, 1975.

Roosevelt, Archie, Jr. "The Kurdish Republic of Mahabad." *Middle East Journal* 1 (July 1947): 247–69.

Iraq

Adamson, David. C. *The Kurdish War*. New York: Praeger, 1964.

Ali, Othman. "British Policy and the Kurdish Question in Iraq, 1918–1932." Ph.D. diss., University of Toronto, 1993.

Andrews, F. David, ed. *The Lost Peoples of the Middle East: Documents of the Struggle for Survival and Independence of the Kurds, Assyrians, and Other Minority Races in the Middle East*. Salisbury, N.C.: Documentary Publications, 1982.

Attar, Kerim Abdul-Razzak. "The Minorities of Iraq during the Period of the Mandate, 1920–1932." Ph.D. diss., Columbia University, 1967.

Beck, Peter J. "A Tedious and Perilous Controversy: Britain and the Settlement of the Mosul Dispute, 1918–1926." *Middle Eastern Studies* 17 (April 1981): 256–76.

Bengio, Ofra. "The Iraqi Kurds: The Struggle for Autonomy in the Shadow of the Iran–Iraqi Conflict." *Immigrants and Minorities* (Great Britain) 9 (November 1990): 249–68.

Bruinessen, Martin van. "The Kurds between Iran and Iraq." *MERIP/Middle East Report* 16 (July–August 1986): 14–27.

Dann, Uriel. "The Kurdish National Movement in Iraq." *Jerusalem Quarterly* 9 (Fall 1978): 131–44.

Eagleton, William. "Iraqi Kurdistan: A Little Known Region." *World Today* 12 (October 1956): 417–32.

Edmonds, Cecil John. "The Kurdish National Struggle in Iraq." *Asian Affairs* 58 (June 1971): 147–58.

———. "The Kurds and the Revolution in Iraq." *Middle East Journal* 13 (Winter 1959): 1–10.

———. "The Kurds of Iraq." *Middle East Journal* 11 (Winter 1957): 52–62.

———. *Kurds, Turks and Arabs: Politics, Travel and Research in North-Eastern Iraq, 1919–1925*. London: Oxford University Press, 1957.

Emanuelsson, Ann-Catrin. "Chasing the Rainbow: Historical and Economic Constraints Affecting Kurdish National Aspirations in Iraq." *International Journal of Kurdish Studies* 8, nos. 1–2 (1995): 110–25.

Field, Michael, and James Kinsman. "Iraq and the Kurds." *World Survey* no. 22 (1970): 1–20.

Fieldhouse, D. K. *Kurds, Arabs and Britons: The Memoir of Col. W. A. Lyon in Iraq, 1918–1945*. London: Tauris, 2001.

Gunter, Michael. "Mulla Mustafa and the Kurdish Rebellion in Iraq: The Intelligence Factor." *International Journal of Intelligence and CounterIntelligence* 7 (Winter 1994): 465–74.

Husry, Khaldun S. "The Assyrian Affair of 1933 (I) and (II)." *International Journal of Middle East Studies* 5, no. 2 (1974): 161–76; no. 3 (1974): 344–60.

Jawad, Sa'ad. "Recent Developments in the Kurdish Issue." In *Iraq: The Contemporary State,* ed. Tim Niblock, 47–61. New York: St. Martin's, 1982.
————. *Iraq and the Kurdish Question, 1958–1970.* London: Ithaca, 1981.
Kanaani, Nauman M. al-. *Limelight on the North of Iraq.* Baghdad: Dar al-Jumhuriya, 1965.
Karadaghi, Kamran. "The Two Gulf Wars: The Kurds on the World Stage, 1979–1992." In *A People without a Country: The Kurds and Kurdistan,* ed. Gerard Chaliand, 214–30. New York: Olive Branch, 1993.
Korn, David A. "The Last Years of Mustafa Barzani." *Middle East Quarterly* 1 (March 1994): 12–27.
MacDonald, Charles G. "The Impact of the Gulf War on the Iraqi and Iranian Kurds." *Middle East Contemporary Survey* 7 (1982–1983): 261–72.
Malek, Mohammed H. "Kurdistan in the Middle East Conflict." *New Left Review,* no. 175 (May–June 1989): 79–94.
Naamani, Israel. "The Kurdish Drive for Self-determination." *Middle East Journal* 20 (Summer 1966): 279–95.
National Foreign Assessment Center (U.S. Central Intelligence Agency). *The Kurdish Problem in Perspective.* August 1979.
Nehme, Michel G., and Lokman I. Meho. "Pawns in a Deadly Game: Iraqi Kurds and the United States, 1972–1975." *International Studies* 32 (January–March 1995): 41–55.
O'Ballance, Edgar. *The Kurdish Revolt, 1961–70.* London: Faber & Faber, 1973.
Olson, Robert. "The Churchill–Cox Correspondence regarding the Creation of the State of Iraq: Consequences for British Policy towards the Nationalist Turkish Government, 1921–1923." *International Journal of Turkish Studies* 5 (Winter 1990–1991): 121–36.
Schmidt, Dana Adams. "The Kurdish Insurgency." *Strategic Review* 2 (Summer 1974): 51–58.
————. "Recent Developments in the Kurdish War." *Journal of the Royal Central Asian Society* 53 (February 1966): 23–31.
————. *Journey among Brave Men.* Boston: Little, Brown, 1964.
Sherzad, A. "The Kurdish Movement in Iraq, 1975–88." In *The Kurds: A Contemporary Overview,* ed. Philip G. Kreyenbroek and Stefan Sperl, 134–42. London: Routledge, 1992.
Sluglett, Peter. "The Kurds." In *Saddam's Iraq: Revolution or Reaction?* 177–202. 2d ed. London: Zed, 1989.
Spencer, William. "The Mosul Question in International Relations." Ph.D. diss., American University, Washington, D.C., 1965.
Thawra, ath- (Central Organ of the Baath Party). *Settlement of the Kurdish Problem in Iraq: Discussion and Documents on the Peaceful and Democratic Settlement of the Problem.* Baghdad: Ath-Thawra, 1974.

U.S. Congress. Senate. Committee on Foreign Relations. *Kurdistan in the Time of Saddam Hussein.* 102d Cong., 1st sess., November 1991.

————. *Civil War in Iraq.* By Peter W. Galbraith, 102d Cong., 1st sess., May 1991.

————. *Chemical Weapons Use in Kurdistan: Iraq's Final Offensive.* A staff report by Peter W. Galbraith and Christopher Van Hollen Jr., 100th Cong., 2d sess., September 21, 1988.

Vanly, Ismet Cheriff. "Kurdistan in Iraq." In *People without a Country: The Kurds and Kurdistan,* ed. Gerard Chaliand, 153–210. London: Zed, 1980.

————. *Le Kurdistan irakien: Entité nationale. Étude de la Révolution de 1961.* Neuchatel: Editions de la Baconnière, 1970.

Viotti Paul R. "Iraq: The Kurdish Rebellion." In *Insurgency in the Modern World,* ed. Bard E. O'Neill, William R. Heaton, and Donald J. Alberts, 191–201. Boulder, Colo.: Westview, 1980.

Yapp, Malcolm. "The Mice Will Play: Kurds, Turks and the Gulf War." In *The Gulf War: Regional and International Dimensions,* ed. Hanns Maull and Otto Pick, 103–18. London: Pinter, 1989.

Lebanon

Meho, Lokman I. "The Kurds in Lebanon: A Social and Historical Overview." *International Journal of Kurdish Studies* 16, nos. 1–2 (2002): 59–82.

Turkey

Bruinessen, Martin van. "The Kurds in Turkey." *MERIP/Middle East Report* 14 (February 1984): 6–12, 14.

————. "Popular Islam, Kurdish Nationalism and Rural Revolt: The Rebellion of Shaikh Said in Turkey (1925)." In *Religion and Rural Revolt,* ed. Janos M. Bak and Gerhard Benecke, 281–95. Manchester: Manchester University Press, 1984.

Natali, Denise. "Kurdayeti in the Late Ottoman and Qajar Empires." *Critique: Critical Middle Eastern Studies* 11 (Fall 2002): 177–99.

Nezan, Kendal. "Kurdistan in Turkey." In *A People without a Country: The Kurds and Kurdistan,* ed. Gerard Chaliand, 38–94. New York: Olive Branch Press, 1993.

————. "The Kurds under the Ottoman Empire." In *A People without a Country: The Kurds and Kurdistan,* ed. Gerard Chaliand, 11–37. New York: Olive Branch Press, 1993.

Olson, Robert. "The Sheikh Said Rebellion: Its Impact on the Development of the Turkish Air Force." *Journal of Kurdish Studies* 1, no. 1 (1996): 77–83.

———. "The Sheikh Said Rebellion in Turkey in 1925: Estimates of Troops Employed." *Turcica: Revue d'Études Turquies* 24 (1992): 263–75.

———. "Five Stages of Kurdish Nationalism, 1880–1980." *Journal of Muslim Minority Affairs* 12, no. 2 (1991): 392–410.

———. "Kurds and Turks: Two Documents Concerning Kurdish Autonomy in 1922 and 1923." *Journal of South Asian and Middle Eastern Studies* 15, no. 2 (1991): 20–31.

———. "The International Consequences of the Sheikh Said Rebellion." In *Naqshbandis: Historical Developments and Present Situation of a Muslim Mystical Order,* ed. Marc Georieau, Alexander Popovic, and Thierry Zarcone, 379–406. Paris: Isis, 1990.

———. *The Emergence of Kurdish Nationalism and the Sheikh Said Rebellion, 1880–1925.* Austin: University of Texas Press, 1989.

———. "The Kocgiri Kurdish Rebellion in 1921 and the Draft Law for a Proposed Autonomy of Kurdistan." *Oriente Moderno* 8 (January–June 1989): 41–56.

———. "The Second Time Around: British Policy towards the Kurds (1921–22)." *Die Welt des Islams* 27, nos. 1–3 (1987): 91–102.

Ozoglu, Hakan. "'Nationalism' and Kurdish Notables in the Late Ottoman–Early Republican Era." *International Journal of Middle East Studies* 33 (August 2001): 383–409.

———. "Unimaginable Community: Nationalism and Kurdish Notables in the Late Ottoman Era." Ph.D. diss., Ohio State University, 1997.

———. "State–Tribe Relations: Kurdish Tribalism in the 16th- and 17th-Century Ottoman Empire." *British Journal of Middle Eastern Studies* 23, no. 1 (1996): 5–27.

White, Paul J. "Ethnic Differentiation among the Kurds: Kurmanci, Kizilbash, and Zaza." *Journal of Arabic, Islamic, and Middle Eastern Studies* 2 (November 1995): 67–90.

POLITICS

General

Ahmed, Mohammed M. A., and Michael M. Gunter, eds. *The Kurdish Question and International Law: An Analysis of the Legal Rights of the Kurdish People.* Oakton, Va.: Ahmed Foundation for Kurdish Studies, 2000.

Barkey, Henri J. "Kurdish Geopolitics." *Current History* 96 (January 1997): 1–5.

Bozarslan, Hamit. "Etats et modes de gestion du problème kurde et mouvement kurde." *Peuples Méditerranéens,* nos. 68–69 (July–December 1994): 185–214.

———. "La regionalisation du problème kurde." In *La Nouvelle Dynamique au Moyen-Orient,* ed. Elizabeth Picard. Paris: L'Harmattan, 1993.

Bring, Ove. "Kurdistan and the Principle of Self-Determination." *German Yearbook of International Law* 35 (1992): 157–69.

Bruinessen, Martin van. *Kurdish Ethno-Nationalism versus Nation-Building States.* Istanbul: Isis, 2000.

Eccarius–Kelly, Vera. "Political Movements and Leverage Points: Kurdish Activism in the European Diaspora." *Journal of Muslim Minority Affairs* 22 (April 2002): 91–118.

Entessar, Nader. "Kurdish Conflict in a Regional Perspective." In *Change and Continuity in the Middle East: Conflict Resolution and Prospects for Peace,* ed. M. E. Ahari, 47–73. New York: St. Martin's Press, 1996.

———. *Kurdish Ethnonationalism.* Boulder, Colo.: Rienner, 1992.

———. "Kurdish Identity in the Middle East." *Current World Leaders* 34 (April 1991): 27–82.

———. "The Kurdish Mosaic of Discord." *Third World Quarterly* 11 (October 1989): 83–100.

———. "The Kurds in Post-Revolutionary Iran and Iraq." *Third World Quarterly* 6 (October 1984): 911–33.

Falk, Richard. "Problems and Prospects for the Kurdish Struggle for Self-Determination after the End of the Gulf and Cold Wars." *Michigan Journal of International Law* 15 (Winter 1994): 591–603.

Frankland, E. "A New Nationalism for a New World Order? The Kurds." *Small Wars and Insurgencies* 6 (Fall 1995): 183–208.

Fuller, Graham E. "The Fate of the Kurds." *Foreign Affairs* 72 (Spring 1993): 108–21.

Gunter, Michael M. "The Bane of Kurdish Disunity." *Orient* 42 (December 2001): 605–16.

———. "The Kurdish Question and International Law." In *The Kurdish Conflict in Turkey: Obstacles and Chances for Peace and Democracy,* ed. Ferhad Ibrahim and Gulistan Gurbey, 31–56. New York: St. Martin's, 2000.

———. "United States Foreign Policy toward the Kurds." *Orient* 40 (September 1999): 427–37.

———. "Turkey and Iran Face Off in Kurdistan." *Middle East Quarterly* 5 (March 1998): 33–40.

———. "The Kurdish Factor in Middle Eastern Politics." *International Journal of Kurdish Studies* 8, nos. 1–2 (1995): 94–109.

Harris, George. "Whither the Kurds?" In *Global Convulsions: Race, Ethnicity, and Nationalism at the End of the Twentieth Century,* ed. Winston A. Van Horne, 205–23. Albany: State University of New York Press, 1997.

Hussein, Fuad Mohammad. *The Legal Concept of Self-Determination and the Kurdish Question.* Amsterdam: Janny Oei, 1985.

Ibrahim, Ferhad. "The Development of the Kurdish Question Since the Outbreak of the Gulf War." In *Yearbook of the Kurdish Academy 1990,* 41–58. Ratingen, Germany: Kurdish Academy, 1990.

Ignatieff, Michael. *Blood and Belonging: Journeys into the New Nationalism.* New York: Farrar, Straus and Giroux, 1994.

Kazak, Amin M. "The Kurds and Kurdistan: The Struggle for Statehood." In *Indigenous Peoples' Politics: An Introduction,* ed. Marc A. Sills and Glenn T. Morris, 147–62. Denver: Fourth World Center for the Study of Indigenous Law and Politics; University of Colorado, 1993.

Khashan, Hilal. "The Labyrinth of Kurdish Self-Determination." *International Journal of Kurdish Studies* 8, nos. 1–2 (1995): 5–32.

Khashan, Hilal, and Judith Harik. "The Plight of the Kurds." *Bulletin of Peace Proposals* 23, no. 2 (1992): 147–58.

Khosrowshahi, Manouchehr Rostamy. "Management of Communal Conflict in the Middle East: The Case of the Kurds." Ph.D. diss., North Texas State University, 1983.

Kutschera, Chris. *Le Mouvement National Kurde.* Paris: Flammarion, 1979.

MacDonald, Charles. "The Kurds." In *The Ethnic Dimension in International Relations,* ed. Bernard Schechterman and Martin Slann, 123–40. Westport, Conn.: Praeger, 1993.

———. "The Kurdish Question in the 1980s." In *Ethnicity, Pluralism, and the State in the Middle East,* ed. Milton J. Esman and Itamar Rabinovitch, 233–52. Ithaca, N.Y.: Cornell University Press, 1988.

MacDonald, Scott B. "The Kurds in the 1990s." *Middle East Insight* 7 (January–February 1990): 29–35.

Mayall, James. "Non-intervention, Self-determination and the 'New World Order.'" *International Affairs* 67 (July 1991): 421–29.

McDowall, David. "The Kurdish Question in the 1990s." *Peuples Méditerranéens,* nos. 68–69 (July–December 1994): 77–94.

Naamani, Israel. "The Kurdish Drive for Self-determination." *Middle East Journal* 20 (Summer 1966): 279–95.

Nagel, Joane P. "The Conditions of Ethnic Separatism: The Kurds in Turkey, Iran and Iraq." *Ethnicity* 7 (September 1980): 279–97.

Nehme, Michael G., and Hilal Khashan. "Institutionalization and the Enigma of Kurdish Statelessness." *Ethnic Forum* 15 (Spring–Fall 1995): 131–52.

Olson, Robert. "The Kurdish Question and Geopolitic and Geostrategic Changes in the Middle East after the Gulf War." *Journal of South Asian and Middle Eastern Studies* 17 (Summer 1994): 44–67.

———. "The Kurdish Question Four Years On: The Policies of Turkey, Syria, Iran and Iraq." *Middle East Policy* 3, no. 3 (1994): 136–44.

————. "The Creation of a Kurdish State in the 1990s?" *Journal of South Asian and Middle Eastern Studies* 15 (Summer 1992): 1–25.

————. "The Kurdish Question in the Aftermath of the Gulf War: Geopolitical and Geostrategic Changes in the Middle East." *Third World Quarterly* 13, no. 3 (1992): 475–99.

O'Shea, Maria T. "Between the Map and the Reality: Some Fundamental Myths of Kurdish Nationalism." *Peuples Méditerranéens,* nos. 68–69 (July–December 1994): 77–94.

Otis, P. "Political and Military Considerations of the Kurdish Case 1991: A Window of Opportunity?" *Small Wars and Insurgencies* 2, no. 1 (1991): 61–90.

Qazzaz, Shafiq. "Nationalism and Cultural Pluralism: The Kurdish Case." Ph.D. diss., American University, Washington, D.C., 1971.

Saeedpour, Vera Beaudin. "Kurdish Hopes, Kurdish Fears: A Survey of Kurdish Public Opinion." *Kurdish Studies: An International Journal* 5 (Spring–Fall 1992): 5–28.

————. "Kurdish Times and the New York Times." *Kurdish Times* 2, no. 2 (1988): 39–58.

Sheikhmous, Omar. "The Kurdish Question: Conflict Resolution Strategies at the Regional Level." In *Building Peace in the Middle East: Challenges for States and Civil Society,* ed. Elise Boulding, 147–61. Boulder, Colo.: Rienner, 1994.

Whitley, Andrew. "The Kurds: Pressures and Prospects." *Round Table* 279 (July 1980): 245–57, 279.

Yavuz, Hakan M., and Michael M. Gunter. "The Kurdish Nation." *Current History* 100 (January 2001): 33–39.

Iran

Ahmadi, Hamid. "The Politics of Ethnic Nationalism in Iran (Kurdish, Azari, Baluchi Identity)." Ph.D. diss., Carleton University, Canada, 1995.

Coyle, James John. *Nationalism in Iranian Kurdistan.* Ph.D. diss., George Washington University, 1993.

Farzanfar, Ramesh. "Ethnic Groups and the State: Azaris, Kurds and Baluch of Iran." Ph.D. diss., Massachusetts Institute of Technology, 1992.

Koohi–Kamali, Fereshteh. *Economic and Social Bases of Kurdish Nationalism in Iran.* Ph.D. diss., Oxford University, 1995.

O'Shea, Maria T. "The Question of Kurdistan and Iran's International Borders." In *The Boundaries of Modern Iran,* ed. Keith McLachlan, 47–56. New York: St. Martin's, 1994.

Yalda, Nariman. "Federalism and Self-Rule for Minorities: A Case Study of Iran and Kurdistan." Ph.D. diss., Claremont Graduate School, 1980.

Iraq

Abd al-Jabbar, Faleh. "Why the Intifada Failed." In *Iraq Since the Gulf War: Prospects for Democracy,* ed. Fran Hazelton, 97–117. London: Zed, 1994.

Awadani e. V., ed. *Irakisch–Kurdistan: Status und Perspektiven.* Berlin: Awadani e. V.: 1999.

Batatu, Hanna. *The Old Social Classes and the Revolutionary Movements of Iraq: A Study of Iraq's Old Landed and Commercial Classes and of Its Communists, Ba'athists, and Free Officers.* Princeton, N.J.: Princeton University Press, 1978.

Bengio, Ofra. "Nation Building in Multiethnic Societies: The Case of Iraq." In *Minorities and the State in the Arab World,* ed. Ofra Bengio and Gabriel Ben–Dor, 149–69. Boulder, Colo.: Rienner, 1999.

———. "The Challenge to the Territorial Integrity of Iraq." *Survival: The International Institute for Strategic Studies Quarterly* 37 (Summer 1995): 74–94.

———. "Experimentation in Kurdish Self-Rule." In *Middle East Contemporary Survey, Vol. XVII: 1993,* ed. Ami Ayalon, 381–88. Boulder, Colo.: Westview, 1995.

———. 'Iraq's Shi'a and Kurdish Communities: From Resentment to Revolt." In *Iraq's Road to War,* ed. Amatzia Baram and Barry Rubin, 51–66. New York: St. Martin's, 1993.

Benjamin, Charles. "The Kurdish Nonstate Nation." In *Nonstate Nations in International Politics: Comparative System Analyses,* ed. Judy S. Bertelsen, 69–77. New York: Praeger, 1977.

Bhattacharya, Sauri P. "The Situation of the Kurds in the Post–Gulf War Period and U.S. Policy toward It." *Asian Profile* 22 (April 1994): 151–60.

Dann, Uriel. *Iraq under Qassem: A Political History, 1958–1963.* New York: Praeger, 1969.

Farouk–Sluglett, Marion, and Peter Sluglett. *Iraq since 1958: From Revolution to Dictatorship.* London: Kegan Paul International, 1987.

Francke, Rend Rahim. "The Opposition." In *Iraq since the Gulf War: Prospects for Democracy,* ed. Fran Hazelton, 153–77. London: Zed, 1994.

Freij, Hanna Yousif. "Tribal Identity and Alliance Behaviour among Factions of the Kurdish National Movement in Iraq." *Nationalism & Ethnic Politics* 3 (Autumn 1997): 86–110.

Ghareeb, Edmund. *The Kurdish Question in Iraq.* Syracuse, N.Y.: Syracuse University Press, 1981.

Goldberg, Jeffrey. "The Great Terror." *New Yorker,* 25 March 2002, 52–75.

Graham–Brown, Sarah. "Intervention, Sovereignty and Responsibility: The Iraq Sanctions Dilemma." *Middle East Report* 25 (March–April 1995): 2–12, 32.

Gunter, Michael M. "The Iraqi Opposition and the Failure of U.S. Intelligence." *International Journal of Intelligence and CounterIntelligence* 12 (Summer 1999): 135–67.

————. *The Kurdish Predicament in Iraq: A Political Analysis*. New York: St. Martin's, 1999.

————. "The Foreign Policy of the Iraqi Kurds." *Journal of South Asian and Middle Eastern Studies* 20 (Spring 1997): 1–19.

————. "The Iraqi National Congress (INC) and the Future of the Iraqi Opposition." *Journal of South Asian and Middle Eastern Studies* 19 (Spring 1996): 1–20.

————. "The KDP–PUK Conflict in Northern Iraq." *Middle East Journal* 50 (Spring 1996): 225–41.

————. "A Kurdish State in Northern Iraq?" *Humboldt Journal of Social Relations* 20, no. 2 (1995): 45–94.

————. "A Trip to Free Kurdistan." *PS: Political Science and Politics* 27 (March 1994): 146–48.

————. " A *de facto* Kurdish State in Northern Iraq." *Third World Quarterly* 14, no. 2 (1993): 295–319.

————. "Foreign Influences on the Kurdish Insurgency in Iraq." *Orient* 34 (March 1993): 105–19.

————. *The Kurds of Iraq: Tragedy and Hope*. New York: St. Martin's, 1992.

————. "The Iraqi Kurds after the 1991 Gulf War." *Crossroads: A Socio-Political Journal*, no. 32 (1991): 3–29.

Harris, George S. "The Kurdish Conflict in Iraq." In *Ethnic Conflict in International Relations*, ed. Astri Suhrke and Lela Garner Noble, 68–92. New York: Praeger, 1977.

Heraclides, Alexis. *The Self-Determination of Minorities in International Politics*. London: Cass, 1991.

Hoagland, Jim. "How the CIA's Secret War on Saddam Collapsed." *Washington Post*, 26 June 1997: A21, A28–A29.

Hunter, Shireen T. "Two Years after the Gulf War: A Status Report on Iraq and the Region." *Security Dialogue* 24 (March 1993): 21–36.

Keen, David. *The Kurds in Iraq: How Safe Is Their Haven Now?* London: Save the Children, 1993.

Khalil, Samir al- (Kanan Makiya). *The Republic of Fear: The Politics of Modern Iraq*. Berkeley: University of California Press, 1989.

Korn, David A. "Democracy for the Kurds." *Freedom Review* 25 (May–June 1994): 16–18.

Kutschera, Chris. "Kurds in Crisis." *Middle East*, no. 253 (November 1995): 6–10.

Makiya, Kanan. *Cruelty and Silence: War, Tyranny, Uprising and the Arab World*. New York: Norton, 1993.

Malanczuk, Peter. "The Kurdish Crisis and Allied Intervention in the Aftermath of the Second Gulf War." *European Journal of International Law* 2, no. 2 (1991): 114–32.

Morad, Munir. "The Situation of Kurds in Iraq and Turkey: Current Trends and Prospects." In *The Kurds: A Contemporary Overview*, ed. Philip G. Kreyenbroek and Stefan Sperl, 115–33. London: Routledge, 1992.

Mylroie, Laurie. "After Saddam Hussein." *Atlantic* 270 (December 1992): 36–38; 49–52.

Nagel, Joane, and Brad Whorton. "Ethnic Conflict and the World System: International Competition in Iraq (1961–1991) and Angola (1974–1991)." *Journal of Political and Military Sociology* 20 (Summer 1992): 1–35.

Natili, Denise. "Manufacturing Identity and Managing Kurds in Iraq." In *Rightsizing the State: The Politics of Moving Borders*, ed. Brendan O'Leary, Ian S. Lustick, and Thomas Callaghy, 253–88. Oxford: Oxford University Press, 2001.

———. *International Aid, Regional Politics, and the Kurdish Issue in Iraq Since the Gulf War*. Occasional Series, no. 31. Abu Dhabi: Emirates Center for Strategic Studies and Research, 1999.

Ofteringer, Ronald, and Ralf Backer. "A Republic of Statelessness: Three Years of Humanitarian Intervention in Iraqi Kurdistan." *MERIP/Middle East Report* 24 (March–April/May–June 1994): 40–45.

O'Leary, Carole A. "The Kurds of Iraq: Recent History, Future Prospects." *Middle East Review of International Affairs (MERIA)* 16, no. 4 (December 2002). At meria.idc.ac.il (accessed December 10, 2002).

Olson, Robert. "The Creation of a Kurdish State in the 1990s?" *Journal of South Asian and Middle Eastern Studies* 15 (Summer 1992): 1–25.

Pelletiere, Stephen. *The Kurds and Their Agas: An Assessment of the Situation in Northern Iraq*. Carlisle Barracks, Pa.: Strategic Studies Institute, 1991.

Prince, James M. "A Kurdish State in Iraq?" *Current History* 92 (January 1993): 17–22.

Rudd, Gordon William. "Operation Provide Comfort: Humanitarian Intervention in Northern Iraq, 1991 (Kurds, Military)." Ph.D. diss., Duke University, 1993.

Sahagun, Felipe. "The New Kurdish Protectorate." *European Journal of International Affairs* 12, no. 2 (1991): 82–106.

Salih, Barham. "Sources of Conflict in the Middle East: The Kurds." In *Powder Keg in the Middle East: The Struggle for Gulf Security*, ed. Geoffrey Kemp and Janice Gross Stein, 237–46. Lanham, Md.: Rowman & Littlefield, 1995.

Salih, Khaled. "Demonizing a Minority: The Case of the Kurds in Iraq." In *Nationalism, Minorities and Diasporas: Identities and Rights in the Middle East*, ed. Kirsten E. Schulze, Martin Stokes, and Colm Campbell, 81–94. New York: Tauris, 1996.

Schmidt, L. "New Politics in Southern Kurdistan." *Argument* 36 (May–June 1994): 419–30.

Shackelford, Collins Guyton. "The Politics and Dilemmas of Humanitarian Assistance (Operation Provide Comfort, Operation Sea Angel, Operation Restore Hope, Military Operations, Disaster Relief)." Ph.D. diss., University of Illinois at Urbana–Champaign, 1995.

Stromseth, Jane E. "Iraqi Repression of Its Civilian Population: Collective Response and Contingency Challenges." In *Enforcing Restraint: Collective Intervention in Internal Conflicts,* ed. Lori Fisler Darmosch, 76–117. New York: Council on Foreign Relations Press, 1993.

Talabany, Nouri. *Arabization of the Kirkuk Region.* Uppsala, Sweden: Kurdistan Studies Press, 2001.

Waterbury, John. "Strangling the Kurds: Saddam Hussein's Economic War against Northern Iraq." *Middle East Insight* 9 (July–August 1993): 31–38.

Wenner, Lettie M. "Arab–Kurdish Rivalries in Iraq." *Middle East Journal* 17 (Winter–Spring 1963): 68–82.

Zeltzer, Moshe. *Aspects of Near East Society.* New York: Bookman Associates, 1962.

Lebanon

Meho, Lokman I. "The Kurds in Lebanon: An Overview." In *Kurdish Culture and Society: An Annotated Bibliography*, ed. Lokman I. Meho and Kelly L. Maglaughlin, 27–47. Westport, Conn.: Greenwood, 2001.

Soviet Union, Russia

Aristova, T. F. "Kurds." In *Encyclopedia of World Cultures, Volume VI: Russia and Eurasia/China,* ed. Paul Friedrich and Norma Diamond, 224–27. Boston: Hall, 1994.

———."The Reflection of Ethnic Processes in the Traditional Domestic Culture of the Kurds of Azerbaijan and Turkmenia." *Soviet Anthropology and Archaeology* 20, no. 1 (1981): 3–24.

———. "Kurds of the Turkmen SSR." *Central Asian Review,* no. 4 (1965): 302–9.

———. "The Kurds of Transcaucasia." *Central Asian Review,* no. 2 (1959): 163–74.

Dziegel, Leszek. "The Kurds Today: Between Local, Regional and National Identity." *Studia Ethnologica Croatica* 6 (1994): 105–17.

Gasratyan, M. "The Great October Revolution and the Kurds." In *The October Socialist Revolution and the Middle East: A Collection of Articles by Soviet Scholars,* 83–97. Lahore: People's Publishing House, 1987.

Hensel, Howard M. "Soviet Policy towards the Kurdish Question, 1970–75." *Soviet Union* 6, no. 1 (1979): 61–80.

Howell, Wilson Nathaniel, Jr. "The Soviet Union and the Kurds: A Study of National Minority Problems in Soviet Policy." Ph.D. diss., University of Virginia, 1965.

Marlay, Ross. "Kurds." In *An Ethnohistorical Dictionary of the Russian and Soviet Empires,* ed. James S. Olson, 408–12. Westport, Conn.: Greenwood, 1994.

Naby, Eden. "The Iranian Frontier Nationalities: The Kurds, the Assyrians, the Baluchis and the Turkmens." In *Soviet Asian Ethnic Frontiers,* ed. William O. McCagg Jr. and Brian D. Silver, 83–114. New York: Pergamon, 1979.

Nadirov, Nadir. "Population Transfer: A Scattered People Seeks Its Nationhood." *Cultural Survival Quarterly* 16 (Winter 1992): 38–40.

———. "What Do the Soviet Kurds Want?" *Asia and Africa Today,* no. 1 (January–February 1991): 74–76.

[Nezan], Kendal. "Kurdistan in the Soviet Union." In *A People without a Country: The Kurds and Kurdistan,* ed. Gerard Chaliand, 202–210. New York: Olive Branch, 1993.

Olson, Robert. "Foreign Policy of the Soviet Union toward the Turkoman Rebellion in Eastern Iran in 1924 and the Kurdish Rebellion of Shaikh Said in Eastern Turkey in 1925: A Comparison." *Central Asian Survey* 9, no. 4 (1990): 75–83.

Vanly, Ismet Cheriff. "The Kurds in the Soviet Union." In *The Kurds: A Contemporary Overview,* ed. Philip G. Kreyenbroek and Stefan Sperl, 193–218. London: Routledge, 1992.

Syria

Feili, Imran Yahya. "The Status of the Kurds in Syria." In *The Syrian Arab Republic: A Handbook,* ed. Anne Sinai and Allen Pollack, 63–65. New York: American Academic Association for Peace in the Middle East, 1976.

Lescot, Roger. "Le Kurd Dagh et le mouvement mouroud." *Studia Kurdica* (1988): 101–25.

McDowall, David. *The Kurds of Syria.* London: Kurdish Human Rights Project, 1998.

Nazdar, Mustafa (Ismet Cheriff Vanly). "The Kurds in Syria." In *A People without a Country: The Kurds and Kurdistan,* ed. Gerard Chaliand, 194–201. New York: Olive Branch Books, 1993.

Vanly, Ismet Cheriff. "The Oppression of the Kurdish People in Syria." In *Kurdish Exodus: From Internal Displacement to Diaspora,* ed. Mohammed M. A. Ahmed and Michael M. Gunter, 49–61. Sharon, Mass.: Ahmed Foundation for Kurdish Studies, 2002.

———. "The Kurds in Syria and Lebanon." In *The Kurds: A Contemporary*

Overview, ed. Philip G. Kreyenbroek and Stefan Sperl, 143–70. London: Routledge, 1992.

———. *The Kurdish Problem in Syria: Plans for the Genocide of a National Minority.* [Europe]: The Committee for the Defence of the Kurdish People's Rights, 1968.

Turkey

Abramowitz, Morton I. "Dateline Ankara: Turkey after Ozal." *Foreign Policy,* no. 91 (Summer 1993): 164–85.

Aras, Bulent, and Gokham Bacik. "The Mystery of Turkish Hizballah." *Middle East Policy* 9 (June 2002): 147–60.

Arbuckle, Tammy. "Winter Campaign in Kurdistan." *International Defense Review* 28 (February 1995): 59–61.

Ataman, Muhittin. "Ozal Leadership and Restructuring of Turkish Ethnic Policy in the 1980s." *Middle Eastern Studies* 38 (October 2002): 123–42.

Avebury, Lord Eric. "Turkey's Kurdish Policy in the Nineties." *International Journal of Kurdish Studies* 9, nos. 1–2 (1996): 3–34.

Aykan, Mahmut Bali. "Turkey's Policy in Northern Iraq, 1991–95." *Middle Eastern Studies* 32 (October 1996): 343–66.

Barkey, Henri J. "The People's Democracy Party (HADEP): The Travails of a Legal Kurdish Party in Turkey." *Journal of Muslim Minority Affairs* 18 (April 1998): 129–38.

———. "Turkey, Islamic Politics, and the Kurdish Question." *World Policy Journal* 13 (Spring 1996): 43–52.

———. "Under the Gun: Turkish Foreign Policy and the Kurdish Question." In *The Kurdish Nationalist Movement in the 1990s: Its Impact on Turkey and the Middle East,* ed. Robert Olson, 65–83. Lexington: University Press of Kentucky: 1996,

———. "Turkey's Kurdish Dilemma." *Survival* 35 (Winter 1993): 51–70.

Barkey, Henri J., and Graham E. Fuller. *Turkey's Kurdish Question.* Lanham, Md.: Rowman & Littlefield, 1998.

———. "Turkey's Kurdish Question: Critical Turning Points and Missed Opportunities." *Middle East Journal* 51 (Winter 1997): 59–79.

Besikci, Ismail. *Kurdistan & Turkish Colonialism: Selected Writings.* London: Kurdistan Solidarity Committee and Kurdistan Information Centre, 1991.

Bolugiray, Nevzat. *Separatist Terror during the Ozal Era (1983–1991).* Ankara: Tekin Yayinevi, 1992.

Bolukbasi, Suha. "Turkey Challenges Iraq and Syria: The Euphrates Dispute." *Journal of South Asian and Middle Eastern Studies* 16 (Summer 1993): 9–32.

———. "Ankara, Damascus, Baghdad, and the Regionalization of Turkey's Kurdish Secessionism." *Journal of South Asian and Middle Eastern Studies* 14 (Summer 1991): 15–36.

———. "Turkey Copes with Revolutionary Iran." *Journal of South Asian and Middle Eastern Studies* 13 (Fall–Winter 1989): 94–109.

Border, Jake. "Orphan Guerrillas: Lonely Struggle of Kurdish Freedom Fighters." *Soldier of Fortune* (October 1992): 38–43, 80.

Bowing, Bill. "The Kurds of Turkey: Defending the Rights of a Minority." In *Nationalism, Minorities and Diasporas: Identities and Rights in the Middle East,* ed. Kirsten E. Schulze, Martin Stokes, and Colm Campbell, 23–38. New York: Tauris, 1996.

Bozarslan, Hamit. "Why the Armed Struggle? Understanding the Violence in Kurdistan of Turkey." In *The Kurdish Conflict in Turkey: Obstacles and Chances for Peace and Democracy,* ed. Ferhad Ibrahim and Gulistan Gurbey, 17–30. New York: St. Martin's, 2000.

———. "Political Crisis and the Kurdish Issue in Turkey." In *The Kurdish Nationalist Movement in the 1990s: Its Impact on Turkey and the Middle East,* ed. Robert Olson, 135–53. Lexington: University Press of Kentucky, 1996.

———. "Turkey's Elections and the Kurds." *Middle East Report,* no. 199 (April–June 1996): 16–19.

———. "Political Aspects of the Kurdish Problem in Contemporary Turkey." In *The Kurds: A Contemporary Overview,* ed. Philip G. Kreyenbroek and Stefan Sperl, 95–114. London: Routledge, 1992.

Brown, James. "The Turkish Imbroglio: Its Kurds." *Annals of the American Academy of Political and Social Sciences,* no. 541 (September 1995): 116–29.

Bruinessen, Martin van. "Shifting National and Ethnic Identities: The Kurds in Turkey and the European Diaspora." *Journal of Muslim Minority Affairs* 18 (April 1998): 39–52.

———. "Turkey's Death Squads." *Middle East Report,* no. 199 (April–June 1996): 20–23.

———. "The Kurds in Turkey: Further Restrictions of Basic Rights." *International Commission of Jurists: The Review,* no. 45 (December 1990): 46–52.

———. "The Ethnic Identity of the Kurds." In *Ethnic Groups in the Republic of Turkey,* ed. Peter Alford Andrews, 613–21. Wiesbaden, Germany: Reichert, 1989.

———. "Between Guerrilla War and Political Murder: The Workers' Party of Kurdistan." *Middle East Report,* no. 153 (July–August 1988): 40–42, 44–46, 50.

———. "The Kurds in Turkey." *MERIP/Middle East Report,* no. 121 (February 1984): 6–12.

Button, Stephen H. "Turkey Struggles with Kurdish Separatism." *Military Review* 75 (December 1994/January–February 1995): 70–83.

Criss, Nur Bilge. "The Nature of PKK Terrorism in Turkey." *Studies in Conflict and Terrorism* 18 (January–March 1995): 17–37.

Criss, Nur Bilge, and Yavuz Turan Cetiner. "Terrorism and the Issue of International Cooperation." *Journal of Conflict Studies* 20 (Spring 2000): 127–39.

Gunter, Michael M. "The Continuing Kurdish Problem in Turkey after Ocalan's Capture." *Third World Quarterly* 21 (October 2000): 849–69.

———. "Turkey Suspends Ocalan's Execution." *Cultural Survival Quarterly* 24 (Summer 2000): 26–27.

———. "Should Turkey Execute Ocalan?" *Cultural Survival Quarterly* 23 (Fall 1999): 13–14.

———. "An Interview with the PKK's Ocalan." *Journal of Conflict Studies* 18 (Fall 1998): 104–109.

———. "Susurluk: The Connection between Turkey's Intelligence Community and Organized Crime." *International Journal of Intelligence and CounterIntelligence* 11 (Summer 1998): 119–41.

———. "Interview: Abdullah Ocalan, Head of the PKK." *Middle East Quarterly* 5 (June 1998): 79–85.

———. *The Kurds and the Future of Turkey*. New York: St. Martin's, 1997.

———. *The Changing Kurdish Problem in Turkey*. Research Institute for the Study of Conflict & Terrorism, no. 270. London: Research Institute for the Study of Conflict & Terrorism, 1994.

———. "The Kurdish Factor in Turkish Foreign Policy." *Journal of Third World Studies* 11 (Fall 1994): 440–72.

———. "The Gulf War and Turkey: New Attitudes towards the Kurds." *Journal of Asian and African Affairs* 4 (Fall 1992): 60–78.

———. "Transnational Sources of Support for the Kurdish Insurgency in Turkey." *Conflict Quarterly* 11 (Spring 1991): 7–29.

———. "Turkey and the Kurds: New Developments in 1991." *Journal of South Asian and Middle Eastern Studies* 15 (Winter 1991): 32–45.

———. "The Kurdish Insurgency in Turkey." *Journal of South Asian and Middle Eastern Studies* 13 (Summer 1990): 57–81.

———. *The Kurds in Turkey: A Political Dilemma*. Boulder, Colo.: Westview, 1990.

———. "The Suppression of the Kurds in Turkey." *Kurdish Times* 3, no. 2 (1990): 5–16.

———. "Kurdish Militancy in Turkey: The Case of PKK." *Crossroads: A Socio-Political Journal,* no 29 (1989): 43–59.

———. "The Kurdish Problem in Turkey." *Middle East Journal* 42 (Summer 1988): 389–406.

Gurbey, Gulistan. "Peaceful Settlement of Turkey's Conflict through Autonomy." In *The Kurdish Conflict in Turkey: Obstacles and Chances for Peace and Democracy*, ed. Ferhad Ibrahim and Gulistan Gurbey, 57–90. New York: St. Martin's, 2000.

Houston, Christopher. *Islam, Kurds and the Turkish Nation State*. Oxford: Berg, 2001.

———. "Shortcut?" *New Perspectives on Turkey* 16 (Spring 1997): 1–22.

Ibrahim, Ferhad. "The 'Foreign Policy' of the PKK: Regional Allies and Enemies." In *The Kurdish Conflict in Turkey: Obstacles and Chances for Peace and Democracy*, ed. Ferhad Ibrahim and Gulistan Gurbey, 103–18. New York: St. Martin's, 2000.

Ibrahim, Ferhad, and Gulistan Gurbey, ed. *The Kurdish Conflict in Turkey: Obstacles and Chances for Peace and Democracy*. New York: St. Martin's, 2000.

Imset, Ismet G. "The PKK: Terrorists or Freedom Fighters?" *International Journal of Kurdish Studies* 10, nos. 1–2 (1996): 45–100.

———. *The PKK: A Report on Separatist Violence in Turkey (1973–1992)*. Ankara: Turkish Daily News, 1992.

Izady, Mehrdad. "Persian Carrot and Turkish Stick: Contrasting Politics Targeted at Gaining Loyalty from Azeris and Kurds." *Kurdish Times* 3 (Fall 1990): 31–47.

Jung, Dietrich. "Turkey in the 1990s: Democratic Consolidation, Kurdish Insurgency, and the Rise of Civil Society." *Orient* 43 (March 2002): 143–58.

Kadioglu, Ayse. "The Paradox of Turkish Nationalism and the Construction of Official Identity." *Middle Eastern Studies* 32 (April 1996): 177–93.

Kehl–Bodrogi, Krisztina. "Kurds, Turks, or a People in Their Own Right? Competing Collective Identities among the Zazas." *Muslim World* 89 (July–October 1999): 439–54.

Kesic, Obrad. "American–Turkish Relations at Crossroads." *Mediterranean Quarterly* 6 (Winter 1995): 97–108.

Kirisci, Kemal. "Turkey and the Kurdish Safe-Haven in Northern Iraq." *Journal of South Asian and Middle Eastern Studies* 19 (Spring 1996): 21–39.

Kirisci, Kemal, and Gareth M. Winrow. *The Kurdish Question and Turkey: An Example of a Trans-state Ethnic Conflict*. London: Cass, 1997.

Kolars, John. *The Euphrates River and the Southeast Anatolia Development Project*. Carbondale: Southern Illinois University Press, 1991.

Kutschera, Chris. "Mad Dreams of Independence: The Kurds of Turkey and the PKK." *Middle East Report* 24 (July–August 1994): 12–15.

Laber, Jeri. "The Hidden War in Turkey." *New York Review of Books* 41 (June 23, 1994): 47–50.

———. "Turkey's Nonpeople." *New York Review of Books* 35 (4 February 1988): 58–62.

Makovsky, Alan. "Western Dreams and Eastern Problems: Turkey's Long-Cherished Goal of European Integration Is Threatened by Its Kurdish Quandary." *Middle East Insight* 11 (May–June 1995): 23–28.

Mango, Andrew. *Turkey: The Challenge of a New Role.* New York: Praeger, 1994.

———. "Turks and Kurds." *Middle Eastern Studies* 30 (October 1994): 975–97.

Marcus, Aliza. "With the Kurdish Guerrillas." *Dissent* 41 (Spring 1994): 178–81.

———. "Turkey's Kurds after the Gulf War: A Report from the Southeast." In *A People without a Country: The Kurds and Kurdistan,* ed. Gerard Chaliand, 238–47. New York: Olive Branch, 1993.

Muftuler–Bac, Meltem. "Addressing Kurdish Separatism in Turkey." In *Theory and Practice in Ethnic Conflict Management: Theorizing Success and Failure,* ed. Marc Howard Ross and Jay Rothman, 103–19. Houndmills, England: Macmillan, 1999.

Muller, Mark. "Nationalism and the Rule of Law in Turkey: The Elimination of Kurdish Representation during the 1990s." *International Journal of Kurdish Studies* 10, nos. 1–2 (1996): 9–44.

Nestor, Carl E. "The Southeast Anatolian Project (GAP) and Turkey's Kurdish Question: Part II." *International Journal of Kurdish Studies.* 9, nos. 1–2 (1996): 35–78.

———. "Dimensions of Turkey's Kurdish Question and the Potential Impact of the Southeast Anatolian Project (GAP): Part I." *International Journal of Kurdish Studies* 8, nos. 1–2 (1995): 33–78.

Nigogosian, Aram. "Turkey's Kurdish Problem: Recent Trends." In *The Kurdish Nationalist Movement in the 1990s: Its Impact on Turkey and the Middle East,* ed. Robert Olson, 38–49. Lexington: University Press of Kentucky, 1996.

Ocalan, Abdullah. *Declaration on the Democratic Solution of the Kurdish Question.* London: Mesopotamian, 1999.

Olson, Robert. "Turkey–Iran Relations, 2000–2001: The Caspian, Azerbaijan and the Kurds." *Middle East Policy* 9 (June 2002): 111–29.

———. *Turkey's Relations with Iran, Syria, Israel, and Russia, 1991–2000: The Kurdish and Islamist Questions.* Costa Mesa: Calif.: Mazda, 2001.

———. "Turkey–Iran Relations, 1997–2000: The Kurdish and Islamist Questions." *Third World Quarterly* 21 (October 2000): 871–90.

———. *The Kurdish Question and Turkish–Iranian Relations: From World War I to 1998.* Costa Mesa, Calif.: Mazda, 1998.

———. "Turkish and Russian Foreign Policies, 1991–1997: The Kurdish and Chechnya Questions." *Journal of Muslim Minority Affairs* 18, no. 2 (1998): 209–27.

———. "Turkey–Syria Relations: Kurds and Water." *Middle East Policy* 5, no. 2 (1997): 168–95.

———. "The Impact of the Southeast Anatolian Project (GAP) on Kurdish Nationalism in Turkey." *International Journal of Kurdish Studies* 9, nos. 1–2 (1996): 95–102.

———, ed. *The Kurdish Nationalist Movement in the 1990s: Its Impact on Turkey and the Middle East.* Lexington: University Press of Kentucky, 1996.

———. "The Kurdish Question and Chechnya: Turkish and Russian Foreign Policies Since the Gulf War." *Middle East Policy* 4 (March 1996): 106–18.

———. "The Kurdish Question and Turkey's Foreign Policy, 1991–95: From the Gulf War to the Incursion into Iraq." *Journal of South Asian and Middle Eastern Studies* 19 (Fall 1995): 1–30.

———. "The Kurdish Question and Geopolitic and Geostrategic Changes in the Middle East after the Gulf War." *Journal of South Asian and Middle Eastern Studies* 17 (Summer 1994): 44–67.

Pancio, Christopher. "Turkey's Kurdish Problem." *Jane's Intelligence Review* 7 (April 1995): 170–74.

Robbins, Philip. "More Apparent Than Real? The Impact of the Kurdish Issue on Euro–Turkish Relations." In *The Kurdish Nationalist Movement in the 1990s: Its Impact on Turkey and the Middle East,* ed. Robert Olson, 114–32. Lexington: University Press of Kentucky, 1996.

———. "The Overlord State: Turkish Policy and the Kurdish Issue." *International Affairs* 69 (October 1993): 657–76.

Rouleau, Eric. "Turkey beyond Ataturk." *Foreign Policy,* no. 103 (Summer 1996): 70–87.

Rugman, Jonathan. *Ataturk's Children: Turkey and the Kurds.* New York: Cassell, 1996.

Skutel, H. J. "Turkey's Kurdish Problem." *International Perspectives* 16 (1988): 22–25.

Teimourian, Hazhir. "Turkey—The Challenge of the Kurdistan Workers' Party." *Jane's Intelligence Review* 5 (January 1993): 29–32.

Thompson, Peter. "United States–Turkey Military Relations: Treaties and Implications." *International Journal of Kurdish Studies* 9, nos. 1–2 (1996): 103–13.

Verrier, Michel. "Kurdes: Le dilemme turc." *Cahiers de l'Orient,* no. 30 (1993): 49–56.

White, Paul. *Primitive Rebels or Revolutionary Modernizers? The Kurdish National Movement in Turkey.* London: Zed, 2000.

———. "Citizenship under the Ottomans and Kemalists: How the Kurds Were Excluded." *Citizenship Studies* 3 (February 1999): 71–102.

———. "The March 1990 Uprising in Turkish Kurdistan & Its Effects on Turkish Politics." *Kurdish Times* 4 (Summer–Fall 1991): 97–106.

Yalcin–Heckmann, Lale. "Ethnic Islam and Nationalism among the Kurds in Turkey." In *Islam in Modern Turkey: Religion, Politics, and Literature in a Secular State,* ed. Richard Tapper, 102–20. New York: Tauris, 1991.

Yavuz, M. Hakan. "Five Stages of the Construction of Kurdish Nationalism in Turkey." *Nationalism & Ethnic Politics* 7 (Autumn 2001): 1–24.

———. "Search for a New Social Contract in Turkey: Fethullah Gulen, the Virtue Party, and the Kurds." *SAIS Review* 19 (Winter 1999): 114–43.

———. "Towards an Islamic Liberalism? The Nurcu Movement and Fethullah Gulen." *Middle East Journal* 53 (Autumn 1999): 584–605.

———. "A Preamble to the Kurdish Question: The Politics of Kurdish Identity." *Journal of Muslim Minority Affairs* 18 (April 1998): 9–18.

———. "Turkish Identity and Foreign Policy in Flux: The Rise of Neo-Ottomanism." *Critique* 7 (Spring 1998): 19–41.

Yegan, Mesut. "The Turkish Discourse and the Exclusion of Kurdish Identity." *Middle Eastern Studies* 32 (April 1996): 216–29.

ECONOMICS

Dziegiel, Leszek. *Rural Community of Contemporary Iraqi Kurdistan Facing Modernization.* Krakow: Agricultural Academy of Krakow, 1981.

Emanuelsson, Ann–Catrin. "Chasing the Rainbow: Economic and Social Constraints Facing Kurdish National Aspirations in Iraq." *International Journal of Kurdish Studies* 8, no. 1–2 (1995): 110–25.

Fleming, Glenn. "The Ecology and Economy of Kurdish Villages." *Kurdish Times* 4 (Summer–Fall 1991): 28–41.

Gotlieb, Yosef. "Irreconcilable Planning: The Transformation of Lifeplace into Economic Space in Iraqi and Turkish Kurdistan." *Progress in Planning* 47, no. 4 (1997): 321–32.

———. "Geo-Ethnic Imperatives of Development: The Inter-Dynamics of Territory, Society and State in the Third World (Political Geography, Kurdistan)." Ph.D. diss., Clark University, 1991.

Hama, A. "Towards the Reconstruction of the Rural Territory of Kurdistan." *Space and Society* 18 (April–June 1996): 54–61.

Hussein, Fuad, Michiel Leezenberg, and Pieter Muller. *The Reconstruction and Economic Development of Iraqi Kurdistan.* Amsterdam: Stichting Nederland–Koerdistan, 1993.

Jafar, Majeed R. *Under-Underdevelopment: A Regional Case Study of the Kurdish Area in Turkey.* Helsinki: Social Policy Association in Finland, 1976.

Jaff, Akram. *Economic Development in Kurdistan.* Tallahassee, Fla.: Badlisy Center for Kurdish Studies, 1993.

Kurdistan Committee of Canada. *The Economic and Human Dimensions of Ten Years of War in Kurdistan.* Ottawa: Kurdistan Committee of Canada, 1995.

Nezam–Mafi, Mansoureh E. "Merchants and Government Tobacco and Trade: The Case of Kordestan, 1333 A.H./1919 A.D." *Iranian Studies* 20, no. 1 (1987): 1–15.

Sajjadi, Mansour. "The State of the Economy in Kurdistan." In *Kurdistan: Political and Economic Potential,* ed. Maria T. O'Shea, 36–61. London: GIBRC, SOAS, 1992.

White, Paul. "The Economic Marginalization of Turkey's Kurds: The Failed Promise of Modernization and Reform." *Journal of Muslim Minority Affairs* 18 (April 1998): 139–58.

Yalcin–Heckmann, Lale. "Sheep and Money: Pastoral Production at the Frontiers." In *Culture and Economy: Changes in Turkish Villages,* ed. P. Stirling, 17–26. Hemingford Grey, United Kingdom: Eothen, 1993.

HUMAN RIGHTS

General

Amnesty International. *Amnesty International Report.* London: Amnesty International, 1975/76–.

Bruinessen, Martin van. "Genocide of the Kurds." In *The Widening Circle of Genocide,* ed. Israel W. Charny, 165–91. New Brunswick, N.J.: Transaction, 1994.

Fertig, Ralph. "International and U.S. Laws and the Kurdish Question." In *The Kurdish Question and International Law,* ed. Mohammed M. A. Ahmed and Michael M. Gunter, 75–80. Oakton, Va.: Ahmed Foundation for Kurdish Studies, 2000.

Gunter, Michael. "The Kurdish Question and International Law." In *The Kurdish Conflict in Turkey: Obstacles and Chances for Peace and Democracy,* ed. Ferhad Ibrahim and Gulistan Gurbey, 31–56. New York: St. Martin's, 2000.

Human Rights Watch. *Human Rights Watch World Report.* New York: Human Rights Watch, 1993–.

Paech, Norman. "International Law and the Kurdish Struggle for Freedom." In *The Kurdish Conflict in Turkey: Obstacles and Chances for Peace and Democracy,* ed. Ferhad Ibrahim and Gulistan Gurbey, 159–79. New York: St. Martin's, 2000.

U.S. Department of State. *Country Reports on Human Rights Practices.* Washington, D.C.: Government Printing Office, 1979–.

Iraq

Akhavan, Payam. "Lessons from Iraqi Kurdistan: Self-Determination and Humanitarian Intervention against Genocide." *Netherlands Quarterly of Human Rights* 11, no. 1 (1993): 41–62.

Amnesty International. *Iraq: Human Rights Abuses in Iraqi Kurdistan Since 1991.* London: Amnesty International, 1995.

Bonner, Raymond. "A Reporter at Large: Always Remember." *New Yorker* 68 (28 September 1992): 46–51.

Bruinessen, Martin van. "Genocide in Kurdistan? The Suppression of the Dersim Rebellion in Turkey (1937–1938) and the Chemical War against the Iraqi Kurds (1988)." In *Genocide: Conceptual and Historical Dimensions,* ed. George J. Andreopoulos, 141–70. Philadelphia: University of Pennsylvania Press, 1994.

Connors, Jane. "Humanitarian Legal Order and the Kurdish Question." In *The Kurds: A Contemporary Overview,* ed. Philip G. Kreyenbroek and Stefan Sperl, 84–94. London: Routledge, 1992.

Farer, Tom J. "Human Rights and Foreign Policy: What the Kurds Learned." *Human Rights Quarterly* 14 (November 1992): 62–77.

Human Rights Watch/Middle East. *Iraq's Crime of Genocide: The Anfal Campaign against the Kurds.* New Haven: Yale University Press, 1995.

Kurdish Program. "The Destruction of Iraqi Kurdistan." *Kurdish Times* 2, no. 2 (1988): 1–6.

Makiya, Kanan. "The Anfal: Uncovering an Iraqi Campaign to Exterminate the Kurds." *Harper's* 284 (May 1992): 53–61.

Middle East Watch (written by Joost Hiltermann). *Bureaucracy of Repression: The Iraqi Government in Its Own Words.* New York: Human Rights Watch, 1994.

——— (written by Kenneth Anderson). *The Anfal Campaign in Iraqi Kurdistan: The Destruction of Koreme.* New York: Human Rights Watch, 1993.

——— (written by George Black). *Genocide in Iraq: The Anfal Campaign against the Kurds.* New York: Human Rights Watch, 1993.

——— (written by Eric Goldstein). *Endless Torment: The 1991 Uprising in Iraq and Its Aftermath.* New York: Human Rights Watch. 1992.

———. *Hidden Death: Land Mines and Civilian Casualties in Iraqi Kurdistan.* New York: Human Rights Watch, 1992.

——— (written by Eric Stover). *Unquiet Graves: The Search for the Disappeared in Iraqi Kurdistan.* New York: Human Rights Watch, 1992.

Miller, Judith. "Iraq Accused: A Case of Genocide." *New York Times Magazine* (3 January 1993): 12–17.

Pepper, William F. "Iraq's Crimes of State against Individuals, and Sovereign Immunity: A Comparative Analysis and a Way Forward." *Brooklyn Journal of International Law* 18, no. 2 (1992): 313–84.

Physicians for Human Rights. *Winds of Death: Iraq's Use of Poison Gas against Its Kurdish Population: Report of a Medical Mission to Iraqi Kurdistan.* Somerville, Mass.: Physicians for Human Rights, 1989.

Saeedpour, Vera Beaudin. "Establishing State Motives for Genocide: Iraq and the Kurds." In *Genocide Watch,* ed. Helen Fein, 59–69. New Haven: Yale University Press, 1992.

Talabany, Nouri. "Southern Kurdistan in International Law." In *The Kurdish Question and International Law,* ed. Mohammed M. A. Ahmed and Michael M. Gunter, 95–103. Oakton, Va.: Ahmed Foundation for Kurdish Studies, 2000.

Soviet Union, Russia

Flint, Julie. *The Kurds of Azerbaijan and Armenia.* London: Kurdish Human Rights Project, 1998.

Syria

Middle East Watch (written by Virginia Sherry). *Syria: The Silenced Kurds.* New York: Human Rights Watch, 1996.
———. *Syria Unmasked: The Suppression of Human Rights by the Asad Regime.* New Haven: Yale University Press, 1991.

Vanly, Ismet Cheriff. "Genocide in Syria: Anguish of the Kurds." *Atlas* 16 (August 1968): 43–45.
———. *The Kurdish Problem in Syria: Plans for the Genocide of a National Minority.* [Europe]: The Committee for the Defence of the Kurdish People's Rights, 1968.

Turkey

Amnesty International. *Human Rights and U.S. Security.* New York: Amnesty International, 1995.
———. *Turkey: A Policy of Denial.* New York: Amnesty International, 1995.
———. *Turkey: Unfulfilled Promise of Reform.* New York: Amnesty International, 1995.
———. *Turkey: Dissident Voices Jailed Again.* New York: Amnesty International, 1994.
———. *Turkey: Human Rights Defenders at Risk.* New York: Amnesty International, 1994.
———. *Turkey: Walls of Glass.* New York: Amnesty International, 1992.

Helsinki Watch. *Turkey: Censorship by Assassination Continues.* New York: Helsinki Watch Committee, 1994.

————. *Free Expression in Turkey, 1993: Killings, Convictions, Confisca-tions.* New York: Helsinki Watch Committee (Human Rights Watch), 1993.

————. *Kurds Massacred: Turkish Forces Kill Scores of Peaceful Demon-strators.* New York: Helsinki Watch Committee, 1992.

————. *Turkey: Censorship by Assassination.* New York: Helsinki Watch Committee, 1992.

————. *Turkey: Eight Journalists Killed Since February: A Ninth Critically Wounded.* New York: Helsinki Watch Committee, 1992.

————. *Freedom of Expression in Turkey: Abuses Continue.* New York: Helsinki Watch Committee, 1991.

Human Rights Watch. *Forced Displacement of Ethnic Kurds from Southeast-ern Turkey.* New York: Human Rights Watch, 1994.

Human Rights Watch Arms Project. *Weapons Transfers and Violations of the Laws of War in Turkey.* New York: Human Rights Watch, 1995.

Kemal, Yasar. "The Dark Cloud over Turkey." *Index on Censorship* 24 (Janu-ary–February 1995): 141–46.

Korn, David A. "Turkey's Kurdish Rebellion." *Freedom Review* 26 (May–June 1995): 33–35.

Korn, David A., and Gerald Robbins. "Turkey: Repression and Opportunities." *Freedom Review* 25 (July–August 1994): 15–18.

Laber, Jeri, and Lois Whitman. *Destroying Ethnic Identity: The Kurds of Turkey.* New York: U.S. Helsinki Watch Committee, 1988.

Magnarella, Paul J. "The Legal, Political and Cultural Structures of Human Rights Protections and Abuses in Turkey." *Journal of International Law and Practice* 3 (1994): 439–67.

Marcus, Aliza. "Turkey, the Kurds, and Human Rights." *Dissent* 43 (Summer 1996): 104–107.

McKiernan, Kevin. "Turkey Terrorizes Its Kurds." *Progressive* 57 (July 1993): 28–31.

Parker, Karen. "The Kurdish Insurgency in Turkey in Light of International Humanitarian Law." In *The Kurdish Question and International Law,* ed. Mohammed M. A. Ahmed and Michael M. Gunter. Oakton, Va.: Ahmed Foundation for Kurdish Studies, 2000.

Pope, Nicole. "A Culture Denied." *Index on Censorship* 25 (May–June 1996): 120–21.

————. "Open to Change." *Index on Censorship* 25 (March–April 1996): 155–59.

————. "Letting Go." *Index on Censorship* 24 (January–February 1995): 124–26.

Whitman, Lois. *The Kurds of Turkey: Killings, Disappearances and Torture.* New York: Helsinki Watch, 1993.

———. *Broken Promises: Torture and Killings Continue in Turkey*. New York: Helsinki Watch, 1992.

———. *Paying the Price: Freedom of Expression in Turkey*. New York: Helsinki Watch, 1989.

Whitman, Lois, and Jeri Laber. *Destroying Ethnic Identity: The Kurds of Turkey: An Update*. New York: Human Rights Watch, 1990.

———. *State of Flux: Human Rights in Turkey*. New York: U.S. Helsinki Watch Committee, 1987.

Zana, Leyla. *Writings from Prison*. Watertown, Mass.: Blue Crane, 1999.

Zana, Mehdi. *Prison No. 5: Eleven Years in Turkish Jails*. Watertown, Mass.: Blue Crane, 1997.

LANGUAGE, LITERATURE

Abdulla, Jamal Jalal, and Ernest Nasseph McCarus. *Kurdish Basic Course: Dialect of Sulaimania, Iraq*. Ann Arbor: University of Michigan Press, 1967.

———, ed. *Kurdish Readers, Vol. I: Newspaper Kurdish. Vol. II: Kurdish Essays. Vol. III: Kurdish Short Stories*. Ann Arbor: University of Michigan Press, 1967.

Ahmad, Abdul–Majeed Rashid. "The Phonemic System of Modern Standard Kurdish." Ph.D. diss., University of Michigan, 1986.

Ahmed, Abdullah Mohammed. "Essai sur l'histoire de la littérature kurde au Kurdistan méridional (1820–1920)." Ph.D. diss., University of Paris III, 1988.

Akrawy, F. R. *Standard Kurdish Grammar*. United Kingdom: privately published, 1982.

Allison, Christine. *The Yezidi Oral Tradition in Iraqi Kurdistan*. Richmond, England: Curzon, 2001.

———. "Oral History in Kurdistan: The Case of the Badinani Yezidis." *Journal of Kurdish Studies* 2 (1996–1997): 37–56.

———. "Old and New Oral Tradition in Badinan." In *Kurdish Culture and Identity*, ed. Philip G. Kreyenbroek and Christine Allison, 29–47. London: Zed, 1996.

———. "Views of History and Society in Yezidi Oral Tradition." Ph.D. diss., London School of Oriental and African Studies, 1996.

Amin, Abdul-Kader, comp. *Kurdish Proverbs*. New York: Kurdish Program, 1989.

Asatrian, Garnik D. "Dimili." In *Encyclopaedia Iranica*, Vol. 7, 405–11. Costa Mesa, Calif.: Mazda, 1996.

Blau, Joyce. "Kurdish Written Literature." In *Kurdish Culture and Identity*, ed. Philip G. Kreyenbroek and Christine Allison, 20–28. London: Zed, 1996.

———. "The Poetry of Kurdistan: Language Embodies Kurdish National Unity." *World and I* 6 (August 1991): 623–37.

———. "La Reforme de la Langue Kurde." In *Language Reform: History and Future,* Vol 4, ed. Istvan Fodor and Claude Hagege, 63–85. Hamburg: Helmut Buske, 1989.

———. *Mémoires du Kurdistan: Recueil de la tradition littéraire orale et écrite*. Paris: Editions Findakly, 1984.

———. *Le Kurde de 'Amadiya et de Djabal Sindjar: Analyse linguistique, textes, folkloriques, glossaires*. Paris: Klincksieck, 1975.

Blau, Joyce, and Yasir Suleiman. "Language and Ethnic Identity in Kurdistan: An Historical Overview." In *Language and Identity in the Middle East and North Africa,* ed. Yasir Suleiman, 153–64. Richmond, England: Curzon, 1996.

Bois, Thomas. "[Kurdish] Folklore and Literature." In *Encyclopedia of Islam*. Vol. 5, 480–86. Leiden, Netherlands: Brill, 1986.

———. "Coup d'oeil sur la littérature kurde." *Al-Machriq* (1955): 201–39.

Bordie, John. "Kurdish Dialects in Eastern Turkey." In *Linguistics and Literary Studies in Honor of Archibald A. Hill, Vol. II: Descriptive Linguistics,* ed. M. A. Jazayery et al., 205–212. The Hague: Mouton, 1978.

Bozarslan, Emin. "Three Short Stories." *International Journal of Kurdish Studies* 7, nos. 1–2 (1994): 71–82.

Bruinessen, Martin van. "Les Kurdes et leur langue au XVIIeme siècle: Notes d'Evliya Celebi sur les dialectes kurdes." *Studica Kurdica*, no. 5 (1988): 13–34.

Bynon, Theodora. "The Ergative Construction in Kurdish." *Bulletin of the School of Oriental and African Studies* 42, part. 2 (1979): 211–24.

Chaliand, Gerard, and Roger Lescot, ed. *Anthologie de la poésie populaire kurde*. Paris: Stock, 1980.

Chyet, Michael L. "'And a Thornbush Sprang Up between Them': Studies on 'Mem u Zin,' a Kurdish Romance." Ph.D. diss., University of California at Berkeley, 1991.

Driver, G. R. "The Name Kurd and Its Philological Connexions." *Journal of the Royal Asiatic Society* (1923): 393–403.

Edmonds, Cecil John. "Prepositions and Personal Affixes in Southern Kurdish." *Bulletin of the School of Oriental and African Studies* 17 (1955): 490–502.

———. "Some Developments in the Use of Latin Characters for the Writing of Kurdish." *Journal of the Royal Asiatic Society* (July 1933): 629–42.

———. "Suggestions for the Use of Latin Characters in the Writing of Kurdish." *Journal of the Royal Asiatic Society* (January 1931): 27–46.

Ferhadi, Ahmed. "Some Morphological and Morphophonemic Features of Arbili Kurdish." Ph.D. diss., University of Michigan, 1990.

————. "Boosters in the Interlanguage of Kurds." *PALM* 3 (Fall 1987): 23–45.

Friend, Robyn Christine. "Some Syntactic and Morphological Features of Suleimaniye Kurdish." Ph.D. diss., University of California, Los Angeles, 1985.

Fuad, Kamal. "On the Origins, Development and State of the Kurdish Language." In *Yearbook of the Kurdish Academy 1990*, 11–21. Ratingen, Germany: Kurdish Academy, 1990.

Haig, Geoffrey. "On the Interaction of Morphological and Syntactic Ergativity: Lessons from Kurdish." *Lingua: International Review of General Linguistics* 105 (August 1998): 149–73.

Hasanpour, Jafar. *A Study of European, Persian, and Arabic Loans in Standard Sorani*. Uppsala, Sweden: Uppsala University, 1999.

Hassanpour, Amir. "The Internationalization of Language Conflict: The Case of Kurdish." In *Language Contact–Language Conflict*, ed. Eran Fraenkel and Christina Kramer, 107–55. New York: Peter Lang, 1993.

————. "The Pen and the Sword: Literacy, Education and the Revolution in Kurdistan." In *Knowledge, Culture and Power: International Perspectives on Literacy as Policy and Practice*, ed. Peter Freebody and Anthony R. Welch, 35–54. Pittsburgh, Pa.: University of Pittsburgh Press, 1993.

————. *Nationalism and Language in Kurdistan, 1918–1985*. San Francisco: Mellen Research University Press, 1992.

————. "State Policy on the Kurdish Language: The Politics of Status Planning." *Kurdish Times* 4 (Summer–Fall 1991): 42–85.

Hitchens, Keith. "Kurdish Literature." In *Encyclopedia of World Literature in the 20th Century*. Vol. 2, 683–84. 3d ed. Farmington Hills, Mich.: St. James, 1999.

————. "Goran, Abdulla." In *Encyclopedia of World Literature in the 20th Century*. Vol. 5, 263–64. New York: Continuum, 1993.

Izady, Mehrdad. "A Kurdish Lingua Franca?" *Kurdish Times* 2, no. 2 (1988): 13–24.

Kahn, Margaret. "Borrowing and Variation in a Phonological Descriptive of Kurdish." Ph.D. diss., University of Michigan, 1976.

Karim, D. L. "A Comparative Study of Free Verse in Arabic and Kurdish: The Literary Caress of al-Sayyab and Goran." Ph.D. diss., University of Glasgow, 1985.

Khanaka, Shayee. "Kurdish Humor." Master's thesis, University of California at Berkeley, 1990.

Khaznadar, Marouf. "Kurdish Prose (1945–1961)." *Journal of Kurdish Studies* 2 (1996–1997): 65–70.

Kreyenbroek, Philip G. "On the Kurdish Language." In *The Kurds: A Contem-*

porary Overview, ed. Philip G. Kreyenbroek and Stefan Sperl, 68–83. London: Routledge, 1992.

———. "Kurdish Identity and the Language Question." In *Kurdistan in Search of Ethnic Identity: Papers Presented to the First Conference on Ethnicity and Ethnic Identity in the Middle East and Central Asia,* ed. Turaj Atabaki and Margreet Dorleijn. Utrecht, Netherlands: University of Utrecht Press, 1991.

Lennox, Gina, ed. *Fire, Snow and Honey: A Collection of Essays, Life Stories, Poetry, Fables and Short Fiction.* Sydney: Halstead, 2001.

Lescot, Roger. "Littérature kurde." In *Histoire des Littératures. I. Littératures Anciennes, Orientales et Orales,* ed. Raymond Queneau, 795–805. Paris: Gallimard, 1977.

MacKenzie, David N. "The Kurdish of Mulla Sa'id Samdinani." *Journal of Kurdish Studies* 1 (1995): 1–27.

———. "The Role of the Kurdish Language in Ethnicity." In *Ethnic Groups in the Republic of Turkey,* ed. Peter Alford Andrews, 541–42. Wiesbaden: Ludwig Reichert, 1989.

———. "Kurdish Language." In *Encyclopedia of Islam.* New ed. Vol. V, 479–80. Leiden, Netherlands: Brill, 1986.

———. "Some Gorani Lyric Verse." *Bulletin of the School of Oriental and African Studies* 28 (1965): 255–83.

———. Kurdish *Dialect Studies, I & II.* London: Oxford University Press, 1961–62.

———. "The Origins of Kurdish." *Transactions of the Philological Society* (1961): 68–86.

———. "Gender in Kurdish." *Bulletin of the School of Oriental and African Studies* 16 (1954): 528–41.

Mahamedi, Hamid. "Notes on Some Phonological Developments in Kurdish." *International Journal of Kurdish Studies* 8, nos. 1–2 (1995): 79–93.

Matras, Y. "Ergativity in Kurmanji (Kurdish): Notes on Its Use and Distribution." *Orientalia Suecana,* nos. 41–42 (1992–1993): 139–54.

McCarus, Ernest N. "Kurdish." In *International Encyclopedia of Linguistics.* Vol. 2, 289–94. New York: Oxford University Press, 1992.

———. "Kurdish Language Studies." *Middle East Journal* 14 (Summer 1960): 325–35; 15 (1961): 123–25.

———. *A Kurdish Grammar: Descriptive Analysis of the Kurdish of Sulaimaniya, Iraq.* New York: American Council of Learned Societies, 1958.

Minorsky, Vladimir F. "Folklore, Literature, Newspapers." In *Encyclopedia of Islam,* 1154–55. London: Brill, 1927.

———. "The Kurdish Language." In *Encyclopedia of Islam,* 1151–54. London: Brill, 1927.

Monch–Bucak, Yayla, "The Kurdish Language in Turkey between Repression and Resistance." *Plural Societies* 21, nos. 1–2 (1991): 75–87.

Nikitine, Basile. "Kurdish Stories from My Collection." *Bulletin of the School of Oriental and African Studies* 4 (1926): 121–38.

Nikitine, Basile, and E. B. Soane. "The Tale of Suto and Tato." *Bulletin of the School of Oriental and African Studies* 3 (1923): 69–106.

Noel, Edward William Charles. "The Character of the Kurds as Illustrated by Their Proverbs and Popular Sayings." *Bulletin of the School of Oriental and African Studies* 1 (1920): 79–90.

Oran, Baskin. "Linguistic Minority Rights in Turkey, the Kurds and Globalization." In *The Kurdish Conflict in Turkey: Obstacles and Chances for Peace and Democracy,* ed. Ferhad Ibrahim and Gulistan Gurbey, 151–58. New York: St. Martin's, 2000.

Pierse, Catherine. *Cultural and Language Rights of the Kurds: A Study of the Treatment of Minorities under National Law in Turkey, Iraq, Iran and Syria in Light of International Human Right Standards.* London: Kurdish Human Rights Project, 1997.

Pikkert, P. A. *A Basic Course in Modern Kurmanji.* Genk, Belgium: Alev, 1991.

Resho, Hemresh. "On the History and Development of Writing the Kurdish Language in the Latin Alphabet." In *Yearbook of the Kurdish Academy 1990,* 78–84. Ratingen, Germany: Kurdish Academy, 1990.

Rizgar, Baran. *Learn Kurdish: A Multi-Level Course in Kurmanji.* London: Rizgar, 1996.

Rondot, Pierre. "Trois essais de latinisation de l'alphabet kurde: Iraq, Syrie, U.R.R.S." *Bulletin d'Études Orientales* 5 (1935): 1–31.

Schmid, Estella, et al., ed. *Anthology of Contemporary Kurdish Poetry.* London: Kurdistan Solidarity Committee, 1994.

Skutnabb–Kangas, Tove, and Sertac Bucak. "Killing a Mother Tongue: How the Kurds Are Deprived of Linguistic Human Rights." In *Linguistic Human Rights: Overcoming Linguistic Discrimination,* ed. Tove Skutnabb-Kangas and Robert Phillipson, 347–71. Berlin: de Gruyter, 1994.

Soane, Ely Bannister. "Short Anthology of Guran Poetry." *Journal of the Royal Asiatic Society* (1921): 57–81.

———. *Grammar of the Kurmanji or Kurdish Language.* London: Luzac, 1913.

———. "Notes on a Kurdish Dialect, Sulaimania (Southern Turkish Kurdistan)." *Journal of the Royal Asiatic Society.* (October 1912): 891–940.

———. "Notes on a Kurdish Dialect, the Shadi Branch of Kurmanji." *Journal of the Royal Asiatic Society* (1909): 895–922.

Soltani, Anwar, ed. *Anthology of Gorani Kurdish Poetry.* London: Soane Trust for Kurdistan, 1998.

Todd, Terry Lynn. "A Grammar of Dimili (Also Known as Zaza)." Ph.D. diss., University of Michigan, 1985.

Tofiq, Mohammed, and Wheeler McIntosh Thackson. *Kurdish Folktales.* New York: Kurdish Library, 1999. (Published as vol. 13, no. 2, of *International Journal of Kurdish Studies.*)

Vanly, Ismet Cheriff. "Regards sur les origines des Kurdes et leur langue." *Studia Kurdica,* no. 5 (1988): 39–58.

REFUGEES

Adelman, Howard. "The Ethics of Humanitarian Intervention: The Case of the Kurdish Refugees." *Public Affairs Quarterly* 6, no. 1 (1992): 61–88.

Ahmad, Abdulbaghi. "Symptoms of Posttraumatic Stress Disorder among Displaced Kurdish Children in Iraq: Victims of a Man-Made Disaster after the Gulf War." *Nordic Journal of Psychiatry* 46, no. 5 (1992): 315–19.

Ahmad, Abdulbaghi, and Mohammad Kirmanj. "The Socioemotional Development of Orphans in Orphanages and Traditional Foster Care in Iraqi Kurdistan." *Child Abuse and Neglect* 20, no. 12 (1996): 1161–73.

Ahmed, Mohammed M. A. "The Chronic Problem of Kurdish Refugees and Internally Displaced Kurds in Southern Kurdistan–Iraq." In *Kurdish Exodus: From Internal Displacement to Diaspora,* ed. Mohammed M. A. Ahmed and Michael M. Gunter, 24–42. Sharon, Mass.: Ahmed Foundation for Kurdish Studies, 2002.

Ahmed, Mohammed M. A., and Michael M. Gunter, eds. *Kurdish Exodus: From Internal Displacement to Diaspora.* Sharon, Mass.: Ahmed Foundation for Kurdish Studies, 2002.

Babille, Marzio, et al. "Post-Emergency Epidemiological Surveillance in Iraqi-Kurdish Refugee Camps in Iran." *Disasters* 18 (March 1994): 58–75.

Black, Richard. "Political Refugees or Economic Migrants: Kurdish and Assyrian Refugees in Greece." *Migration,* no. 25 (1994): 79–109.

Bruinessen, Martin van. "Shifting National and Ethnic Identities: The Kurds in Turkey and the European Diaspora." *Journal of Muslim Minority Affairs* 18 (April 1998): 39–52.

Fernandes, Desmond. "The Targeting and Criminalization of Kurdish Asylum Seekers and Refugee Communities in the United Kingdom and Germany." In *Kurdish Exodus: From Internal Displacement to Diaspora,* ed. Mohammed M. A. Ahmed and Michael M. Gunter, 133–91. Sharon, Mass.: Ahmed Foundation for Kurdish Studies, 2002.

Freedman, L., and D. Boren. "Safe Havens for the Kurds in Post-War Iraq." In *To Loose the Bands of Wickedness: International Intervention in Defence of Human Rights,* ed. N. Rodley, 43–92. London: Brassey's, 1992.

Frelick, Bill. "Protection and Durable Solutions for Internally Displaced Persons: The Case of Northern Iraq." In *Kurdish Exodus: From Internal Displacement to Diaspora,* ed. Mohammed M. A. Ahmed and Michael M. Gunter, 192–204. Sharon, Mass.: Ahmed Foundation for Kurdish Studies, 2002.

———. "The False Promise of Operation Provide Comfort: Protecting Refugees or Protecting State Power?" *Middle East Report* (May–June 1992): 22–27.

———. "Kurdish Refugees and the New World Order." *Kurdish Studies: An International Journal* 5 (Spring–Fall 1992): 45–53.

Gardner, Sheena, Eleoussa Polyzoi, and Yvette Rampaul. "Individual Variables, Literacy History, and ESL Progress among Kurdish and Bosnian Immigrants." *TESL Canada Journal* 14 (Winter 1996): 1–20.

Gunter, Michael M. "The Legal Rights of Refugee and Internally Displaced Kurds under International Law." In *Kurdish Exodus: From Internal Displacement to Diaspora,* ed. Mohammed M. A. Ahmed and Michael M. Gunter, 111–32. Sharon, Mass.: Ahmed Foundation for Kurdish Studies, 2002.

Gurbey, Gulistan. "Internally Displaced Kurds in Turkey with Special Focus on Women and Children." In *Kurdish Exodus: From Internal Displacement to Diaspora,* ed. Mohammed M. A. Ahmed and Michael M. Gunter, 3–23. Sharon, Mass.: Ahmed Foundation for Kurdish Studies, 2002.

Higgitt, Nancy C., and Lena Horne. "Resettlement Experiences: Refugees from Kurdistan and Vietnam." *Canadian Home Economics Journal* 49, no. 1 (1999): 24–31.

Hooglund, Eric. "The Other Face of War." *MERIP/Middle East Report* 21 (July–August 1991): 3–7, 10–12.

Jones, James L. "Operation Provide Comfort: Humanitarian and Security Assistance in Northern Iraq." *Marine Corps Gazette* 75 (November 1991): 98–107.

Kahn, Margaret. "Kurds." In *Harvard Encyclopedia of American Ethnic Groups,* ed. Stephan Thernstrom, 606–8. Cambridge, Mass.: Belknap, 1980.

Karadaghi, Pary. "Kurdish Diaspora in North America." In *Kurdish Exodus: From Internal Displacement to Diaspora,* ed. Mohammed M. A. Ahmed and Michael M. Gunter, 102–7. Sharon, Mass.: Ahmed Foundation for Kurdish Studies, 2002.

Karasapan, Omer. "Gulf War Refugees in Turkey." *Middle East Report* 19 (January–February 1989): 33–35.

Kelley, Ron. "Kurds." In *Irangeles: Iranians in Los Angeles,* ed. Ron Kelley et al., 150–57. Berkeley: University of California Press, 1993.

Kirisci, Kemal. "Provide Comfort and Turkey: Decision Making for Refugee

Assistance." *Low Intensity Conflict and Law Enforcement* 2 (Autumn 1993): 227–53.

———. "Refugee Movements and Turkey." *International Migration* 29, no. 4 (1991): 545–60.

Kneller, R. W., K. Ingolfsdottir, and J. P. Revel. "The Mortality Experience of Kurdish Refugees Remaining in Turkey." *Disasters* 16, no. 3 (1992): 249–54.

Laird, Elizabeth. *Kiss the Dust*. New York: Dutton Children's Books, 1992.

Laizer, Sheri. "And the Refugees Suffer." *Kurdish Times* 3 (Fall 1990): 26–29.

Lawyers Committee for Human Rights. *Asylum under Attack: A Report on the Protection of Iraqi Refugees and Displaced Persons One Year after the Humanitarian Emergency in Iraq*. New York: Lawyers Committee for Human Rights, 1992.

Leggewie, Claus. "How Turks Became Kurds, Not Germans." *Dissent* 43 (Summer 1996): 79–83.

MacDonald, Charles. "Kurdish Refugees and Internally Displaced Kurds in Iran." In *Kurdish Exodus: From Internal Displacement to Diaspora*, ed. Mohammed M. A. Ahmed and Michael M. Gunter, 63–69. Sharon, Mass.: Ahmed Foundation for Kurdish Studies, 2000.

Medico International. "Deportations in Iraqi Kurdistan and Kurdish Refugees in Iran." In *Yearbook of the Kurdish Academy 1990*, 59–77. Ratingen, Germany: Kurdish Academy, 1990.

Mockaitis, Thomas R. "Peacekeeping in Intra-State Conflict." *Small Wars and Insurgencies* 6 (April 1995): 112–25.

O'Connor, Karen. *A Kurdish Family*. Minneapolis: Lerner, 1996.

Ostergaard–Nielsen, Eva. "Trans-state Loyalties and Politics of Turks and Kurds in Western Europe." *SAIS Review* 20 (Winter–Spring 2000): 23–38.

Peralta, Judith B. *The Kurds in Canada: A Question of Ethnic Identity*. Master's thesis, Carleton University, 1997.

Porter, J. D. G., and F. L. van Loock. "Evaluation of Two Kurdish Refugee Camps in Iran, May 1991: The Value of Cluster Sampling in Producing Priorities and Policy." *Disasters* 17, no. 4 (1993): 341–47.

Robson, Barbara. *Iraqi Kurds: Their History and Culture*. Washington, D.C.: Center for Applied Linguistics, 1996.

Saeedpour, Vera Beaudin. "From the Lion to the Fox: Iraqi Kurdish Refugees in Turkey." *Kurdish Times* 3 (Fall 1990): 17–23.

———. "The Real Victims of the Iran–Iraq War." *Cultural Survival Quarterly* 12, no. 2 (1988): 55–57.

Sheikhmous, Omar. "The Kurds in Exile." In *Yearbook of the Kurdish Academy 1990*, 88–114. Ratingen, Germany: Kurdish Academy, 1990.

Smith, C. "Kurds." In *Encyclopedia of Canada's Peoples*, ed. Paul Robert Magocsi, 890–93. Toronto: University of Toronto Press, 1999.

Van Hear, N. "Mass Flight in the Middle East: Involuntary Migration and the Gulf Conflict, 1990–1991." In *Geography and Refugees: Patterns and Processes of Change,* ed. R. Black and V. Robinson, 64–83. London: Belhaven, 1993.

Vanly, Ismet Cheriff. "The Forgotten Faili Kurds of Iraq." *In Kurdish Exodus: From Internal Displacement to Diaspora,* ed. Mohammed M. A. Ahmed and Michael M. Gunter, 43–48. Sharon, Mass.: Ahmed Foundation for Kurdish Studies, 2002.

Wahbeck, Osten. "Kurds in Europe: From Labor Migrants to Asylum Seekers." In *Kurdish Exodus: From Internal Displacement to Diaspora,* ed. Mohammed M. A. Ahmed and Michael M. Gunter, 73–101. Sharon, Mass. Ahmed Foundation for Kurdish Studies, 2002.

————. *Kurdish Diasporas: A Comparative Study of Kurdish Refugee Communities.* New York: St. Martin's, 1999.

————. "Community Work and Exile Politics: Kurdish Refugee Associations in London." *Journal of Refugee Studies* 11 (Summer 1998): 215–30.

————. "The Kurdish Diaspora and Refugee Associations in Finland and England." In *Exclusion and Inclusion of Refugees in Contemporary Europe,* ed. Philip Muus, 171–86. Utrecht, Netherlands: European Research Centre on Migration and Ethnic Relations, 1997.

Wayman, Richard. "Bright Lights Big City: Turkey's Crackdown on Kurdish Guerrillas Forces Kurdish Migration into Cities." *Geographical Magazine* 70 (April 1998): 79–82.

Yip, R., and T. W. Sharp. "Acute Malnutrition and High Childhood Mortality Related to Diarrhea: Lessons from the 1991 Kurdish Refugee Crisis." *Journal of the American Medical Association* 270, no. 5 (1993): 587–94.

RELIGION

General

Bois, Thomas. "La religion des Kurdes." *Proche Orient Chrétien* 11, no. 2 (1961): 105–36.

Bruinessen, Martin van. *Mullas, Sufis and Heretics: The Role of Religion in Kurdish Society.* Istanbul: Isis, 2000.

————. "Religion in Kurdistan." *Kurdish Times* 4 (Summer–Fall 1991): 5–27.

Kreyenbroek, Philip G. "Religion and Religions in Kurdistan." In *Kurdish Culture and Identity,* ed. Philip G. Kreyenbroek and Christine Allison, 85–110. London: Zed, 1996.

Leezenberg, Michiel. "Between Assimilation and Deportation: The Shabak and the Kakais in Northern Iraq." In *Syncretistic Religious Communities in the Near East: Collected Papers of the International Symposium "Alevism in Turkey and Comparable Syncretistic Religious Communities in the Near East in the Past and Present," Berlin, 14–17 April 1995,* ed. Krisztina Kehl–Bodrogi, Barbara Kellner–Heinkele, and Anke Otter–Beaujean, 155–74. Leiden, Netherlands: Brill, 1997.

Moosa, Matti. *Extremist Shiites: The Ghulat Sects.* Syracuse, N.Y.: Syracuse University Press, 1988.

Ahl-i Haqq

Bruinessen, Martin van. "When Haji Bektash Still Bore the Name of Sultan Sahak: Notes on the Alh-i Haqq of the Guran District." In *Bektachiyya: Études sur l'ordre mystique des Bektachis et les groupes relevant de Hadji Bektach,* ed. Alexandre Popovic and Giles Veinstein, 117–38. Istanbul: Isis, 1995.

Edmonds, Cecil John. "The Beliefs and Practices of the Ahl-i of Iraq." *Iran* 7 (1969): 89–106.

Halm, H. "Ahl-e Haqq." In *Encyclopaedia Iranica,* Vol. 1, 635–637. London: Routledge & Kegan Paul, 1982.

Hamzeh'ee, M. Reza. *The Yaresan: A Sociological, Historical, and Religio-Historical Study of a Kurdish Community.* Berlin: Schwarz, 1990.

Ivanow, Wladimir, ed. *The Truth-Worshipper of Kurdistan.* Leiden, Netherlands: Brill, 1953.

Mir–Hosseini, Ziba. "Faith, Ritual and Culture among the Ahl-e Haqq." In *Kurdish Culture and Identity,* ed. Philip G. Kreyenbroek and Christine Allison, 111–34. London: Zed, 1996.

———. "Redefining the Truth: Ahl-i Haqq and the Islamic Republic." *British Journal of Middle Eastern Studies* 21, no. 2 (1995): 211–28.

———. "Inner Truth and Outer History: The Two Worlds of the Ahl-i Haqq of Kurdistan." *International Journal of Middle East Studies* 26 (May 1994): 267–85.

Alevis

Bruinessen, Martin van. "The Shabak: A Kizilbash Community in Iraqi Kurdistan." *Les Annales de l'Autre Islam* 5 (1998): 185–96.

———. "Aslini Inkar Eden Haramzadedir! The Debate on the Ethnic Identity of the Kurdish Alevis." In *Syncretistic Religious Communities in the Near East: Collected Papers of the International Symposium "Alevism in Turkey and Comparable Syncretistic Religious Communities in the Near East in the Past and Present," Berlin, 14–17 April 1995,* ed. Krisztina Kehl–Bodrogi, Barbara Kellner–Heinkele, and Anke Otter–Beaujean, 1–23. Leiden, Netherlands: Brill, 1997.

————. "Kurds, Turks and the Alevi Revival in Turkey." *Middle East Report* 26 (July–September 1996): 7–10.

Bumke, Peter J. "The Kurdish Alevis: Boundaries and Perceptions." In *Ethnic Groups in the Republic of Turkey,* ed. Peter Alford Andrews, 510–18. Wiesbaden: Reichert, 1989.

Jacobson, C. M. "The Alevi Religion." In *Kurdish Culture: A Cross-Cultural Guide,* ed. Denise L. Sweetnam, 209–217. Bonn: Verlag für Kultur und Wissenschaft, 1994.

Kehl–Bodrogi, Krisztina. "Rediscovering the Alevi Community in Turkey: Myth of History and Collective Identity." *Orient* 34, no. 2 (1993): 267–82.

Christians

Blincoe, Robert. *Ethnic Realities and the Church: Lessons from Kurdistan, a History of Mission Work, 1668–1990.* Pasadena, Calif.: Presbyterian Center for Mission Studies, 1998.

Dodd, Edward M. "By the Grace of the Kurds." *Moslem World* 10 (May 1920): 420–25.

Husry, Khaldun S. "The Assyrian Affair of 1933 (I) & (II)." *International Journal of Middle East Studies* 5, no. 2 (1974): 161–76; no. 3 (1974): 344–60.

Joseph, John. *Muslim–Christian Relations and Inter-Christian Rivalries in the Middle East: The Case of the Jacobites in an Age of Transition.* Albany: State University of New York Press, 1983.

————. *The Nestorians and Their Muslim Neighbors: A Study of Western Influence on Their Relations.* Princeton, N.J.: Princeton University Press, 1961.

Kreyenbroek, Philip G. "The Lawij of Mor Basilios Shim'un: A Kurdish Christian Text in Syriac Script." *Journal of Kurdish Studies* 1 (1995): 29–53.

Rooy, Silvio E. van. "Christianity in Kurdistan." *Star of the East* 23 (July 1962): 10–14.

Sabar, Yona. "The Christian Neo-Aramaic Dialects of Zakho and Dihok: Two Text Samples." *Journal of the American Oriental Society* 115 (January–March 1995): 33–51.

Yacoub, Joseph. "The Assyrian Community in Turkey." In *Contrasts and Solutions in the Middle East,* ed. Ole Hoiris and Sefa Martin Yurukel. Aarhus, Denmark: Aarhus University Press, 1997.

Jews

Baharav, G. "Mountain Jews of Kurdistan." *Jewish Digest* 12 (June 1967): 45–48.

Beller, J. "Jews of Kurdistan." *Jewish Digest* 20 (May 1975): 32–36.

Ben–Yacob, Abraham, and Edith Gerson–Kiwi. "Kurdistan." *Encyclopaedia Judaica.* Vol. 10, 1295–1301. New York: Macmillan, 1972.

Blau, Joyce. "Les Juifs au Kurdistan." In *Mélanges Linguistiques offerts à Maxime Rodinson,* ed. Ch. Robin, 123–32. Paris: Geuthner, 1985.

Brauer, Eric. *The Jews of Kurdistan.* Completed and edited by Raphael Patai. Detroit: Wayne State University Press, 1993.

Chyet, Michael L. "Neo-Aramaic and Kurdish: An Interdisciplinary Consideration of Their Influence on Each Other." *Israel Oriental Studies* 15 (1995): 219–52.

Cohen, David. "Neo-Aramaic." *Encyclopaedia Judaica.* Vol. 12, 948–51. New York: Macmillan, 1972.

Epstein, Shiftan. "The Jews of Kurdistan." *Ariel* 51 (1982): 65–78.

Feitelson, Dina. "Aspects of the Social Life of Kurdish Jews." *Jewish Journal of Sociology* 1, no. 2 (1959): 201–16.

Fischel, Walter J. "The Jews of Kurdistan: A First Hand Report on a Near Eastern Mountain Community." *Commentary* 8 (December 1949): 554–59.

———. "The Jews of Kurdistan: A Hundred Years Ago." *Jewish Social Studies* 6 (1945): 195–226.

Garbell, Irene. "The Impact of Kurdish and Turkish on the Jewish Neo-Aramaic Dialect of Persian Azerbaijan and the Adjoining Regions." *Journal of the American Oriental Society* 85 (1965): 159–77.

Gerson-Kiwi, Edith. "The Music of Kurdistan Jews: A Synopsis of Their Musical Styles." In *Contributions to a Historical Study of Jewish Music,* ed. Eric Werner, 266–79. New York: Ktav, 1976.

Gerstein, Mordicai. *The Shadow of a Flying Bird: A Legend of the Kurdistani Jews.* New York: Hyperion Books for Children, 1994.

Herman, Robert D. *The Syntax and Semantics of Verb Morphology in Modern Aramaic: A Jewish Dialect of Iraqi Kurdistan.* New Haven, Conn.: American Oriental Society, 1989.

Krotkoff, Georg. *A Neo-Aramaic Dialect of Kurdistan: Text, Grammar, and Vocabulary.* New Haven, Conn.: American Oriental Society, 1982.

Magnarella, Paul J. "Jewish Kurds of Iran." *Jewish Digest* 15 (April 1970): 17–20.

———. "A Note on Aspects of Social Life among the Jewish Kurds of Sanandaj, Iran." *Jewish Journal of Sociology* 11 (June 1969): 51–58.

Miller, E. "The Jewish Village That Moved to Israel." *Jewish Digest* 25 (April 1989): 33–37.

Rand, Barukh, and Barbara Rush. *Jews of Kurdistan.* Toledo, Ohio: Toledo Board of Jewish Education, 1978.

Rejwan, Nissim. *The Jews of Iraq: 3000 Years of History and Culture.* Boulder, Colo.: Westview, 1985.

Sabar, Yona, "Jews of Kurdistan." In *Encyclopedia of World Cultures, Volume IX: Africa and the Middle East,* ed. John Middleton and Amal Rassam, 144–47. Boston: Hall, 1995.

———. "Multilingual Proverbs in the Neo-Aramaic Speech of the Jews of Zakho, Iraqi Kurdistan." *International Journal of Middle East Studies* 9 (1978): 215–35.

———. "A Survey of the Oral and Written Literature of the Kurdish Jews." In *Pesat Wayehi Besallah. A Neo-Aramaic Midrash on Beshallah (Exodus)*, ed. Yona Sabar, 161–78. Wiesbaden, Germany: n.p., 1976.

———. "First Names, Nicknames and Family Names among the Jews of Kurdistan." *Jewish Quarterly Review* 65 (1974–1975): 43–51.

Schwartz–Be'eri, Ora. "Kurdish Silversmiths and Their Craft." *International Journal of Kurdish Studies* 6 (Fall 1993): 12–24.

———. "Jewish Weaving in Kurdistan." *Journal of Jewish Art* 3–4 (1977): 74–89.

———, trans. *The Folk Literature of the Kurdistani Jews: An Anthology Translated from Hebrew and Neo-Aramaic Sources*. New Haven, Conn.: Yale University Press, 1982.

Sered, Susan Starr. "The Religious World of Jewish Women in Kurdistan." In *Jews among Muslims: Communities in the Precolonial Middle East*, ed. Shlomo Deshen and Walter P. Zenner, 197–214. New York: New York University Press, 1996.

Shai, Donna. "Family Conflict and Cooperation in Folksongs of Kurdish Jews." In *Jewish Societies in the Middle East*, ed. S. Deshen and W. P. Zenner, 273–84. Washington, D.C.: University of Press America, 1982.

———. "Wedding Customs among Kurdish Jews in Zakho (Kurdistan) and in Jerusalem (Israel)." *Studies in Marriage Customs, Folklore Research Center Studies* 4 (1974): 253–66.

Soen, Dan, and Ruth Ezrachi. "Kurdish Immigrants, Culture Contact and Social Adjustment in Israel." *Sociologus* 40, no. 2 (1990): 97–120.

Sufis

Bruinessen, Martin van. "The Naqshbandi Order in 17th Century Kurdistan." In *Naqshbandis: Cheminements et situation actuelle d'un ordre mystique musulman. Acte de la Table Ronde de Sevres, 2–4 mai 1985*, ed. Marc Gaborieau, Alexandre Popovic, and Thierry Zarcone, 337–60. Paris: Institut Français d'Études Anatoliennes, 1990.

Le Gall, Dina. "The Ottoman Naqshbandiyya in the Pre-Mujaddidi Phase: A Study in Islamic Religious Culture and Its Transmission." Ph.D. diss., Princeton University, 1992.

Singer, Andre. "The Dervishes of Kurdistan." *Asian Affairs* 61 (June 1974): 179–82.

Yezidis

Ahmed, Sami Said. "A Study of the Yazidis: An Introduction." *Iliff Review* 30 (Fall 1973): 37–48.

Allison, Christine. *The Yezidi Oral Tradition in Iraqi Kurdistan.* Richmond, England: Curzon, 2002.

Bois, Thomas. "Les Yezidis: Essai historique et sociologique sur leur origine religieuse." *Al-Machriq* 55 (1961): 109–28, 190–242.

Edmonds, Cecil John. *Pilgrimage to Lalish.* London: Royal Asiatic Society, 1967.

Empson, Ralph H. W. *The Cult of the Peacock Angel: A Short Account of the Yezidi Tribes of Kurdistan.* London: Witherby, 1928.

Fuccaro, Nelida. *The Other Kurds: Yazidis in Colonial Iraq.* London: Tauris, 1999.

————. "Communalism and the State in Iraq: The Yazidi Kurds, c.1869–1940." *Middle Eastern Studies* 35 (April 1999): 1–26.

————. "Ethnicity, State Formation, and Conscription in Postcolonial Iraq: The Case of the Yazidi Kurds of Jabal Sinjar." *International Journal of Middle East Studies* 29 (November 1997): 559–80.

————. "Aspects of the Social and Political History of the Yazidi Enclave of Jabal Sinjar (Iraq) under the British Mandate, 1919–1932." Ph.D. diss., University of Durham, England, 1994.

Guest, John S. *Survival among the Kurds: A History of the Yezidis.* Rev. and expanded ed. London: Kegan Paul International, 1993.

Kreyenbroek, Philip G. *Yezidism: Its Background, Observances, and Textual Tradition.* Lewiston, N.Y.: Mellen, 1995.

CULTURE

General

Busby, Annette. "Kurds: A Culture Straddling International Borders." In *Portraits of Culture: Ethnographic Originals,* ed. Melvin Ember, Carol Ember, and David Levinson. Englewood Cliffs, N.J.: Prentice–Hall, 1994.

Dziegiel, Leszek. "Iraqi Kurdish Traditional Costume in Its Process of Europeanization." *Acta Ethnografisca Academiae Scientiarum Hungaricae* 33, nos. 1–4 (1984–85): 93–112.

————. "Traditional Food and Daily Meals in Iraqi Kurdistan Today." *Ethnologia Polona* 7 (1981): 99–113.

Hassan, Mohammed Khalis. "Notes on Urban and Domestic Architecture of Central Kurdistan, Iraq." *International Journal of Kurdish Studies* 9, nos. 1–2 (1996): 79–94.

Hassanpour, Amir, T. Skutnabb–Kangas, and M. Chyet. "The Non-Education of Kurds: A Kurdish Perspective." *International Review of Education* 42, no. 4 (1996): 367–79.

Kren, Karin. "Kurdish Material Culture in Syria." In *Kurdish Culture and Identity,* ed. Philip G. Kreyenbroek and Christine Allison, 162–73. London: Zed, 1996.

Kreyenbroek, Philip G., and Christine Allison, eds. *Kurdish Culture and Identity.* London: Zed, 1996.

O'Shea, Maria T. "Kurdish Costume: Regional Diversity and Divergence." In *Kurdish Culture and Identity,* ed. Philip G. Kreyenbroek and Christine Allison, 135–55. London: Zed, 1996.

Research Institute of Oppressed People, ed. *The Importance of Cultural Elements in the Struggle of the Kurdish People.* Amsterdam: Research Institute of Oppressed People, 1983.

Sweetnam, Denise L. *Kurdish Culture: A Cross-Cultural Guide.* Bonn: Verlag fur Kultur und Wissenschaft, 1994.

Journalism

Davidson, L. "Rising from the Ruins: Local TV Helps Define a New Kurdish Identity." *Independent* 16 (April 1993): 24–28.

Edmonds, Cecil John. "A Kurdish Newspaper: 'Rozh-i-Kurdistan.'" *Journal of the Royal Central Asian Society* 12 (1925): 83–90.

Gundem, Ozgur, and Yeni Ulke. *How Journalists Are Murdered in Kurdistan.* Cologne, Germany: Representation of Özgür Gündem Newspaper in Europe, 1993.

Hassanpour, Amir. "The MED-TV Story: Kurdish Satellite TV Station Defies All Odds." *Inter Radio* 10 (December 1998): 8–9.

———. "Satellite Footprints as National Borders: MED-TV and the Extraterritoriality of State Sovereignty." *Journal of Muslim Minority Affairs* 18 (April 1998): 53–72.

———. "The Creation of Kurdish Media Culture." In *Kurdish Culture and Identity,* ed. Philip G. Kreyenbroek and Christine Allison, 48–84. London: Zed, 1996.

Human Rights Watch. *Turkey: Violations of Free Expression in Turkey.* New York: Human Rights Watch, 1999.

International Association for Human Rights in Kurdistan. *The Kurds and Kurdistan: Thinking Is a Crime: Report on Freedom of Expression in Turkey.* Bonn: International Association for Human Rights in Kurdistan, 1996.

Petley, J. "Dishing the Dirt—Satellite Television in Kurdish Language: MED-TV." *Index on Censorship* 28 (July–August 1999): 27–30.

Woker, M. "Press Freedom under Attack in Turkey." *Swiss Review of World Affairs* 12 (December 1994): 21–22.

Zimmerman, Ann. "Culture after Saddam: Video Artists Restore a Country's Identity in Iraqi Kurdistan." *High Performance* 17 (Spring 1994): 32–35.

Music

Baksi, Mahmut. *The Kurdish Voice: Shivan Perwer*. Stockholm: Helin House, 1986.

Blum, Robert Stephen, and Amir Hassanpour. "The Morning of Freedom Rose Up: Kurdish Popular Song and the Exigencies of Cultural Survival." *Popular Music* 15 (October 1996): 325–43.

During, Jean. "The Sacred Music of the Ahl-i Haqq as a Means of Mystical Transmission." In *Manifestations of Sainthood in Islam,* ed. G. M. Smith and C. W. Ernst, 27–41. Istanbul: Isis, 1993.

Hassan, Schehrazade Qassim. "The Long Necked Lute in Iraq." *Asian Music* 13, no. 2 (1982): 1–18.

Mokri, Mohammad, ed. *Kurdish Songs*. Tehran: Ketab–Khaneh Danesh, 1951.

Nezan, Kendal. "Kurdish Music and Dance." *Le Monde de la Musique/The World of Music* 21, no. 1 (1979): 19–32.

Ozturk, U., and S. Perwer. "Singing of Home: Shivan Perwer Talks about Banned Kurdish Music in Turkey." *Index of Censorship* 27 (November–December 1998): 124–27.

Salihi, Nur al-Din al-. "Some Remarks and Investigations on the History of Kurdish Music." In *Yearbook of the Kurdish Academy 1990,* 85–87. Ratingen, Germany: Kurdish Academy, 1990.

Shiloah, Amnon. "Kurdish Music." In *The New Grove Dictionary of Music and Musicians,* ed. Stanley Sadie, 314–18. London: Macmillan, 1980.

Tatsumura, Ayako. "Music and Culture of the Kurds." *Senri Ethnological Studies* 5 (1980): 75–93.

Rugs

Akasheh, Anahid. *The Archaeology of the Kurdish Rugs*. New York: Kurdish Library, 1992.

Biggs, Robert D., ed. *Discoveries from Kurdish Looms*. Evanston, Ill.: Mary and Leigh Block Gallery, Northwestern University, 1983.

Criel, Jean-Marie, and Pervine Jamil. *Costume et Tapis kurdes*. Brussels: Institut Kurde de Bruxelles, 1995.

Eagleton, William. "Kurdish Rugs and Kelims: An Introduction." In *Kurdish*

Culture and Identity, ed. Philip G. Kreyenbroek and Christine Allison, 156–61. London: Zed, 1996.

———. *An Introduction to Kurdish Rugs and Other Weavings.* New York: Interlink, 1988.

Eiland, Murray L. *Oriental Rugs: A New Comprehensive Guide.* 3d ed. New York: Graphic Society, 1982.

Ford, P. R. J. *The Oriental Carpet: A History and Guide to Traditional Motifs, Patterns, and Symbols.* New York: Abrams, 1981.

Gans–Ruedin, E. *Splendeur du Tapis Persan.* Fribourg, Switzerland: Office du Livre, 1978.

Housego, Jenny. *Tribal Rugs: An Introduction to the Weavings of the Tribes of Iran.* New York: Van Nostrand Reinhold, 1991.

Hull, Alastair, and Jose Luczyc–Wyhowska. *Kilim: The Complete Guide. History, Pattern, Technique, Identification.* London: Thames and Hudson, 1993.

Zipper, Kurt, and Claudia Fritzsche. *Oriental Rugs: Vol. 4: Turkish.* Woodbridge, Suffolk: Antique Collectors' Club, 1981.

SOCIAL

Barth, Fredrik. *Principles of Social Organization in Southern Kurdistan.* Oslo: Brodrene Jorgensen Boktrykkeri, 1953.

Bois, Thomas. "Kurdish Society." In *Encyclopedia of Islam.* Vol. V, 470–79. New ed. Leiden, Netherlands: Brill, 1986.

Daponte, B. O., J. B. Kadane, and L. J. Wolfson. "Bayesian Demography: Projecting the Iraqi Kurdish Population, 1977–1990." *Journal of the American Statistical Association* 92 (December 1997): 1256–67.

Dziegiel, Leszek. "Life Cycle within the Iraqi Kurd Family." *Ethnologia Polona* 8 (1982): 247–60.

Gol-Anbar, Jalil. "A Descriptive Survey of Psychotherapy in Kurdistan and Western Cultures." Ph.D. diss., United States International University, 1983.

Hassan, Mohammed Khalis. "Notes on Urban and Domestic Architecture of Central Kurdistan, Iraq." *International Journal of Kurdish Studies* 9, no. 1–2 (1996): 79–94.

Hassanpour, Amir. "The Creation of Kurdish Media Culture." In *Kurdish Culture and Identity,* ed. Philip G. Kreyenbroek and Christine Allison, 48–84. London: Zed, 1996.

Kramer, Carol. "Ethnographic Households and Archaeological Interpretations: A Case from Iranian Kurdistan." *American Behavioral Scientist* 25 (July–August 1982): 663–75.

Lamb, Harold. "Mountain Tribes of Iran and Iraq." *National Geographic Magazine* (March 1946): 385–408.

Leezenberg, Michiel. "The Kurds and the City." *Journal of Kurdish Studies* 2 (1996–1997): 57–62.

Mardin, Serif. *Religion and Social Change in Modern Turkey: The Case of Bediuzzaman Said Nursi.* Albany: State University of New York Press, 1989.

Masters, William Murray. "Rowanduz: A Kurdish Administrative and Mercantile Center." Ph.D. diss., University of Michigan, 1954.

Mutlu, Servet. "Ethnic Kurds in Turkey: A Demographic Study." *International Journal of Middle East Studies* 28 (November 1996): 517–41.

———. "Population of Turkey by Ethnic Groups and Provinces." *New Perspectives on Turkey,* no. 12 (Spring 1995): 33–60.

Vasil'eva, Eugenia. "The Social Aspect of Genealogical Descent among the Kurds." *Acta Kurdica: The International Journal of Kurdish and Iranian Studies* 1 (1994): 73–76.

Wolfram, Eberhard. "Nomads and Farmers in Southeastern Turkey: Problems of Settlement." *Oriens* 6 (1953): 32–49.

Yalcin–Heckmann, Lale. *Tribe and Kinship among the Kurds.* Frankfurt am Main, Germany: Peter Lang, 1991.

———. "Kurdish Tribal Organisation and Local Political Processes." In *Turkish State, Turkish Society,* ed. Andrew Finkel and Nukhet Sirman, 289–312. London: Routledge, 1990.

———. "On Kinship, Tribalism and Ethnicity in Eastern Turkey." In *Ethnic Groups in the Republic of Turkey,* ed. Peter Alford Andrews, 622–32. Wiesbaden: Reichert, 1989.

WOMEN

Bruinessen, Martin van. "Matriarchy in Kurdistan? Women Rulers in Kurdish History." *International Journal of Kurdish Studies* 6 (Fall 1993): 25–39.

Fuad, Tania. "National Liberation: Women's Liberation." *Freedom Review* 26 (September–October 1995): 31–33.

Gearing, Julian. "The Ones Left Behind." *The Middle East,* no. 218 (December 1992): 43–45.

Hansen, Henry Harald. *The Kurdish Woman's Life: Field Research in a Muslim Society, Iraq.* Copenhagen: National Museum, 1961.

———. *Daughters of Allah: Among Moslem Women in Kurdistan.* London: Allen & Unwin, 1960.

Kurdistan Solidarity Committee. *Resistance: Women in Kurdistan.* London: Kurdistan Solidarity Committee, 1995.

Mojab, Shahrzad, ed. *Women of a Non-State Nation: The Kurds.* Costa Mesa, Calif.: Mazda, 2001.

————. "Crossing the Boundaries of Nationalism, Patriarchy, and Eurocentrism: The Struggle for a Kurdish Women's Studies Network." *Canadian Woman Studies* 17, no. 2 (Spring 1997): 68–72.

————. *Women in Politics and War: The Case of Kurdistan.* Working paper no. 145. Lansing: Michigan State University, 1987.

Mojab, Shahrzad, and Amir Hassanpour. "Thoughts on the Struggle against 'Honor Killing.'" *International Journal of Kurdish Studies* 16, nos. 1–2 (2002): 83–98.

Yalcin–Heckmann, Lale. "Gender Roles and Female Strategies among the Nomadic and Semi-Nomadic Kurdish Tribes of Turkey." In *Women in Modern Turkish Society: A Reader,* ed. Sirin Tekeli. London: Zed, 1995.

WEB SITES

Although web sites are ephemeral compared to the hard bibliographic sources listed above and are more lacking in quality control, many of them are still quite excellent, and of course they are increasingly being used. Therefore, a listing of some of the more important ones dealing with the Kurds seems appropriate. All of the following web sites were accessible as of 21 December 2002. All are prefixed with <http://www> except the second entry for the Kurdistan Workers Party (PKK), as also noted below.

AKA Kurdistan. akakurdistan.com.
American Kurdish Information Network. kurdistan.org.
Democratic Party of Iranian Kurdistan Canada. pdki.org *or* pdk-iran.org.
eBarzan Com for Kurdistan. krds.net *or* ebarzan.com.
Encyclopaedia of Kurdistan, The. kurdistanica.com.
Incore Guide to Internet Sources on Conflict and Ethnicity in Kurdistan. incore.ulst.ac. uk/cds/countries/kurdistan.html.
Institut Kurde de Paris. institutkurde.org *or* fikp.org.
Iraq Foundation. iraqfoundation.org.
Iraqi National Congress. inc.org.uk.
Kurdish Human Rights Project (London). khrp.org.
Kurdish Human Rights Watch, Inc. (USA). khrw.com.
Kurdish Scientific and Medical Association. ksma.org.
Kurdish Worldwide Resources. kurdish.com.

Kurdistan Democratic Party (KDP). kdp.pp.se.

Kurdistan Information Network. xs4all.nl/~tank/kurdish/thdocs.

Kurdistan News. kurdishnews.com.

Kurdistan Observer. kurdistan.com.

Kurdistan Regional Government (Iraq). krg.org.

Kurdistan Web. humanrights.de/~kurdweb.

Kurdistan Web Org. kurdistanweb.org.

Kurdistan Workers Party. pkk.org *or* burn.ucsd.edu/~ats/PKK/pkk.htm (no www.).

MED-TV. med-tv.be/med.

MEDYA-TV. medyatv.com.

Patriotic Union of Kurdistan (PUK). puk.org.

Washington Kurdish Institute (USA). kurd.org.

About the Author

Michael M. Gunter (B.A. Columbia University; M.I.A. Columbia University; Ph.D. Kent State University) is a professor of political science at Tennessee Technological University in Cookeville, Tennessee, USA, where he has been a member of the faculty since 1972. Earlier, he taught at Kent State University in Kent, Ohio. In 1978–79, he taught as a Senior Fulbright Lecturer in International Relations at the Middle East Technical University in Ankara, Turkey. Recently, he also has taught at Fisk University in Nashville, Tennessee; the International University in Vienna, Austria; and Shanghai Xuhui College of Education in Shanghai, China. Professor Gunter is the author of a number of scholarly, acclaimed books dealing with the Kurds, including *The Kurdish Predicament in Iraq: A Political Dilemma* (1999); *The Kurds and the Future of Turkey* (1997); *The Kurds of Iraq: Tragedy and Hope* (1992); and *The Kurds in Turkey: A Political Dilemma* (1990). He also coedited *Kurdish Exodus: From Internal Displacement to Diaspora* (2002) and *The Kurdish Question and International Law* (2000). In addition, he has published numerous scholarly articles on the Kurds in such prestigious journals as the *Middle East Journal, Orient, Current History, Middle East Quarterly, Third World Quarterly, Cultural Survival Quarterly,* and *PS: Political Science and Politics,* among many others. Professor Gunter has been invited to speak on various aspects of the Kurdish issue by a number of different government agencies in the United States, as well as many scholarly conferences both in the United States and abroad.